AF760250

Social Security Reform in Transition Economies

Social Security Reform in Transition Economies

Lessons from Kazakhstan

Charles M. Becker, Grigori A. Marchenko,
Sabit Khakimzhanov, Ai-Gul S. Seitenova,
and Vladimir Ivliev

palgrave
macmillan

SOCIAL SECURITY REFORM IN TRANSITION ECONOMIES
Copyright © Charles M. Becker, Grigori A. Marchenko, Sabit Khakimzhanov, Ai-Gul S. Seitenova, and Vladimir Ivliev, 2009.

All rights reserved.

First published in 2009 by PALGRAVE MACMILLAN® in the United States - a division of St. Martin's Press LLC, 175 Fifth Avenue, New York, NY 10010.

Where this book is distributed in the UK, Europe and the rest of the world, this is by Palgrave Macmillan, a division of Macmillan Publishers Limited, registered in England, company number 785998, of Houndmills, Basingstoke, Hampshire RG21 6XS.

Palgrave Macmillan is the global academic imprint of the above companies and has companies and representatives throughout the world.

Palgrave® and Macmillan® are registered trademarks in the United States, the United Kingdom, Europe and other countries.

ISBN-13: 978-0-230-60736-1
ISBN-10: 0-230-60736-5

Library of Congress Cataloging-in-Publication Data

Social security reform in transition economies : lessons from Kazakhstan / Charles M. Becker ... [et al.].
p. cm.
Includes bibliographical references.
ISBN 0-230-60736-5
1. Social security—Kazakhstan. 2. Kazakhstan—Economic policy—1991–
I. Becker, Charles M., 1954–

HD7212.563.S63 2009
368.4'30095845—dc22 2008021791

A catalogue record of the book is available from the British Library.

Design by Macmillan Publishing Solutions

First edition: January 2009

10 9 8 7 6 5 4 3 2 1

Printed in the United States of America.

For my parents

—Sabit Khakimzhanov

For my parents, Vladimir and Inna, my wife Tanya, my sons, Vladimir and Michael, my tutors, the first pilot-instructor Igor Baliberdin, the tutors and colleagues, David Bardsley and Darrell Brown, who are brave and capable lawyers, and for my spiritual director, priest Sergey Konoplev

—Vladimir Ivliev

For my *alma mater,* the Economic Cybernetics Department of Timiryazev State Agricultural University in Moscow and, above all, to my dissertation advisor Professor Akhyar Muginovich Gataulin and my diploma advisor Professor Kopjenkin Urij Ivanovich

—Ai-Gul Seitenova

For Erbolat Musabek, a world-class demographer and a true scientist

—Charles Becker

Contents

List of Figures

List of Tables

Foreword

Dear readers,
For me this is a very important book about the introduction and performance of an Accumulative pension system in Kazakhstan. It all started in October 1996 when I, then deputy governor of the National Bank of Kazakhstan, drafted the first three-page concept of the system, which was in principle approved by the president of the country. Then the whole preparatory process started that included a lot of people and a lot of hard decisions. The system was introduced in January 1998 and now, 12 years after the process started and over 10 years of the system's performance behind us, I am quite happy to say that it was one of the most important reforms in the history of independent Kazakhstan and, probably, the most successful one.

With assets of accumulative pension funds being around 12% of GDP and growing steadily and with a working population coverage of around 90 percent, this could also be the most successful Accumulative pension system in all of the countries of Latin America and Eastern Europe that tried this approach.

Not everyone fully realizes what a change it has produced for our financial system and for the country as a whole. Not only it did secure better, funded pensions for the bulk of the country's employed population, but it also boosted dramatically our banking system and our securities markets by creating a whole class of institutional investors with a pool of long-term funding available. For instance, Kazakh banks have been consistently able to issue long-term bonds, sell them mostly to pension funds, and then use the proceeds to fund either mortgage loans for the public or investment loans for local companies. Previously, long-term funding was available only from the budget or from foreign direct investment, which made our options limited.

I am deeply thankful to my coauthors for working on this book, which was quite long in the making, and especially to my old friend Charles Becker, who is the principal inspiration and force behind this effort. We do not agree on everything among us, and I do not necessarily agree with some of their conclusions, mostly because they view the whole process from the outside and I was involved in it very intimately from the very start. Also, my involvement was on either the regulatory side, when I was the governor of the central bank in 1999–2004, or as a market practitioner, as our Halyk bank (where I have been the CEO since January 2005) owns the largest pension fund in the country with a market share of almost 30%. My partners were mostly involved as analysts and did a great job at that, but our different positions explain most of our difference in points of view.

I enjoyed working on this book almost as much as I enjoyed participating in this important set of financial sector reforms, which made a lot of difference for my country, Kazakhstan, and I do hope that this book will be interesting for English-speaking readers.

Grigori Marchenko

Acknowledgments

There are many who helped in the preparation of this book and who raised important questions along the way. Foremost recognition goes to Ms. Dina S. Urzhumova, who developed and programmed both the KAZAK1 and KAZAK2 macroactuarial models upon whose simulations we rely heavily. Dina was heavily involved in pension reform policy analysis for many years, was founding president of both the Kazakhstan Actuarial Center and the Actuarial Society of Kazakhstan, and contributed many of the ideas that have emerged in this book through countless discussions with all of the authors.

Ms. Aigul Sultanbekova, Ms. Azhar Krukpaeva, and Mr. Aibek Bekzhanov were instrumental in collecting, organizing, and assessing data from many sources. Their dedication and statistical skills contributed greatly to the quality of the information presented. We also appreciate advice from Mr. Dossym Bespaev and Mr. Alimuhamedov Nurzhan Erzhanovich.

Space constraints prevent us from naming all of those who contributed to the pension reform itself, and to a range of technical analyses. This omission does not signal an unawareness or lack of appreciation of their contributions. On the contrary, we recognize the extent to which the reform built on and benefited from a lively internal debate within Kazakhstan, and also emphasize that the Accumulative system reform was generated and planned by Kazakhstanis, with international institutions and advisors playing no more than a supportive role.

However, many international counterparts did contribute substantially to the reform. These include Dr. Paul Davis, Mr. William Baldridge, and Mr. Rick Gurley from USAID and Dr. Emily Andrews and Dr. Sandor Sipos from the World Bank. Prior to Pragma, the USAID contractor in place was IMCC, and its technical staff made important contributions as well: Mr. David Bardsley, Mr. Darryl Brown, Mr. Mitchell C. Wiener, Mr. Jean Noel Martineau, Ms. Rosa Chiappe, Mr. Pedro Souss, Mr. Juan Carlos Chekay, Mr. Andreas Kern, Ms. Victorya Olskaya, Mr. Mike McWherter, and Mr. David Weig merit special mention.

We especially appreciate the support of the Pragma Corporation family, with which all of us worked—Grigori Marchenko as a counterpart and the rest of us as professional staff—for many years. Pragma was both tolerant and supportive in countless ways. Dr. Mohammad Fatoorechie, president of Pragma, and Mr. David Lucterhand, who served as Chief of Party on its financial sector projects in Kazakhstan from 2000 to 2005 are responsible for Pragma's commitment to ensuring the reform's success through the total engagement of the firm's and for creating a wonderful team. Mr. Stephen Moody, Pragma's lead financial advisor in

Kazakhstan from 2000 to 2007, both contributed to the reform and helped in the creation of this book with comments, ideas, and technical analysis, while Dr. Michael Sze was responsible for creating Kazakhstan's actuarial profession. Their contributions and ideas run throughout this book, though neither they nor any of the others mentioned here, nor anyone not mentioned, are responsible for errors or mistaken interpretations.

Finally, we would be remiss in not acknowledging the exceptionally prompt and efficient Palgrave Macmillan editorial staff, including the staff of Macmillan Publishing Solutions and Ms. Emma Hamilton and Ms. Erin Ivy at the Palgrave Macmillan New York office.

List of Abbreviations

ADB	Asian Development Bank
AERI	annual expected retirement income
AFK	Association of Financiers of Kazakhstan
AGI	average gross income
AMC	asset management company
APF	Accumulative Pension Fund
BE	bank's equity capital
CBR	Central Bank of Russia
CL	contingent liabilities
CRPFA	Committee on Regulation of Pension Funds Activity
DAI	Development Alternatives, Inc.
EAMCI	estimated average monthly contributor's income
EBO	estate beneficial ownership
EDI	Economic Development Institute
ESR	effective support ratio
FSA	Financial Supervision Authority
GoK	Government of Kazakhstan
HSA	Health Savings Account
HMOE	historically market-oriented economies
IMF	International Monetary Fund
IMWG	Inter-ministerial Working Group
IPA	individual pension accounts
IR	investment returns
IRIS	Institute for Research on the Informal Sector
KAZAK I	Kazakhstan Actuarial Model I
KAZAK II	Kazakhstan Actuarial Model II
L	liability
LA	liquid assets
LBMA	London Bullion Market Association
LFPR	labor force participation rate
LOS	length of service
MinFin	Ministry of Finance
MLSP	Ministry of Labor and Social Protection
MMIF	Mandatory Medical Insurance Fund
MREC	minimum required equity capital
MSP	Ministry of Social Protection

mT	millions of Tenge
MW	minimum wages
NBK	National Bank of Kazakhstan
NDC	notional defined contribution
NFR	no further reform
NFRK	National Fund of the Republic of Kazakhstan
NPA	National Pension Agency
NSAPF	nonstate accumulation pension funds
NSC	National Securities Commission
OSI	Obligatory social insurance
OSL	official subsistence level
PA	pension assets
PAMC	pension asset management companies
PAYGO	pay-as-you-go
PC	pension contribution
PENMODEL	Kazakhstan Pension Reform Model
PF	Pension Fund
PROST	Pension Reform Options Simulation Toolkit
RCI	regulatory calculation index
REER	Real exchange rate
SAPF	State Accumulative Pension Fund
SARK	Statistical Agency of the Republic of Kazakhstan
SPPC	State Pension Payments Center
SIC	Social Individual Codes
SIF	State Insurance Fund
SIPC	Securities Investor Protection Corporation
SME	small and medium enterprise
SOE	state-owned enterprises
SRO	Self-Regulating Organization
SSA	Special State Allowance
SSIF	State Social Insurance Fund
TFR	total fertility rate
USAID	U.S. Agency for International Development

1

The Road to Kazakhstan's Pension and Social Reform

It is rare that cataclysmic social events in human history are addressed calmly and with deliberate consideration of a range of alternative responses. It is also uncommon outside economically advanced nations that the forces generating these events, the policy reforms, and their aftermath are documented in detail. Thus, Kazakhstan's pension reform is an almost unique event, as it was undertaken with a large amount of initial and ongoing study and has been documented exhaustively.

This book documents Kazakhstan's pension reform experience. It details the pressures that made the Soviet-era social security system unsustainable without large changes to the parameters of the system; it also discusses the options that were considered and presents the reforms actually undertaken. Forecasts of different scenarios are presented along with simulations of likely outcomes for different groups. We also analyze political and popular reactions to the reform (often sufficiently loud and negative to belie assertions that Kazakhstan's politicians are cowed and its press muzzled) and evaluate the underlying fears. Finally, this volume examines the pension system as it stands today, and addresses remaining shortcomings.

Because Kazakhstan's social security reform is so recent, the chapters that follow lie somewhere between history and diary—but are written from an analytical perspective based on economic and actuarial assessments. The volume is aimed primarily at social security policy analysts and technical specialists in these areas. At the same time, it should be of interest to political scientists and transition nation researchers who want to explore the way in which a major political decision was taken and who are interested in how anticipated consequences modified or restricted choices. First and foremost, the book is aimed at policymakers and technicians from other middle- and upper-middle-income countries who are considering pension system reforms. From China to Russia to Ukraine to Thailand to the Czech Republic, major structural changes are under consideration or are already under way. For these and other countries, Kazakhstan's experience should provide a valuable guide.

Ultimately, this book attempts to present a very recent economic history. As with all histories, the purpose is to analyze the motivations that drove major human decisions, to assess the consequences of those acts, and to serve as a guide to others who might be confronted with similar choices. Social policy decisions are often portrayed as the consequences of conflicting political forces or as game theoretic equilibria resulting from decisions taken by various players, and in most cases interpretations along these lines may be accurate. But during periods characterized by national crises, as was much of Kazakhstan's immediate post-independence period, decisions are made in a very different environment. Parallels to the "fog of war" should not be overdrawn. Yet, it is apparent that social policy decisions in Kazakhstan and elsewhere, taken under pressure of economic deterioration and transformation to a market basis, were often made by a handful of government officials and advisors in a hurried rather than deliberative manner, and with a highly imperfect grasp of the likely consequences of their actions. Given this environment, we argue below that the decision-making process in Kazakhstan was highly careful and, while often imperfect, overall presents a highly professional model for making policy choices under considerable pressure.

Some ten years into the process, the pension reform in Kazakhstan and the associated financial sector development both appear to be highly successful. Three major and many small pension funds compete in an increasingly professional environment. Assets are being carefully recorded, problems of duplicate accounts are being addressed, initial withdrawals are being handled without incident, and portfolios are being diversified (to the extent possible, given limited investment opportunities and the lack of viable collateral among many potential investors). Confidence in the pension system has risen dramatically; confidence in the financial sector as a whole is dramatically greater than it was only a few years ago.

These remarks are not intended to be self-serving, though we are open in acknowledging our own roles in the reform. Among the authors, Grigori Marchenko was the leading architect of the reforms that were instituted and, as chairman of Halyk (People's) Bank and an advisor to the president of Kazakhstan, remains one of the nation's most senior economic policymakers. The other authors all took part in the policy analysis that supported the decision making and were involved in prior demo-economic research that drew attention to the impending crises.

Rather, it is important to recognize that many decisions that appear successful ex post facto were not obvious at the time. The authors did not always agree with one another during the process, and all worried about many of the consequences. Nor did others who disagreed more fundamentally necessarily have flawed visions; for that matter, many of the reform's supporters had a fairly limited grasp of its implications. Because this is an economic rather than a political history, we do not dwell on the motivations or roles of individual actors. It will suffice to mention that many people took many important steps and that one of the main reasons for the success of the reforms is that a large number of mutually supporting measures were adopted within a reasonably short period. Kazakhstani and international advisors share credit for the design of these reforms. Credit for implementation and effective decision making belongs to the government of Kazakhstan (GoK). Ultimately, the decision to proceed with a series of bold pension and financial reforms lies with Kazakhstan's president, Nursultan Nazarbayev, who remained committed to reforms that initially were deeply unpopular.

1.1 Macroeconomic Pressures for Reform

The fundamental problems with the reformed Soviet (and then Kazakhstani) pay-as-you-go (PAYGO) defined benefit pension system emerged only in the post-independence era. In part, the Kazakhstan government's structural reforms in the areas of privatization generated new economic principles that conflicted with the "solidarity of generations" objective inherent in existing pension legislation, which remained a social principle even following the collapse of the Soviet Union. In the absence of incentives to be concerned with employees' future benefits, the growing private sector quickly learned how to evade paying mandatory pension contributions. More importantly, the Kazakhstan economy contracted dramatically during this period, and that in turn led to falling formal sector employment and wage and social payments arrears by those enterprises that did remain intact.

Kazakhstan emerged as an independent nation at the end of 1991 under conditions of complete dependence on ruble zone partners, especially Russia. With the collapse of interrepublican trade and simultaneous transition to the market economy, the starting point of which was the liberalization of prices in early 1992, inflation took off. Demand and production collapsed, and formal sector employment fell dramatically. In 1992 alone, consumer price inflation exceeded 3,000%, and GDP decreased by 11.3%. Worse was yet to come, as in 1993 Russia ended the ruble zone and stopped supplying other former Soviet republics with rubles, necessitating the creation of local currencies. Thus, the fall in social contribution compliance was accompanied by declining production even during the last years of the USSR and then by a collapsing GDP during the first years of independence. Since Kazakhstan's Pension Fund was sustained by payroll contributions, these factors together ensured that real contributions imploded.

As the share of workers employed in private and individual sectors rose from 32% in 1994 to 57.8% in 1997, the Pension Fund deficit increased from 12% to 53%. While individuals with non-payroll earnings are in principle obligated to make contributions, including 5% social tax payments, in reality contributions from individuals in small business and professional activities have been insignificant, especially in the early post-independence years (for example, in 1994 such contributions comprised only 0.14% of total Pension Fund revenue). Given rampant noncompliance, it is easy to understand the growth of the accumulated pension debts of nearly 40 billion tenge—nearly 3% of GDP—by the end of 1996 (table 1.1).

The desperate employment situation inevitably had a large, adverse impact on the pension system's dependency ratio, defined as the ratio of pension and other social benefit recipients to the number of social insurance contributors. While there were slightly fewer than 30 pensioners and beneficiaries per 100 workers paying insurance contributions in 1980, this number rose to 73 in 1997 and then to 83 in 1998. During this period, the proportion of pensioners and other social benefit recipients in Kazakhstan's population rose from 11.9% in 1980 to 17.1% in 1997.

Table 1.1 Kazakhstan's pension system: Main indicators, 1994–97

	1994	*1995*	*1996*	*1997*
Wage bill, billion tenge	111.0	271.7	335.3	339.3
Pension Fund revenue				
billion tenge	18.5	51.0	71.5	78.9
as % of wage bill	16.6%	18.8%	21.3%	23.2%
Mandatory contribution rate to the Pension Fund	27.0%	25.5%	25.5%	25.5%
Total amount of granted pensions and allowances:				
billion tenge	21.0	59.3	111.4	113.9
as % of wage bill	18.9%	21.8%	33.2%	33.6%
Total amount of paid pensions and allowances:				
billion tenge	18.5	52.8	79.8	139.0
as % of wage bill	16.6%	19.4%	23.8%	41.0%
Pension Fund deficit:				
billion tenge	25	8.2	39.9	60.2
as % of total amount of granted pensions and allowances	11.9%	13.9%	35.8%	52.8%
Accumulated pension debt, billion tenge	25	8.2	39.9	35.0
As % of GDP:				
Wage bill	26.2%	26.8%	23.7%	20.3%
Pension Fund revenues	4.4%	5.0%	5.1%	5.6%
Total amount of granted pensions and allowances	4.9%	5.8%	7.9%	6.8%
Accumulated pension debt	0.6%	0.8%	28%	21%
Amount of debt paid at the expense of transfers from Republican budget, billion tenge				35.0

Source: Seitenova and Becker, 2004

The surging system dependency ratio also reflected post-independence liberalization of pension eligibility. While nominal retirement ages (55 for females and 60 for males) did not change from Soviet levels, relaxed early retirement rules increased the numbers eligible for pensions. Before independence, less than 20% of new retirees received early retirement pensions or other favorable terms, but this share jumped to more than 30% during the period 1992–96 (Seitenova and Becker, 2004; also see Becker and Urzhumova, 1998). To its credit, the Kazakhstani government then took strict measures to restrict new retirement on favorable terms.

Overall, the 25% increase in the number of pension beneficiaries between 1988 and 1993, coupled with declining real contributions, gave rise to an increase in government pension expenditures from 5.5% of GDP in 1989 to 7.9% in 1996, though not before temporarily collapsing to 4.1% in 1993 as individual pension payments shrank. Worse, these expenditures would have been much higher if the government had completely indexed the benefit payments in accordance with inflation. In reality, replacement rates oscillated, generally increasing after independence (from 39% for all pensions in 1989 to 63% in 1994, before declining to 45% in 1997), but not nearly sufficiently to maintain real pension values.

Taken together, increased payroll tax burdens, growing numbers receiving early and favorable pensions, and the deteriorating macroeconomic situation created a powerful impetus for reform of the Soviet-style, defined benefit, PAYGO Solidarity pension system. This growth in the number of pensioners and recipients of social allowances was accompanied by a fall in the numbers of social insurance contributors, making pension security an increasingly critical issue for Kazakhstan's government. Moreover, the demographic situation, while not unfavorable by European, other former Soviet, or East Asian standards, also left little reason to be optimistic. On the contrary, cohort effects encouraged quick rather than delayed reform, especially if the reform involved switching to an Accumulative system. Something had to be done: maintenance of Kazakhstan's Solidarity system, with its current levels of funding as of January 1, 1998, was simply not an option.

An ironic consequence of Kazakhstan's dramatic economic recovery dating from mid-1999—with growth beyond anyone's wildest expectations in the preceding years when the pension reform decisions were taken—is that while this growth has been contributed to the Accumulative system's success, it would have made the Solidarity system look even (temporarily) better. The reason is simple: PAYGO pyramid schemes do best when the base is expanding, because both the contributor pool and their earnings (and hence social tax payments) are rising. In contrast, an Accumulative reform inevitably will be most unattractive at the outset, when taxes remain high and Solidarity payments are repressed to balance the transition budget. If the economy grows smoothly forever, net liabilities need never be repaid, and doing so is an unnecessary cost of an Accumulative system. But not only was the extent of Kazakhstan's surge unanticipated, it is neither guaranteed to continue indefinitely, nor is making social policy on the basis of optimistic assumptions good economics. Social protection is most important during poor economic conditions: virtually any reasonable policy will be effective during boom times.

1.2 Reform Options and the Experience of Other Countries

The global movement to reform public pension systems began in Chile and spread to other Latin American countries (for a superb summary, see Devesa-Carpio and Vidal-Meliá, 2002; for an overview of the Chilean reform and its aftermath, see Acuña and Iglesias, 2001). Introduced in 1981 under the Pinochet dictatorship as part of a multipronged liberalization policy aimed at spurring a lagging economy, the new individual accumulation account, defined contribution system was intended to fully supplant the old PAYGO public pension system.

Conditions in 1980 Chile were quite different from those in 1998 Kazakhstan. While Chile's economy was not flourishing, real per capita GDP was higher than in Kazakhstan; more importantly, its "formal sector" enterprises were stable, rather than reeling from economic dislocation and collapse. Transition costs in Chile were bound to be lower as well—as a typical dualistic society, much of the labor force was not covered by the preexisting state PAYGO system. In contrast, Kazakhstan retained the salient features of the Soviet welfare state, including virtually universal pension coverage. This system in the Soviet era entailed significant transfers from the central government to low-income, low-productivity agricultural and service sector workers, who comprised more than 40% of Kazakhstan's labor force, thus creating far higher transition costs than in Chile. Kazakhstan had both an older population and a younger retirement age than Chile, though it also had the "advantage" of higher elderly mortality. On the investment side also, the situation differed: Chile was a private enterprise economy with potentially diverse demand for pension fund assets; Kazakhstan initiated its pension reform with virtually no demand for these savings, other than to cover public sector deficits.

During the 1981–2000 period, the Chilean pension reform appeared to be highly successful and won much praise. Real rates of return to invested funds averaged nearly 11% annually and were negative in only two years (1995 and 1998). While returns to broad Chilean portfolios appear to have been even greater, such portfolios have had higher volatility (Srinivas, Whitehouse, and Yermo, 2001). Thus, the new system was both high return but conservative; the outcome has been that replacement rates (average pension as a percentage of average wage) have been far higher—nearly 80%—under the Accumulative system than under its PAYGO predecessor. On the other hand, this performance was strongly bolstered by conscious Chilean government policy, including high interest rates on public debt during the 1980s (which led to a concentration of pension fund assets in such debt), financial sector assistance during the 1983–84 crisis, and a generous recognition bond for past PAYGO contributions for workers who switched to the new system (Devesa-Carpio and Vidal-Meliá, 2002).

The Chilean system's limitations have included declining returns since the mid-1990s and high fees by U.S. (although not Latin American) standards, driven in large part by high marketing costs by competing pension funds. This fierce competition has resulted in high asset transfer rates (nearly 11% of all accounts in 2000) also, further adding to administrative costs. Against these limitations are Chile's overall very high growth rate of real GDP, its government's success in eliminating a vast and growing liability, and the system's surprisingly high coverage.

Chile's reform was eventually followed by several other Latin American countries, including Peru (1993), Colombia (1994), Argentina (1994), Costa Rica (1995), Uruguay (1996), Mexico (1997), Bolivia (1997), and El Salvador (1998). Coupled with gradual recognition from demographic projections of rapid aging in both developed and many developing countries, as well as an emphasis on controlling public expenditures, the World Bank (1994) began to emphasize social security reform as well. These reforms were especially important in the more developed and urbanized Latin American nations.

The Latin American reforms have been broadly similar, while varying in detail. The switch to an Accumulative system has been mandatory in Chile, Mexico, Bolivia, and El Salvador, but voluntary elsewhere. Payroll contribution rates range from 7.72% (Argentina) to 12.32% (Uruguay), except in Costa Rica, where no amount is specified. Nearly all countries have a minimum pension; several also have minimum rates of return guarantees. As of 2000, the proportion of assets invested in government debt ranged from 9% in Peru to 93% in Mexico; the proportion held as foreign assets ranged from zero (several countries) to 11% (Chile); total portfolio values ranged from US$482 million in El Salvador to US$36 billion in Chile (Devesa-Carpio and Vidal-Meliá, 2002).

The Latin American experience had a profound impact on the transition nations in Eastern Europe and the former Soviet Union. The Eastern European countries were the first to consider reforms, in part because of a more rapid political transition and in part because an older and more rapidly aging population made significant reform more urgent. Moreover, while Eastern European countries did not suffer economic collapses to the same extent as most former Soviet republics, they had aspirations of joining the European Union, and therefore faced great pressure to curb public expenditures.

Hungary became the first country to implement reforms, with initial planning in 1996, followed by the passing of an Accumulative system conversion law in the middle of 1997. Hungary faced intense pressure to reform: by 1995, pension recipients had risen to 75% of the employed population (Palacios and Rocha, 1998). With a replacement rate in excess of 60%, pension expenditures in the early 1990s ranged from 10% to 11% of GDP. Inasmuch as Hungary's working age population is set to shrink, and its elderly population will grow rapidly in the next half century, reform was inevitable. The resulting plan included an Accumulative pillar, a reformed PAYGO system, and increased retirement ages for both men and women.

Poland followed Hungary shortly thereafter and did so for roughly the same reasons. As in Hungary, the first PAYGO pillar was not dismantled. Despite having a younger population (and so fewer long-run demographic problems) and slightly lower replacement rates, Poland's pension system costs rivaled those of Hungary, averaging some 12% of GDP during the period 1992–98. While the reform adopted was complex, it was similar in spirit to the Latin American reforms and in addition converted the defined benefit PAYGO system with limited links to individual contributions to a more overt, "notional" defined contribution (NDC) system in which individual accounts are maintained (Chlon et al., 1999).

Bulgaria followed with a pension reform as well, with an Accumulative pillar coming into place in 2000, along with increased retirement age. As elsewhere, the objective was to curtail government transfers to cover pension fund deficits (Tafradjiyski, 2002). Bulgaria's problems were slightly less critical than those of Poland or Hungary, but pension expenditures as a share of GDP nonetheless reached 9.6% by 2000—a large figure, given pension replacement rates in recent years of 33% to 36%.

Elsewhere in the region, pension reform is getting under way more slowly. Russia considered a wide range of options between the mid-1990s and the early 2000s, and ultimately chose a complex three-pillar system (described in Chapter 11), but with a healthy fiscal system, faced little pressure to abandon the Solidarity system. Reforms are also being implemented in Estonia, Lithuania, and Croatia (Anusić et al., 2003), and we discuss these in later chapters. In Kyrgyzstan, the World Bank convinced the government to implement a notional defined contribution reform in late 1997, but economic difficulties that emerged in the middle of 1998 have prevented the reform from being effectively realized (for a detailed discussion, as well as of nascent reforms in Uzbekistan, see Becker et al., 2006). A three-pillar reform similar to that in Hungary is now being implemented in Romania as well (Zaman and Vasile, 2001).

In short, pension reform has spread from Latin America and swept through Eastern Europe and the former USSR—and is now spreading further to China (especially Laioning Province) and Southeast and South Asia. Kazakhstan, along with Hungary, became the first country outside Latin America to implement a substantial reform and, as suggested above, did so under circumstances that were, on net, far more challenging.

In addition to the graver economic situation and near absence of investment opportunities beyond government debt, Kazakhstan undertook its reforms with only a tiny financial sector and legal infrastructure underlying the new institutions. In effect, the country took an considerable chance, betting that the reform not only would relieve long-run public expenditures without bankrupting a shaky government budget during the transition but that it would also contribute to the emergence of a flourishing private financial sector. Yet, while the risks were substantial, the social payoff also had exceptional potential, since the new pension funds meant great institutional development in banking and finance, and also a potential flow of funds to sectors starved of capital. It was, in short, a high-risk/high-return choice; as in nearly all games with a substantial element of risk, it helped that the key movers remained calm and resolute.

A decade on, this decision appears to be paying off quite well, though we emphasize that a ten-year period is nowhere near conclusive in terms of social security reform. The number of events that had to have reasonably favorable outcomes for such success to be achieved is considerable, and Kazakhstan has been blessed both with good fortune, especially in the form of high minerals' prices (though there is a downside, since pension fund returns have been depressed severely) and skilled economic policy during this period. While one cannot count on a repetition elsewhere of surging export prices, much less the presence of competent policymakers, Kazakhstan's setting and outcome are sufficiently instructive that the case merits study by others considering reform.

At the same time, it is important to ask whether Kazakhstan in fact had to adopt a multipillar structure with a mandatory Accumulative system. Put purely in terms of pension reform and maintaining macroeconomic balances, the answer is negative—though the more difficult question, which cannot be answered in an introductory chapter, is whether a Solidarity system reform would have been easier in terms of meeting these objectives. This latter question is addressed in the coming chapters, as is an assessment of the importance of the Accumulative system's contribution to the nation's financial market development—a key strength that is easily recognized but difficult to quantify. It is also essential to put these questions in the context of 1997, and without the hindsight of seven years of rapid growth.

1.3 The Reforms and Initial Aftermath

The obvious point of departure is to consider contributions to Accumulative pension funds following the reforms and to compare them with social tax collections, since in principle the two types of contributions should be in fixed proportion (correcting for changes in social tax collection rates). The year 1998 serves as a base, in part because it was the first year of the pension reform and also because the State Center for Benefit Payments' (SCBP's) collection rate of pension contributions in 1998 (76.1%) did not differ markedly from those collected by Accumulative pension funds (71.1%). In the early postreform period, social tax compliance exceeded payment of pension contributions to the Accumulative pension funds (APFs). Some of this difference can be attributed to changes in legislation, according to which (since March 15, 1999) employers pay APF contributions from wage deductions rather than from their own funds, but the differences also in part reflected an initial lack of confidence in the Accumulative system and, hence, rampant evasion. That uncertainty as to the effectiveness of the Accumulative system should have been great in 1998–99 is hardly surprising in light of the Russian debt crisis, collapse of the ruble, and the shock effects that were quickly transmitted to the Kazakhstan economy, in particular to the consumer goods' industrial sector. The appreciation of the tenge vis-à-vis the ruble slowed economic recovery and added to hardships for many firms, thereby inducing at least some of them to delay social tax and, especially, Accumulative pension payments.

Indeed, confidence in the efficacy of any reform will inevitably reflect the underlying economic situation. Marked improvements in macroeconomic indicators (including rapid real GDP growth and controlled inflation) by 2002 had a positive effect on compliance with required pension contributions. Pension contributions collection rose by 42% in 2002 compared with 2001, while the social tax collection grew by less than 2%. By early 2003, the number of contributors of social tax and pension contributions were nearly identical, and APF contributions rose a further 65% between 2002 and 2005, as opposed to only 20% for social tax payments.

In addition to rapid growth of APFs as a whole, there has been an even more dramatic rise in contributions to private pension funds. This accelerating rise of share of non–state accumulation pension funds (NSAPFs) in total volume of pension contributions (from around 20% of total contributions and 24% of total assets in 1998 to 77% of total assets by the end of 2003: see Chapter 7) indicates increased interest by individual Kazakhstanis in independent selection of pension funds to which they can entrust accumulation of future pensions. At least in major urban centers, it is clear that workers near the top of the income distribution now regard their pension accumulations as real assets to be guarded carefully. A telling indicator of this phenomenon is the currently high rate of transfer of assets by individuals from one fund to another.

By 2002, the fifth year of the reform, there was increasing confidence in sustained economic growth, and at the same time, Kazakhstan's regulatory, legal, and oversight system had become increasingly mature, and also was regarded with increased confidence. By the end of the 2002, sixteen pension funds were functioning stably. Total net pension assets of these APFs equalled 258.6 billion tenge (approximately US$1.6 billion); two years later, assets had surged to 484.0 billion tenge (US$3.7 billion: see Moody, 2005). As of January 2003, 36.6% of assets of the pension funds were invested into short-term, medium-term, and long-term securities of the Ministry of Finance (MinFin); 12.7% were in notes of the the

National Bank of Kazakhstan (NBK); and 27.5% were held in shares and "A-listed" bonds. The share of APF assets invested in state securities and NBK notes declined from 98% in 1998 to 48% in 2002 and hit a low point of 22.5% in October 2006 (NBK, 2007). The corresponding rise of the investment share into corporate bonds can be regarded as a major step toward pension funds' participation in investment in Kazakhstan's real sector, though, as we shall see, it also reflects a healthy government fiscal situation, and hence little debt emission.

Indeed, the Russian crisis resulted in an early crisis for Kazakhstan's nascent pension fund accumulations that prompted GoK intervention on April 5, 1999. Kazakhstan had introduced a floating exchange rate for the tenge in early 1999, largely in response to the collapse of the Russian ruble, and this caused a sharp decline in the value of GoK T-bills. In response, the GoK offered APFs the option of converting part of their tenge T-bills into five-year U.S. dollar T-bills at the pre-devaluation exchange rate. This move demonstrated GoK's commitment to ensure a comparatively high level of protection to pension accumulations from the influences of unforeseen inflation and devaluation.

From a macrofinancial standpoint, Kazakhstan's pension reforms were a key element of the establishment of its international credibility. In 2002, Kazakhstan became the first Central Asian nation to receive investment grade status ratings on its sovereign debt. While high oil prices may have had some impact on Fitch rating agency's decision, rating agencies do not anticipate permanently high oil prices, and efforts to achieve long-term macroeconomic structural balances were critical as well. Indeed, Fitch forecast GoK deficits to be in the 2.1% to 3.3% of GDP range for 2001–3, and these forecasts proved pessimistic. But the key point is that the rating agency greatly discounted its importance, since its analysis made clear that the APFs could easily absorb that much debt, and more.[1]

Markets are less certain about the desirability of the growing concentration of Kazakhstan's financial sector, including both in banking (where the top three banks control the majority of assets) and in similarly concentrated pension funds. Because of the system's openness to new domestic entrants and the regulators' policy of actively encouraging potential foreign entrants throughout the financial sector, the consolidation that has taken place to date seems positive. Its main effect appears to have been the elimination of very small entities that had no potential to become viable. At the same time, the pension fund industry is characterized by several aggressive small funds that seek to either gain market niches or find new approaches that will enable them to compete aggressively with the large, established funds.

Taking all factors together, domestic and international financial analysts are optimistic about developments in Kazakhstan's financial sector in recent years, and also clearly attribute much of the success to the emergence of APFs and the underlying pension reforms. Yet, much remains to be achieved. Monetization of the Kazakhstan economy grew slowly in the initial transition and recovery stages: even through the end of 2002, total banking system assets (around US$7 billion) were only about 30% of GDP; M3/GDP was only 20.4%.[2] The recorded monetization since (M3/GDP rose to over 25% by the end of 2004, over 30% by 2005, and to 38% by the end of 2006) reflects surging oil revenues, leading to a new, unanticipated problem, namely, that of excess liquidity and inflationary pressure (Moody, 2007).

Given Kazakhstan's rapid GDP growth, very rapid APF asset accumulation (especially in dollar terms, given the appreciation of the tenge from 153 per dollar in 2002 to 124 per dollar in early 2007) has translated into only modest growth in the ratio of assets to GDP. At the end of the first five years of the Accumulative system, with steady collections and virtually no payments, assets equalled 7.1% of GDP. Over the next three years, the GDP share rose gradually to 8.54% before jumping to 9.34% by the end of 2006 (NBK, 2007). Between 2002 and February 2007, real assets grew at an annualized rate of nearly 26%, in nominal terms from 270 to 947 billion tenge. The comparable rise in dollar terms was from US$1.76 billion to US$7.62 billion.

Whether this annual absorption capacity of Kazakhstan's pension funds increases further will depend on overall economic growth, compliance with legal contribution requirements (and, in aggregate, the "re-formalization" of the economy), returns on existing assets, and withdrawals from the system, currently mainly due to emigration to Russia (at which point contributors are allowed to cash in their assets), but in the future due to growing retirements of contributors.

A long-term problem for Kazakhstan's pension funds has been lack of asset diversity (Fitch, 2002: 11), which in turn reflects low levels of investment demand outside the nation's petrochemical industry (which taps international resources of a completely different scale). Low aggregate investment demand means few bond issues by firms or local governments; given limited international asset holdings of pension funds, this inherently means great asset concentration (especially when one considers that bank deposits by the funds ultimately are largely investments in government debt). As of September 2001, pension fund holdings included 62% sovereign eurobonds and GoK paper, as against 20% invested in corporate bonds and 7% in A shares. While development of a mortgage market, new municipal bond issues, and economic growth all will contribute to asset diversification, there has been a significant lag in APF holdings' diversification. In several aspects, though, 2005 and 2006 appear to have been breakthrough years. The percentage of assets held in shares rose from 7% at the end of 2004 to more than 9% at the end of 2005, to an average of about 20% in late 2006 and early 2007 (NBK, 2007). The corporate bond share rose from slightly less than 25% in 2004 to nearly 31% in 2005, before declining to around 28% in late 2006 and early 2007. Perhaps most impressive is the rise of mortgage assets: from virtually nil in 2002, to almost 4% of assets by the end of 2004, to about 5.5% by the end of 2006.

However, the picture painted is slightly rosier than reality. APFs have reduced their shares of government debt not because of a deliberate diversification strategy, but because there is excess demand for T-bills. Pension funds still provide semicaptive savings to the Kazkahstan government—which at present does not need these resources, since high oil prices have at least temporarily eliminated deficits. In principle, this asset structure problem is solvable, given the infrastructure demand that exists. If the Republican and local governments exhibit good budgetary management and transparent, open procurement behavior, their vast potential demand for funding will find willing suppliers from the nation's pension funds. However, the APFs today hold no municipal bonds.

Indeed, an irony of the current situation is that the architects of pension reform quite reasonably envisioned that the Kazakhstani government would in fact have great need for pension savings and that it would be willing to pay high interest rates to secure these funds. High oil prices and rapid economic growth have enabled the Kazakhstani government to weather the initial pension reform period with declining deficits that, if one includes oil fund savings, have since turned to surpluses—despite the fact that reduced social contributions create a short-term deficit balloon. Limited demand for savings from the Republican and local governments, and from private investors, when coupled with growing supply of pension fund assets, inevitably causes a crash in yields, and this is exactly what has happened. Yields on GoK T-bills plummeted to below 6% by the end of 2002; by mid-2005 they fell further still, and were negative in real terms. Returns have oscillated since, but in real terms are close to zero and often negative. The same is true for returns on interbank lending, where interest rates on dollar loans have exceeded those on tenge transactions since February 2005 (NBK, 2007: 41). While these developments greatly reduce long-term debt service costs for the Kazakhstani government, they simultaneously greatly reduce short-term profitability of the nation's Accumulative pension funds.

This situation was completely unforeseen in the early years of the reform. Initial concerns were that the move from the Solidarity system would simply cause the "marketizing" of the nation's social expenditures and that in a high-demand, low-savings environment, GoK would pay high and possibly unsustainable yields to fund asset holders. With economic growth and high oil prices, the reverse is now the overwhelming concern. Since the oil sector has been funded through direct foreign investment, this growth did not result in an increase in the supply of corporate debt or equity instruments. At the same time, liquid funds accumulated in both banking and pension funds. Because of a shortage of sound investments in non-oil sectors, banks could not significantly increase their loan portfolios and hold additional securities instead, thereby competing with APFs for financial instruments.

Excess demand for securities resulted in negative real returns on short-term instruments. The situation was further exacerbated by the low rates of return in international markets and an appreciating *tenge*, the national currency, so that Kazakhstan's pension funds could not easily escape low domestic demand for funds and hence low domestic interest rates by buying foreign assets—even though the proportion of foreign assets a pension fund may hold in its portfolio is now 25%.

The nation's pension funds also can be accused of mismatching assets and liabilities. Confident until fairly recently that the tenge would continue to depreciate against the dollar, funds have tended to hold dollar-denominated assets. Yet, APF liabilities are denominated in tenge. As the dollar declines, pension funds then find themselves exposed. This is not presently a critical problem, since payments are still low. However, it does point to an unanticipated risk, and hence to a need to more carefully hedge assets. Overall, though, the problems that have arisen for the most part cannot be solved by the pension system: the true underlying limitation is a low level of investment demand outside the petrochemical industry, and addressing this "real sector" problem is one of the nation's greatest tasks.

These problems to date are largely academic, and the reform thus far has been rather painless if not easy, since payouts to pensioners are to date very small. This will change in the coming years as the contributing population ages. Even given the substantial amount of churning (moving from one pension fund to another) and withdrawal of accumulations in the event of emigration, current payouts are modest and are greatly exceeded by inflows. Recent financial losses, while far from trivial in light of falling interest rates and the tenge's appreciation against the dollar, therefore are unpleasant but not critical. In ten or fifteen years, a similar squeeze would be far more burdensome.

Nor have most of the social issues been fully sorted out. The initial reform appeared to be highly regressive, and one that would disfavor women. With rapid economic growth and budgetary stability, GoK has greatly increased Solidarity pension payments and has introduced a guaranteed minimum "demogrant" payment. These steps will substantially reverse the initial regressiveness. Still, it is important to remember that these steps are being taken during good times: it remains to be seen whether the government's social resolve will be maintained in more difficult periods.

1.4 And So the Story Unfolds: An Outline of the Remainder of the Book

The setting and the reforms have already been outlined. The next chapter moves to a more detailed discussion of the underlying economic and demographic situation in Kazakhstan. There can be no doubt that maintaining the status quo was not an option, but the situation is worth documenting fully in order to understand the pressures for reform. Chapter 3 provides both a discussion of the reform and a chronology of events. Political pressures, support, and opposition are discussed, though with limited reference to individual actors. The first of the reform's key goals—restoring macroeconomic stability—is considered in Chapter 4. We provide macroactuarial forecasts of the reform as expected at the time (that is, prior to the oil price boom and rapid economic growth) and explain how these projections were important in selecting key reform parameters.

The next three chapters consider the actual performance of the pension system during the period 1998–2005. Chapter 5 provides a macroeconomic background. Chapters 6 and 7 then examine the Solidarity and Accumulative systems, respectively. An important aspect of the public system is continued state provision of disability pensions, which are a large share of total pension payments in Kazakhstan and other formerly socialist nations. Chapter 6 addresses both disability patterns and state commitments along with options for supplemental private insurance. The Accumulative system as it has evolved is detailed in the following chapter.

Chapter 8 then turns to legal issues and institutional changes. Those who focus on economic, financial, and actuarial issues often overlook needed development of the legal and regulatory structures: this chapter provides both a sobering list of necessary changes and a blueprint for further developments. Chapter 9 addresses administrative issues generated by the reform, many of which were not fully anticipated. These included matters of pension fund and asset management companies' regulation and supervision, payout mechanisms, and the emergence of duplicate accounts. While the State Accumulative Pension Fund (SAPF) is no longer dominant today, there was a period when the emergence of successful private funds was in doubt and when SAPF management issues abounded.

Chapter 10 addresses social questions, and in particular the distributional consequences of the reform. It also examines forecasts for different genders and income groups, and addresses difficult questions relating to retirement age, interregional transfers, and the structure of retirement payouts. These issues set the stage for Chapter 11, which summarizes some of the key lessons learned from Kazakhstan's experience. These lessons touch on a range of sensitive topics, from the adequacy of the Accumulative pillar alone to distributional issues to the choice of retirement age. It also places the pension reform in the context of broader financial sector development.

Chapter 11 also places Kazakhstan in context. We discuss achievements and failures in Latin America and other transition countries with major reforms, such as Hungary. This chapter also summarizes the public/defined benefit/PAYGO vs. private/defined contribution/Accumulative system debate.

2

The Unsustainable Welfare State

2.1 Macroeconomic and Social Security System Post-Independence Trends

As discussed in Chapter 1, Kazakhstan was economically unprepared for independence when it came in 1991. Table 2.1 provides key macroeconomic indicators from 1990 to 1997. The years 1992–93 were characterized by economic collapse: by 1995, Kazakhstan's real GDP had fallen to 52.6% of its 1990 level, and the number of formal sector workers (and especially the number making regular social insurance contributions) fell rapidly and steadily. Formal sector employment was 30% lower in 1995 than in 1991; by 1997 the decline was by more than 50%. Thus, while real wages were fairly stable from 1994, when Kazakhstan became financially independent, to the onset of pension reform in 1998, this stability pertained only to a rapidly dwindling share of Kazakhstan's labor force (Becker and Urzhumova, 1998).

Of greater importance from the perspective of the Pension Fund, wage stability in the mid-1990s did not mean healthy receipts from payroll taxes, and hence a healthy Fund budgetary situation. Among enterprises that submitted reports to statistical authorities, the proportion that were unprofitable rose from a moderate 11% in 1991 to almost 60% by 1997. This rise translated directly into postponed tax payments to the state budget and accumulating wage arrears (so that recorded wages and actual wage receipts diverged sharply). Collection efforts also appear to have deteriorated, a point stressed by Auty (1998), Andrews (2000), and Baimateyeva (2002). By 1997, enterprises' overdue debt to the state budget reached 7.3% of GDP, and wage arrears reached 16% of the total wage bill. Largely as a result, GoK revenue as a share of GDP declined from 38.3% in 1990 to 16.7% by 1997.

The desperate employment situation inevitably had a large, adverse impact on the pension system's dependency ratio. While there were almost 30 pensioners and beneficiaries per 100 workers paying insurance contributions in 1980, this number rose to 73 in 1997 and then to 83 in 1998 (figure 2.1). During this period, the proportion of pensioners and other social benefit recipients in Kazakhstan's population rose from 11.9% in 1980 to 17.1% in 1997. The surging system

Table 2.1 Key macroeconomic indicators, Kazakhstan 1990–97

	1990	*1991*	*1992*	*1993*	*1994*	*1995*	*1996*	*1997*
Real GDP index	111.0	100.0	94.7	86.0	75.2	69.0	69.3	70.5
Consumer prices (annual average, % change)		190.9	1614.8	1758.4	1977.4	276.2	139.2	117.4
Market Exchange Rate, tenge per U.S. dollar (annual average)				5.31	36.35	61.12	67.76	75.56
State budget revenues as % of GDP	38.3	31.6	20.8	24.1	21.7	21.6	17.2	16.7
Consolidated budget deficit as % of GDP			−7.3	−1.4	−6.5	−3.7	−2.4	−3.8
Actual number of employees in formal sector of economy, 1991 = 100		100.0	97.2	86.8	78.0	69.6	60.1	48.3
Share of unprofitable enterprises as % of enterprises that submitted reports to Statistical Agency		10.7	14.1	23.8	35.3	45.7	53.2	57.2
Enterprises overdue debt to the State budget as % of GDP						5.50%	6.85%	7.27%
Enterprises wage arrears as % of wage bill						12.0%	15.0%	16.1%

Note: These figures exclude revenues of extrabudgetary funds (and do not include privatization receipts, which are treated as a financing item).
SARK or Pragma
Source: Pragma database

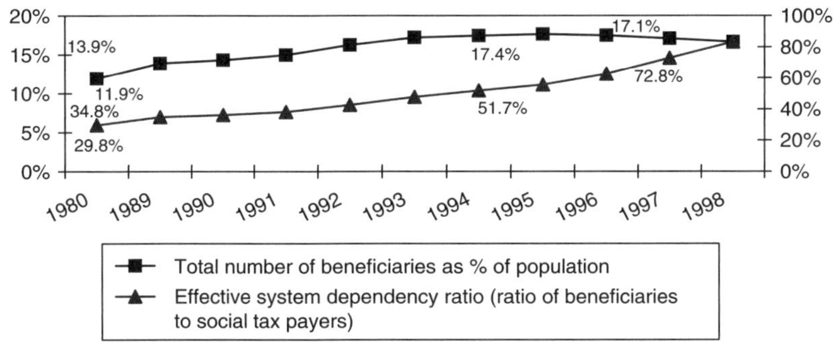

Figure 2.1 System dependency ratio dynamics
Source: Pragma database

dependency ratio also reflected post-independence liberalization of pension eligibility. While nominal retirement ages (55 for females and 60 for males) did not change from Soviet levels, relaxed early retirement rules increased the numbers eligible for pensions.

Shortly after independence, the Kazakhstan government amended the nation's Soviet-era 1991 pension law with Provision N1521-XII of July 3, 1992, according to which the eligibility for early retirement (53 for females and 58 for males) was extended to those Kazakhstani citizens with at least 25 years of service for men or 20 years for women, and who were unable to find new employment after being discharged from their prior job owing to layoffs or enterprise closure. Given the prevailing hyperinflation and deteriorating economic outlook during 1992–93, this amendment provoked significant early retirement, increasing the number of old-age pensions granted on standard and favorable terms by 19% and 30%, respectively, and decreasing the number of pensions with incomplete service by 27% in comparison with that during 1991.

These rule changes also changed the structure of Kazakhstan's pensioner population. The proportion of pensioners receiving supplemental payments (on "privileged" or favorable terms) increased from 20% in 1991 to 25% in 1996, while the proportion receiving the legal minimum pension (typically due to incomplete service) fell from 4.3% to 2.5%. While this latter decline at least in part could have reflected decreasing voluntary turnover in light of general economic uncertainty, there were no structural labor market or demographic reasons for the sudden jump in favorable pensions.[1] Rather, 1992 was a year of explosive growth in Kazakhstan's pensioner population overall: the number of new pensions due to standard years of service, old-age favorable pensions, and pensions to individuals prior to normal retirement age on the basis of "special merit" rose by 19%, 80%, and 139%, respectively. This abrupt jump is astonishing: almost half of those who retired in 1992 did so under favorable terms (table 2.2), and the effect was to destabilize the entire Solidarity system, even though the demographic structure was still reasonably favorable (Becker and Urzhumova, 1998). This surge of retirements under favorable conditions appears to lie in imperfections in old pension assignments legislation. Article 44 of the 1991 pension law greatly loosened standards of evidence of

Table 2.2 Structure of pensioner population and pension expenditures

	1989		*1993*		*1997*	
	Number of pensioners as % of total	*Amount of pensions as % of total*	*Number of pensioners as % of total*	*Amount of pensions as % of total*	*Number of pensioners as % of total*	*Amount of pensions as % of total*
Pensions,						
Of which	74.6%	81.0%	76.4%	82.4%	77.3%	81.9%
Old age pensions granted on standard terms	58.3%	62.5%	57.5%	62.5%	56.7%	59.5%
Old age pensions with incomplete service	3.9%	2.5%	2.0%	1.3%	1.9%	1.2%
Pensions granted on favorable terms						
Of which:	12.4%	16.0%	16.8%	18.7%	18.8%	21.3%
Old age pensions	11.1%	14.5%	15.4%	16.8%	16.7%	18.6%
Pensions for sufficient number of service	0.3%	0.4%	0.7%	0.7%	1.5%	1.7%
Pensions for special merit	0.9%	1.2%	0.8%	1.2%	0.6%	1.0%
Social allowances						
Of which:	25.4%	19.0%	23.6%	17.6%	22.7%	18.1%
All types of disability social allowances, including those received for military service	12.8%	10.9%	11.8%	9.1%	13.1%	10.0%
Survivorship social allowances	12.3%	7.9%	9.2%	7.5%	8.5%	7.5%
Old age social allowances	0.2%	0.1%	2.6%	1.0%	1.1%	0.5%
Total pensions and social allowances	100.0%	100.0%	100.0%	100.0%	100.0%	100.0%

Source: Pragma database

employment and social insurance contributions, including acceptance of unspecified "testimony" in the absence of records.

Not surprisingly, the existence of many different ways of establishing one's employment record was conducive to falsification. These came not only from employees but also from employers interested in shifting older workers to the state pension payroll in order to reduce salary burdens during the economic crisis. A simple method was simply to declare the loss of one's labor book; the worker could then get a new one and, with the connivance of management, list more advantageous service records on the basis of forged documents. Outright corruption almost certainly contributed as well to the jump in the number of new pensioners. Social welfare workers themselves received very low wages, but had limited supervisory and auditing control over their activities; there was also a very low level of computerization of record keeping and reporting with regard to pension payments.[2] Thus, these workers had ample opportunity and need to solicit bribes in exchange for altering documents, and it would be most surprising if they did not do so liberally. Privatization of state enterprises added further to chaos, making falsification easier still and creating still greater incentives to do so. Accelerating early retirement in the early and mid-1990s eventually resulted in an increase in the proportion of pension recipients in the total age 45+ population from less than 50% in the late Soviet period to more than 60% by 1994. Pension and social allowance recipients together as a share of the 45+ population rose from 61% in 1991 to 71% only four years later.

Unlike the situation prevailing for pensioners, the share of adult social allowance recipients in the 45+ population was relatively stable during period from 1983 to 1997, except in 1991, when the population share jumped 2.3 percentage points. There also has been a gradual (but accelerating during 1990–93) increase in the number of disability social allowances that began before Kazakhstan's independence. This rise appears to have been driven by the enactment of the USSR 1990 Law on Pension Provision. Thanks to this law, social pensions (i.e., allowances) began to be assigned to those citizens who lacked the right to labor service pensions, namely, old-age pensioners without sufficient work history, along with disabled individuals and survivors. By implication, the previous Soviet pension system did not cover all people who needed social support, despite the generally recognized claim that the USSR had for a long time provided comprehensive pension coverage. Consequently, Kazakhstan's post-independence pension problems stemmed not only from the drastic expansion of beneficiaries because of massive early retirement in 1992–93 but also because the Soviet government had just made a generous commitment in 1990 to provide *all* elderly people, disabled individuals, and survivors with either adequate labor or social pensions. While these promises were well intentioned, they ultimately became a Soviet legacy to be borne by the successor independent republics, including Kazakhstan.

In short, the 25% rise in pension beneficiaries between 1988 and 1993 plus the rising pension system dependency rate resulted in government pension expenditures growing from 5.45% of GDP in 1989 to 7.87% in 1996 (table 1.1). Moreover, this growing share of GDP committed to pensions occurred despite a sharp decline in real pension payments.

Replacement rate dynamics reflect the decline in value of the minimum old-age social pension. By 1997, the replacement rate of the maximum, favorable-term pension relative to average replacement rates had returned to the 1989 ratio. In contrast, social old-age pensions for those with inadequate length of service were consistently relatively smaller after independence than they were in 1989. This deterioration mainly reflected GoK's inability to maintain all categories of pensions and allowances. Moreover, stable replacement rates during a period of declining real wages mask falling real pensions: the maximum replacement rate fixed in 1994 (58.3%) was far from being identical in terms of its real content to the one in 1989. On the other hand, the low replacement rate during the waning years of Soviet power cannot but be a surprise: 35.4% in 1980 and 36.6% in 1989 (although, one must recognize that Soviet pensioners enjoyed a vast range of unpriced benefits). However, if one compares this figure with pension contributions by multiplying the average replacement rate by the average system dependency ratio, it appears that this replacement rate is consistent with social budget balance based on insurance contribution rates at that time.[3]

For the economy as a whole, the balanced average payroll tax necessary to maintain the social security system in fiscal balance—the required rate of pension contributions from the wage bill—had a sharp long-run upward trend from 1980 through 1998. Defining the payroll tax rate required for a balanced budget as the product of the average replacement rate and the system dependency ratio, it is apparent that the secular increase in the dependency ratio has been the main force in the trend. The year 1993 is the main anomaly, when the average replacement rate (28.6%) declined markedly, although, as we know, there was no sudden fall in the number of pensioners and hence in the system dependency ratio (47.7%).[4]

As large deficits emerged, the Kazakhstan government did take a series of steps aimed at increasing revenue. Prior to 1992, insurance contributions were accumulated in the State Social Insurance Fund (SSIF) budget, which was part of the State Insurance Fund (SIF) and had been used for different types of social security, including pension payments. After establishing the Pension Fund (PF) of the Republic of Kazakhstan in 1993, GoK began dividing total public social insurance contributions between the PF and SSIF according to proportions approved annually in the Republican budget. Moreover, with the establishment of the PF, its funds were no longer included in the state budget. Standard social contributions in 1992 amounted to 30% of the wage bill, of which 80.5% went to the PF and 19.5% went to the SSIF. Thus, the payroll tax for pension contributions in 1992 was 24.15%. In 1993, owing to escalating economic crisis, the payroll rate was increased to 27% and was maintained at that level until 1995. From 1995 through 1997, owing to the establishment of the Mandatory Medical Insurance Fund (MMIF), public social insurance contributions were divided among the PF, SSIF, and MMIF in 85:5:10 proportions. As a result, pension contribution payroll tax rate decreased to 25.5%, further contributing to the Pension Fund's surging deficit.

In summary, increased payroll tax burdens on Kazakhstan's contributing workers, rising numbers of pensioners, and the deteriorating macroeconomic situation combined to create a powerful impetus for reform of the PAYGO pension system. During the period 1989–97, growth of the number of pensioners and recipients of social allowances was accompanied by a fall in the numbers of social insurance contributors, making pension security a critical issue. By the beginning of 1998, maintaining Kazakhstan's Solidarity system with its current levels of funding was not an option. The question, then, was whether the PAYGO system could or should be retained in a reformed manner, or whether a completely new approach should be adopted.

2.2 Demographics and Growth: Was the Crisis Temporary?

One possibility, of course, is that the explosive growth of Kazakhstan's pension and social allowance recipients between 1990 and 1997 simply reflected economic deterioration, and that normalcy would return with economic recovery. Obviously, the rising pension population was linked to economic decline, as were the shrinking contributor base and shrinking real wages. From the GoK perspective in 1997, though, it was far from clear when sustained recovery would take place. The pension reform decisions were made during a time of nascent but highly tentative recovery—a recovery soon to be halted by the Russian crisis.

Furthermore, the horizon was troubling as well. The reason for this was simple: Kazakhstan has a gradually aging population, with declining birth rates more than offsetting rising adult and elderly mortality rates. The population projections in table 2.3, reproduced from Becker, Seitenova, and Urzhumova (2000, chap. 3, table 24), are difficult for any pension system. While these figures are forecasts, it

Table 2.3 Kazakhstan's population structure, 1999–2050 (*Baseline* actuarial simulation)

Year	*Total population (million)*	*Retirement age population (million)*	*Retirement age population growth rate (%)*	*Support ratio: Work age population/ retirement age population*
1999	14.96	1.66		5.4
2000	14.92	1.57	−5.9	5.9
2001	14.90	1.58	1.0	5.9
2002	14.91	1.58	−0.4	6.0
2003	14.94	1.57	−0.6	6.1
2004	14.99	1.56	−0.4	6.2
2005	15.07	1.57	0.7	6.3
2006	15.15	1.59	1.1	6.3
2007	15.25	1.60	0.5	6.4
2008	15.37	1.61	0.8	6.4
2009	15.50	1.63	1.3	6.4
2010	15.64	1.67	2.4	6.3
2015	16.49	1.95	3.4	5.5
2020	17.40	2.34	4.0	4.6
2025	18.17	2.80	3.0	4.0
2030	18.84	3.12	2.0	3.7
2035	19.50	3.51	2.4	3.4
2040	20.16	3.90	2.1	3.1
2045	20.82	4.36	2.4	2.8
2050	21.42	4.88	2.2	2.5

Source: Becker, Seitenova and Urzhumova (2000)

should be realized that those retiring in 2050 already have been born (in fact, 2050 will be the first year when most new regular-age retirees will not have been born in the Soviet era, in the unlikely case that retirement ages remain unchanged over the next half century). Thus, the trends depicted for the most part reflect demographic events that already have taken place or are under way. Underlying table 2.3 is the assumption of a gradual recovery of the total fertility rate (TFR, the expected number of live births per woman who survives her entire fecund life span, at current age-specific birth rates) from the below-replacement level to which it fell in the late 1990s and hence increased labor force growth after 2020.[5] The forecasts more optimistically assume gradually recovering life expectancy (for which evidence is weaker: see Becker and Urzhumova, 2005). If adult mortality does not decline considerably in the years to come, then the retirement age population will grow more slowly.

Presuming that economic recovery will bring demographic recovery, Kazakhstan's population should have reached a trough in 2001 and then begun to grow, despite total fertility rates still slightly below replacement level. The large number of young adults, reflecting high birth rates in the 1980s, drives this growth. The combination of a rapidly growing labor force in coming years due to demographic momentum, and small cohorts of new retirees, causes Kazakhstan's pension population to stagnate in the coming decade. Overall, the number of old-age pensioners in 2010 will be virtually identical to the number in 1999, despite significant mortality recovery. However, starting at the end of this decade, the pension population will begin to grow rapidly, peaking at an annual growth rate of 4.0% in 2020.[6]

These trends imply heavy burdens for a PAYGO system. This is not to say that such a system could not have been fashioned, but it would have to be based on rapidly rising retirement ages, more stringent social allowance eligibility, or rapid formal sector employment growth—which was not evident in 1997. Whether these conditions could have been met is addressed in subsequent chapters. But the impetus for moving away from the Solidarity system toward a defined contribution Accumulative system is easy to understand.

So, too, was the timing of the reform. As table 2.3 shows, the period from the mid-1990s through 2004 was a period of declining (old-age) retirement age population, because this is the retirement era for the very small cohort born during the Second World War. If Kazakhstan was going to make a switch from its Solidarity system toward an Accumulative system and intended to lower PAYGO payroll tax rates as part of that reform, then the obvious time to do so would be during a trough in the elderly population. Whenever the transition takes place, the country in question will experience a period of declining social contributions relative to obligations during the transition to an Accumulative system; its burden will be minimized during a small retirement cohort era. This is true regardless of whether one uses demographic projections from the late 1990s, with higher levels of emigration and higher mortality, or projections based on older historic data. In short, the stage was set in 1997 for a dramatic reform.

Ironically, the economic deterioration of the 1990s largely forestalled the impact of this impending demographic crunch on the Solidarity system. Indeed, Seitenova and Urzhumova, (2003, figure 2.4.2) in their actuarial simulations find that the required social tax necessary to ensure a 40% replacement in a PAYGO system will fall from about 22% today to about 13% in 2015 before gradually rising to 28% by the middle of the twenty-first century. While their results are obviously sensitive to underlying demographic, economic, and financial values chosen, one of the most critical assumptions is that social contribution compliance gradually grows from 43% to 58% of the employed population, and in particular to 56% by 2015. In effect, their economic recovery scenario implies extra growth in the number of contributing workers by 2.2% per annum between 2003 and 2015, so that while the working age population grows by only 8% over this period, the number of effective contributors grows by more than 43%. The simple moral to be gleaned is that pyramid schemes work well when the base grows rapidly, making any reasonable PAYGO scheme attractive during a period of economic recovery. Stated differently, Kazakhstan's economic collapse created a vast pool of labor that could be drawn into the formal sector, and doing just that during a period of economic recovery prevents demographic constraints from binding.

However, in the late 1990s, when the pension reform decisions were taken, the picture was one of continued formal sector job losses rather than of expansion. To base policy on what would have been super-optimistic forecasts would have been untenable. While Kazakhstan's boom has made the Accumulative system look better than it would have had economic crisis been maintained, it also would have been an exceptionally favorable era had a reformed Solidarity system been implemented. Eventually, however, this beneficent era would have to have ended.

To summarize, at the advent of Kazakhstan's pension reform, its pensioner population was expected to continue growing (even given an anticipated three-year increase in retirement age). However, the dual impact of small new retirement populations from World War II birth cohorts together with further reductions in the number of new retirees given the increase in old-age retirement eligibility from 55 to 58 for women and from 60 to 63 years for men, implied growth in the number of projected pensioners by only 0.7% annually from 1996 to 2010. In contrast, from 2010 to 2015, the annual increase was expected to rise to 2.4%. Given that moving from a PAYGO to an Accumulative system implied heavy transition costs, if Kazakhstan was going to make such a move, an obvious time to do so would be during a window of limited pressure on the Republican government's recurrent budget. From this perspective (though it was not a major force in the decision), the timing of Kazakhstan's reform was ideal.

In the long run, demographic structure matters less. Holding compliance and participation rates constant, as well as assuming fixed growth rates of individuals' real wages (w^*) and interest rates (r^*), PAYGO systems benefit from high population growth (p^*) environments. As pyramid schemes, PAYGO systems inherently benefit from demographic structures that generate a wide base. Of course, as Brown (1997) notes, to some extent this is misleading, since w^*, r^*, and p^* are interdependent. In particular, a society with higher p^* will generate higher returns r^* to relatively scarcer capital, for any given labor productivity growth rate. Consequently, if one chooses consistent parameter values, there is relatively little, if any, long-run benefit to maintaining a PAYGO system in a high population growth environment, or switching to an Accumulative system in a falling population setting—at least in a closed economy without globally determined interest rates.

Kazakhstan has neither fully open nor completely closed capital markets. To some extent, its gradually narrowing population pyramid makes a funded

Accumulative system attractive, *given fixed labor force participation, net emigration, retirement ages, and social tax or own pension accumulation fund compliance rates.* In fact, however, these rates had not been constant prior to Kazakhstan's pension reform; nor were they assumed to be in the various actuarial simulations. Differences in these assumptions have heavily influenced the three sets of actuarial forecasts (Mitchell Wiener's PENMODEL, which is used in Anderson et al., 1997, and Weiner, 1997; the World Bank's PROST-based KAZAK1 [Kazakhstan Actuarial Model] of Becker, Seitenova, and Urzhumova, 2000; and the more sophisticated KAZAK2 created by Seitenova and Urzhumova, 2003), as we detail in Chapter 4.

Given the weak economic performance of the period 1995–98, an assumption of rapid compliance improvements or growing labor force participation would have been irrationally optimistic. The initial PENMODEL was in fact highly optimistic, but KAZAK1 was much less so, thereby creating a demographic setting for several decades that would be unfavorable to a maintained PAYGO system.[7]

The rapid growth since 2000 has created a very different setting, and demographic forces are essentially unimportant in KAZAK2, since they are overwhelmed by the impact of rapid formal sector labor force growth and rising compliance. Especially given slow mortality recovery, but rapid wage growth, an environment that virtually demanded either radical PAYGO Solidarity reform or its abandonment has given way to one that is unusually favorable to a modified Solidarity system. But this could not have been known at the time reform options were being considered in the mid-1990s, nor would it have been appropriate to choose a permanent system based on a highly favorable medium-run macroeconomic and demographic environment. The prudent interpretation at the time was one of moderate long-run demographic pressure on the Solidarity system, coupled with a window of opportunity for a transition to a funded Accumulative structure.

2.3 Maintaining the Solidarity System

While there can be no doubt that the Solidarity system was under severe pressure by the mid-1990s, its fate was not clear. In part, this uncertainty stemmed from a weak information base: forecasts of Solidarity pension expenditures were made on the basis of wild guesses about future earnings growth rates, replacement rates, survival rates, compliance rates, and disability rates. Given that the environment was an unstable one in which many of these variables changed dramatically—age-specific mortality, for example, often changed by more than 10% from one year to another—it is not surprising that the forecasts have varied greatly.

Somewhat ironically, the initial forecasts of Anderson et al. (1997) of DAI seem incredibly optimistic given the times, with assumed 3% annual real GDP growth between 1996 and 2005, but only 0.76% real pension growth and 2% growth in the number of pensioners, and a stable old-age dependency rate. Under these conditions, it is not surprising that Solidarity pension expenditures as a share of GDP actually falls from 4.9% in 1996 to 4.4% in 2005, before rising gradually to 5.0% in 2010, 5.9% in 2025, and 7.3% in 2040—even without the gradual three-year rise in retirement age introduced in 1996. It is easy to design reforms that would have made simple Solidarity reforms quite adequate in such an environment; despite that, and perhaps bowing to the World Bank and USAID enthusiasm with a three-pillar system then prevailing, the DAI team recommended adopting a full, three-pillar system, including both mandatory and voluntary Accumulative systems.[8]

Subsequent analysis by Becker, Seitenova, and Urzhumova (1999, 2001) was based on more refined demographic and system financial estimates, and the numbers in turn were far more pessimistic. The 2001 report estimates total Solidarity system payments of 6.2% of GDP for 1999, requiring a Republican government transfer of 2.9% of GDP, despite introduction of the Accumulative system (which would have reduced both expenditures and, depending on social contribution rate assumptions, contributions). Even with the Accumulative system, and even assuming large savings by eliminating privileged Solidarity pensions (a gain of 1.4% of GDP in 2015, for example), they forecast a continued Solidarity deficit until at least 2008, and under pessimistic conditions until as long as 2025. Indeed, their 1999 study forecast, under some circumstances there might be a need for permanent support from the Republican government budget. Thus, they conclude:

> The implication of these demographic facts is that delayed pension reform would have been courting disaster. Kazakhstan could have controlled pension expenditures for the coming decade simply by raising retirement ages and cutting privileged pensions. Together with rapid labor force growth and economic recovery, these steps would have been sufficient to eliminate nearly all of the deficit.
>
> But that victory would have been a transitory one. The second decade of the 21st century will be characterized by a surge in retirements, and the numbers of pensioners will roughly double between 2010 and 2030. This growing elderly population—and stagnating labor force, since new work age adults will have been born in the low fertility 1990-2010 era—would put an untenable burden on even a reformed PAYGO Solidarity system. (Becker, Seitenova, and Urzhumova, 2001: 61).

There is indeed an irony in these contrasting findings. The Anderson et al. studies used parameter values exceptionally favorable to a reformed PAYGO system, but nonetheless accepted for less than obvious reasons the need for a "second pillar", that is, a mandatory, defined contribution Accumulative system. On the other hand, Becker, Seitenova and Urzhumova were highly skeptical about the new Accumulative system, but used updated parameters that made a continued PAYGO system far more problematic, especially in the medium term. For example, the Weiner PENMODEL inputs implied a doubling of the effective labor force between 1997 and 2012, and with that sort of broadening of the base, the system dependency ratio was forecast to decline by 30% between 1996 and 2002, and not to regain the 1996 level (0.39) until roughly 2025. KAZAK1 had a far more dismal view—effective contributors were projected to grow by only 30% during the first 15 years of the simulation; the old-age dependency ratio declined only by about 10% (owing to the small wartime-retiree cohort) from its base value of nearly 46%, and by 2027 had reached an alarming 65% level.

In effect, KAZAK1 painted a grim demographic and compliance scenario. By 1997, it was clear that Kazakhstan's TFR had fallen below replacement levels, and while the model assumed eventual recovery to replacement, its capturing of the fertility bust of the 1990s, and assumed low fertility during the first decade of the third millennium, together meant a stagnant labor force between 2010 and 2050. Becker, Seitenova, and Urzhumova (1999) also assumed bleak economic scenarios, in part because there was no basis for assuming otherwise at the time, and in part because they argued that the design of a social safety net should be predicated on its performance during difficult times—after all, any reasonable system will work well if economic growth of 7% is sustained.

The Kazakhstan government, and in particular the MinFin, was irritated by KAZAK1's pessimism, perhaps because it was unpleasant to accept such a gloomy picture. However, GoK's actions have been consistent with steps being taken in anticipation of just such a dismal outcome. The pension reform took place at a time of continued formal sector employment shrinkage, deteriorating tax compliance by the firms that remained, and rapid growth in the number of pensioners. Pension payments were often delayed and were sometimes paid in kind rather than in cash. The bottom-line motivation for the pension reform was simple: key policymakers in Kazakhstan's government almost certainly feared that they would not be able to get a handle on Solidarity obligations, and simultaneously would be unable to raise adequate funds—and absorbing a transfer from the Republican budget of 3% of GDP also seemed unsustainable. Government officials may have wanted macroactuarial modelers to use rosier parameter values that promised an imminent Solidarity turnaround, but clearly did not believe in the inevitability, or even likelihood, of such a recovery.

The irony is accentuated by the fact that the Kazakhstan government took clear steps to improve the Solidarity system's performance well prior to the main reform. Growth in early retirements halted, as did the surge in favorable retirements. The medium-term damage, however, largely had been done, as previous retirements could not be reversed.

As the chronology in Chapter 3 discusses in detail, as early as 1995 there was serious consideration of a dramatic pension reform, and agreement in principle by 1996. This initial engagement preceded rather than followed careful macroactuarial analysis of alternatives; indeed, one might argue that truly careful analysis did not occur until the third generation of models (KAZAK2) in 2002. This should not be taken as a severe criticism of the Kazakhstan government, but rather as a key to understanding its priorities. Short-term budget imbalance seems likely to have been the main driving force in the reform, which promised shedding of long-term government expenditure commitments, in concert with the short- to medium-term measures aimed at reducing premature and favorable retirements. The transition to a funded system inevitably would be expensive, but international development bank loans were anticipated.

It is difficult to know to what extent the World Bank's enthusiasm for a multipillar system, or Russia's interest at the time in a defined contribution Accumulative system, furthered Kazakhstan's interest in such a reform. Certainly, these were not negative factors. But desire to bring under control an extensive social security system was surely key: Kazakhstani policymakers in the mid-1990s could not have been sure of their success in curbing obligations or of increasing revenues, and the chance to remove a permanent threat to macroeconomic fiscal stability must have been most inviting.

3

The Political Economy of the Reform

"The cement never sets on British pensions legislation!"

(David Blake, Pension Schemes and Pension Funds in the United Kingdom, 2003)

3.1 Initial Efforts to Reform the Solidarity System

The first steps to reform Kazakhstan's pension system were actually taken before the USSR's collapse. Following discussion in the late 1980s, the Soviet government enacted new pension legislation in 1990 in order to establish the USSR Pension Fund and its republican branches.[1] The USSR Pension Fund was funded by contributions from enterprises and organizations and was established as an independent "financial-banking system." The separation of the pension system from the state budget that the act represented was a step toward more explicit recognition of pension liabilities of the state. While the 1990 legislation can be seen as an initial step toward a funded system, the USSR Pension Fund continued to operate on PAYGO principles.

The law elaborated a system of rather liberal pension benefits, but failed to specify a proper mechanism for collecting pension contributions.[2] The disorder of early 1990s made collection of pension fund contributions increasingly difficult. Creation of the Pension Fund of the Republic of Kazakhstan by a 1993 decree did little to improve collection of the fund's revenues.[3] Although the decree specified the PF's revenue sources, including pension insurance premiums to be made by the employers and the employees, it failed to adequately delineate the functions of collecting, enforcing, and auditing bodies. These essentially tax administration measures were left to the Ministry of Social Protection (MSP) and the PF itself, which had no institutional capacity to perform these functions. Nominally mandatory, the contributions could not be enforced in the same way as taxes because few credible penalties to noncompliant employers were specified in the legislation. As contribution rates declined further, the PF began to delay pension payments by several months. Because of hyperinflation, delayed payments greatly reduced the real value of pensions relative to contributions. When inflation was brought under control in late 1994, pension arrears began to accumulate again.

Most measures taken during 1993–1996 consisted of efforts to improve PF operations (Orenstein, 2000). Government tried to increase compliance rates by specifying the deadlines for transferring payments and imposing fines for the delays,[4] by mandating transfer of collections from the regional branches of the MSP to the PF and by motivating the collectors,[5] by charging the MinFin to pay arrears from the central Republican government budget and by improving the payments mechanism,[6] by increasing personal responsibility for untimely transfer of contributions,[7] by increasing late-payment fines imposed on delinquent contributors,[8] by granting delinquent contributors a once-off fine amnesty in November 1995,[9] and then by granting it again just fifteen months later.[10]

As a result of these efforts, the process of collection began to involve a number of government agencies that traditionally were not associated with running a pension system. If in 1993 the operation of the PF was a sole prerogative and responsibility of the MSP, by the end of 1995 it involved MinFin, the NBK, the Ministry of Labor, regional branches of these agencies, and local administration. Although compliance improved, the resultant system of revenue collection remained somewhat inefficient and ineffectual, and demanded continuous attention from top government officials. Meanwhile, pensioners, who saw the real value of their pensions decline as a result of pension arrears, became increasingly vocal critics of the government. Dissatisfied with the futility of earlier attempts to fix the pension system, the government also began to look for more radical ways to address the problems of the pension system.

Thus, it was not surprising that in late 1995, Prime Minister Kazhegeldin, a staunch supporter of market reforms, directed the MSP to prepare draft legislation for pension reform within two months, including creation of the system of voluntary pension insurance.[11] This initiative was further supported by a presidential edict.[12] Eventually, the representatives of the ministries and of the NBK formed a working group charged with drafting two law proposals in spring 1996, one of which was intended to establish the legal basis for voluntary private pensions, while the other aimed at addressing the immediate problems of Solidarity pensions.[13]

Most likely, the notion of voluntary pension provision was borrowed from Russia, where a corresponding bill "On Non-Government Pension Funds" was introduced into the Duma in April 1995. Under the proposal on voluntary non-government pension funds, workers and employers could make contributions to private pension funds on a voluntary basis, with the rate determined by both sides in a pension contract. Pension contributions in turn would be accumulated by pension funds on individual accounts and be invested in available instruments.

The government agreed to the proposal. During parliamentary discussions, some MPs proposed that the pension funds be licensed and regulated by the national bank. The NBK governor agreed to these demands during parliamentary discussions despite concerns about the resulting burden on the bank's supervision department. NBK's reluctance was well justified—the law failed to outline properly the legal and regulatory environment in which the voluntary pension funds were supposed to operate. This was not surprising given the short history of investment financing in Kazakhstan and the lack of special regulatory experience on the part of the authorities. The lack of clear specification placed both NBK and the MLSP in an awkward position, as the law assigned them supervisory functions and responsibilities without spelling these out clearly. The development of a proper regulatory framework and the procedures for private industry did not really begin until after the law had been enacted.

The Kazakhstan voluntary pensions' proposal was approved and signed within six months of introduction, unlike the Russian voluntary pensions' bill, which took more than three years until passed by the Duma.[14] Prepared and adopted in a rush, the Kazakh law had little impact, and hardly any private accounts were created before the new pension law superseded it on June 20, 1997. However, this was not a failure by the 1996 reform's designers. In fact, neither the government in general nor the NBK in particular wanted to promote a voluntary contributions approach, which even then was widely recognized as pointless. The subsequent experience of neighboring Kyrgyzstan with voluntary funds, which attracted only a trivial number of contributors, confirmed their skepticism.

In Kazakhstan, voluntary pension funds played only a tiny role in the design of the pension fund industry. This limited role is unsurprising, since the newly established funds had little time to develop the capacity for representing and defending their institutional interests.[15] Cross-country study by James and Brooks (2001) finds evidence that "well-established voluntary pension plans facilitate the move toward a mandatory funded plan, with substantial private management, providing it is shaped in such a way that their role is maintained and extended, rather than displaced." They argue that Hungary's voluntary pension funds "lobbied successfully for regulations that matched their organizational structure." While Kazakhstan's voluntary pension funds could hardly advance the interests of the industry at the time, their establishment raised the issues of ownership and regulation of pension funds,[16] taxation of contributions,[17] and annuity provision (DAI, 1996c) before the launch of pension privatization reform in 1997.

Immediately after the adoption of the law, international consultants (from the U.S. consultancy DAI, with funding from the U.S. Agency for International Development (USAID)) began delineating the rights and the responsibilities of the pension funds and the beneficiaries, exploring the payout options, and assessing tax implications for pension plans, all of which were made available to the concerned parties within the government (DAI, 1996c). In that sense, the law on the voluntary pension funds facilitated the development of a pension fund industry as early as the summer of 1996 by initiating the discussions between GoK and the prospective pension funds. However, GoK largely ignored the expatriate consultants' recommendations on voluntary pension funds in preparation of a more radical initiative.

The second set of legislative proposals included a number of amendments to the pension law, originally adopted in 1991. The proposal called for a gradual increase in the age of retirement from 55 to 58 for women and from 60 to 63 for men. The increases were to be made in half-year increments over the period July 1996–July 2001. By reducing pension obligations of the state, this step moved the pension system towards fiscal sustainability. It was also unpopular and met fierce resistance in parliament, to the extent that the government resorted to a confidence vote to pass it.

In retrospect, these amendments paved the way for the nation's subsequent radical pension reform. In addition to being generally beneficial to the pension system, higher retirement age reduced political hurdles for the transition from PAYGO to private pension accounts.[18] Introduction of voluntary pension funds, while not successful on its own, initiated the discussions of the idea of private pensions and raised issues of pension fund regulation. Activity of the intergovernmental working group increased the awareness of the various parties involved about other actors and helped consolidate their efforts. The failure of voluntary pension funds also underscored the importance both of developing a mature stock market and of mandating defined contributions, rather than basing pension reform on the development of private pension funds.

Early retirement ages and generous benefits created negative incentives for continued labor force participation and hence contributions to the Solidarity pension system. The large informal sector meant that the system old-age dependency ratio (ratio of elderly population to working-age population) of 0.18, a value quite favorable to a PAYGO system, translated into a very high pensioners-to-contributors dependency ratio of .56 (Andrews, 2001). This high dependency ratio in turn necessitated high payroll contribution rates, further worsening incentives for workers to participate in the formal labor market and for firms to make regular contributions. As a result, the tax base kept shrinking and tax evasion became pervasive.

Parallel to these developments, the World Bank and USAID began providing what proved to be ongoing technical assistance in the area of pension reform. USAID strongly encouraged reforms, emphasizing both improvements to the Solidarity system and ultimate implementation of a multipillar system. The World Bank engaged various ministries in discussions of pension reforms, advocating a multipillar pension system and cost reduction of the Solidarity component. GoK also received analytical reports from the IMF and from the Asian Development Bank (ADB), in addition to ADB technical assistance. The initial major international advisory group was funded by the World Bank, which contracted with DAI to provide technical support for development of pension funds. DAI's various reports from 1996 cited excessive benefits and poor compliance as the main threats to the sustainability of the pension system. Based on these diagnostics, DAI recommended improving compliance through improved administration of contributions, better intergovernmental structure of pension collections, and an improved incentive structure by establishing a clearer connection between wages and pensions (Evans-Young, 1996). However, all recommendations referred to the existing unfunded pension system and discussed no alternatives to Solidarity systems (DAI, 1996a).

3.2 Pension Reform Preparation: The Concept Paper

3.2.1 New Players

Rising retirement age did not improve the compliance rate. Because of poor coordination between the MSP and the Tax Administration, the PF collected less than 45% of planned revenues in 1996, and by the end of the year pension arrears reached 2% of GDP. In addition to low compliance, the pension system lacked procedural uniformity in collection of contributions and allocation of payments, and suffered from excessively broad eligibility and poorly differentiated benefits. Specifically, full-service benefits could reach a maximum of 60% of highest wage within any twelve consecutive months for workers with twenty years' work history for women and twenty-five years' for men, assuming that this effort had been properly recorded in a person's "Individual Labor Book." In addition to formal employment, work history recognized military service, childcare for up to three years for nonworking persons, and invalid care, university, vocational, and professional training, and other activities that justified nonparticipation in the labor force. These terms were inherited from Soviet pension laws; in addition, credit for periods of private business activity was added in the early 1990s, as was a tripling of the years credited for those exposed to radiation from nuclear tests.

The inability of the MSP to address problems that plagued the PF since its creation in 1993 only heightened government's frustration with the PAYGO system. By late 1995, top government officials were beginning to realize the extent of the problems, while the ability of MSP to address the problem without the involvement of MinFin and the NBK was seriously questioned.

By 1996, USAID had emerged as the leading provider of technical assistance to GoK in the area of economic policy. USAID began actively participating in a number of economic policy reforms as early as 1993, and in so doing forged close links with senior MinFin and NBK officials. In 1995, the government produced sweeping economic reforms that largely liberalized Kazakhstan's economy, thereby providing the institutional foundations for future economic success (Chapter 5). USAID initially provided technical assistance in tax administration, intergovernmental finance, budget reform, and, from early 1996, social security reform. USAID contracted with DAI, whose consultants began to work with the MSP on pension provision and administration. DAI did not last long: USAID was dissatisfied for many reasons, and in April 1997 awarded the pension work to the consultancy IMCC, whose staff were key counterparts on the reform for about three years. IMCC in turn was replaced by the consultancy Pragma in 2000, but virtually all local staff and several expatriates were retained, and remained engaged as the projects moved from pension reform to financial and insurance institution development. Staff turnover was remarkably low, so that many technical members were involved from 1998 to 2000 up until the end of 2005, when the successor projects concluded. This stability, along with comparable stability on the GoK side, prevented long gaps in activity and loss of institutional knowledge.

When the NBK first became involved in the administration of the pension system in 1994, its role was limited to "accepting pension contributions," but expanded with the adoption of the law on voluntary pension funds. The National Bank had to delineate its own responsibilities as the regulator of these funds and started working on a concept paper outlining voluntary pension funds' development in the summer of 1996. The NBK worked with an ADB-funded consultant whose literature raised its awareness of alternatives to a PAYGO pension system, and also confirmed its skepticism with respect to the ability of the voluntary pension funds to replace the insolvent Solidarity system. In consequence, NBK staff began to see mandatory contributions combined with private pension funds as the defining principle of the much-needed reform.

In August 1996, the prime minister created an Inter-ministerial Working Group (IMWG), chaired by Grigori Marchenko and charged with preparation of the pension reform concept paper. Although the working group received recommendations from expatriate consultants working with the Ministry of Labor aimed at improving the viability and efficiency of Solidarity-type pensions, the group nevertheless proposed that Kazakhstan move to a new three-tier system. According to their proposal, this system would combine (1) a mandatory public PAYGO pension system providing basic old-age, invalidity, and survivor benefits; (2) a mandatory system of individual contributions to funded pension accounts that would be managed and invested by private pension funds; and (3) a framework for private voluntary supplemental pension plans that would be provided with tax incentives and be regulated by the state. However, this proposal did not advance to legislators.

The current and former chairman of the NBK, the Minister of Social Protection, and a deputy chairman of the NBK were the highest-ranking officials in the group. It was then that the NBK management learned of the USAID-funded pension reform project working independently with the Ministry of Labor. DAI, the lead consultancy, was disheartened by lack of progress with Ministry of Labor senior management—presumably, because the ministry strongly resisted abandonment of the Solidarity system. Discussions with these consultants further strengthened the belief of NBK team in the mandatory private pensions. In order to convince GoK of advantages of a funded Accumulative pension system, the expatriate advisors composed a number of papers regarding private and public pension systems. These papers were intended to serve as the basis for a series of seminars designed to educate all interested parties on the basics of pension plans. These studies were wide ranging, covering the role of insurance companies and actuaries, pension fund management, annuity payout options for private pensions, the effect of demographic factors on pension plan funding, the role of actuarial analysis in management of pension fund cash flows, and actuarial analysis of the public pension system. The effect of these papers was to strengthen the intellectual basis for a radical reform.

3.2.2 The NBK Proposal

In late October 1996, two members of the IMWG, Oraz Jandosov and Marchenko, then chairman and deputy chairman of the NBK, respectively, prepared and presented a note on pension reform to the president of Kazakhstan, Nursultan Nazarbayev. This note proposed an alternative plan for a pension system reform, tightly integrating three components of a pension-cum-broad privatization reform. The elements included establishment of private pension funds, the development of a securities market, and privatization of the nation's state-owned enterprises (SOEs). The revenues from privatization of SOEs would finance the transition from a PAYGO to a fully funded pension system; public offering of SOE shares would boost the activity of a shallow stock market, while SOE shares would become the major investment instrument for the private pension funds, promising healthy returns on pension contributions.

Originating in the NBK, the Jandosov-Marchenko proposal emphasized private pensions and integrated the individual Accumulative system with stock market development, sharply differentiating this proposal from the proposal of the IMWG. It would be hard to imagine such a reform conceived in the MSP, which was interested mainly in fixing the Solidarity system, or in MinFin, which would be more cautious about the fiscal costs of transition. However, the NBK proposal won the approval of Prime Minister Akiezhan Kazhegeldin on the strength of its privatization component, which could legitimize the results of earlier privatization efforts and make these results irreversible through mass involvement of pension plan participants. In a series of meetings with Jandosov and Marchenko in November 1996, President Nazarbayev agreed to the general concept of the proposed pension reform. The note became the prototype for the pension reform Concept.

As technical support to the IMWG, DAI delivered educational seminars organized by the MLSP and sponsored by USAID, the World Bank's Economic Development Institute (EDI), and the ADB. DAI consultants prepared a concept paper on multipillar pension reform in Kazakhstan and presented it at one such meeting in Washington, D.C., in late November 1996. Kazakhstani delegation members Marchenko, by now chairman of the National Securities Commission (NSC), and Senator Daulet H. Sembaev (also a former chairman of the NBK) criticized it for lack of detailed actuarial and financial analysis of the cost of alternative structures. Subsequently, DAI prepared fairly crude computations of the financial costs of alternative multipillar pension systems to back the concept paper and presented them to the IMWG the following month. While limited confidence in international advisors might have induced many governments to delay reforms, in Kazakhstan it had the reverse effect, building self-confidence and leading to a determination to forge ahead.

While at the conference, Kazakh officials informed the World Bank of the government's plans to introduce a multipillar system in 1998. However, given the state of financial and economic development, the Bank representatives were skeptical about the prospects for such a reform. The experience of working on pension systems reforms in over 20 countries dictated that it would take at least four to five years just to prepare the introduction of such a reform in Kazakhstan. Despite the cool reception, the Kazakhstan government proceeded to design the main features of the reform.[19]

The list of blue-chip state-owned enterprises that were intended to form a backbone of the investment portfolio of the pension funds was agreed upon consultation with President Nazarbayev. However, it was repeatedly revised, as there were a number of attempts to replace blue chips with less attractive or even failing enterprises. The privatization list was at the center of struggle between the privatization party and a party opposing large-scale privatization. The opponents represented the interests of top SOE managers and the ministries overseeing large SOEs. In December 1996, the list of enterprises slated for privatization eventually appeared in a government decree.[20] The list reflected a compromise, with either the most attractive enterprises removed from the list or the shares slated for privatization significantly reduced.

3.2.3 Concept Preparation

In January, 1997, Prime Minister Kazhegeldin replaced the initial Pension Reform Concept working group with a new one (*Order of the Prime Minister #16-p*, January 30, 1997), even though the first group had been in operation for only five months.[21] This document imparted a sense of urgency to the task of the Concept preparation. The new group was smaller, higher ranking, had fewer representatives from MLSP and the Majilis (the lower chamber of parliament) and more representative of government financial institutions (MinFin, Ministry of the Economy, NSC, and NBK), voluntary pension funds, and the Senate (the upper branch of parliament).[22] The new timetable was extremely tight, allowing less than 45 days for preparation of the final draft of the Concept, as opposed to five months given to the first working group. The MLSP was directed to "provide the data for actuarial forecasts" within 24 hours (these forecasts are discussed in Chapter 4). Along with the tasks given to the working group, *Order 16-p* obligated the heads of the ministries and departments participating in development of the Concept to organize departmental workgroups, and to organize their interaction with other working groups.

As the only members of the old working group who remained in the new one were Jandosov, Sembaev, and Marchenko (the present, former, and future NBK chairmen, respectively), it is not surprising that they became the new group's informal leaders. Their first objective was to secure the support of MinFin by downplaying the fiscal costs of the reform for both the pension system and the Treasury. Other ministries had their doubts too, but many members of the group had already tried and failed to address the problems of the pension system, which hardly positioned them to criticize the proposed social security privatization. Tight deadlines and the lack of technical expertize also thwarted the emergence of potential criticism. However, the most decisive factor in swaying the group was backing for the radical reforms from both the president and the prime minister.

Once the Concept paper was prepared, all members of the working group signed it, staking their personal reputations on the success of the reform. The unwavering support and active involvement of every ministry that was part of the working group during the next two years should be credited to this early commitment-building effort. GoK's practice of using working groups as a commitment-building technique was shrewd, and it seems to have been a novel idea save for in a few mature, wealthy democracies. The pension working groups were not the first intergovernmental working groups, as by 1996 this practice had become standard in Kazakhstan—though they were not always successful, as earlier attempts at reforming the pensions indicated.

In early March 1997, the working group distributed the first draft of the Concept. It proposed to split the original Solidarity pension contributions (equal to 25.5% of the gross wage bill) between public Solidarity pensions (15.5%; later amended to 15.0%) and mandatory contributions to the individual accounts in private pension funds (10%). The rights of current Solidarity pension recipients would be honored, but mandatory contribution private pensions were to eventually replace Solidarity pensions as the number of workers with work experience prior to the reform declined over time. Offering workers a choice between a defined-benefit Solidarity system and a defined-contribution Accumulative system was not envisioned. Privatization and oil revenues would be used for financing the resulting shortage of public pension revenues during the transition period. Other features of the Concept's recommendations for plan design and financing included complete elimination of public pension system benefits over a period of 30 years; financing of the state pension system through a combination of public pension system contributions by employers, and financing from the Republican budget; continued Solidarity social, disability, and survivor benefits, but to be paid out of the Republican budget; a private pension fund tier funded by voluntary contributions by employees and employers; and a minimum guaranteed pension for individuals with at least thirty years of participation, equal to the minimum living cost in Kazakhstan.

As the government worked in earnest on the draft pension law in early 1997, a complex issue that arose concerned safety of pension fund assets, both in legal and financial respects. One of the solutions in the legal environment of Kazakhstan was to create asset management companies (AMCs), a legal entity in addition to the pension fund. Even though many believed that it would be possible to create a structure without management companies, the Concept recommended adoption of a system with dual entity pension funds. According to the Concept, the AMCs were designed to guard against financial fraud and embezzlement still fresh in the memory of contributors. This debate was complex, and the legal solutions and possible implications of adopting them are considered in Chapter 8. At the time, the both the DAI and IMCC advisers supported the proposed AMCs.

While it seems difficult to imagine today, given the emergence of a vibrant (if still small) actuarial profession, in 1997 there were no Kazakhstani actuaries whatsoever. In their absence, the IMWG had to rely on the DAI and then IMCC projections in their development of a pension reform concept paper. Mitchell Weiner, DAI's actuarial consultant, and the rest of DAI or IMCC team directly supported the IMWG by preparing fiscal analysis of the various proposed pension reform scenarios. Thus, the IMWG was given estimates of accrued liabilities, annual benefit payments and contributions, and emerging deficits. The working group also received detailed analysis of the savings generated by each proposed change in design features. However, the IMWG often disregarded Weiner's advice, in part because of different views on pension reform among members of group and in part because of the very short time given by GoK for the Concept's preparation, but mainly because financial and actuarial considerations were of secondary importance to the designers. The designers believed that the reform was required and also felt that the window of opportunity would close if reform opponents were to regain influence on or within the government and, eventually, on the president. Thus, the reformers viewed imperfections of the proposed Concept to be secondary; meeting the deadline was the priority.

While IMCC and DAI worked on their response to the Concept, members of the working group headed by Deputy Prime Minister (and previous Minister of Finance)

Aleksandr Pavlov and Senatorial Budget Committee Chairman Sembaev visited provincial centers and had intensive discussions with the public, the trade unions, and the employers to promote the concept and receive feedback on the proposal. As a result, more than 200 amendments were introduced in the Concept, the most important one being the introduction of a government-run pension fund, in addition to private pension funds.

The SAPF, as it was called, would be a default option for workers who did not indicate a preferred private pension fund; it also represented a sensible alternative for workers who mistrusted private financial institutions. The fund would provide explicit government guarantees on pension contributions and help build public trust in the pension fund industry by investing in government bonds. The contributors could transfer their balances to private pension funds at a later date. This idea found universal support, although a 1997 World Bank mission warned of potential monopolization of the industry.

The pace of work was such that the expatriate consultants provided their comments on the Concept only after a draft version for public discussion had already been published in newspapers.[23] As a result, they addressed an earlier version of the Concept. The most important of their recommendations included introduction of unique social security numbers; centralized pension payment processing; transfer of the responsibility for the collection of public pension contributions to the tax authorities in order to improve compliance rates; care in the development of pension fund regulation to ensure both sufficient diversity of pension funds and their meeting the fiduciary requirements for investments; establishment of an effective supervisory body; and other measures aimed at improving the public pensions' efficiency. Most recommendations were not included in the Concept, but were later incorporated at the implementation stage and proved decisive in the success of the reform.

In late March 1997, a second draft of the Concept together with a plan of action for development of pension legislation was approved by the prime minister (*Order of the Prime Minister #70-p*, March 19, 1997) and published in the media for nationwide discussions. This version described the proposed SAPF and incorporated some of the recommendations made by the foreign advisors. Quite likely to avoid the confusion between the SAPF and the PF of the Republic of Kazakhstan, which collected social contributions and provided unfunded Solidarity pensions, the group gave the latter the more fitting name of State Pension Payments Center (SPPC) after its reorganization (see section 3.4 of this chapter). Prime Minister Kazhegeldin charged the working group with the development of actuarial and financial simulations and estimation of borrowing needs by the end of March. Meanwhile, the government (including MinFin, MSLP, Ministry of Economy and Trade, Ministry of Justice, NBK, NSC, and the State Insurance Regulator) was given time until the end of April to draft the pension laws and amend a number of earlier laws and regulations. On the basis of the DAI and IMCC comments and less strident proposals from the public, the Concept was revised, refined, and approved by the government on May 12, 1997.

The resulting law proposal required centralized collection of the contributions from the employers to the SPPC, regardless of the accumulation pension fund (APF) responsibility for administering the savings. Centralized collection was intended to reduce fraud and improve compliance while forcing GoK to accelerate the introduction of unique social security identification numbers, without which centralized collection and countrywide consistency could not have been achieved. The law also limited the fees charged by the pension funds. Limits on the rates pension funds could charge were part of a screening mechanism designed to deter the entry of actors with "very short-term profit expectations."

3.2.4 World Bank Support

With plans to evaluate the preparation for the reform and possibility of a loan, the first World Bank mission arrived in May 1997, six months after the government requested technical assistance from the World Bank at a Washington conference. The World Bank mission expressed its opinion on Pension Reform Concept in an *Aide-Memoire* (WBPRM, 1997). The mission sought to understand the key features of the government reform strategy and to explore the possibilities for operational support that the Bank could provide in conjunction with the ADB and USAID. The USAID team urged the World Bank to use loan conditionality to promote the creation of an effective legal and regulatory environment. USAID consultants, who had developed long-standing relations with the government working group, also met with the ADB and the IMF to share information and to harmonize their positions. Throughout the past decade, the various international bodies involved have in fact been mutually reinforcing and devoid of the interinstitutional conflict that sometime appears.

While IMCC and World Bank comments on the Concept did not provide unreserved support for the reform, they were broadly supportive. The Bank's *Aide-Memoire* cautioned that the timetable of the reform was "exceedingly ambitious," but indicated a willingness to provide financial and technical assistance conditional on a number of "design and implementation issues." These mostly coincided with the IMCC recommendations. In particular, the *Aide-Memoire* stressed the need for better social analysis of the reform impact, the importance of properly chosen minimum pensions, the need for pension indexation, the absolute necessity of universally assigned identification numbers, and the need to centralize collection of pension contributions and administer them as payroll taxes. Similar to the USAID-sponsored IMCC recommendations, World Bank staff advocated utilization of foreign expertise and foreign companies for fund management, actuarial estimations, accounting and auditing, and especially for development of the regulations for the nonstate pension funds. In terms of organization of the pension funds, the World Bank experts did not rule out the use of internal asset managers, thus differing from the USAID or IMCC team's advocacy of allowing only external asset managers (operating via AMCs). The World Bank also proposed that the NBK act both as a custodian for pension funds and as an AMC for the SAPF, which would be especially important in the first years of the reform. This latter suggestion was implemented by the reformers as the only reasonable response, given the dearth of financial institutions. Last but not least, the Bank mission advised taking a deliberate approach to resolving remaining problems, arguing that current problems in legislation, poor compliance, and enforcement of the regulation could be resolved gradually.

Public opposition to the reform quickly emerged, and while the groups did not initially enjoy access to sophisticated counteranalysis, their opinions were vehement nonetheless. The primary opposition came from the Pokoleniie (Generation) movement, which was formed to represent the interests of pensioners, and from the opposition movement Azamat (Citizen). In their joint statement in April 1997, they argued that the reform was not warranted in Kazakhstan, where "the age of retirement was recently raised above the life expectancy," blamed government reforms for low pension contributions by enterprises, and expressed doubts in the ability of the financial sector to preserve the value of individual pension contributions.[24] They also demanded that the government halt discussions of the pension reform and pay off pension arrears.

To counter the misperceptions of the reforms, the government initiated an aggressive public education campaign, which commenced in May 1997. This campaign also received technical assistance from USAID. It included publication of articles in newspapers, preparation and distribution of brochures, radio and TV shows, public service announcements, and incorporated some elements into soap opera scripts, while monitoring media materials regarding pension reform, press conferences, seminars, and newspapers.

3.3 Pension Reform Preparation: The Pension Law

Once the first version of the Concept had been approved by the prime minister, the second IMWG, assisted by USAID consultants, began drafting the new pension law in late March 1997. The working group worked against a difficult deadline set by President Nazarbayev to have the law prepared by the end of April, and then submitted it to parliament; the law was to be enacted by June 1, 1997. The expatriate consultants were to ensure the legislation's quality and its conformance to international norms. The law had to meet fiduciary standards, specify regulatory requirements to ensure financial soundness of the new Accumulative pension funds, and provide for a smooth transition from the old Solidarity system to the new Accumulative system. Both the domestic and expatriate teams needed to coordinate their work with existing laws as well as other legislation under development. The latter included the Commercial Law, amendments to the Investment Law, the proposed Joint Stock Companies' Law, and the Civil Code.[25]

In early April, the working group developed several iterations of the draft law, each time distributing them to the expatriate consultants for comments, and later circulating them among the government agencies involved, namely, the NSC and the MLSP. In terms of fiduciary standards, the consultants were particularly concerned about the interpretation of the proposed dual-entity structure, consisting of pension funds and management companies. This required extensive preparation and coordination with other laws, since no entity remotely like the proposed AMCs existed in Kazakhstan or other former Soviet republics. However, the consultants were hindered by limited direct access to the working group. This prompted them to develop their own version of the law. Thus, by the end of April there existed two competing versions of the law.

A point of contention in the establishment of pension system's legal structure was the status of the pension funds (IMCC, 1997a). Formally, the emerging pension law established three types of legal entities: private pension funds, AMCs, and custodians. The law proposed that the pension funds (hereafter, termed APFs) were to be established as for-profit legal entities, namely, closed joint-stock companies. The law further established minimum capital requirements and provisions for payment of commissions from pension contributions (no more than 1%) and investment income (no more than 10%). The for-profit status of the pension funds contained the risk that, despite segregation of the assets of the founders of an APF from the assets of pension contributors, the founders, as shareholders of a for-profit venture, could reasonably claim their share of investment income under existing legislation.

The second type of entity was the AMC. These firms also were to be closed joint stock companies, whose primary objective would be management of a pension fund's assets, in effect providing investment advisory services. Minimum charter requirements and provision for the payment of commissions from the pension funds were envisioned. It was anticipated that some funds could act as their own asset managers, provided they had adequate technical capacity. The role of the custodian was to hold an APF's assets and monitor the AMC's legislative compliance with respect to its investment directives.

Although USAID supported the creation of two separate legal entities in the pension system, its consultants were critical of the for-profit status of the pension funds and were not comfortable with the functional delineations between pension funds and management companies. Their concerns for proper corporate governance structure were motivated by the objectives of transparency, cost efficiency, and protection of beneficiaries' interests. As Chapter 8 details, the main concern surrounded the dual entity, for-profit status of the pension funds contained in the government draft. The Civil Code of Kazakhstan did not contain a trust fund form of corporate governance prevalent in English-speaking countries, and GoK was unwilling to amend the Code. Thus, the trust fund single entity approach that would effectively segregate assets and secure the rights of the beneficiaries in all contingencies was not an option for the emerging legislation.

In the absence of a single-entity structure, IMCC proposed establishing APFs as public funds under Article 107 of the Civil Code. According to this scheme, the AMC would found the pension fund, but not contribute any authorized capital for its establishment. The AMC would be established as a closed-end joint stock company and be responsible for the administration of the fund. Pension assets would have to be held as a public fund, that is, only on paper, without a physical address. The assets of the pension fund, including contributions and investment gains and losses, would entirely belong to the beneficiaries. A mandatory custodian would ensure safekeeping of fund assets, payments from APF, record keeping, and reporting to the AMC and to the regulatory authorities. This approach would have achieved the same results as a trust fund in terms of costs to the contributors and protection of their claims.

However, other legal issues further compounded the asset security problem, since the introduction of the new pension system could not be accomplished in isolation. Most critically, the Joint-Stock-Company Law addressed corporate governance, disclosure requirements, shares' conditions, and the entrance of new shareholders—all affecting the Accumulative pension system. Another complication came from the Bankruptcy Law, which, under Article 19, allowed for separation of assets for purposes of liquidation, but did not imply that the separation extended to a going concern.

Tight deadlines, technical limitations of the working group members (who, after all, had never before drafted a comprehensive social security reform!), and poor communication with IMCC consultants resulted in a draft that did not meet organizational and fiduciary standards. In late April, when the working group's first draft was completed, the MLSP requested IMCC to review it article-by-article. IMCC dismissed the draft as requiring "too many major revisions" and presented the MLSP with its own version of the law. While technically superior to the working group's, IMCC version did not fit seamlessly into the existing legal structure, and was not adopted. The working group, under intense pressure and with professional reputations at stake, proceeded with its own version despite the lack of an adequate legal structure for pension funds and AMCs. The fourth draft dated May 13, 1997, was adopted as final, was submitted to parliament, and became law.

By the end of May, when the expatriate consultants realized that their proposed structure was not under consideration, they changed tactics. Some members of the working group were attentive to their suggestions, exchanged opinions with IMCC consultants informally, and indicated a willingness to incorporate changes at the implementation stage.

By then the law was already in parliament. The parliament wanted to resolve the issue of pension arrears, which at the time stood at some US$500 million, but did not want to be responsible for a radical pension law. The legislation, which was lacking in many ways, could have been stopped on reasonable objections or on technicalities. To the parliamentarians, it appeared that the problems with the Solidarity system at the time did not merit a reform as radical as proposed. In fact, the reform would have made it more difficult to pay the pension arrears off because of the proposed 40% payroll tax reduction. Yet the parliament adopted an almost universally unpopular and hastily prepared law within a month without major changes.

How could this happen? The simplest explanation—that it was imposed on a voiceless parliament—is not accurate.[26] While it is true that Kazakhstan does not have a tradition of strong parliamentary opposition to government proposals, and while it is clear that the reforms had President Nazarbayev's support and that parliamentarians were reluctant to oppose him, it is also the case that parliament did not regard the proposed law as nondebatable. Further, although President Nazarbayev put his full political weight behind the reform, there is no evidence that he tried to restrain the parliamentarians. Indeed, given the vast amount of hostile press following the reforms, it is clear that GoK did not seek to squelch dissent, and also that opposition would have been politically popular. Thus, the reasons for the quick adoption must lie elsewhere.

First, the reformers clearly had much more expertise and more information about the state of the pension system and the potential implications of the reform than did the parliamentarians. The reformers also had access to the expertise of international consultants and shared a vision of a radical reform, which at once addressed several issues and had the potential of becoming more than merely an institution of old-age income security. In particular, the Concept of the reform was unique in consolidating into a tight reform package private individual pensions, financial market development, and blue-chip privatization. Each of these had its own merit, but their synergy made the proposed reform particularly attractive to the designers.

Second, the reformers built a powerful and robust coalition by aligning top officials from key ministries behind the reform Concept. GoK officials were well aware that the major problem of the Solidarity pension system was low social tax compliance, not long-term insolvency driven by aging.[27] Those implicated in failed attempts at improving compliance were not willing to make another good-faith attempt at fixing it unless it was tied with some radical conceptual change. Ironically, some of those responsible for mismanagement of social tax collection used pension arrears to justify the need for radical departure from the Solidarity pension system. Others were interested in private pension funds as a vehicle for development of the financial markets. Still others were concerned about the social unrest that pension arrears were producing. Finally, the members of the working group jointly authored and signed both the Concept and the pension law, which cemented their commitment to the reform.

Whatever their motivation, the decision to privatize pensions proved prescient and shrewd in retrospect. Even *ex ante*, the decision was supported by sound economic arguments. If low compliance was the main problem of the pension system, the obvious solution was to raise collection of contributions by tax administration methods. However, it could be argued that low compliance was only a symptom reflecting disincentives caused by a high dependency ratio and proliferation of an informal labor market. High dependency demanded high pension taxes, creating disincentives that hindered compliance. Breaking this vicious circle called for delinking its elements, and the switch to the individual accounts did just that.

Third, despite flaws in the adopted law, the international consultants did not publicly express their disagreement with the government version, as they did not want to jeopardize the working relations with their Kazakhstani government counterparts, and also because they felt that the flaws could be ameliorated through the supporting regulations and later revisions at the stage of implementation (IMCC, 1997a). The consistent perspective of USAID—from its mission directors down to short-term consultants—has been that the working group members and other Kazakhstani officials involved in the reform were exceptionally competent and honest. Thus, the failure to adopt ideal legislation was seen as a secondary matter, and USAID was confident that remaining problems would be addressed subsequently.

As a result, the reform proceeded at the originally mandated schedule, leaving the potential opposition little time for reaction. Within less than a year, GoK achieved significant progress in all aspects of the reform. Although pensioners and workers with significant work experience opposed the reform because they felt it reduced their old-age entitlements, they lacked organization and the analytical resources.[28] The strongest opposition came from parties that opposed privatization and that appeared to be gaining greater influence with President Nazarbayev.[29] The original short- and long-term financing plans for the reform depended critically on privatization of blue-chip enterprises. In the short run, proceeds from privatization of key SOEs would provide more than enough revenues to replace the foregone payroll taxes. In the long run, it was expected that privatization of SOEs would jump-start the stock market and provide investment opportunities for the pension funds. Ultimately, the reformers had to shed the privatization plans so as not to jeopardize the other components. In the fall of 1997, large-scale privatization plans were abandoned, but by then it was no longer critical to implement the Accumulative pension reform, as the World Bank had come through with a US$300-million Pension Reform Transition Loan. However, from a longer-term perspective, the political decision to stop privatization was highly damaging, as it seriously hindered the development of the pension-fund industry and the financial system as whole.

Fourth, and probably the most decisive factor, was the political will and unequivocal support of President Nazarbayev, who gave an "urgent" status to the draft. This meant that the parliament had to make a decision on it within one month or face the risk of dismissal, a feature of Kazakhstan's constitution and not an empty threat, given the fate of the previous parliament. The carrot was provided by Prime Minister Kazhegeldin, who allegedly promised to the Speaker of the Majilis to pay off all pension arrears should the law be adopted promptly and without major revision. Although parliament was not entirely impressed by the arguments of the working group, it was ultimately cajoled into adopting the law on June 20, 1997.

The legislation adopted by the parliament did in fact have some populist modifications compared with the edition submitted to the body. Parliament lowered the retirement age to 58/63 (for women and men, respectively, against the 60/65 originally proposed), changed death benefits in the public component of the plan (i.e., the remnants of the Solidarity system), and maintained benefits for citizens in the regions of radiation risk (namely, in the Semipalatinsk nuclear polygon). While the adopted law was not as comprehensive as the expatriate advisors had hoped, their comments were in fact reflected in successive legislative drafts. Indeed, almost every year since 1997, various changes have been inserted into the pension law, and certain problematic provisions have been withdrawn without replacement. In addition to changes to the body of the law, comprehensive supporting regulations helped make pension system functional. For example, subsequent amendments to the Tax Code provided for deferred taxation and tax deductions for different types of contributions.

The enacted law incorporated some of IMCC recommendations, but fell short of being comprehensive, instead outlining the intended relationships between the principle actors in a rather declaratory way. More importantly, the cornerstone of the Accumulative pension system, the private financial institutions and regulatory agencies, did not exist at the time of enactment and had to be created virtually from the scratch. Their creation presented opportunities to correct the omissions and shortcomings of the 1997 law through the adoption of detailed regulations. Following the informal advice of the first World Bank mission, the reform had to be implemented flexibly, with international advisors "continuously monitoring the implementation of prerequisites and sequencing the introduction of component elements of the reform based on their role in the pension system" (WBPRM, 1997).

3.3.1 Kazakhstan versus Chile: Fiscal Details

Similarities of the design call for a comparison of Kazakhstan's reform with the 1981 Chilean reform. As in Chile, current pensioners in Kazakhstan were assured that their pensions would not be affected by the reform. In Kazakhstan, where the government had recently revised downward its obligations to the pensioners, this promise could not have been accepted at face value. Even the increase in Solidarity pensions after 2000, when oil revenues filled treasury coffers, raised fears that GoK could cut benefits as quickly as it raised them. In that sense, PAYGO pensions in Kazakhstan were never "defined benefits" and could not possibly be so, given their unfunded nature and high variability of government revenues.

A second difference with the Chilean reform appeared in the treatment of current generation of workers. Chilean workers were given the choice of staying in PAYGO or opening individual pension accounts. Unlike Chileans, the current generation of Kazakhstani workers did not have a PAYGO option, and all were required to switch to individual retirement accounts. Hence, virtually all Kazakhstani workers will receive both types of pensions at retirement for many years to come, while Chileans would receive only one type, which they chose.

A third difference was how pension rights of current workers were recognized. Chilean workers who switched to individual accounts were credited with "recognition bonds." These bonds transformed unfunded pension rights earned under PAYGO into funded pensions. Kazakhstan instead promised to pay PAYGO pensions according to the work history of current workers up to the date of the reform. This choice left the Solidarity component of the current workers' pensions unfunded.

The choices made by Kazakhstan's reformers reflected preference for a design that was easy to prepare, implement, and administer. Given the speed with which the reform was implemented, their decisions were not surprising. Besides simplicity, the decision to keep the Solidarity component unfunded provided the flexibility to adjust PAYGO pensions in either direction, as needs and capacity dictated. Chilean-style recognition bonds, on the contrary, would have required GoK to commit early on to the size of Solidarity pensions to be paid decades after the reform was implemented—a commitment which fiscal authorities had good reasons to avoid.

3.4 Implementation

3.4.1 Financing

A central issue to be resolved before the beginning of the reform concerned financing the shortfall in Solidarity system revenues. At the time of the reform, the projected loss of revenues in 1998 due solely to the reduction in the social contribution rate from 25.5% to 15.0% was in the order of US$395 million, or 1.7% of GDP (Andrews, 2001). Expenditure adjustments promised to reduce the financing needs by 0.7% of GDP. The working group proposed a plan according to which the pension funds themselves would finance the transition by buying government bonds equal to the remaining 1.0% of GDP. However, to ensure that these bonds would be sold (without resorting to market pricing of the yield in what was a very thin and not terribly liquid market), the plan called for GoK to impose a cap on pension fund portfolios requiring at least 50% to be invested in government bonds. Other options called for a slower transition, either mandating participation in the Accumulative system only for the new labor force entrants or lowering the rate of Accumulative contributions for all employed persons (and hence raising the social contribution rate).

Ultimately, these slower transition proposals were not chosen. The potentially great number of minimum pension applicants at the mature stage of the reform was one reason for eschewing these options, and in addition the former option implied a much larger number remaining in the Solidarity system, while the latter meant that fewer workers would generate substantial Accumulative fund accounts. That these alternatives amounted to delay in pension funds' and financial sector development also discouraged their adoption. Most critically, the new World Bank loan, conditionally secured in July–August 1997, reduced the need for internal financing and also made the government bond minimum option unnecessary.

3.4.2 Building Institutions

After financing the fiscal costs of the transition, the most urgent tasks in order of implementation were the development of custodial bank regulations, the development of pension fund laws and regulations, and creation of institutional capacity of the pension fund regulatory authority. At the same time, the issue of legal status of pension funds needed to be resolved in a manner consistent with the existing legislation, either through amendments to the Civil Code or through creation of the new legal entities.

The essential elements of the system had to be established before January 1998, the launch date of the new pension system. This in turn meant that regulations with direct impact on the minimum terms and conditions had to be in place by September 1997. Those planning the reform anticipated needing at least four months for entities considering participation to review the regulations, assess costs and benefits, and file for licenses with enough time for approval and commencement of operations.

As part of this plan, two new government institutions were created. The State Pension Payments Center (formed under GoK *Decree #926*, June 4, 1997) absorbed the erstwhile PF, while the National Pension Agency (NPA) was given the supervisory and regulatory functions in the pension fund industry. Both the NPA and the SPPC were reformed as units under the MLSP, an institution with limited regulatory and tax collection experience, rather than being placed in an independent government agency such as the NSC or the NBK. Moreover, the

NPA was given only ten positions in the central administration of the MLSP, while the SPPC received forty staff in addition to the network of subnational offices inherited from the PF.

3.4.3 State Pension Payments Center

Neither the MLSP nor SPPC could possibly develop the capacity to perform all functions specified in the pension law by January 1998. Hence, priority had to be assigned to the development of functions required for the launch of the redesigned pension system. These included benefit payments, contributions receipts, control and allocation of contributions, processing of applications for pensions, and building and maintaining the contributor database.

Forming the database in turn required assigning a unique identification number to every employee and pensioner in the system, processing registrations on an employer basis, and establishing a procedure to receive and reallocate contributions received from employers and employees. The SPPC wanted to accomplish this task on a decentralized basis, through local district offices, just as had been done by the existing system of collection of PAYGO contributions. In reality, the SPPC was unequipped to fulfill its duties even in a centralized fashion, and decentralization would have been even more chaotic, as it had limited staff and little competence in banking operations, information systems, and tax collection and decentralized management of financial operations. Each of these institutional competencies was held by organizations not directly under SPPC supervision.

The international consultants proposed an alternative scheme (documented in an unpublished memo to USAID from Stephen Lewarne). Under their plan, the accounts would be opened on behalf of employees at the custodian bank of each employee's APF. Employers would transfer 15% of the wage bill from their bank accounts to the SPPC account at the NBK. Simultaneously, employers would also transfer 10% of gross wages to the custodian banks of their employees' pension funds, together with the list of employees. The SPPC would receive monthly invoices from the service bank, with the list of employees, their choices of the pension funds, and amounts of contributions. Custodian banks would supply the SPPC with a monthly report on the contribution payments received in aggregate from each employer, as well as lists of employees, including the amount of contributions placed in their accounts. An added benefit was that the employer would provide a tax registration number, leaving an auditing trail. Under this scheme, the SPPC would not hold the 10% individual account contributions.

The debate over the role and functions of the SPPC continued until September 1997. Eventually, a scheme with centralized operations was adopted, except that the SPPC wanted to keep 10% individual contributions on its account for one day and then remit them to the pension funds. By December, the SPPC and the NPA convinced GoK to charge the SPPC with responsibility for controlling the 10% mandatory pension contributions, on the grounds that doing so was necessary to identify delinquent employers and enforce payment of contributions.[30] But, critically, responsibility for collection of social taxes was assigned to the Tax Inspectorate, in effect rendering moot any rationale for depositing individual account funds with the SPPC. By inserting this unnecessary step, the act complicated and lengthened the transfer of contributions from employer accounts to pension funds' accounts by two business days. The NPA and the SPPC also sought to position the SPPC as the only record-keeper for the Accumulative pension funds. However, in a joint meeting of members of the working group with representatives of all government agencies involved (and attended by international consultants), an alternative plan was adopted, according to which APFs could choose among a number of record-keepers.

3.4.4 Fiduciary Concerns and Regulations

During the fall of 1997, the SPPC developed forms and records for the Accumulative system and developed regulations and procedures for assignment of Social Individual Codes (SICs). By the end of the year, employers began submitting registration forms for the issuance of SICs on behalf of their employees. Over the course of 1998, the SPPC would receive and process this information, design and develop the database, and commence the transition to a comprehensive centralized system. During 1998, SPPC assigned SICs to all pensioners and current employees. This was a remarkable achievement, and completing the task was essential to the Accumulative system's operation. While duplicate numbers for individuals has been an inevitable issue, it has been addressed at various times since the reform was undertaken, and is no longer a significant problem.

In addition to implementing the necessary accounting infrastructure, the involved government agencies (NPA, NSC, MLSP, SPPC, NBK) had to separate and coordinate their regulatory roles within the new system. This called for the development of regulatory norms starting with licensing, day-to-day operations' practices and regulations, and reorganization and liquidation procedures. These regulations and agreements incorporated fundamental principles that were not included in the pension law, but had to be in place before the launch of the new pension industry to ensure its effective functioning, and to provide legal protection of participants' assets.

Licensing regulations were the first step in establishing regulatory oversight of pension funds. To this end, ADB and USAID-funded consultants jointly developed model documents such as management procedures, pension fund and AMC charters, contracts, record-keeping requirements, custodian and asset manager agreements, and other supplementary documentation. The consultants proposed that the model charter, the core document upon which the others would be based, be given legal force, while leaving other provisions to the consideration of APF founders. Within the proposed model charter, the pension fund was treated as a nonprofit entity. Unfortunately, this conflicted with the already-enacted NPA regulation on equity requirements. In particular, the arrangement whereby commissions could be paid to the AMC was one that envisioned commissions paid to APF, from which a separate commission would be allocated to the AMC. However, if APFs had nonprofit status, the management company would have to receive the commission directly.

As the NSC and the NPA continued developing regulations for the pension funds and AMCs, the legal status of the pension funds remained a central concern. The two institutions found themselves in disagreement over the nonprofit status of pension funds, which, if adopted, could reduce conflicts of interests and improve protection of beneficiaries' rights. International advisors suggested that a nonprofit structure could be implemented in Kazakhstan without changes to the Civil Code, joint-stock company law or the pension law. Given this interpretation, the NSC was willing to accept the idea that APFs be incorporated as nonprofit entities, but the NPA was less enthusiastic and refused to go along with the proposal.

The structure eventually approved by the NPA was a management agreement, which followed the basic structure of the proposed pension fund model charter.[31] It was designed as a tripartite agreement among the fund, the manager, and the custodian. The agreement set out terms respecting the appointment of the manager; the powers, rights, and obligations of the manager; obligations of the fund; allocation of expenses; conflicts of interest; resignation or removal of the manager; and the fee structure. Protection of beneficiary's rights was reflected both in the *Rules of Reorganization and Liquidation of Private Pension Funds* (NPA Order #16-P, November 3, 1997) and in the model tripartite custodial agreement. As with the management agreement, the custodial agreement was drafted as a three-party agreement, but with the focus on relations between the manager and the custodian. It established obligations regarding the transfer and payment of contributions and other assets, the investment of pension and assets, accounting and record keeping, distributions and disbursements, fees and expenses, and the resignation or removal of the custodian (NPA Order #17-P, February 17, 1998).

Close monitoring of compliance with the adopted model documents at the registration and liquidation stages also would imply legal protection of a participant's assets during the interim contributing (and earning) period. However, this approach required much more staff and expertise than the NPA had on hand at the outset of the reform. Staff requirements were at a maximum at this point, since the system's credibility rested on the successful registration of more than one million accounts—by a tiny staff with no prior experience. Thus, time was of the utmost importance, as regulatory staff had to be trained prior to offering training to the market participants, and ultimately to explaining the system in detail to the citizens of Kazakhstan. Almost incredibly, the training was achieved on schedule, and a capable if small NPA staff was assembled. By the end of 1997, regulations were enacted, licenses were issued to the pension funds, and employers began submitting registration forms for the issuance of SICs on behalf of their employees.

This task was alleviated somewhat by the creation of the Association of Pension Funds (with European Union TACIS (Technical Assistance to the Commonwealth of Independent States) funding, which helped to reproduce the technical experience needed for registration and operation of the pension funds as pension fund regulatory models were being developed.[32] Later, the association became a vocal supporter of the interests of the private pension funds. Eventually, through incremental improvements in the regulations, supporting legislation, operational changes in the SPPC, and effective financial and legal counseling to participants in the new system, the original problems were largely resolved.

At the time—roughly 1997–2000—this massive institutional and legal development effort appeared somewhat superfluous. After all, a sophisticated asset management system was hardly needed to invest in Treasury bills—the only practical choice during the first years of the pension funds' history. However, the economic recovery and healthy government coffers have since given the pension reform a far firmer footing, while the institutional reforms have transformed the public's confidence in its financial and pension institutions. Indeed, these institutional developments were essential for the long-term sustainability of the Accumulative pillar and, despite its haphazard origin, helped develop pension fund industry—though, as Chapter 8 details, much remains to be done.

3.4.5 Minimum Capital and Minimum Return Requirements

Another danger in the government drafts of the Accumulative pension system regulations was the attempts to insert the guarantees of minimum pension payments and minimum returns into the defined-contribution pensions. These attempts generally came through proposed regulations regarding pension fund rules and prototype contracts that had been drafted earlier by USAID-funded advisors.[33] At the insistence of some of the working group members, backed by IMCC consultants, the most offensive provisions of unfunded guarantees were removed from the regulations before they were adopted.[34] The only guarantee that found a way into the regulation was the requirement of nonnegative real rate of return on pension contributions for corporate pension funds. This mandated guarantee forced AMCs to hold additional capital to cover the guarantees; by raising the costs for the pension industry, this would eventually translate into lower returns on pension investments. In retrospect, these guarantees appear even more misplaced in light of the initial (but long since modified) portfolio caps on pension investments that were adopted. By requiring that pension funds hold at least 50% of their portfolio in government debt while limiting international investments, the regulation made it difficult for the companies to preserve the real value of contributions.[35] Costs were further raised by unnecessarily burdensome demands of daily reports on investment positions, profitability indicators, and other prudential norms.[36] The regulation also failed to outline adequate conflict of interest and fiduciary standards.

In addition to the NPA's minimum return guarantees, the NSC drafted regulations introducing penalties for deviations from average returns of the all AMCs.[37] For example, AMCs with returns on pension assets exceeding a function of the national average return on pension assets had to contribute the difference to its reserve capital. Specifically, this function was defined as Max($R/2$, R-2%), where R is defined as the national average return on pension assets. Conversely, if the return on pension assets fell below some other function of average return—Min($R/2$, R-2%)—the AMC had to compensate the difference at its own expense. By placing these contingent claims on AMC capital, the regulation exposed the companies to a risk not unlike that composed by writers of a detective novel—a combination of options, each with complex risks made more obscure still by anticipated ongoing changes to the regulatory environment. The outcome of this piece of prudential regulation was to greatly increase the systemic risk facing the pension industry and, ultimately, the prospective pensioners. However, at the time, these risks were partly alleviated by the portfolio caps that leveled out the performance of the pension funds.

Another difficult though hardly urgent issue confronting the regulators concerned the nature of Accumulative pension payments. When the system was introduced, the NPA regulations made no mention of annuities (a completely new concept in Kazakhstan and other transition nations), fixed payment schedules from accumulated funds, or other actuarial schemes. Instead, there was a reference to "life pension provision from voluntary pension contributions for the period stipulated by the pension contract." While this provision did not provide details as to the form of pension payout, it recognized in passing its actuarial nature. In effect, the problem of payout mechanisms was tabled until pension accounts accumulated the amounts that would warrant payout schemes more sophisticated than lump-sum payments.[38]

As implementation of the Accumulative system unfolded in 1998, another review of the Pension Law was proposed. The basis for the review stemmed from the central role that the supplementary legislation had quickly assumed in the operation and proper functioning of the pension industry. However, for political reasons the proposed legislative changes expected by the end of 1998 were never realized.

3.4.6 Setting up the Accumulation Pension Funds

While development of regulations continued through the fall of 1997, the Accumulative system's administrators had to begin establishing the necessary private sector institutions. To this end, the plan of action called for meetings with private sector organizations interested in participation to specify the licensing and other requirements under the laws and regulations still under development. This work was initiated in September and began in earnest in October 1997, when the prospective personnel began training on the pension fund and management company financial models. In November, private banks assisted by the expatriate advisors worked intensively to develop a private pension fund sector. At approximately same time, the Association of Pension Funds was created.

One of the first private movers was the local branch of the international bank ABN-AMRO, which moved to create one large multiemployer fund covering KazTelekom, AES, Ispat Karmet, Vneshinvest, Almaty Merchant Bank, and other companies. This move was relatively easy for ABN-AMRO, which could draw on parent company expertise and capital, and for which the investment, as part of a global strategy on a vast scale, offered little risk. Moreover, ABN-AMRO sought to capture the valuable high end (large firms paying high wages to a stable labor force) of the market.

Of course, getting financial institutions to set up APFs and AMCs was only part of the challenge. A main concern among employers was a loss of control if they joined a combined fund, in contrast to establishing their own, single-firm fund.

In December 1997, the international advisors held a series of education and information seminars for potential PF and AMC founders. The purpose was to assist with the licensing, preparation of development of required legal documentation, and assistance with the development of business plans and financial projections using the private pension fund model. These companies were Phillip Morris, Dostar Capital Markets, Caspiyskiy Bank, ABN-AMRO, Turan-Alem Bank, AES, Kunaev Fund, MEDEU Insurance Group, Kazcommerce Bank and Intergas Central Asia. As the launch day of the reform neared, public education and awareness campaign accelerated, massive numbers of booklets and posters were distributed, and mass media announcements urged the public to receive their SIC numbers.

3.4.7 The Stalled Privatization Component

In November 1997, Prime Minister Kazhegeldin, who had been a strong supporter of both pension reform and capital market development through the "blue chip" privatization, left the country and his position, ostensibly for medical treatment. Soon, the post of prime minister was assumed by Nurlan Balgimbaev, an avowed opponent of privatization. Thereafter, the privatization program, which was supposed to propel development of capital markets and other investment vehicles for the nascent pension fund industry, decelerated markedly.

The true reasons for Kazhegeldin's departure and its relation to the move away from rapid privatization remain murky. Clearly, Prime Minister Kazhegeldin had emerged as a potential competitor of President Nazarbayev. Indeed, with ties to managers of large enterprises and a KGB background, while at the same time being regarded favorably by the international community as an active, promarket reformer, Kazhegeldin was a plausible threat (Olcott, 2002). However, the privatization being pushed was not broadly popular, and most Kazakhstanis were appalled at the way privatization had proceeded in Russia, with vast resources ending up in the hands of a few clever and well-connected oligarchs. President Nazarbayev surely felt this opposition keenly, and may have been reacting to Kazhegeldin's growing unpopularity, as much or more than to his prospective popularity. It seems plausible that the move to stall privatization was intended to prevent the emergence of an oligarchy of industrialists. Although the Accumulative pension system was envisioned as creating a natural source of demand for blue-chip enterprises' shares, President Nazarbayev and his advisors may well have believed that APFs would not immediately be large enough to compete with prospective oligarchs.

It is apparent from political histories of the era (and it should be noted that the most informed analysts do not tend to be impartial; for a recounting that is equally critical of all parties, if occasionally naïve, see Olcott, 2002) that the period was one of intense political jockeying. Balgimbaev came from the oil industry, and was primarily interested in its development; he also brought in his own coterie of prospective oligarchs. Most of the leading pension reformers were eclipsed from power during this period, though hardly entirely. More importantly, after less than a year in office, Balgimbaev was dismissed and returned to his former post as head of the state oil company; with the new Prime Minister Kasymzhomart Tokaev most of the reformers returned, with Jandosov taking a variety of key positions, and Marchenko emerging for a long stint as chairman of the NBK.

In retrospect, some privatization delay was favorable to the pension industry, as its assets have indeed grown rapidly. However, with the economic boom that has ensued, the value of Kazakhstan's large industrial concerns also has soared, and for the most part until recently pension funds have not been important shareholders or sources of funding.

3.5 Launching the New Pension System: 1998

3.5.1 Processing Contributions

As the new system was launched, both GoK and its advisors began focusing on implementation, including record keeping, SPPC administration, introducing the notion of a trust, and considering interest-bearing accounts in the absence of adequate custodial agreements. They also recognized the need to expand the public-education campaign to increase employee and employers' awareness of their rights and responsibilities within the new system. As the reformers struggled to make the system operational, USAID, the World Bank, and ADB continued providing technical assistance. Their experts and consultants advised the government agencies in virtually every aspect of implementation, emphasizing the importance of setting up a proper institutional structure for efficient operation of the new Accumulative system. World Bank conditionalities linked to the release of its implementation loan served to emphasize the advisors' messages.

The main concern in 1998 was the operation of the SPPC and its inability to handle all transactions. Low contribution rates, backlogs of unprocessed contributions, high error rates and other organization problems afflicting the SPPC limited the amount of transfers to the newly established pension funds. The SPPC fell behind schedule in assigning Social Identification Codes to all contributors.

However, the SPPC gradually developed a unique database of value in assessing other tax obligations as well as social and pension contributions. With more than 270 branches and the mandate to process the contributions from all employers and for all their employees, the SPPC gained information on all officially complying employers'. Prior to the SPPC, no single authority had detailed knowledge of all taxpayers. At the same time, improvement in collection of social taxes required that the SPPC work closely with the Tax Inspectorate and share pertinent information. However, the tax authorities were somewhat reluctant to enforce collection of pension contributions, as two-thirds of the amount was not considered public revenue.

A high error rate also marred the SPPC's early days. Hard copies of all transactions were required for backup, despite the use of advanced electronic processing. The difficulties stemmed in part from lack of attention to the organizational aspects of processing administrative records. Payment orders arrived in various ways, including the bank clearing system, gross payments system, electronic mail, and paper documents. Almost all of them would be initially rejected by the processing software due to some type of error.

As the reform unfurled, SPPC's inability to process payment orders became all too evident. It was exacerbated by the low level of contributions and the high error rates on payment orders remitted. Underlying these problems was a lack of information among the enterprises and banks. For example, mistakes in allocating the contributions from SPPC to SAPF instead of nonstate pension funds were not sorted out until late 1998. A common error with major implications was that enterprises did not properly indicate whether or not a payment order was written regarding a 10% Accumulative contribution or a 15% Solidarity system payment. SPPF responded by preparing a booklet to provide specific information for employers on how to fill out payment orders for mandatory pension contributions. Gradually, SPPC reduced the error rate and developed error-correction procedures, and its staff improved the standard software used for processing employer remittance forms. Organizational and public education campaigns reduced the error rates in the forms submitted. The popular soap opera *Perekrestok* (*Crossroads*) continued to incorporate into its storylines pension reform subjects such as the need for SIC registration and the importance of choosing a proper pension fund.

3.5.2 *Regulation of Pension Funds*

Despite teething pains, the reformers could claim several major accomplishments in 1998. The government cleared past pension arrears. Basic regulations for pension industry were developed. All regulatory agencies were staffed and operational. Seven nonstate and one state pension accumulation funds, two AMCs, and four custodial banks were licensed. Thus, as a February 1998 World Bank mission *Aide-Memoire* noted, the main elements of the investment infrastructure for the Accumulative pension system were largely in place.

On the other hand, merely providing licenses did not constitute an immediately effective pension system, as necessary contracts between the funds, management companies, custodian banks, and contributors were not implemented. By the end of February, only two funds, Kaztelekom-Umit and Halyk Bank Fund, signed agreements with asset management firms and a custodial bank. The limited number and mutual affiliation of nonstate custodial banks meant that the NBK was compelled to serve as a temporary custodian for nonstate pension funds not affiliated with the three nonstate custodians.

While most pension fund regulations were developed by 1998, the regulatory agencies continued to introduce amendments and additions to the laws and regulations in response to further developments in the Civil Code, international experts' recommendations, and as a result of regulatory experience. Licensing procedures for pension funds and management companies, which were relatively lenient at the outset of the reform, were originally issued only for one year. With relicensing, the NPA implemented more strict requirements. While there was little distinction between licensing and supervision at the outset, after permanent licenses were issued to pension funds, the role of the NPA was evaluated.

The upshot was that the NPA was recommended either for closure or for merger, which, in turn, needed to train its staff and develop regulatory procedures. Concurrently, the NBK served both as asset manager and custodian for the SAPF. Over time these activities were taken over by the commercial banks and AMCs. These private sector players learned from NBK's experience, which was also instrumental for further development of regulations for the pension funds and their relationships with management companies.

Even at this early stage of pension system development, lack of investment instruments for pension funds became a concern. The securities markets could barely cope even with the relatively small demand generated by the SAPF. The demand for instruments was bound to surge as accumulations grew and private APFs entered the market. Options were exacerbated by restrictive portfolio requirements also, and the pension funds became the advocate of both less restrictive regulations and financial market development.

3.5.3 *World Bank Conditionalities*

In February, a World Bank team reviewed the reform's progress prior to releasing a US$400 million pension reform financing loan. The mission listed several conditions, most of which had been suggested by USAID consultants the previous summer, as prerequisite for loan approval by the Bank, including:

(a) payment of all pension arrears;
(b) establishment of actuarial capacity within the Ministry of Finance;
(c) a public information plan with implementation timetable;
(d) issuance of licenses to at least four nonstate AMCs and four nonstate APFs, plus evidence of contracts to ensure that the funds were operational;
(e) development of acceptable budgets, organizational charts, and staffing plans for the NPA, NSC, NBK custodial monitoring unit, SAPF, and SPPC;
(f) development and revision of regulations for the SAPF, nonstate APFs, and AMCs, concerning licensing, commissions, reporting and disclosure, accounting and auditing, assert transfers, prudential regulation, portfolio limits, and minimum capital requirements, with provisions satisfactory to the World Bank;
(g) development of prototype pension contracts;
(h) installation of a SPPC computer system to provide a central data base for recording individual account contributions;
(i) assignment of SICs to all current contributors; and
(j) introduction of a clearance system by the SPPC to ensure quick transfer of contributions from the employer to the accumulation fund.

The mission concluded that the proposed pension reform loan was not yet ready for negotiation. By this time, most of those involved in the reform realized that its implementation was far more complex than has been previously assumed. The problems at this early stage of implementation were in the areas of fiscal management and social protection, the regulation framework for pension funds, and administration. The problems identified by the World Bank mission were sufficiently serious to threaten the reform's viability and required immediate attention. The mission suggested a reappraisal in late March, and that, given sufficient progress, negotiations resume in May. In taking this fairly hard line, there was some danger that GoK might reject the World Bank loan conditionalities as too stringent. Kazakhstan's government viewed USAID assistance as sufficient and seemed likely to reject the technical assistance loan insisted upon as part of the World Bank loan package. Consequently, and in recognition of the objective difficulty of trying to achieve everything demanded, the conditions were softened. In particular, the subsequent mission reduced the unique ID number assignment to only half of the contributors prior to loan approval, though other conditions remained.

Pension contribution collections also improved in March, but remained low, at approximately half of the amount expected from 1997 social security contributions. The legal division of payroll contributions into 15% and 10% components was maintained. However, some of the 10% contributions that should have been directed toward Accumulative accounts were directed to Solidarity pension accounts as 15% contributions. In April, the amount of requisitioned accumulation fund transfers began decreasing as 15% social contribution collections improved.

SPPC proved unable to process more than about two-thirds of the 6000 forms submitted daily, resulting in a backlog of transfers to the pension funds that could be cleared up only during the following weekend at best. Payments that were made to the SAPF and six private funds from SPPC were not transferred to the pension funds promptly, and commonly sat in SPPC accounts for up to ten days. By March, average arrears of unprocessed returns reached 700 million tenge. Despite transfers from the budget expressly designated for liquidating arrears, pension arrears persisted through 1998. Overall, though, after the initial two months of problems, operation of the pension system began to improve gradually.

In March, the SPPC reported that 1.5 million temporary accounts had been established, given a total of some 4 million hired workers. Actual compliance was somewhat lower because of assignment of more than one identification number to persons working for multiple employers. This raised the importance of issuing unique identification numbers by SPPC, the SICs, of which only 130,000 had been issued. Other issues regarding the transfer of individual Accumulative contributions were less urgent and hence persisted far longer. For example, the choice of the pension fund was largely limited to the employer and not to the employee, an arrangement that the World Bank strongly discouraged.

3.5.4 Pension Funds during the Currency Crisis

By August 1998, the primary infrastructure of Kazakhstan's pension fund industry was already in place, while rapidly growing pension funds' assets reached US$160 million. Their portfolios, rigidly controlled by regulations, consisted mainly of tenge-denominated GoK debt. The pension funds did not hold Kazakhstan government Eurobonds because regulations did not explicitly permit it, although they did not explicitly forbid it either. At the time, the face value of outstanding Eurobonds placed by the GoK within previous two years stood at US$550 million, and the preparation for the new placement was well underway.

Following the Russian default in August, the price of Kazakhstan's outstanding Eurobonds fell, although by less than Russian paper, reflecting Kazakhstan's dependence on trade with Russia, but also its better fiscal position. Kazakhstan's Eurobonds issued in October reflected this change in market perceptions, and offered a coupon rate that was 5¼% higher than a year prior. Default fears reflected both continuing declines in export prices and the ruble devaluation, which reversed 1997's small GDP gains. During the fall of 1998, pension funds began expressing interest in acquiring the Eurobonds on the secondary market as way to diversifying their largely tenge-denominated assets. The share of Eurobonds in pension funds assets grew from 0% in June 1998 to 2% in September 1998, to 23% in March 1999, and peaked to 66% at the end of 2000 (NBK *Statistical Bulletin* 11(96), 2002).

As of April 1999, the bulk of pension fund assets remained tenge-denominated, making them vulnerable to devaluation. Yet, following devaluation, the pension funds actually realized extremely high returns (approximately 180% on an annualized basis). A group of expatriate government advisors claimed that GoK decided to bail out the funds during the devaluation by pretending that the funds had originally been invested in dollar-denominated assets (Hoffman et al., 1999).

Hoffman et al. (1999) also claimed that GoK considered reversing the reform or at least reducing the accumulation portion of the payroll contribution once it realized the cost of the bailout. If so, it was perhaps the only time that the Kazakhstan government got cold feet. Indeed, while the Accumulative pension reform may have been questioned by the Ministry of Finance during the 1998–99 crisis, the interests of the fiscal authorities and reformers were not inconsistent. The pension funds were seeking foreign currency investments while GoK needed foreign currency financing. After this episode, the fiscal authorities began to see the pension funds as a dependable source of deficit financing.

Yet, the bailout charge is not implausible. The government never fully explained why it took so long to decide to devalue the tenge, and the effect of possible devaluation on pension funds undoubtedly played a role in the decision to delay. From the contributors' perspective, these actions appeared only fair and sensible given that GoK kept rigid regulatory control over the portfolio. It was only natural that the authorities resisted devaluation until pension funds were protected from it. The episode demonstrated that the new pensions, although fully-funded and managed by nonstate pension funds, remained in the domain of fiscal responsibility to the extent that their assets contained government obligations.

In the early 2000s, fiscal policy remained the dominant factor affecting the performance of the pension funds. Soaring budget revenues allowed the Ministry of Finance curtail new debt issues; rapidly expanding banks and pension funds found themselves in a bidding war for increasingly scarce government paper. As real interest rates turned negative, pension funds began desperately looking for alternatives to investing in government debt and began lobbying for the relaxation of portfolio regulations. As later chapters discuss, the subsequent development of the pension reform was dominated by issues of pension funds regulation and their performance.

3.6 Lessons

Kazakhstan's radical pension reform phased out an insolvent Solidarity scheme in order to replace it with a system of individual investment accounts financed by mandatory contributions. Such a sweeping change was bound to affect almost everyone. The reform emphasized the role of the market institutions in provision of old-age pensions by reducing direct involvement of the government; it rationalized labor market incentives, but cut entitlements for the unemployed and the self-employed; it created a sector of institutional investors and, according to the original plan, was intended to spur the privatization of large state-owned enterprises. The story of the early stage of the pension reform in Kazakhstan, narrated in this chapter, illuminates several aspects of policy making in Kazakhstan, with a focus on how competing ideas and institutions shaped the development of the current pension system.

Although the need for pension reform was universally recognized, older workers and many international experts were opposed to what they saw as excessive reliance on markets and unfair preference given to younger urban workers. Fiscal authorities were concerned with the fiscal costs of the transition, but were swayed by the promise of World Bank financial support. Social security administrators were naturally skeptical of the privatization proposal, but hardly able to voice criticism after failing to revive the Solidarity scheme. Parliament's endorsement of the reform was achieved by tactics that employed information rationing and a threat of parliamentary dissolution. More decisively, firm and consistent support of the president ensured that the government position was aligned with that of the reformers. Only top management of large SOEs was able to defend own interests by appealing directly to the president to halt blue-chip privatization.

The pace of execution was unprecedented in transition nations. The difficult timetable mobilized the reformers but contributed to flaws in the statutory legislation and a high error rate at the start of implementation. Despite assistance from the international donor organizations, technical challenges abounded. Successful implementation in this environment required the reformers and the technical advisors to be flexible when possible and resolute when it mattered. For example, fiduciary concerns over the pension law were corrected through the use of nonstatutory legislation rather than through revisions to the law itself, which would have been politically unacceptable.

It is ironic that a reform adopted and executed with limited regard for popular opinion in fact prepared the soil for greater stakeholder involvement in the formulation of pension policy. The reform created a mass of people for whom the old-age pensions would be a right earned by decades of contributions rather than a privilege financed by other people's earnings. These people's financial interests to a large degree were represented by the pension funds. Pension funds began to promote the interests of their account holders, most immediately by voicing concerns, through the APFs, over excessively restrictive regulations.

Although much was chaotic and did not go as planned, it is difficult to look back on the initial reform period, 1996—98, without sensing that it was an extraordinary time. A great deal had to go right, and it did. The reformers turned out both to have a coherent vision and to be highly competent managers—and these two features often do not go together. Both they and the staff they employed enjoyed a reputation for transparency and honesty; remarkably, none of the key agencies involved in the reform has been tainted by corruption, while the regulatory system has been designed for exceptional openness within the pension industry.

In addition to being supportive, President Nazarbayev imposed deadlines that seemed utterly unrealistic at the time, but that turned out to be feasible. This rapid pace was important because it kept opposition from solidifying (Orenstein, 2000). It also placed the new Accumulative system at the vanguard of an ongoing series of developments that together amounted to the creation of a fairly sophisticated financial system on a tabula rasa. Indeed, it seems likely that the Accumulative system would have bogged down in detail and debate had an expedited timetable not been imposed. In his study contrasting pension reform in Kazakhstan, Poland, and Hungary, Orenstein (2000) reports that interministerial conflict and public debate in Poland resulted in a forty-eight-month period between the onset and implementation of pension reform, nearly seven times as long as in Kazakhstan. However, Kazakhstan's pace would have resulted in chaos in the absence of competent administration, since so many modifications had to be made once reforms were underway.

The working group members also made effective use of their international advisor counterparts. At the time, USAID, ADB, and the World Bank, all were ardent advocates of individual account, defined-contribution pension systems, and the IMWG's general vision was shared by all three supporting international bodies. However, the pace of change caught the international institutions by surprise, and they found themselves being pulled along. Rather than finding themselves trying to persuade an uncertain or recalcitrant government, and therefore often "pushing on a string," the international agencies and their consultants found themselves doing the job for which they were well suited: giving advice on competing options, modifying legislation and regulations to conform to international norms, offering critical commentary on proposals, and alerting the reformers to additional steps that were needed.

Thus, the international advisors were unusually effective. This was enhanced because they were dealing with able GoK counterparts with whom they had a shared vision, and who came from a variety of constituencies. The international community also spoke with a (generally) consistent voice. This sort of collaboration is rarer than it should be, and was further enhanced by the ongoing involvement for many years of key players from both the Kazakhstani and international sides.

The fact that GoK took the lead was important for another reason as well. Most of the international advisors had expertise limited to a very narrow aspect of social security systems, few had experience in transition nations, and fewer still had a sense of the general macroeconomic consequences of their actions, or even whether their efforts were suited to the existing financial system. On the other hand, the agencies had an ideological commitment to shrinking the state, along with a naïve view of Kazakhstani politics and political figures. These limitations are inherent to teams of international advisors, and explain why they are better at supporting policy than making it. Fortunately, GoK had the necessary global vision, and was able to modify proposed measures to fit with local reality and constraints. The key reformers were able to make use of the advisors' expertise, and, as trust quickly built up on both sides, were able to engage in productive give-and-take discussion.

These points are intended not as empty praise, but rather as a warning to future reformers. As this and later chapters indicate, the Accumulative reform in Kazakhstan has not been without problems, even with the extremely favorable environment for implementing the reforms, and the even more favorable oil-led boom. Had the reform not been artfully implemented, it is easy to imagine many scenarios in which it would have collapsed. Skillful management and a coherent, unified vision almost certainly are prerequisites for success.

4

Macroactuarial Forecasts

This chapter examines three "macroactuarial" models of Kazakhstan critical to informing policymakers' decisions. Naturally, the initial model—Mitchell Wiener's PENMODEL, constructed in 1997 under a USAID contract—was created hurriedly, with little time to explore available data or even to determine the sorts of data that existed. Two years later, a larger, primarily Kazakhstani, team modified the World Bank's PROST model to create a more sophisticated picture.[1] Termed KAZAK1 (Kazakhstan Actuarial model 1), this model was built on an already sophisticated software package and more fully utilized the nation's considerable information database. While KAZAK1 gave analysts a much better picture (and looming pitfalls) of pension options in 1999–2001 than its predecessor, it in turn is primitive in comparison with Dina Urzhumova and Ai-Gul Seitenova's KAZAK2 model.

The most critical policy choices were made early on, at a time of minimal information and crude actuarial modeling. Our purpose here is not to identify the preferred actuarial simulation model (a trivial choice), but rather to examine the models' predictions, discuss their similarities and differences, and explore the extent to which policymakers' decisions were compatible with the forecasts then available. Thus, this chapter provides an overview of the social security forecasts at the macro level and explores as well how these forecasts informed policy choices. The chapter concludes by suggesting a sequence of social security–related decisions during a reform, with the aim of deferring complex choices that require vast data and careful modeling.

4.1 The Players

We begin by summarizing the objectives of different agents, whose roles are outlined in detail in the preceding chapter. It is of particular interest to grasp what information they sought, and how they responded to different news. While decisions relating to national security, relocating the national capital, and oil development are highly centralized and are not matters of major national debate, social policy tends to be highly pluralistic in Kazakhstan, and this pluralism extended to social security reform, with major interest factions both inside and beyond the GoK.

A reason for the cacophony of voices is that many ministries and key government agencies are affected by pension policies, and often have divergent interests. As is true for most of its counterparts around the world, Kazakhstan's MinFin was concerned with maintaining macroeconomic balance and could be seen as a force for restraining pensions, including future obligations. MinFin thus could be seen as a force for pension reform, though not necessarily of a particular type, as long as it appeared likely to reduce deficits. It was also concerned that its macroeconomic projections be used, and was the only ministry that sought to replicate the simulations by developing in-house actuarial modeling capacity.

The MLSP is similar to its counterparts elsewhere, and consistently fought to maintain Solidarity payments at the maximum feasible level. Pensioners, to the extent that they have an advocate within the government, regard MLSP as their voice—and the ministry certainly tries to advance their cause. Finance ministries and central banks around the world tend to be more powerful than labor ministries, and again Kazakhstan is no exception. MLSP therefore emphasized analysis that examined the fate of the poor, but perhaps because of limited analytical capacity, never showed interest in technical analysis to the extent that MinFin or the national bank did.

Kazakhstan differs from the vast majority of transition and other middle-income countries in that its central bank, the NBK, is influential and highly autonomous—and became stronger during the period 1997–2003. The NBK was a strong proponent of pension reform and disinflationary macroeconomic policy, and in fact became the first proponent of switching to an Accumulative system. Since the IMWG chairman, Grigori Marchenko, was instrumental in building the NBK during his four-year term as governor, the bank's interest is understandable though in fact it antedated his appointment. Moreover, as Kazakhstan's financial system developed, the National Bank became the regulator of virtually all activities, until a separate agency was created in 2004, making it in effect a superregulator. Given the NBK's authority, bodies such as the SAPF and the now-defunct NPA have not played a strong independent role in recent years, but rather have been voices consistent with the National Bank. NBK has remained most actively involved in pension reform of any public body, demanding a vast array of technical reports, and creating an in-house pension reform working group.

At the same time, Kazakhstan's Majilis (lower house of parliament) was not a pushover, and often has been hostile both to the Accumulative pension reform and to efforts to curtail Solidarity payments. Parliamentarians are naturally sensitive to their constituents' preferences, and both the media and popular organizations initially reacted to the Accumulative reforms with sentiments ranging from suspicion to extreme hostility. While technical presentations were made to parliamentarians, these were not critically evaluated. The Majilis has no technical evaluation agency comparable with the U.S. Congressional Budget Office or various congressional committee permanent staff and therefore was not able to play a major role in the technical design or evaluation of various pension reform options.

Had Kazakhstan's major pension reforms been put to a popular vote, they almost certainly would have been defeated. Ultimately, the voices of reform prevailed, with the quiet but consistent and strong support of President Nazarbayev. President Nazarbayev was committed to building a stable society and, specifically, to restoring competent macroeconomic policy; as such, he could hardly reject a key reform backed by both the Ministry of Finance and the National Bank. The presidential administration itself did not demand technical reports, but rather depended on advice generated by the IMWG and the NBK.

Even if President Nazarbayev and the parliament had been willing to reject their macroeconomic bodies, they would have been hard-pressed to reject the proreform voices coming from international agencies. While their opinions have not remained entirely unchanged, the World Bank, ADB, and USAID all strongly advocated pension reform—and, generally, the adoption of an Accumulative system. The IMF tends to be nervous about funded systems, mainly because of the transition costs, but in Kazakhstan's case did not intervene to oppose the other bilateral and multilateral agencies.

In short, pension issues engaged many interested and powerful parties. All had access to the forecasts described in this chapter. Most technical work was conducted for the NBK, MinFin, or the MLSP; USAID regularly sponsored its own analysis as well. Parliamentarians were briefed, as were other major political figures, and the international agencies were regularly informed of results, either directly or through contracted consultancies. In this sense, Kazakhstan's policymakers made informed choices. While the decisions made were hurried, there was an impressive effort to analyze various options, and results from the actuarial forecasts were disseminated. Along with independent analyses within MinFin and NBK, senior officials broadly understood these results, though they did not grasp many details, and were not equipped to provide technical rebuttals. Regardless of whether or not one likes the decisions taken, it is difficult not to be impressed with the professionalism and clarity with which the choices were made. Indeed, we argue that an important force contributing to the success to date of the reforms is the effective coordination of proreform Kazakhstani policymakers and international agencies.

A more difficult question is whether enthusiasm for reform resulted in unduly hasty decisions. Did the forecasts described in this chapter contain information that was ignored? For some interested parties, the answer must be yes, since neither the MLSP nor the parliament fully understood all of the issues and options surrounding pension policy. Since greater information most likely would have intensified opposition, MinFin, NBK, and their international supporters made no effort to broadcast or explain detailed results. In effect, the reforms were rammed through, mainly because of the enormous sense of urgency felt by the proponents. Was this haste justified? More specifically, was it justified based on the macroeconomic stability criteria that preoccupied the reform's proponents?

4.2 Economic and Demographic Parameter Assumptions

While Chapter 1 notes that Kazakhstan was economically unprepared for independence when it came, Chapter 2 documents the pressure for pension system reform. Six fairly grim years of independence were followed by a brief window of economic recovery, during which time the pension reform was enacted. The window appeared to slam shut with the Russian crisis of August 1998, as its effects spread almost instantly to Kazakhstan. While Kazakhstan did not default on its international obligations, and did not seek to negotiate, the collapse of the ruble resulted in the tenge's dramatic appreciation, in both in nominal and real terms, against the nation's most important trading partner.

GDP in constant 1993 prices declined from 42.5 billion tenge in 1990 to 23.6 billion in 1995 (Asian Development Bank, 2002: 186), a fall of some 44%. The economy then stagnated, growing by 2% in 1997, before declining virtually to the 1995 level by the end of 1998. GoK's current deficit was large, though not quite out of control, ranging from 5.6% to 5.9% of GDP between 1995 and 1997. Employment in industry steadily declined following the collapse of the USSR, and by 1997, at 0.92 million, was 35% below its 1992 peak. Birth rates declined markedly, and adult and elderly mortality rose sharply during this period, while premature retirements due to disability also surged. Thus, the setting for the first actuarial model was one of stagnation, at best, and rapid socioeconomic collapse, at worst, leaving the PENMODEL forecasters with an awkward choice. In essence, the modelers could regard Kazakhstan's postindependence crisis as a prolonged but transitory phenomenon and choose parameter values arbitrarily. Alternatively, they could use recent historical values that portended an extraordinarily dark future. As is detailed, the parameters ultimately chosen represented a mix.

Although they began working after the worst of the post-Soviet collapse had ended, the KAZAK1 modelers were even more pessimistic. The model was parameterized on the basis of 1998–99 reality, which indicated either stagnation or slow (3% in 1999) economic growth. The GoK deficit as a share of GDP peaked at 6.5% in 1998, but receded to 4.2% in 1999, suggesting structural difficulties that were, nonetheless, being aggressively treated. Industrial employment stagnated during this period as well.

By the time KAZAK2 was created, Kazakhstan was clearly experiencing a robust recovery. Real GDP rose by more than 9% in 2000 and 13.2% in 2001, and as the model was parameterized, it was apparent that comparable growth would continue in the near future. The NBK forecast a recovery in real per capita incomes to the Soviet-era peak by 2004, and that projection turned out to be on target. Moderately heavy borrowing from the IMF (1998 debt reached US$653 million) was reversed: in 2000, and ahead of schedule, Kazakhstan repaid its entire IMF debt. With rising oil prices, and hence booming exports and government revenues, public budgetary deficits ceased to be a major issue—a minor current deficit was recorded in 2000, while a small surplus was realized in 2001. Less optimistically, industrial employment continued to decline, albeit more slowly than in the past. However, other formal sector employment clearly rose, and indicators of unemployment declined substantially.

Unlike conventional econometric models, simulation models tend to have large numbers of variants. This is certainly the case for actuarial models, for several reasons. First, while there is great uncertainty as to the underlying value of many input parameter values, only in rare cases—and, in practice, never in a model of a developing or transition economy—is there an effort to characterize these parameter values in terms of an underlying probability distribution. If there were, one could conduct Monte Carlo simulations, running the actuarial model a large number of times, and ultimately generate a distribution on the values of key output values. But since this is not common in practice, the second best (if dramatically inferior) practice is to consider a range of scenarios with differing key input values. In addition, actuarial models tend to be living creatures that are used for a considerable period. Input values during initial runs are often quite different from those used a year or two later.[2] Finally, government and international agencies often request simulations based on "their" specific assumed parameter values. Thus, it is impractical to present all variants of each model's parameter assumptions, and we instead provide an impressionistic feel for the manner in which they differ.

The initial PENMODEL simulates Kazakhstan for thirty-one years, from 1997 through 2027. The economic assumptions are conservative: real wages are assumed to be stable or to rise at 1% annually; Solidarity pensions are maintained at a constant value in real terms or are assumed to grow slowly. However, the underlying demographic and labor force assumptions are more optimistic and, ultimately, are favorable to an Accumulative system reform. The working age population grows at 1.16% annually between 1997 and 2013, and essentially is stable thereafter, growing at an annual rate of 0.05%. The 1989 Census data are used to calculate labor force participation rates—surely an extremely optimistic choice. The number of payroll tax contributors grows at 1.71% between 1997 and 2013, with growth falling to 0.05% thereafter. While this may well be close to the realized outcome, it seems wildly optimistic from the perspective of the 1990s.

In essence, the PENMODEL assumptions embody rapid employment growth but neither substantial wage growth nor health recovery. Assumed high mortality means that the over-65 population of 2013 is actually 16.4% smaller than in 1997, implying a decline in the old-age dependency ratio from 10.7% in 1997 to a low of 7.2% in 2012 (and 7.5%% in 2013). The ratio rises thereafter, but does not recover to its 1997 level until 2024. An assumption of reasonably high fertility underlies this—the fertility collapse that actually took place, to below replacement, is not recognized. So, too, does high mortality: 1994–95 rates were used in initial simulations; 1996–97 values were used when they became available.

The KAZAK1 parameters initially were extremely pessimistic, but its economic assumptions (determined by the MinFin for the *Baseline* simulations) gradually grew more optimistic as the economy recovered. Actual values for GDP growth were used in initial years (2.7% in 1999 and 9.6% in 2000); thereafter, growth of 3 to 4% was assumed for simulations out to 2050. Corresponding real formal-sector wage growth assumptions were 7.3% in 1999; 5% in 2000; 3% in 2001–05; 1.5% in 2006–11; 2.5% in 2012–36; 2.7% in 2037–39; 3.8% in 2040–45; and 4.0% after 2045. The modelers also assumed great improvements in compliance within the formal (government and registered enterprise) sector, even more so than did the PENMODEL forecasters.

This optimism was undercut by generally less favorable demographic and employment assumptions. By 2000, it was clear that Kazakhstan's total fertility rate (TFR, the number of live births a woman who survives her entire fecund lifespan can expect to have if she experiences current age-specific birth rates) was well below replacement. Therefore, for KAZAK1, the 1999 TFR of 1.76 was maintained to 2005, with gradual recovery to 2.10 by 2050, and constant fertility thereafter. From the perspective of forecasting, this fertility slowdown means a smaller labor force in the future, with the strongest effects occurring in later years, since the impact is cumulative. The decline is most disadvantageous to a Solidarity system, since the base of the pyramid scheme is forced to shrink.

The "unfavorable" mortality assumption was that life expectancy would gradually recover, implying a larger pension population to be supported. The basis for this was the gains observed between 1997 and 1999 in age-specific mortality rates, especially in the prospering regions. The modelers also anticipated that mortality improvements surely would follow in the wake of the high per capita income and wage growth projected, and therefore assumed annual decline of 2% (but only 1% in *Pessimistic* scenarios) in age-specific mortality. This combination of low fertility and recovering mortality meant that KAZAK1's simulations generate higher old-age dependency ratios in the long run than those emerging from PENMODEL forecasts, thereby increasing social welfare burdens.

Employment growth has several dimensions. Ignoring outright unemployment (assumed to gradually decline from 13.5% in 2000 to 7% in 2010 in KAZAK1, and stay constant thereafter), employment growth will equal the growth of the working-age population multiplied by the labor force participation rate. However, only a fraction of these people will work in registered firms, so that modelers must make assumptions about (a) the proportion in registered firms, (b) the proportion in unregistered firms who pay social taxes, and (c) the proportion in registered firms who fully pay social taxes. The simulation models all assume rising compliance (albeit very modest levels in the unregistered sector), with key differences centering on overall labor force growth and the proportion of those who end up in "formal" sector jobs. Following assumptions generated by the Ministry of Finance, KAZAK1 assumed in its *Pessimistic* scenario that the share of all employed in legal entities would rise slightly from 46% in 1999 to 50% by 2030, and stay constant thereafter. In its *Baseline* scenario, the formal sector share was projected to rise to 65% by 2030, thereafter remaining constant. These figures are close to the well-documented time series of Venezuela (Bello, 2000), which has a minerals economy with many features similar to the economy of Kazakhstan. Venezuela's formal sector has varied from roughly 45% to 65% of total employment during the past thirty years, growing during periods of economic recovery and shrinking quickly during economic decline. The PENMODEL also has several compliance scenarios. Most pessimistically, formal sector compliance remains constant at 63% throughout the period, while informal sector compliance rises from 2% to 14%. In the most optimistic scenarios, the increase is to 80% in the formal sector and 40% in the unregistered sector. Offsetting these optimistic scenarios, to some extent, is a quite modest projected rise in the formal sector share of total employment from 42.5% to 45% over the simulation period.

These differing demographic assumptions ultimately yield very different visions of tomorrow's Kazakhstan. In PENMODEL, employment in 2025 is 48.3% greater than in 2000; in KAZAK1, the increase is 30.7%. In PENMODEL, the over-65 population in 2025 is 1.621 million, almost exactly twice the number in 2000.

In KAZAK1, the retirement age population initially declines, and does not recover its 2000 level until 2010; it then grows quickly, doubling between 2010 and 2025 to 2.338 million and rising another 86% to 4.348 million by 2050.

KAZAK2 had yet another two years of economic recovery to incorporate into its parameter assumptions. Seitenova and Urzhumova (2003) assume gradually declining real GDP growth, from recorded rates of 13.2% in 2001 and 9.8% in 2002, falling to 6.0% in 2006, thence to 5.0% in 2015, 4.0% in 2025, and 3.5% in 2050. Thus, while the three models assume convergence to a similar rate, the lengthy interim assumptions in the most recent model result in a far larger economy. Real wage growth assumptions are also far more optimistic and, while not identical to one another, are essentially identical to GDP growth assumptions through 2025. This rapid growth generates much higher rates of accumulation, but also smaller replacement rates for those receiving slowly growing Solidarity payments.

Less obviously, the assumptions of KAZAK2 also ensure low replacement rates (defined as the ratio of average pension income to average wage), and in effect make the Accumulative system reform an unattractive option relative to a reformed PAYGO. While the rate of return on pension funds assets is fairly high in KAZAK2, at 4.0% forever after 2006, it is below real wage growth until after 2020; the return to assets during the decumulation (retirement) stage at 2.5% is below real wage growth in perpetuity. This assumption on returns to investment relative to real wage growth is the opposite of that in KAZAK1, which assumes very slow real wage growth for most of the simulation, but has real interest rates declining from 10.0% in 1999 to an asymptotic value of 7.0%, reached in 2005. For PENMODEL, the real return on assets was assumed to be a modest 3.0%, but that still exceeds 1% real wage growth. These asymmetries make it relatively likely in both KAZAK1 and PENMODEL that the Accumulative reform will appear attractive, since individually held and invested assets will grow more rapidly than wages. Compliance, labor force growth, and income distribution (in KAZAK2) all affect the PAYGO base as well, though, making the relative merit of the reform a more complex matter.

The actuarial modelers' choices of appropriate wage growth and return to capital were unconstrained by history. Since Kazakhstan clearly was experiencing disequilibrium during the benchmark period years 1997–2002, the modelers were forced to choose both a rate of recovery and a steady state growth rate for these variables. Even a few years removed, the PENMODEL assumptions seem far too conservative with respect to wage rates and returns to capital. KAZAK2 reflects recent history better than the other models, but it is difficult to imagine indefinite wage growth at the assumed long-run real rate of 4.0% without massive immigration from other countries in the region, which in turn would depress wage growth. KAZAK1 has average real wage growth of 2.66%, which is probably better in an open economy setting, but its capital returns are likely to be overly optimistic. To reiterate, one's view of these rates will affect model variant preferences and, ultimately, will affect one's view of the desirability of the Accumulative reforms.

It is ironic that the forces contributing to KAZAK2's assumption of low returns are precisely those macroeconomic features that characterize Kazakhstan's success. The disappearance of government budget deficits, combined with still stunted investment demand, has helped ensure that Kazakhstan's boom has indeed depressed returns. Indeed, declining returns are a major feature of Kazakhstan's pension funds in more recent years, although an additional driving force in this decline is the tenge's appreciation, which has depressed the tenge equivalent of dollar returns; it has driven asset movement away from dollar holdings, further increasing an excess supply of domestic funds.

KAZAK2's other assumptions are less dramatic refinements. Life expectancy is similar to that in KAZAK1, as is fertility, though the recovery in TFR is more prolonged, and the eventual steady state value at 2.08 is slightly lower. Both KAZAK1 and KAZAK2 assume net migration declines to zero by 2015; PENMODEL assumed a closed society. The growth of effective contributors in KAZAK2 rises from 43% of employment in 2003 to 56% in 2015, and ultimately to 58% in 2050.

In sum, the three models chose strikingly different relative parameter values, and these will inevitably affect the relative attractiveness of the reform and of various options. Before examining their results, it is important as well to contrast the three models.

4.3 Contrasting Kazakhstan's Actuarial Models

Pension system forecasting models tend to be conceptually simple, data-intensive structures that link a limited number of economic and financial assumptions with a detailed demographic-actuarial picture. Typically, the economic and demographic sides of the model are not linked during estimation, giving rise to occasionally inconsistent and hence implausible implications. As today's demographic events and changes in current policy have impacts that will not be entirely felt for decades, these models are usually run for up to fifty years or more. Macroeconomic assumptions are crucial because they determine the pace of economic growth, and hence system contributions. Ideally, these assumptions are taken from economic forecasting models, and alternate pension forecasts are made based on a range of optimistic to less optimistic economic forecasts.

Macroactuarial models project many variables related to pension forecasts, but have easily understood structures. From an economist's perspective, these models appear to be giant, nonbehavioral accounting exercises. Forecasts are built on data for a particular "benchmark" year. Future values of exogenous parameters also must be chosen. Common practices in choosing future parameters include assuming that current values remain constant forever, that recent past trends are maintained forever, or that convergence to long-term trends occurs. Forecasts based on formal econometric estimation are also possible, but virtually nonexistent in analysis of transition pension systems, as these countries have been in disequilibrium, with insufficient time series to estimate equilibrium and convergence rates.

The current generation of macroactuarial forecasting models was developed in 1996–98. The World Bank initially created several models, including for Ukraine, Hungary, and Poland, while USAID sponsored models for Romania and Kazakhstan (see Becker and Paltsev, 2001, on which this section is based). While these models are often criticized as being country-specific, all have similar structures, with Macroeconomic, Population, Labor, and Pension "blocks." They differ in their usage of country-specific accounting formulas for pension systems, assumptions about interaction among macroeconomic variables, and reform scenarios. These models were followed by the World Bank's PROST model, a universal model intended for applications in different countries, and which is becoming increasingly flexible.[3] Unfortunately, PROST's code is proprietary, which means that any modification requires ancillary programs that calculate data in a manner acceptable to PROST—if that is possible.

A typical pension forecasting model contains both an aggregate component, which projects pension fund performance, and an individual statement designed to estimate contributions and benefits under different options for a participating individual. The aggregate module starts from demographic projections; annual pension expenditures and pension fund revenue forecasts then follow. Calculations are based on system averages.

Despite the conceptual simplicity of a pension-forecasting model, it is necessary to obtain a vast amount of age- and gender-specific data. Data for population, fertility, mortality, and immigration are needed for the Population block. The Labor block requires age- and gender-specific labor participation rates, unemployment rates, and earnings profiles. The Pension block stores benchmark year information about a pension system, and also contains projections of contributors; old-age pensioners; disability, survivor, evasion, and exemption rates; and replacement rates. The Macroeconomic block requires information for the base year on GDP, pension fund balance, wages, and pension payments. It also requires forecasts of real GDP growth, inflation, real interest rates, budget transfers to the state pension fund, wage growth elasticity with respect to GDP growth, and retirement ages.

To calculate a pension fund's current balance, one starts with data on payroll contribution rate T, average wage w, the number of contributors L, average pension A, and the number of pensioners P. For a system to be in balance in year t, contributions must equal pension payments:

$$\sum_t \sum_i T w_{it} L_{it} = \sum_t \sum_i A_{it} P_{it} \tag{4.1}$$

where i denotes age group. The number of pensioners is given by

$$P_{it} = \left(r1_{it} + k1_{it} + v1_{it}\right) M_{it} + \left(r2_{it} + k2_{it} + v2_{it}\right) F_{it}, \tag{4.2}$$

where M_{it} and F_{it} are number of males and females of age i in year t; $r1_{it}$ is the male retirement rate for age group i, $r2_{it}$ is the corresponding female retirement rate; $k1_{it}$ and $k2_{it}$ are male and female disability coefficients, respectively; while $v1_{it}$ and $v2_{it}$ are the respective male and female survivor pension coefficients.

The basic formula for average pension benefits of new pensioners in a PAYGO system is:

$$A_{it} = LOS_{it} Z_t W_{it}, \tag{4.3}$$

where LOS_{it} denotes a length of service coefficient at retirement for age group i in given year t; Z is the replacement rate; and W is final average wage. LOS for people retiring at standard retirement age(s) is determined by pension system rules. The model calculates average LOS for those who retire earlier based on age-specific labor force participation rates. If half of persons aged 25 are active, then a basic pension actuarial model will assume that only one-half year of LOS is accumulated on average at age 25. *W* takes into account the wage profile, so the average wage of a person retiring at age 60 is different than the average wage of the person retiring at the age of 55. However, in simple models—and this would include all of the early models for transition nations—the economy-wide average wage (usually broken down by gender, but not age) is the basis of the calculation. Pension benefits to existing pensioners are typically, though not invariably, adjusted for inflation and real wage growth. For estimation of funded system liabilities, calculations are based on standard actuarial techniques.

T is determined exogenously by pension system rules in forecasting models. Typically, wage rates also are set exogenously, and then moved according to the GDP growth rate. The equation,

$$L_{it} = \sum_{h=M,F} LFPR_{h,i,t}(1-U_{h,i,t})(1-E_{h,i,t})h_{it} \tag{4.4}$$

gives the number of effective contributors L_{it}, where *LFPR* is age- and gender-specific labor force participation rate; *U* is the unemployment rate (age- and gender-specific); *E* gives the exemption and evasion rate (age- and gender-specific); and M_{it} and F_{it} give male and female age-specific populations, respectively.

Demographic projections for population of age one and older are simply:

$$M_{t+1,i+1} = M_{t,i}S^{m}_{t,i+1} + IM^{m}_{t,i+1}. \tag{4.5}$$

Here, $M_{t,i}$ is the male population of age *i* at the beginning of year *t*; $S^{m}{}_{t,i}$ is the proportion of the male population of age *i* that survives between year *t* and *t+1*; $IM^{m}{}_{t,i}$ is the net male immigration level of age *i* between year *t* and *t+1*. A similar equation projects the female population. The equation for newborn males is:

$$M_{t+1,0} = \sum_{j} f_{t,j}F_{t,j}mk_{t}S^{m}_{t,0} + IM^{m}_{t,0} \tag{4.6}$$

where $M_{t+1,0}$ is the male population less than a year old in year *t+1*; $f_{t,j}$ is the birth rate in year *t* of women age *j*; $F_{t,j}$ is the number of women of age *j* in year *t*; and mk_t is the male/female birth coefficient. A similar equation projects newborn females. As discussed, *S*, *f*, and *IM* are usually treated as constants over time in actuarial models, while the KAZAK1 and KAZAK2 forecasts permit these demographic parameters to vary.

The PENMODEL is fairly representative of a quickly but competently constructed, first-generation macroactuarial model for a middle-income country. The model was created with only one type of individual—that is, all retirees are assumed identical, other than having mortality risks that vary by gender. Distributional issues therefore cannot be addressed. In fairness to the authors, who worked under great time constraints, relatively little was known about the distribution of earnings at the time, and any overall assessment would have been highly speculative. However, the model did not encourage creation of alternative scenarios, and therefore downplayed distributional problems created by the Accumulative system. The main aim of the model, however, was to project GoK pension liabilities, and not actual replacement rates.[4]

A detailed description of PENMODEL appears in IMCC (1997a). Its focus was on providing public budgetary implications of a continued PAYGO system, the reforms as initially outlined, and alternative reform scenarios (notably, an Accumulative system with retirement age increased to 65 for both men and women). In comparison with both PROST-based models, PENMODEL provides a rich statement of the various types of retirement categories that actually exist in Kazakhstan, including regular length of service, favorable terms, short service, disability retirement, survivorship benefits, and social allowances to those outside the labor force. The model keeps separate track of military retirements, and, usefully, also contains estimates of state contributions for public employees.

The PENMODEL carefully estimates average retirement age for both men and women of different categories. Compared with the PROST-based models that followed, it has great detail in demographic and retirement structural areas. It also has a set of Kazakhstan-specific policy options, and allows the user to play with benefits' taxation and select from alternative population, wage growth, interest rate, compliance, and pension distribution scenarios. Offsetting these attractive features is use of optimistic data that tend to make all pension options seem fairly manageable, and simplistic labor market and contribution assumptions (and, consequently, no sense of the magnitude of contingent liabilities – namely the difference between projected pension earnings and minimum pension incomes guaranteed by GoK – or elderly poverty under alternative regimes). High mortality that is maintained, both prior to and following retirement age, means lower burdens for the Solidarity system—but it also means that smaller savings are needed for a viable Accumulative system. High labor force participation and improved compliance, especially in the informal sector, also reduce burdens both for Solidarity system and Accumulative system reforms. Critical failures to consider interrupted service and pension adequacy, along with higher rates of return to assets than wage growth, further ensure that PENMODEL will give an exceptionally favorable picture of Accumulative reforms.

The original emphasis of PROST was to provide a simple, generic model that could be used for illustrative purposes in a wide range of countries. The World Bank's initial expectation was that countries seriously considering major pension reforms would develop their own models that could capture idiosyncratic pension system design and labor force considerations. It did not actually turn out that way—the initial country-specific models were quite simple, and PROST gradually added features and increased in complexity. KAZAK1 is an application of PROST7, while KAZAK2 is based on PROST11.

KAZAK1 lacks much of the Kazakhstan system detail found in PENMODEL, but contains three major improvements. First, it enables the user to calculate pension payments in both systems, and therefore to get at the issue of replacement rate adequacy. Second, the model uses considerable ancillary analysis of labor force and demographic trends, so that the exceptionally high mortality of the mid-1990s was not presumed to prevail indefinitely. Third, while it is not a PROST7 option, ancillary routines were built in KAZAK1 to estimate contingent liabilities. In effect, KAZAK1 uses PROST7 as its actuarial model, but also involved the construction of several programs to modify input values. In the case of contingent liabilities, the individual account option of PROST7 can be used with information on the distribution of the population into different income classes, with group-specific earnings' projections using PROST's "profile" option.

The first step in a rigorous contingent valuation process is to evaluate noncontingent liabilities separately for each category of pensioners and recipients of social allowances. Payments from the Solidarity system for various categories of workers with different levels of wages are then assessed. To these Solidarity payments—which are time-dependent, since length of service in the old system will diminish for younger cohorts—payments from individual accounts made to current and new participants of the Accumulative pension system, depending upon the wage level, must be added. The last stage, estimation of contingent liabilities, involves several steps:

1. Calculation of a number of new retirees (males and females) participating in the Accumulative system, with delineation by income level and age of joining the Accumulative system (accordingly, with calculation of LOS in the Solidarity system and Accumulative system for each group) from 2000 through 2050
2. Calculation of aggregate replacement rates in relation to a population's average wage, and identification of contingent liabilities at the retirement year for each group
3. Formation of a survival matrix for each of the previously defined groups
4. Calculation of dynamics of replacement rates for surviving pensioners during their pension life spans and, accordingly, dynamics of contingent liabilities

KAZAK1 also analyzed a large number of scenarios, but did not have restricted, preprogrammed options as in PENMODEL. However, in work for MinFin and MLSP, two main development scenarios were emphasized. Relatively high rates of real GDP growth, substantial employment growth, high rates of returns to accumulation funds, and improved compliance system characterize the *Baseline* scenario. The *Pessimistic* scenario is based on lower rates of GDP growth and slow growth of the formal sector. Eventually, two *Optimistic* scenarios also were added.

KAZAK2 included both updated input data and a more sophisticated annuity calculation component. Perhaps most critically, and of particular importance for calculating contingent liabilities, the model used detailed income distribution data, rather than making illustrative projections based on a number of profiles, as in KAZAK1. Ironically, PROST11 is so complex and interdependent that the KAZAK2 programmer, Dina Urzhumova, used it mainly as a subroutine. Thus, while PROST11 has an income distribution component, with a stochastic process generating a distribution given specified moments, the resulting distribution was never consistent with actual data outcomes for each group, when data were given from the SCBP on both contributor and pensioner distributions. SCBP data have very refined delineations, varying from $25/month at low-income levels to $100/month for those with earnings over $600/month. In addition to bypassing PROST11's income distribution component, KAZAK2 also calculates annuities independently. This reduced dependency on PROST also reflected determination to capture Kazakhstani reality more accurately (for example, PROST does not allow disability payments below minimum social allowances, but the fact that partially disabled people receive a modest monthly payment means that this constraint does not hold in Kazakhstan); it also reflected a desire to avoid complex constraints imposed by a large, interdependent package.

Over time, actuarial models of Kazakhstan have become far more sophisticated. Unfortunately, given the time constraints under which they have been constructed, they are either user unfriendly (KAZAK1 and, especially, KAZAK2) or restrictive (PENMODEL). Thus, they reflect the hurry with which decisions were taken, and little consideration was given to how assumptions and structure would drive and ultimately bias results. Rather, key assumptions were dictated (typically by the Ministry of Finance, directly or indirectly), were determined by data availability, or were hastily estimated without painstaking sensitivity analysis. While this situation is far from ideal, Kazakhstan in fact enjoys a far richer model base than most middle-income countries undertaking reforms. Furthermore, as it turns out, these models—especially the more recent ones—have been used to make several important points.

4.4 Initial Macro Forecasts from Penmodel

As noted, PENMODEL was created to analyze GoK social security obligations. Its projections, taken from IMCC (1997a), can be found on a companion data website at http://www.econ.duke.edu/Econ/Faculty/Users/cbecker.html. These figures are striking: the first impression one gets is that they are highly optimistic, from a fiscal burden standpoint, especially for a maintained Solidarity system. An obvious reason for this is the assumption of continued very high mortality. The second point to notice is that the cost of a maintained Solidarity PAYGO system, while quite high for the period 1997–2006 by the standards of a middle-income country, is not out of control. Rather, PENMODEL forecasts that the pressure put on the Republican government budget would be temporary. It is also apparent that there are many Solidarity reforms that would alleviate budgetary pressures more rapidly than the adoption of an Accumulative system. These prospective steps include efforts to improve compliance, reduce the incidence of early retirement, and raise retirement ages further and more quickly.

Indeed, the reduction in GoK budgetary pressure from a move to an Accumulative system is quite modest—and does not show up for the first quarter century of the simulations! A key reason for this is that GoK must now make substantial payments for its own employees: models that do not include this charge will understate the cost of the reform to the Republican government, especially in early years. PENMODEL clearly implies that the high cost of social payments in the first decade of the simulations is inevitable and that, by the time the Accumulative reforms kick in to reduce budgetary pressures, social payment levels already will have decreased to a far more manageable level.

These projections imply that fiscal sustainability could not be the main reason for Kazakhstan's pension reform—or, more accurately, that the actuarial projections at the time the reforms were adopted did not support an Accumulative system for fiscal control reasons. However, as the chronology in Chapter 3 suggests, the commitment to reform was well under way prior to construction of any of the actuarial models. Pension reform advocates largely focused on anticipated financial sector development benefits, and appear not to have been persuaded by the forecasts that the Solidarity system's cost easily could be brought under control. Indeed, anyone pessimistic about improved compliance, curtailed favorable or early retirements, or employment recovery in registered firms would have great reason to doubt the projections and would be tempted to accept the certain reduction in obligations offered by an Accumulative system.

This reaction by IMWG members and other Kazakhstani policymakers seems rational. We know in hindsight that the explosion of early and favorable retirements (outlined by Becker and Urzhumova, 1998) was effectively curtailed within the Solidarity system. The vast arrears and periodic payments in kind that characterized the mid-1990s also are long gone—in fact, they were repaid as a condition of the reform. But improved administration and economic recovery were far from being certainties in 1996, and the PENMODEL forecasts appear to have had no impact. The projections were so optimistic as to strain credulity, and stood in clear juxtaposition to actual conditions of 1996–97. Furthermore, while the user-friendly model encouraged alternative forecasts based on a range of assumptions, in fact it was not used in such a manner, and the studies produced offered little feel for the robustness of the results.

Yet another reason these forecasts did not cause reconsideration is that they also failed to sway the sponsoring international organizations. The mantra of the "three-pillar" system espoused by the World Bank was powerful, especially in the immediate wake of the so-called James Report (World Bank, 1994). Moreover, the PENMODEL designer and programmer himself appeared to ignore the implications of his own forecasts.[5] In fact, USAID did not waver in its commitment to funding the infrastructure of an Accumulative system, as well as the emerging financial sector, while the World Bank worked with Kazakhstani officials on collection improvements. Internal USAID consultancy reports from the period (e.g., Wiener, 1998) contain virtually no criticism of the switch to an Accumulative system, and beyond advocating technical assistance, enthusiastically recommend advocacy and public relations on behalf of the reform. Kazakhstani officials and technocrats who read these varied reports would have rightly interpreted them as being inconclusive, and in any case would have been suspicious of the database quality, and hence the validity of results. Rather, they wanted to know how successful prior reforms had been, notably in Chile, and generally were reassured on that score.

The speed with which the reform was introduced made such an outcome almost inevitable. Prior to any actuarial analysis, USAID, following the recommendation of its contractors, strongly advocated the introduction of a multi-pillar system (e.g., Anderson, 1996; Anderson et al., 1997). As conceived by Anderson et al, this initially involved a mandatory PAYGO component with a payroll tax of 10%, a mandatory second-pillar Accumulative system with a payroll contribution rate of only 6%, and a modest voluntary contribution pillar. Over time, the second pillar's relative importance was strengthened, and a commitment both by GoK and its international supporters was made prior to any serious actuarial analysis. When PENMODEL results became available, institutional reform was already under way, the forecasts were downplayed (though the modest accumulations projected with a 6% contribution may have led to its increase), and there was no turning back.

4.5 Revised Macro Forecasts from Kazak1

In fact, a reasoned case for continuing the reforms could be made, in part stemming from gains from financial sector development, in part by emphasizing the certainty with which the reforms would limit government spending obligations (improved collection efforts and reduced early retirements might not be sustained indefinitely), and in part by noting Penmodel's data and modeling weaknesses. But the reform's design also could have been modified in the light of these actuarial forecasts, and that sort of reconsideration did not occur.

However, USAID did commission another actuarial model, in part to estimate contingent liabilities, in part to examine replacement rate implication of the reforms for different groups, in part to develop a Kazakhstani version of the increasingly standard PROST model, in part to incorporate improved data, and in part to see if a second model would give such tiny budgetary gains to the reforms. The initial results that came back from KAZAK1 are reproduced in table 4.1.

As is apparent from a comparison of table 4.1 with the Penmodel forecasts (and noting that Kazak1 did not estimate government contributions for its own employees independently) the new projections were indeed more to the liking of the reform's advocates, especially as unpublished estimates of a maintained Solidarity system without reforms were extremely grim. There is irony in these results, as the KAZAK1 technical team (Becker, Seitenova, and Urzhumova) regarded the Accumulative reforms with considerable skepticism. Nor did they place much faith in the imminence of economic recovery, and their preferred scenarios differed far less in terms of budgetary implications from those of PENMODEL than did the official, MinFin-approved scenario.

Clearly, it is easy to selectively choose results that differ widely, as a result of marked differences in assumptions. But are legitimate choices really that unrestricted? Becker, Urzhumova, Seitenova, and Golovatsky (1999) and Becker, Seitenova, and Urzhumova (2001) argue otherwise. To start with, there is no need for a complex actuarial model to note that projected deficits as a share of GDP will shrink rapidly in an environment of high economic growth. The pleasant

Table 4.1 KAZAK1-based estimates of the Solidarity system surplus (deficit), excluding contingent liabilities (required Republican government budget transfers), as a percent of GDP

Year	*Official forecast (1)*	*Baseline forecast (2)*	*Optimistic scenario A: high GDP and high employment growth (3)*	*Optimistic scenario B: high GDP but low employment growth (4)*	*Pessimistic scenario (5)*
1998	(4.1)	(4.1)	(4.1)	(4.1)	(4.1)
1999	(3.3)	(3.6)	(3.6)	(3.6)	(3.6)
2004	(1.3)	(2.5)	(1.9)	(1.9)	(2.6)
2009	0.4	(1.9)	(0.3)	(0.7)	(2.4)
2014	0.7	(2.1)	0.1	(0.5)	(2.4)
2019	0.8	(2.3)	0.3	(0.4)	(2.4)
2024	1.8	(2.1)	0.9	0.2	(2.1)
2029	3.6	(1.4)	2.1	1.3	(1.4)
2034	3.0	(1.3)	1.7	1.1	(1.3)
2039	1.7	(1.4)	0.9	0.5	(1.3)
2044	2.3	(0.6)	1.4	0.9	(0.9)
2049	3.0	(0.0)	1.9	1.2	(0.5)

Note:

Official forecast: real per capita GDP growth of –1.5% for 1999, 0.5% for 2000, 1.5% in 2001, 2.0% in 2002–2997, 2.5% in 2008–2011, 3.0% in 2012–2030, 3.5% in 2031–2039, and 4.0% in 2040–2050. Unemployment rate quickly declines from 13% to 4%; inflation gradually declines from 10% to 2%; 5% return to Accumulative system assets; pension contribution and Solidarity obligation compliance rate rising from 63% to 84.5% by 2010; pension system contribution rate (formal sector employment share) of 48% in 1998 rising to 75% by 2030; age/sex mortality rate recovery to 1987 (Soviet era low) by 2010; fertility recovery to replacement (TFR = 2.1) by 2010; net emigration ceases by 2005, followed by net immigration that gradually grows to 0.6% of population by 2015 and is stable thereafter; gradual improvement of female disability rates to equality with male rates; real wage growth of 4.6% in 1998, 2.5% in 1999, and 3.0% during 2000–2050.

Baseline forecast (maintained behavior): constant real per capita GDP; constant unemployment rate of 13%; 6% inflation rate; 5% return to Accumulative system assets; pension contribution and Solidarity obligation compliance rate rising from 63% to 72% by 2010; pension system contribution rate (formal sector employment share) of 48% in 1998 rising to 52.5% by 2030; age/sex mortality rate recovery to 1987 (Soviet era low) by 2020; fertility recovery to replacement (TFR = 2.1) by 2020; net emigration ceases by 2005, followed by net immigration that gradually grows to 0.3% of population by 2015 and is stable thereafter; gradual improvement of female disability rates to remove half of the gap with male rates; zero real wage growth.

Optimistic A forecast: real per capita GDP growth of 3.0%; unemployment rate gradually declines from 13% to 4%; inflation gradually declines from 10% to 3%; 8% return to Accumulative system assets; pension contribution and Solidarity obligation compliance rate rising from 63% to 84.5% by 2010; pension system contribution rate (formal sector employment share) of 48% in 1998 rising to 75% by 2030; age/sex mortality rate recovery to 1987 (Soviet era low) by 2010; fertility recovery to replacement (TFR = 2.1) by 2010; net emigration ceases by 2005, followed by net immigration that gradually grows to 0.6% of population by 2015 and is stable thereafter; gradual improvement of female disability rates to equality with male rates; wage bill/GDP rises from 41% in 1998 to 45.4% by 2050, implying annual real wage growth of 2.36%.

Optimistic B forecast: real per capita GDP growth of 3.0%; constant unemployment rate of 13%; inflation gradually declines from 10% to 3%; 8% return to Accumulative system assets; pension contribution and Solidarity obligation compliance rate rising from 63% to 84.5% by 2010; pension system contribution rate (formal sector employment share) of 48% in 1998 rising to 62.5% by 2030; age/sex mortality rate recovery to 1987 (Soviet era low) by 2010; fertility recovery to replacement (TFR = 2.1) by 2010; net emigration ceases by 2005, followed by net immigration that gradually grows to 0.6% of population by 2015 and is stable thereafter; gradual improvement of female disability rates to equality with male rates; wage bill/GDP rises from 41% in 1998 to 43.3% by 2050, implying annual real wage growth of 2.06%.

Pessimistic forecast: initial era declining per capita GDP of 2.5% per annum followed by constant real per capita GDP; unemployment rate gradually rises from 13% to 23%; inflation rises from 10% to 12% (Solidarity pension elasticity of 0.78 with respect to CPI); 3% return to Accumulative system assets; pension obligation compliance rate of 63%; pension system contribution rate (formal sector employment share) of 48% in 1998 falling to 40% by 2030; stable mortality, fertility, and net emigration rates; stable disability rates (excluding effect of 1942–44 cohort); elasticity of real wage/GDP = 1.

Source: Becker, Urzhumova, Seitenova, and Golovatsky (1999)

economic world and formal sector employment boom envisioned in the *Official* and *Optimistic A* scenarios could hardly fail to generate budgetary surpluses, especially given relatively slow Solidarity pension growth. With restricted obligations and a flourishing contribution base, the social security system becomes a net source of funds for government, to no surprise.

This point serves as the foundation for a major departure by the KAZAK1 modeling team. They argue that, in the absence of information on the underlying distributions of actuarial model parameter input values, the simple point estimates of greatest value are those for which relatively unfavorable values are chosen. The rationale is simple: Accumulative and, especially, Solidarity pensions are intended to provide a safety net for the elderly and disabled. Should Kazakhstan experience 10% real GDP growth for the next quarter century, living standards of all will be almost unimaginably better than at present, and state social payments surely will be far larger than presently expected. The choice of pension system is of relatively minor importance in such a setting, since under almost any conceivable outcome, poverty rates will diminish greatly, even for the elderly and disabled. Indeed, the events of the past nine years illustrate this point.

Rather, the test of a social security system's effectiveness occurs when the economy is generally stressed—this, after all, is when a safety net is most needed. Consequently, the KAZAK1 modelers were most interested in the *Baseline* (and its closer variants, *Optimistic B* and *Pessimistic*) simulations. However, they did not use this version to explicitly test the relative merit of reemphasizing the Solidarity system—those experiments remained for KAZAK2.

Thus, the KAZAK1 forecasts preferred by the modelers differed less than from those of PENMODEL than first glance suggests. While Kazakhstan government officials and their international agency counterparts could look at the *Official* forecast figures and see long-run projections of a Solidarity system surplus equal to 3% of GDP, given the Accumulative reform, in contrast to the 3% charge implied for 2021 in the PENMODEL forecasts, a more conservative reading based on *Baseline* does not generate Solidarity system balance until 2050. Worse still, its forecast of necessary Republican budget transfers to SCBP to cover Solidarity costs, at 2.1% of GDP for 2021, are actually greater than those estimated from PENMODEL, once one excludes contributions for public employees for the sake of comparability.

The extended KAZAK1 forecast to 2050 (PENMODEL terminated in 2026) puts a very different spin on the fiscal success of the reforms. The longer duration of the forecasts includes roughly two decades in which regular service-based Solidarity pensions are tiny, so that, assuming a fixed contribution rate, surpluses are the inevitable outcome. However, in an economy as volatile as that of Kazakhstan, 50+ year projections have little meaning, and the potential error dwarfs the projected values.

Another useful point from table 4.1, comparing the two *Optimistic* scenarios, is that while rapid economic growth is useful, employment-oriented growth is especially helpful. Given the compounding effects of differences in growth rates, this effect is modest at first. But by 2014, the high employment version is generating a surplus from payroll contributions, while the high GDP but low employment growth scenario still suffers from a budgetary shortfall of 0.5% of GDP.

4.6 Revised Macro Forecasts from KAZAK2

As it has turned out, Kazakhstan's economic performance since 2000 has surpassed all expectations. The debate has long been put aside about whether to use mildly optimistic MinFin or darkly pessimistic alternative assumptions. In addition, as other budgetary pressures slackened, GoK has greatly increased real pensions. Combined with cost estimates that include contingent liabilities, Kazakhstan thus finds itself with a larger unfunded pension liability that its government must handle—but fears of being able to do so have receded.

Given these different conditions, the actuarial forecasts of Seitenova and Urzhumova (2003) to the World Bank emphasized instead adequacy of pensions for different groups, the subject of Chapter 10. The economic recovery also led to the development of two proposals by the Kazakhstan government, along with a commitment in 2003 to improve pension conditions. These proposals, plus several other options suggested by Seitenova and Urzhumova, are outlined in table 4.2.

The 2003 reforms represented a major step away from government's erstwhile determination to curtail social expenditures. This relaxation is hardly surprising: lagging state pension payments in the face of economic recovery were politically unpopular, while improved payments serve as a clear sign of increased state capacity. In addition, the reforms corrected a glaring injustice, by linking Solidarity payments to comparable current earnings rather than to individuals' histories—this practice being ruinous because of the high inflation of the 1990s.

As the boom continued, further social welfare spending commitments were made. In early 2004, the fifth year of high GDP growth, GoK undertook additional steps that would increase state pension payments. One proposal was to link the Solidarity system's Minimum Pension to an estimated subsistence level, with an old-age social allowance set at 65% of subsistence level even for those with no Solidarity service years from 2006 onward, while the Minimum Pension gradually increases to 85% of subsistence (table 4.3). A second proposal has been to provide demogrants (fixed payments) to all citizens of retirement age, with this amount equal to at least 65% of subsistence level from 2006 onward. The demogrant option was adopted in 2005 (Chapter 6), and while there was no formal commitment to its level, it was intended to quickly rise to the subsistence level.

The Seitenova-Urzhumova proposals go further in several dimensions. *Proposal 3* links both the Minimum Pension (at 24%) and the social allowance (at 12%) to the average wage, thereby ensuring stable growth of pensions along with economic growth. For the same reason, it also raises the wage ceiling used in calculating Solidarity pension entitlements from three to four Minimum Wages. A further variant (*Proposal 3A*) also raises pension age for women by six months per year starting in 2004, until parity with men's retirement age (63) is reached at the end of 2013. The rationale for doing so is that an Accumulative system is disadvantageous for women if they have restricted working years. A more complex alternative (*Proposal 3B*) develops *3A* further, as it compares the Minimum Pension with the Solidarity entitlement for workers who have made funded-system contributions in at least 75% of the years between 1998 and their retirement. It then proposes to pay the greater of the Minimum Pension and the Solidarity pension for

Table 4.2 Proposed pension system options simulated in KAZAK2

No [further] reform: committed 2003 reforms	2003	Recalculation of pensions of those who retired prior to January 1, 2003 based on 2002 wages by branches of the economy and personal participation coefficients (distribution determined from data maintained in SPPC pension files). The new pension is set as the maximum of the old pension, recalculated pension, and the minimum pension, with a maximum pension equal to 75% of 15 RCI (regulatory calculation index units). The new pensions are paid effective July 1, 2003. Minimum pension is set at 5500 tenge effective July 1, 2003.
	All years	Minimum pension and the old-age social allowance (3 RCI) are indexed to the past year average annual inflation. Minimum pension guarantee applies to retirees with either 25/20 years of PAYGO service for males/females, respectively, or with contributions to the Accumulative system during at least 75% of the period from January 1, 1998 to retirement. The minimum pension is compared against the sum of the calculated prorated PAYGO pension and the annuitized monthly pension from the Accumulative system. Social allowance guarantee applies to retirees with low or no service years in either PAYGO or the funded system. All pensions are fully indexed to the past year average annual inflation. Wage ceiling is maintained at 15 RCI for the whole projection period and is indexed to the past year average annual inflation.
Government of Kazakhstan	2003	Same changes as above
***Proposal 1*: Minimum pensions**	2004	Recalculation of maximum pensions in 2004 based on the wage ceiling of 15 RCI (increased to compensate for 2003 inflation) and personal participation coefficients. Indexation of all pensions to 2004 projected inflation. The new pension is set at the maximum of the inflation-adjusted recalculated pension and 75% of 15 RCI.
	2005	Minimum pension is set at 70% of a new subsistence level estimate. Recalculation of maximum pensions in 2005 based on the personal participation coefficients. Indexation of all pensions to 2005 projected inflation. Introduction of a new wage ceiling of 3 Minimum Wages. The new Solidarity pension is set at the maximum of the inflation-adjusted recalculated pension and 75% of 3 Minimum Wages.
	2006 and thereafter	Minimum pension is set at 85% of calculated Subsistence Level. Indexation of all pensions to 2006 projected inflation. A new minimum Old Age Social Allowance (OASA) is set at 65% of Subsistence Level for retirees with no service years in PAYGO (to replace the old social allowance of 3 RCI).
Government of Kazakhstan ***Proposal 2*: Demogrant**	2003	Recalculation of all pensions of those who retired prior to January 1, 2003 based on either 1997 wages by branches of the economy or 1997 nationwide average wage (8,541 tenge) and personal participation coefficients with a maximum value of 2.25 (to be calculated based on data maintained in SPPC pension files: service years and pre-retirement wages as submitted on the date of retirement). Indexation of the recalculated pensions to CPI from January 1, 1998 to July 1, 2003 (CPI of 1.53).

Continued

Table 4.2 (*Continued*)

		The new pension is set as the maximum of the old pension, recalculated pension, and the minimum pension, with a maximum pension equal to 75% of 15 RCI and paid effective June 1, 2003. If the old pension is higher than the recalculated pension (and higher than the minimum pension), the difference between the old and the recalculated pension is paid as the OASA. If the recalculated pension is lower than the minimum pension, then the difference between the two values is paid as the OASA. The demogrant is paid to all citizens at ages 58/63 and over. Effective July 1, 2003, new retirees are to submit papers for year 1997 or earlier years for the calculation of new pensions.
	2004	Indexation of all pensions to 2004 projected inflation. The new OASA is set at the maximum of 20% of Subsistence Level and the OASA granted in 2003.
	2005	Indexation of all pensions to 2005 projected inflation. The demogrant is set at the maximum of 40% of Subsistence Level and the OASA granted in 2004.
	2006 and thereafter	Indexation of all pensions to 2006 projected inflation. The demogrant is set at the maximum of 65% of Subsistence Level and the OASA granted in 2005.
Proposal 3 (Seitenova – Urzhumova)		Minimum pension is indexed to the past year nominal wage growth effective 2004 and stays at 24% of the average wage for the whole projection period. The social allowance is maintained at 12% of the average wage through indexation to the past year nominal wage growth. Eligibility for the minimum pension and the social allowance is the same as in *No Reform Scenario*. Wage ceiling is increased to 4 Minimum Wages effective January 1, 2004. In 2004, all pensions for those who retired prior to January 1, 2004 are recalculated based on 2003 wages and personal participation coefficients, with the maximum pension of 75% of 4 Minimum Wages. All pensions are inflation indexed.
Proposal 3a		Same as *Proposal 3* but with female pension age being gradually increased from age 58 to age 63 by six months per year, starting January 1, 2004.
Proposal 3b		Same as *Proposal 3a*, but with the minimum pension guarantee compared to the PAYGO pension for retirees who have made contributions to the funded system during at least 75% of the period from January 1, 1998 to retirement. If the pro-rated Solidarity pension is below the minimum pension or if it equals zero in later years, the minimum pension is paid irrespective of the annuitized pension from the Accumulative system. This means that the minimum pension of 24% of the average wage becomes a demogrant (or a basic pension) for the Accumulative system contributors at later stages, while the social allowance of 12% of the average wage becomes a demogrant for non-contributors.
Proposal 3c		Same as *Proposal 3b*, but a lower wage ceiling of 3 minimum wages is introduced in 2004, and all pensions are indexed to the nominal wage growth from 2004.

Source: Seitenova and Urzhumova (2003)

Table 4.3 Solidarity system expenditures and current account balance, KAZAK1 *Baseline* actuarial simulation (all figures given as a percent of GDP)

Year	*Total benefit payments*	*including payments to:* Old age	Contingent liabilities	Favorable	Survivors	Disabled	*Current balance*
1999	6.2	3.1	0.0	1.8	0.6	0.7	(2.9)
2000	5.3	2.7	0.0	1.5	0.5	0.6	(1.6)
2001	5.0	2.5	0.0	1.4	0.5	0.5	(1.0)
2002	4.7	2.4	0.0	1.3	0.5	0.5	(1.0)
2003	4.5	2.3	0.0	1.2	0.5	0.5	(1.0)
2004	4.3	2.2	0.0	1.1	0.5	0.5	(0.8)
2005	4.2	2.2	0.0	1.0	0.5	0.5	(0.5)
2006	4.1	2.2	0.0	0.9	0.5	0.5	(0.4)
2007	4.0	2.2	0.0	0.9	0.4	0.5	(0.2)
2008	3.9	2.1	0.0	0.8	0.4	0.5	(0.1)
2009	3.8	2.1	0.0	0.8	0.4	0.5	0.1
2010	3.8	2.2	0.0	0.7	0.4	0.5	0.2
2015	4.0	2.5	0.0	0.5	0.5	0.5	0.4
2019	4.3	2.8	0.0	0.4	0.5	0.6	0.3
2020	4.3	2.8	0.0	0.4	0.5	0.6	0.3
2025	4.3	2.9	0.0	0.3	0.4	0.6	0.6
2030	4.3	2.8	0.0	0.5	0.4	0.6	0.8
2035	3.8	2.3	0.1	0.4	0.4	0.6	1.2
2040	3.3	1.8	0.2	0.3	0.4	0.6	1.6
2045	3.0	1.5	0.2	0.3	0.4	0.7	1.9
2050	2.8	1.3	0.3	0.2	0.4	0.7	2.1

Source: Becker, Seitenova, and Urzhumova (2001)

such persons, in effect converting the Minimum Pension and social allowance payments to demogrants. *Proposal 3C* is the same as *3B*, but with a lower wage ceiling of 3 Minimum Wages, and pensions linked to nominal wage growth from 2004.

It should be emphasized that earlier actuarial simulation models could not have addressed these proposals. Calculating payments based on inadequate Solidarity entitlements or Accumulative savings requires both a mechanism for estimating contingent liabilities and data on the distribution of incomes and years of service. In macroactuarial modeling sophistication, between 1997 and 2003, Kazakhstan may be said to have gone from a Yak-40 turbojet to an Ilyushin 86 wide-bodied jet.

Most of the data assumptions are outlined above. Annuity pension benefits are indexed to inflation. Net emigration declines to zero by 2015 and is constant thereafter. The labor force participation rate overall is 76% for males and 65% for females for the whole projection period, except for changes in ages close to retirement, to adjust for ageing retirees on favorable terms and for the increase in female retirement age in *Proposals 3a* and *3b*. The unemployment rate is assumed to be constant at 8% for males and 11% for females for the whole projection period. Finally, the proportion of contributors grows from the current 43% of employment to 56% in 2015 and to 58% in 2050. Macroeconomic and financial assumptions appear in table 4.4.

Table 4.4 KAZAK2 estimates of required GoK expenditures (percent of GDP)

Year	*No further pension system reforms beyond 2003*		*Proposal 3 reforms added: Minimum Pension and Social Allowances linked to average wage (stable lower bound replacement rates implied)*	
	4% real interest rate	*5% real interest rate*	*4% real interest rate*	*5% real interest rate*
2003	3.2	3.2	3.2	3.2
2005	3.1	3.1	4.4	4.5
2010	2.3	2.3	3.2	3.2
2015	1.8	1.8	3.1	3.1
2020	1.5	1.5	3.4	3.4
2025	1.2	1.2	3.5	3.5
2030	1.0	1.0	3.4	3.4
2035	0.7	0.7	3.2	3.2
2040	0.5	0.5	3.2	3.1
2045	0.4	0.4	3.3	3.2
2050	0.3	0.3	3.6	3.4

Source: Seitenova and Urzhumova (2003)

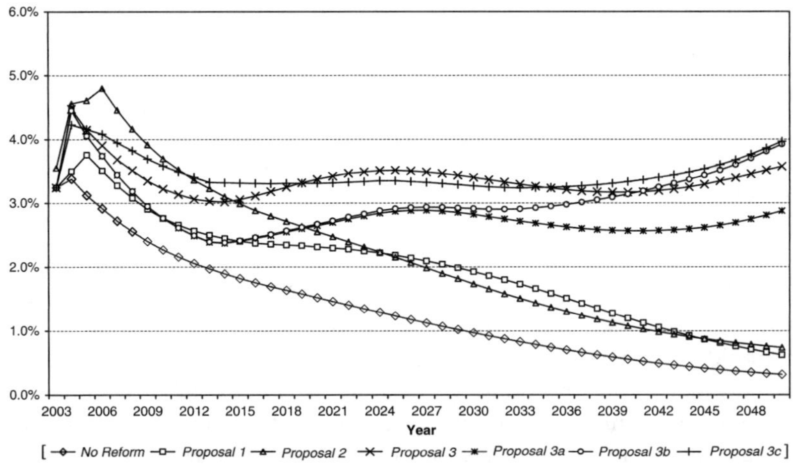

Figure 4.1 Government pension and social allowance expenditures as a percentage of GDP, KAZAK2
Source: Seitenova and Urzhumova (2003)

Figure 4.1 shows government expenditures for the proposed options as a share of GDP. Since pensions in the Accumulative system are projected to be low for the majority of contributor retirees, maintaining state pensions for this group at the level of 24% of the average wage would result in high government expenditures on either supplemental or basic pension payments. If GoK decided to keep the replacement rate for noncontributor retirees at 12% of the average wage, this would also imply high expenditures as this group is projected to account for 40% of all retirees in later years. In *Proposals 3B* and *3C*, which in their mature stages generate a replacement rate of more than 40% for contributors, and 12% for nonparticipant retirees, government expenditures would make 4% of GDP. Without the assumed increase in female retirement age to 63, the expenditures would be higher still, by roughly 0.7% of GDP in the long run.

In *Proposal 3a* with the same long-run retirement ages for both men and women, expenditures still amount to about 3% of GDP in the long run. In this scenario, the total replacement rate for contributor retirees (27%) is very close to the current rate. In other words, strategies that generate stable replacement rates will end up with social security system costs roughly comparable with their current levels, with slight fluctuations driven by demographic cohort shifts, and occasional switches in economic assumptions. As Seitenova and Urzhumova (2003: 87) note, "the so-called 'residual' PAYGO would be comparable with the current PAYGO in terms of expenditures." The surpluses that emerged from some of the KAZAK1 scenarios vanish in light of the higher pension commitments: even with the reforms committed, considerable but sustainable central government budget contributions to the SPPC will be needed for the foreseeable future.

As Chapter 10 details, even the current reforms and the government's other proposals still imply markedly falling replacement rates for most pensioners. Our guess is that this is not tenable in a pluralistic society such as Kazakhstan, especially given that it historically is a welfare state. If it is not, then the long-run impact on the GoK budget of the vast pension reform may be quite small. The reason for this is a mathematical consequence of rapid economic growth. In the government-designed reform scenarios presented in tables 4.1 and 4.2, state support to pensioners is maintained in real terms or indexed to poverty lines that do not rise as rapidly as wages. At the same time, individual contributions to the Accumulative system will occur during eras when wages would have been lower. Barring very high real returns, these also fail to generate high replacement rates, especially as they must be spread over an increasing number of years because of rising life expectancy. Since shrinking replacement rates may be politically untenable in an environment of continued growth, either a *de facto* or *de jure* but in either case substantial demogrant seems likely as long as the public purse can afford these payments.

This conclusion does not mean that the pension reform was unsuccessful or unimportant: it clearly has had major consequences. Rather, the anticipated outcome and *Proposals 3, 3a, 3b, and 3c* reflect the nation's economic recovery. The initial Accumulative reform gave Kazakhstan's government an escape from potentially untenable expenses. The need to escape would have been most acute had the economy continued to stagnate or fail; with economic recovery, it is virtually certain that the escape option will not be exercised. Indeed, one can view Kazakhstan's pension reform in part as a vast effort to ensure budgetary control regardless of the future. Like many financial derivatives, it is complex, and has *ex ante* value whether or not the option is ultimately exercised.

4.7 Contingent Liabilities

Calculation of contingent liabilities is a complex matter. Prior to introduction of the demogrant, GoK was legally committed to guarantee either a Minimum Pension or a Social Allowance to retirees whose combined pension (prorated

Solidarity portion plus monthly scheduled withdrawal amount from Accumulative system funds) would be lower than the amounts cited above. These additional payments are termed contingent liabilities (CL). While no longer relevant with the introduction of the demogrant, they are worth analyzing, as any minimum pension system will have such liabilities.

Contingent liability determination requires data disaggregation and estimation of likely CL values and cohort sizes for various vulnerable groups, including

(1) Retirees from the informal sector (non-contributors) whose Accumulative pension components will equal zero. This group will be especially numerous in low formal sector employment growth scenarios;
(2) Life-long, low-income formal sector employees who do not accumulate enough, especially in pessimistic scenarios with low earnings and low real rates of return on investment;
(3) Retirees from the formal sector who contribute to Accumulative system accounts, but who start doing so at too late an age to accumulate sufficient funds. This group is actually largest in optimistic scenarios, as the formal sector expands.

Neither PENMODEL nor PROST7 has the capacity to compute contingent liabilities, as both models are based on nationwide wage and replacement rate averages. The data demands are also considerable: one needs disaggregated information on the various groups, including on the distribution of their Solidarity entitlements and individual accumulations. The third group is the most complex, since it implies that (ideally) one must have information on the combined distribution of formal sector years of service and Accumulative contributions. Such information is not readily available, though close approximations were available for use in KAZAK2. KAZAK1 made strong, simplifying assumptions and used the individual account component of PROST7 to forecast contingent liabilities, but with far less accuracy than its KAZAK2 successor.

Contingent liabilities would be of trivial importance in the short and medium terms. Because virtually all elderly Kazakhstanis will receive full or nearly full years' of service Solidarity pensions for the next decade, the issue was never a pressing one (and, in particular, will have almost no bearing on the date at which the GoK will no longer have to provide subsidies from the Republican budget). Thus, while contingent liabilities eventually would have become a noticeable if not vast budgetary issue, and matter in the latter decades of the projected period, its cost parameters with regard to GDP would have been insignificant for some time.

Final 2001 fiscal projections from KAZAK1 (Becker, Urzhumova, and Seitenova, 2001), which served as a Ministry of Finance report to the World Bank, appear in table 4.3. The financial success of the reform becomes apparent if one focuses either on total payments, including contingent liabilities as a share of GDP, or on the projected social welfare system current account balance. The current account includes revenues from social tax payments less expenses, and excluding support from the Republican budget to pay pensions and social allowances. The large deficits of the late 1990s—involving a transfer of about 3% of GDP to pensioners *after* workers' payroll contributions—quickly shrink to

1.3–1.4% in the near future. The reduction in required Republican budget subventions is projected to cut the national government budget deficit by roughly one-half. Taken together with other measures, this decreased fiscal burden in the near future effectively ensures that GoK's goal of macroeconomic stability will be realized—or, more accurately, that it would have been realized even in the absence of the oil boom and exceptional growth.

Comparison of table 4.3 and column 2 of table 4.1 reveals a considerable fiscal improvement in the KAZAK1 forecasts between 1999 and 2001, despite the inclusion of contingent liabilities. These differences reflect improved economic conditions and, hence, scenario assumptions. The immediate reasons underlying the surplus forecast to emerge by the end of the current decade lie largely in Kazakhstan's demographics. The newly retired population in the year 2000 consists mainly of women born in 1943–44 and men born in 1938–39. The former is an especially small cohort. These cohorts will begin to grow as baby-boom women start retiring, but an abnormally small pool of male war cohort retirees will offset these increased numbers. The number of new retirees should then accelerate around 2007, and the pool will continue to grow rapidly for several decades. This growth will be augmented by mortality recovery, which we assume to be especially rapid until 2030; both of these forces prevent surpluses from growing more rapidly. Positive migration rates augment tax collections starting in 2015, while labor force entry fluctuates due to highly cyclical behavior in fertility between 1980 and, according to projections, 2015.

Contingent liabilities were not projected to comprise a significant proportion of total pension expenses until toward the end of the 2030s, when they reach 9% in the *Baseline* scenario. However, the number of Solidarity payment recipients does become quite large. The number of contingent liability payment recipients was forecast to increase from 1.9% of all Accumulative system participants in 2025 (of 2.8% of female participants) to 12.0% in 2030 (17.4% of women), to 39.4% in 2040 (52.8% of women), before stabilizing a few years later. However, payments are very small, other than for those in low-income groups or with limited service.

As a practical administrative matter, it would seem that GoK had invited unnecessary administrative expenses by committing to make a large number of very small payments repeatedly, but only after significant documentation and costly calculations. The minimum pension payment system also has the extremely unattractive feature of implying an effective 100% marginal tax on accumulative savings for those with some but inadequate amounts. These considerations make the demogrant more logical, even though it implies payments to some well-off individuals.

The presentation of KAZAK2 output did not emphasize contingent liabilities, although these were included and calculated among the government's anticipated costs. The reason for this is straightforward. The economic growth and financial assumptions, combined with no formal commitment to continue to increase real values of minimum pensions and social allowances, implies plummeting replacement rates (see Chapter 10). Hence, contingent liabilities are also assuredly tiny—even smaller as a share of GDP than in the 2001 KAZAK1 forecasts.

As we have argued, even had a demogrant not been adopted, such an outcome would have been most unlikely for political reasons. Thus, while formal contingent liabilities are trivial, it seems more instructive to consider *implicit contingent liabilities*, which equal formal CLs, plus the difference in cost between the *No Further Reform* and *Proposal 3* (which fixes Minimum Pension and social allowance rates) scenarios in figure 4.1. These costs are presented as well in table 4.4, which also shows their lack of sensitivity to different asset return assumptions.

These figures suggest that in the coming decade, implicit contingent liabilities will equal about 1% of GDP in addition to those already created by the 2003 reforms. The cost rises to somewhat more than 2% during the 2020s, and ultimately to about 3% of GDP. This seems like a moderate cost to pay to maintain the social security portion of a comprehensive welfare state as Kazakhstan moves from being a lower-middle-income to a high-income country during this period.

4.8 Making Policy Strategically

This chapter has charted the GoK budgetary implications of Kazakhstan's pension reforms, starting with estimates made immediately after the commitment to introduce an Accumulative system and continuing to more recent forecasts. Kazakhstan's 2005 economy was roughly 70% larger in real terms than at the outset of the reforms, and the actuarial forecasts reflect both the policy changes that have been made in light of this economic recovery, as well as the growing sophistication of the models themselves.

By 2003–4 it was apparent that a major modification to the Accumulative reform was inevitable, since the initial reform possessed spending restraints that were politically unpopular and unnecessary with continued economic growth. Even six years into the reform, the fiscal implications for public social security spending were very different than at the outset. This should not be seen as a retreat from the initial reforms, but rather as a reflection of new policy options and public preferences that come with being at a higher level of prosperity.

The apparent fact that Kazakhstan may well have its cake and eat it too—that is, the country will end up with both a developed financial sector and an Accumulative system without giving up its welfare state—does not mean that the pension reform decisions and the process by which they were taken were flawless. Positive exogenous shocks, notably with respect to the world oil price and domestic oil finds, played an important role. So did highly competent economic management in pension reform and other spheres: the technical aspects of the reform, and parallel financial development processes, were addressed comprehensively and successfully. But there was little room for error.

Clearly, Kazakhstan's economic and financial system policymakers and political leaders displayed remarkable consistency, nerve, and coolness under pressure. Their daring and self-confidence enabled Kazakhstan to undertake a complex economic liberalization of which pension reform was but a part. On a less flattering note, willingness to curb potential incomes of a poor and dependent part of the population also was important. But economic recovery is not an easy matter, and some social payment repression seemed virtually inescapable.

Indeed, most lower-middle-income countries avoid welfare states and ignore the plight of the elderly and disabled entirely. Kazakhstan appears to have been fortunate in two respects. First, its socialist past continues to affect preferences, and it is clear that there is overwhelming public demand for maintained social payments to the elderly and disabled. Indeed, a dispassionate observer might argue that these resources might be better redistributed, at least in part, to education and public health, which appear to have suffered more severely than pensions during the transition. Yet, there is no clear public support for such a reallocation—though, in an environment of ongoing economic growth, these areas are in fact receiving belated attention.

In addition, Kazakhstan's government contains competing internal interests, and also responds to a wide range of external domestic pressure groups. Thus, policy responds to a variety of demands and, therefore, adapts fairly quickly to new possibilities. Reforms starting out as a severe measure aimed at shrinking state commitments and jump-starting a domestic financial market have now metamorphosed into a continued commitment to significant public welfare spending *plus* individual defined contribution accounts.

This process highlights the importance of a pluralistic society in which policy is formed as an equilibrium outcome of pressures from the polity and a range of interest groups. Middle-income countries lacking this balance may well experience a very different outcome. On the one hand, countries without voices for social welfare may find themselves building a system that ultimately provides old-age security only to a tiny proportion of the population—and the simulations in Chapter 10 document how small this group is likely to be. On the other hand, nations unable to curb comprehensive PAYGO social commitments may find that a new Accumulative system remains stunted.

The manner in which pension reform in Kazakhstan was introduced also points to the cost of haste and, conversely, to the gains from rapid action. The commitment was made prior to any actuarial analysis, and with very little public support. A more deliberate process likely would have resulted in a less radical and more widely accepted reform, if only because the initial actuarial simulations projected (too optimistically) that Solidarity system deficits would naturally diminish quite quickly.

In the case of Kazakhstan, these comments reflect the advantage of hindsight. Unlike countries considering reforms today, the IMWG had virtually no experience of pension reforms in transition economies upon which to build. Government focused on recovering macroeconomic stability and recreating capacity, and it took actions in a wide range of areas. With respect to pensions, it moved to restrict early retirements and improve collections, as well as undertaking the set of reforms that became the Accumulative system. That its measures were crude and lacking in deliberation reflects the period during which they were taken.

We turn now to an in-depth presentation of the reforms, starting with a discussion of the economic background and then analyzing the system's performance and the vast array of steps that comprised the reforms. A key purpose in doing this is to make the reader aware of the enormous complexity of introducing an individually funded Accumulative system in a country with few supporting institutions.

5

Kazakhstan's Economic Transformation, 1989–2007

The story of Kazakhstan's transition offers several insights into the conduct of economic policy and the factors that shape it. Macroeconomic policies usually take center stage in developed countries' economic policy discussions. In transition economies, macroeconomic stabilization is only a part of a larger package of economic reforms aimed at institutional development taken for granted in established market economies. The experience of Kazakhstan and other transition economies suggests that macroeconomic policy effectiveness depends crucially on the success of structural reforms and that neglecting microeconomic and institutional policies jeopardizes the sustainability of macroeconomic achievements. Thus, it is important to place Kazakhstan's macroeconomic patterns in the context of the sweeping restructuring that transformed a centrally planned province of the Soviet Union to an independent, market-based economy.

5.1 Collapse of the Soviet Economy

Soviet economic planners emphasized the development of the USSR's industrial base, beginning in late 1920s with the program of planned industrialization and agricultural collectivization. The ensuing five-year plans directed the lion's share of resources to the development of the investment goods sector. Manufacturing received implicit subsidies through a system of price formation, which tweaked the terms of trade against agricultural producers (Sah and Stiglitz, 1992). The resultant urban-rural inequality was maintained by a combination of political terror and administrative means.

While the Soviet Union did indeed industrialize, the resultant economy proved unsustainable, especially as further growth required increasingly flexible adaptation of technology to meet changing demands. Agricultural, mining, petrochemical, and metallurgical sectors supplied the machine-building and construction sectors with primary commodities at relatively low prices. Although the Soviet economy continued to grow, it used inputs and factors of production increasingly inefficiently. The resultant growth was capital intensive, with low rates of factor productivity growth.

As the problem of slow productivity was recognized, Soviet economists proposed a number of piecemeal solutions that ultimately failed to stimulate productivity. Raising productivity demanded painstaking work on the micro level, yet yielded few political dividends, and so was neglected in favor of grand projects associated with massive reallocation of tangible resources. As a result, only cosmetic changes were introduced, prices remained heavily distorted, workers and managers unmotivated, and productivity stagnant. However, the sheer amount of natural resources and favorable world prices for commodities allowed the economy to maintain growth, albeit at a decreasing rate, of physical output through the 1970s.

For Kazakhstan and the rest of the Soviet Union, the 1980s were a period of increasing inefficiency relative to global productivity norms. In the 1980s, continued pursuit of industrialization worsened the USSR's structural imbalances. As in other republics, Kazakhstan maintained an unsustainably high stock of capital, and was part of the production chain focused on production of investment goods, rather than consumer goods and services.

Pressure on the Soviet economy increased in the 1980s from several sources. At home, low-cost mineral deposits were nearly exhausted, so that mining and metallurgy could no longer supply cheap commodities. Inefficient agriculture further drained financial resources. Internationally, as commodities' prices declined, oil and raw material exports could no longer finance internal imbalances. In the late 1980s, facing rising consumer expectations at home and an arms race with the United States abroad, the Soviet government resorted to monetary expansion. In a market economy the gap between supply and demand for money would lead to inflation, but in an economy held back by price controls, it manifested itself in the form of shortages, proliferation of nonmarket modes of allocation, and involuntary accumulation in savings accounts—a monetary overhang. De Broeck and Kostial (1998) report that the ratio of household monetary assets to monetary income, an indirect indicator of overhang, increased from 50% in 1985 to more than 100% in 1991.

By 1990, the USSR government was too weak financially to maintain customary transfers to the 15 constituent republics and too weak politically to crack down on the regions. However, the Communist Party was not prepared to break up completely with the principles of a command economy, and the party offered a plan of economic liberalization. Not only was this mild liberalization "too little, too late," it antagonized conservative elements within the Soviet government, who staged a coup in 1991. The coup failed, but by then the credibility of the central government was compromised. Within five months, all republics proclaimed independence from the Soviet Union.

5.2 Before the Break-Up: 1989–91

At the time Kazakhstan announced independence, its economy was tightly integrated into the all-union (pan-USSR) production network, mainly as a supplier of primary commodities. Abundant in mineral resources, energy, and land, Kazakhstan's economy was dominated by mining, metallurgy, and agriculture. Machine building and other manufacturing activities were important but secondary. Most final goods were imported from the rest of the Union.

Machine building was represented by relatively independent plants, which were designed as an integral part of the all-union production distribution chain. Executives were appointed by all-union ministries, and financial support came directly from Moscow. The plants typically relied on inputs from Russia, and their output was Russia bound. Most were congregated near the Russian border, with assets complementary to production facilities in western Siberia and the Urals, but not to one another. The sector as a whole relied on unrestricted intraindustry, interrepublican trade, and relied both on massive financial injections and guaranteed orders from USSR defense ministries. Disruption of these in the 1990s proved catastrophic to this sector.

Mines and metallurgical plants depended less on Russian counterparts. Unlike producers of highly specialized intermediate goods, which depended on orders from a single buyer across the border, metallurgical plants produced standardized general-purpose products competitive on international markets. Traditional suppliers could be replaced by others at a relatively low cost. Agriculture, another exporting sector, depended on cheap fuel and direct transfers, while rural infrastructure remained underdeveloped. Technology was land intensive, reflecting Kazakhstan's abundance of land. However, land quality had deteriorated in the preceding three decades owing to unchecked soil erosion and overgrazing. All sectors experienced shortages of skilled labor and suffered from low labor productivity: in manufacturing it was approximately 20% of that in developed countries, and in agriculture barely 10%. The situation in mining was exacerbated by escalating extraction costs as easily accessible deposits neared exhaustion. Education and health care were universal and free, though health care quality was not high by international standards.

The partial autonomy granted to the constituent republics in the late 1980s had little effect on Kazakhstan's economy. Despite a superficially independent republican budget, Kazakhstan kept receiving budget transfers amounting to 10% of the GDP. At the same time, partial liberalization of prices for less important commodities left the prices for Kazakhstan's exports to other republics largely unreformed (IMF, 1993). This measure relieved the pressure on price controls, but did not resolve the deeper structural problems inherent in a system of regulated prices. Economic liberalization in the waning days of the USSR also called for privatization of nonstrategic enterprises. Initiated in 1991, it transferred to workers ownership of a negligible percentage of enterprises. Large metallurgical and mining enterprises as well as a host of medium-sized machine-building plants remained under firm control of Moscow planners. Direct international trade was virtually nonexistent, preserving the inefficiencies of the domestic industrial sector.

5.3 The Disorder of 1992–93

It was at this stage of its development that Kazakhstan approached the daunting tasks of double transition. Not only did the government have to transform itself into an independent state; in addition, to develop a market economy, it had to create new institutions and laws while phasing out the Soviet legacy. While the former task was largely completed within two years, the government's command methods were more difficult to phase out. Without the Communist Party, which imposed enterprise discipline, and with diminishing financial transfers from Moscow, administrative fiat could not sustain inefficient production. Machines and other intermediate goods were no longer in demand; domestic consumer goods could not compete with newly available imports. Economic shock affected even primary goods' producers. Correction of structural imbalances was aggravated by economic mismanagement, including piecemeal liberalization, expansionary macroeconomic policies, and unchecked credit. By mid-1993, the government began to grasp both the importance of market institutions for transforming the economy and the complexity of the required reforms.

5.3.1 Hyperinflation

In 1991, the financial system of Kazakhstan consisted of a central bank, five state banks, and 72 commercial banks, all of which had opened within the preceding two years. A financial system in name only, it lacked the essential elements of a market-based financial system, including the legislation and regulatory capacity. Though officially now a central bank, the NBK reflected its historic republican branch status and performed only a portion of the functions of the Soviet central bank, itself an institution with little decision-making power. Commercial banks did not have the capacity to evaluate commercial projects, issue financial instruments, or make financial plans. Their role was traditionally limited to channeling financial resources from the central bank to production activities according to a plan of allocation of real resources. The payment system contained only basic defenses against fraud and hardly any mechanisms for enforcing and monitoring payments. Financial regulation was lax and inconsistent; its enforcement was weak.

As Kazakhstan was a member of the ruble zone, the NBK did not conduct independent monetary policy. The National Bank received massive transfers from the Central Bank of Russia (CBR) and, in turn, injected liquidity to the economy to shore up failing enterprises and, on two occasions, to clear up interenterprise and banking arrears. The NBK's tools were limited to reserve requirements, economy-wide credit levels, and an ineffective interest rate policy (World Bank, 1993). Because the NBK had little control over the ruble zone's money supply, it was bound to follow Russia's expansionary policy.

The 1992–93 hyperinflation stemmed from several factors compounding the money-supply growth. Forced savings accumulated in the late 1980s as unintended deposits in the USSR Savings Bank (Sberbank) grew because of goods' shortages—a monetary overhang. When price controls were removed in January 1992, the overhang quickly dissipated into 200% per month inflation. Inflation accelerated again in the second half of 1993, when the CBR unexpectedly replaced Soviet rubles and imposed constraints on changing them into Russian rubles. Other republics promptly followed, dumping the old Soviet bills in Kazakhstan, which was among the last of the newly independent states to introduce a national currency. A natural byproduct of the hyperinflation and accompanying inflationary expectations was a crash in the real demand for rubles and increased demand for foreign currency, especially U.S. dollars. Thus, the ruble deposit base decreased from 96% of GDP at the end of 1991 to 20% of GDP two years later.

Hyperinflation turned real interest rates negative and made financial intermediation extremely unprofitable. Kazakhstan's government responded coherently only in mid-1993. While banks continued to receive NBK transfers, enterprises could barely obtain trade and inventory financing; long-term financing virtually disappeared. Large mining and metallurgical enterprises responded by creating their own one-client banks. While banks sprouted, financial intermediation did not develop, despite extension of government credits to the real sector, both under direct instruction or underwritten guarantees (IMF, 1996). Initially, the newly created banks, as intended, channeled financial resources from the NBK to enterprises. But soon they started lending to shareholders and other insiders based on noneconomic considerations. Estimates of the actual share of bad loans made during this period are necessarily rough as such data were not reported at the time. However, even in 1996, classified loans still amounted to a third of the banking system portfolio and accounted for more than a half of all commercial loans (Hoelscher, 1998).

Disruption in traditional modes of financing and weaknesses of the payment system contributed to the "real" (i.e., primary and secondary) sector's deteriorating viability (De Broeck and Kostial, 1998; Calvo and Coricelli, 1993). As financial resources were redirected by banks to other uses, enterprises experienced acute withdrawal from cheap credit and responded by accumulating arrears against suppliers and defaulting on bank loans. These developed into economy-wide interenterprise arrears, bringing the payment system to halt on several occasions. Dependent on a long supply chain, manufacturing enterprises were affected the most, while mining and metallurgical companies coped better.

5.3.2 Mismanaged Fiscal Contraction

The inherited Soviet scale of public services was too big to be sustained by independent Kazakhstan's limited budgetary resources. Its rational downsizing became a major challenge for fiscal policy in early 1990s and indeed continues to dominate budgetary concerns even today. Of particular importance were the comprehensive health care and education systems, which together employed some 70% of more than two million public sector workers (World Bank, 1997d). Relative numbers of teachers and doctors were comparable with those in high-income countries, and the achievements of the Soviet Union in this area were gains that the people of Kazakhstan understandably did not want to lose.

Yet, GoK had to cut expenditures because it could not mobilize sufficient resources. Taxes constituted a declining share of diminishing GDP because of deteriorating compliance and financial disintermediation. In mid-1993, Russia discontinued budget transfers, which in 1992 constituted approximately 10% of Kazakhstan's GDP. As a result, by 1993, budgetary resources declined to 50% of their 1991 level in real terms. By 1995, they fell to 25% of the 1991 level.

The government did not act decisively in response to this catastrophic situation, failing to downsize according to particular programs' relative importance and the availability of budgetary resources. This would have rationalized expenditure structure with minimal impact on the value of public services. Instead, inertia translated into maintained public employment and raises that did not match inflation, so that real wages fell sharply to below subsistence levels. As a result, the quality of education and health services declined while nominally providing the same level of service.

Despite dwindling real revenue, fiscal authorities exercised little control over expenditures at the budget-planning stage, intervening only when presented with bills. Line ministries undertook excessive expenditure obligations at the beginning of the year, while payments were sequestered by the Ministry of Finance or moved to the next fiscal year. Given hyperinflation, the resulting budget arrears constituted a default on government's obligations, contributing to plummeting living standards for fixed income recipients on government payroll. Unchecked credit to SOEs and government guaranteed loans added to rapid accumulation of public debt.

Nor was GoK prepared to address the problem of inefficient taxation in order to raise revenues. Taxation in the Soviet system performed only a superficial function, given the system of direct allocation of resources. Tax rates were not uniform; tax legislation, spread in many documents, contained preferences and loopholes; tax administration was ineffectual; and the tax system as a whole was not geared toward generating revenue with minimal distortion. In summary, government, during the early transition period, was unprepared to cut expenditures, reduce public employment, raise and rationalize taxes, or institute independence macrofinancial management. This unpreparedness did not distinguish it in the slightest from other former Soviet republics outside the Baltic states.

5.3.3 Labor Market Adjustments

Total registered (or, equivalently from our perspective, formal sector) employment began to fall in 1992, as organizational turmoil and declining aggregate demand made it difficult for enterprises to hold onto excess labor. The slide continued for five years, during which employment fell to half of its 1991 level. However, the effect of structural adjustments on employment could have been greater yet were enterprises not able to adjust by cutting the real wages via lagging nominal increases.

As aggregate employment declined, the nature of labor market adjustment varied across sectors. Many industries previously had received effective subsidies, and were unequipped to compete with imports when borders opened and relative prices began to move toward world prices. The machine-building and light industry enterprises were the first to lay off the workers (or to shut down entirely), while the share of services, mining, and metallurgy in total employment increased.

At approximately the same time, open unemployment emerged as a social phenomenon. Actual unemployment was not surveyed until 1994, when it stood at 7.5%, but the rate must have been growing because employment was declining. The officially registered unemployment rate, which is highly correlated with but understates actual unemployment, grew from 0.4% in 1992 to 0.6% in 1993 and to 1.1% in 1994, suggesting similar growth rates in actual unemployment. Yet, despite massive losses of jobs, outright unemployment remained surprisingly low, even in 1994. The muted response reflected migration of laid-off workers to Russia and Germany, declining labor force participation, and as of 1994, rising self-employment. Precipitously declining real wages took the major brunt of labor market adjustment, motivating workers to seek nontraditional alternatives in agriculture and the informal sector.

5.4 The Reforms of 1994–98

The second transition phase involved multifaceted economic liberalization reforms, sweeping changes in the private sector, market institution development, and the establishment of a stable macroeconomic environment. Enterprises had little incentives to make painful adjustments during the era of unchecked credit, but tight monetary and fiscal policies plus enforcement of payment discipline finally compelled firms to face economic reality. GDP bottomed out in 1995, reaching less than 60% of its pretransition peak value. However, real wages began to recover in the second half of 1994, helped by sharp disinflation and rationalization of enterprise incentives, and have continued growing since then, interrupted only during the devaluation in 1999. Meanwhile, real average incomes continued to fall due to continued declines in employment and reduced government transfers. Public employment fell as GoK struggled to mobilize revenues and balance its budget.

5.4.1 Disinflation

While Kazakhstan tried to preserve the ruble zone, Russia, the leading member, had little interest in maintaining it, given its members' fiscal irresponsibility and the large transfers directed to the central banks of zone members, especially the NBK. Rather than bearing the cost of other former Soviet republics' profligacy, in mid-1993 Russia single-handedly abandoned the ruble zone by replacing old USSR notes with new Russian Federation ones and halting transfers to other republics' central banks. This forced other republics to create national currencies of their own, and in November 1993, the NBK introduced tenge and assumed full responsibility for conducting monetary policy.

However, monetary expansions continued. Less than three months after tenge's introduction, the NBK oversaw a massive injection of liquidity into the banking sector to clear up interenterprise arrears. Another bout of hyperinflation, now of newly minted tenge, soon followed. The government began to realize that without resolving the underlying problems causing interenterprise arrears, the temptation to use monetary policy to clear them was irresistible.

In order to prevent the accumulation of further arrears, GoK initiated enterprise restructuring and limited privatization, improving enterprises' budget and payment discipline. Bank regulation reforms, including higher capital requirements, regular evaluation of banks' portfolios, and liquidation and restructuring of insolvent banks also were introduced. Concurrently, NBK began developing legal frameworks for prudential regulation and its own regulatory capacity. GoK granted the NBK operational independence in 1993, with independence from the parliament following in

1995. This allowed the monetary authorities to better resist inflationary pressures and made its disinflation stance more credible. As a result, tight monetary policy reduced inflation from more than 1,000% in 1994 to 60% in 1995 and 11% in 1997.

Simultaneously, the NBK's supervision units began restructuring the financial sector. Bad loans were transferred from the banks' balance sheets to state restructuring institutions, created in 1994 with a mandate to collect debts and rehabilitate indebted enterprises or liquidate residual assets. Many banks, including the largest, were insolvent as a result of unsound banking practices and poor corporate governance; by rough estimates, the share of nonperforming loans reached 50–55% (Tang et al., 2006). Subsequently, GoK had to provide financial support to nonperforming loans that carried government guarantees.

Financial disintermediation continued, albeit at a slower pace and for different reasons. Unlike the "wild banking" era of 1992–93 where the main culprit was hyperinflation, disintermediation of 1994–96 stemmed mainly from monetary tightening. Much of the disintermediation was definitional, as bad loans disbursed before 1994 were restructured and reclassified. The proportion of nonperforming loans declined from 41% in 1995 to 27% in 1998. Tighter financial regulation did not affect depositors significantly. Few people held their savings in banks (a series of bank-related scandals added to the general distrust fostered by an environment of high inflation, low real returns, and extraordinarily user-unfriendly banking practices; declining incomes further deterred all but the most intrepid savers), and most who did kept them in Halyk (former Narodny) Bank, a state savings bank with implicit guarantees.

The NBK discontinued massive transfers to commercial banks, limiting its role to short-term, lender-of-last-resort credit. Most commercial banks were unable and unwilling to raise costly funds from the population. As balance sheets were stripped bare of nonperforming loans, the banks had to curtail loan activity and learn to allocate limited funds based on market considerations.

Over the next few years, a further series of legal acts gave the NBK the authority to develop and implement increasingly strict supervision policies. By 1998, a functional market-oriented banking system supervised by a credible authority had emerged. By then the NBK's experience included liquidation and restructuring of more than a hundred banks (mostly small and short lived, but also at least two large ones). More stringent financial norms had seen the number of banks shrink from 191 in 1994 to 82 in 1997. With disinflation came the gradual remonetization of the economy and declining nominal interest rates.

5.4.2 *Fiscal Reforms*

Fiscal policy in the mid-1990s was shaped by concerns about unchecked government expenditures and attempts to build an accountable and transparent budgetary system. The system suffered from inadequate tax legislation, poor tax administration, and an underdeveloped budgetary system at all government levels. While the aggregate expenditures were soon brought under control, budgetary and taxation reforms proceeded at a slower pace, reflecting institutional challenges.

A new tax code in 1995 reduced the number of taxes, removed tax exemptions, harmonized tax rates, and brought the law in line with modern practices. However, its administration required a large number of qualified tax officers, relied on sophisticated tax administration methods, and presumed firms' use of international accounting standards. None of these prerequisites was in place at the time. However, tax administration was soon strengthened by legislative acts, organizational measures and training programs. Accounting reform sought to replace Soviet bookkeeping with modern accounting practices. Although these reforms could not address the most immediate concerns, they established a foundation for sustained economic growth.

While revenue rose only slowly, the principle economics bodies (MinFin and NBK) were determined to reduce deficits and inflation. However, MinFin lacked control over line ministries' budgetary commitments. The only control it could exercise over fund allocation was at the appropriations stage, when the line ministries already had obligated their spending. When funding was not appropriated, GoK began defaulting on its obligations to civil servants and social security recipients. The line ministries in effect accepted these wage cuts and delays in obligated transfers in lieu of reductions in civil servants or transfers, even though public service quality inevitably deteriorated. Direct attempts at reducing the size of government were not unsuccessful, resulting only in the reduction or rearrangement of government agencies (World Bank, 1997d). Eliminated units and their staff often reappeared under new guises.

This rapid disinflation and fiscal tightening had an inevitably contractionary effect on the nascent private sector. Yet, the hyperinflation alternative was disastrous as well, and had no positive long-term benefits. Price stability slowed and eventually reversed financial disintermediation. However, macroeconomic policy alone could not address the structural problems of the real sector—manufacturing, extractive industries, agriculture, construction, and transportation. As we see in subsequent chapters, these structural constraints created problems for the Accumulative pension system to overcome.

5.4.3 *Dissolution of the Pension Fund*

Among the budgetary reforms, emergence of the Pension Fund (PF) as independent and separate from the budget was a justifiable step toward greater transparency and accountability, as PF transfers differed substantially from public services. However, the assignment of PF revenues to regional oblast governments made its operation unsustainable. As pension liabilities grew, PF revenues did not keep pace, and by 1998 deficits were projected, even though Kazakhstan was a demographically young country. Low wages were a key reason but, more importantly, the PF did not present a credible threat to noncomplying employers. Appeals to the power of local authorities had little effect. Instead of reforming the revenue part of the PF, the government dissolved it into the national budget at the end of 1997 and assigned enforcement of social security tax to national tax administration authorities.

5.4.4 *Privatization and Restructuring*

Enterprise reform started with the restructuring of interenterprise arrears and transfer of their nonperforming loans (some 11% of GDP) from banks to restructuring institutions. Few in number and socially important as the only employer in town, large mining and metallurgical enterprises were downsized and otherwise rehabilitated on a case-by-case basis. By 1997, more than half of 45 large enterprises were privatized, and six were liquidated. The job of restructuring the nonperforming loans of smaller enterprises was left in the hands of commercial banks (Hoelscher, 1998). A cumbersome and politicized enterprise privatization program was put in place for large, restructured enterprises. Small-and medium-scale enterprises were mass privatized through auctions. In theory, the citizenry could participate by using privatization vouchers, but in practice firms ended up in the hands of the managers through insider deals. Despite numerous irregularities, the program succeeded in transferring ownership rights to the private sector and rationalizing production incentives.

Debt restructuring in agriculture was less successful and in many cases amounted to debt forgiveness. Farms were not restructured, partly because staff shortages in the agricultural restructuring institution, which proved incapable of handling the number of insolvent farms, but mainly because of the poor condition of rural enterprises and the risk of rural collapse. In 1992–95, agriculture's terms of trade worsened dramatically following piecemeal price liberalization: agricultural output prices were controlled, while agricultural input prices were liberalized. Contraction of agricultural output and rural impoverishment followed promptly; conditions were further worsened with the virtual cessation of rural public services and infrastructure maintenance. GoK did provide subsidized credit, restricted fuel exports during sowing and harvest seasons, practiced state procurement of agricultural products, and influenced organizational structure by favoring large agricultural partnerships. However, the net effect was strongly negative, and, with agricultural producer viability depending on access to administrative resources, productivity continued to deteriorate. Bad agricultural debts eventually were written off in 1998, creating a heavy fiscal burden (around 6% of GDP) and placing more efficient farms at a financial disadvantage.

5.4.5 *Labor Market*

As discussed, the early independence period was one in which the declining labor demand that accompanied economic contraction resulted mainly in falling real wages. However, from 1994, when monetary policy tightened and enterprise restructuring began in earnest, real wages stopped declining and a period of labor shedding commenced. Unemployment rose from 7.5% in 1994 to 13.0% in 1996. Moreover, Verme (2001) argues that self-employment in the mid-1990s largely represented hidden unemployment, chosen as a subsistence activity in the absence of proper employment. During expansionary 1992–93, self-employment remained low at 7%. However, beginning in 1994, the self-employment rate grew at an annual rate of 7% for the next five years, peaking at 45% of the labor force in 1999. Concurrently, while in 1994 average wages declined by 32% in real terms, they began growing in 1995, gaining on average almost 3.5% per year until 1998.

Overall, GoK's record on liberalization of the labor market remained mixed. In 1995, the government implemented counterproductive wage controls in an attempt to bring inflation down. Rather than curbing inflation, the wage controls induced private sector evasion and further depressed the morale of public sector employees, which in real terms declined even faster than in SOEs and the private sector.

5.5 The Currency Crisis of 1999

By 1998, Kazakhstan had made significant progress in transforming into a market-based economy. Prudent fiscal and monetary policies stabilized macroeconomic environment. Soviet "entrepreneurship" laws were largely replaced by modern business legislation. Privatization of the large mining and metallurgical enterprises, with many sales to foreign investors, reduced the scope for government intervention and created investment incentives. Conventional banking emerged after substantial regulatory overhaul, while financial supervision units gained capacity and experience. The economy was in its third year of a slow and uneven but real recovery, responding to the changes in the business environment and massive foreign investments in petrochemicals. Seven years after independence, the economy's composition had changed markedly, with only the most resilient activities surviving, such as mining and metallurgy, construction, and services. This made the economy more specialized and more vulnerable to external shocks, all of which converged in 1998.

Severe drought halved grain production; external terms of trade worsened as world oil and copper prices fell to a historically low levels in real terms. Then in August, Russia, the principal trade partner and main competitor to Kazakhstan on the European metal markets, defaulted on sovereign debt and devalued the ruble by 80%. As a result, tenge appreciated against the ruble by more than 60% in real terms, making Kazakhstan's exports, which were already losing the battle for Russian markets, even less competitive. These shocks underlined serious fiscal vulnerabilities of Kazakhstan. Enterprises accumulated tax arrears reaching 6.8% of GDP as a way of coping with adverse shocks while weak tax administration was unable to collect them. Capital flight and tax evasion in the form of transfer pricing to off-shore companies further reduced tax revenues. The high share of nondiscretionary spending by local budgets, mostly wages of public servants and solidarity pensions, offered little flexibility in responding to revenue shortfalls. Not allowed to borrow, local governments resorted to sequestrations and wage arrears, amounting to 3.6% of GDP (IMF, 2000).

The spread on Kazakh Eurobonds increased from 0.5% to 2.5%, reflecting the reassessment of country's fiscal vulnerability in the more adverse environment. Real appreciation of tenge raised the pressure on the NBK to devalue as well. In the face of these pressures, government tightened its fiscal policy, notwithstanding resistance from parliament, thus showing serious commitment to fiscal rectitude and macro stability for perhaps the first time. Managing monetary and exchange rate policy was not as simple. A key goal was preventing panic in the domestic market, at least until after the presidential elections in February 1999. The NBK was to maintain a crawling peg against the U.S. dollar, albeit with a faster rate of tenge depreciation than before. The National Bank used unsterilized interventions to keep the supply of tenge and tenge-denominated assets in line with the steadily shrinking demand. As devaluation fears set in, interest rates on tenge-denominated asset were increased. These policies were maintained until April 1999, when export prices began to recover. By then, short-term interest rates on tenge-denominated assets had increased from 17% to 26%, and the stock of broad money had declined by 20% in real terms. The monetary authorities had passed a key test and in so doing gained valuable credibility, but the cost in terms of real economic activity was high.

In April 1999, foreign exchange reserves fell dangerously near a level that would invite a run on tenge. In April 1999, the NBK abandoned its crawling peg and announced that it would not "substantially intervene" in a free float. Tenge immediately fell from 88T/US$ to 115T/US$. Indeed, demand for tenge-denominated assets had slipped gradually since August 1998, suggesting that the market anticipated devaluation but was uncertain of the date. Thus, between June 1998 and April 1999, the ruble/tenge real exchange rate (REER) appreciated by 25% and US$/tenge REER depreciated by almost 30%.

The crisis was a watershed event for Kazakhstan, demonstrating the (relative) resilience of its restructured economy, especially its financial sector, and the maturity and independence of its monetary authority. It also benefited from an unexpected but positive consequence of the 1998 pension reform—pension funds were used by the Treasury as an additional source of deficit financing. The crisis further disassociated Kazakhstan from Russia in the eyes of international investors. While at the beginning of 1998, Russian sovereign ratings exceeded those of Kazakhstan, after 1999 Kazakhstan enjoyed higher sovereign ratings, allowing top commercial banks of Kazakhstan to compete for Russian clients.

In 1999, Kazakhstan emerged as a country with fiscally prudent government and a resilient economy. Several factors contributed to its ability to weather the effects of the Russian crisis. Most critically, oil export volumes, then one-quarter of all exports, were dollar denominated and did not decrease following tenge's real appreciation. Second, the newly created pension funds bought and held on to Kazakhstan's sovereign Eurobonds when international investors' demand sagged, thus demonstrating a new source of savings available for deficit financing. Budget arrears, another hidden source of budget financing, were rolled over into 1999, instead of being reduced as the government pledged a year before. Most importantly, the fiscal authorities scaled down the expenditures as early as the summer of 1998, as signs of falling tax revenues appeared.

5.5.1 *Budget Policy*

Until 1999, tax assignment between local and national governments remained opaque, ad hoc and, therefore, negotiable. The budgetary system motivated local authorities to "hide locally mobilized revenues in extra-budgetary funds, or to reduce their efforts to mobilize revenues locally" (McLure et al., 1999). Budgetary relations between oblasts and the national government remained subservient to the overriding concern of the latter to maintain administrative control over the regions. The state's strong unitary structure rendered fiscal decentralization reforms ineffectual.

In 1999, a new budget law made the budgetary system more transparent and accountable. The assignment of revenues and expenditures between national and subnational government was clearly delineated. Extrabudgetary funds, which included the Social Insurance Fund, the Medical Insurance Fund, and the Employment Fund, previously had been financed by earmarked payroll taxes. These taxes were not included in the Tax Code and the tax administration was not responsible for their collection. With the adoption of a new budget law, these extrabudgetary funds were dissolved and the Social Insurance Fund was replaced with a general budget payroll tax.

5.6 The Oil Boom: 2000–06

Even before 2000, the economy had returned to positive growth, boosted by terms-of-trade improvements and tenge devaluation. Annual real GDP growth during the period 2000–2006 averaged 10%, doubling the economy during the period. By the end of 2003, Kazakhstan had reached its Soviet-era level of GDP, and has since far surpassed that. As population has fallen due to substantial emigration (though undocumented immigration from Central Asia in more recent years has reversed this trend), per capita income today is greater still. However, the oil boom years have been associated with a large increase in income inequality, and the benefits have been felt much more strongly at the top than at the bottom of the income distribution.

Although hydrocarbons served as the driving force, their GDP share, even including related services, was relatively small, reaching only 16% in 2004 (IMF, 2005) despite a decade of rapid growth. Nevertheless, their indirect effects through income growth and via financial and factor markets linkages were profound. Hydrocarbons accounted for the lion's share of FDI, export revenue growth, and borrowing from abroad (against future oil revenues). With these indirect effects, sectoral composition shifted toward construction and services and away from agriculture and manufacturing, betraying classic Dutch disease symptoms. Oil wealth indirectly influenced government policies and, by changing them, affected the rest of the economy. The interplay of these factors determined the path of economic development in the 2000s.

5.6.1 The Dutch Disease

As oil revenues and foreign investments raised incomes, Dutch disease effects manifested themselves, with an appreciating REER depressing nonminerals exports and import competitors. The real sector could not keep up with the pace of growth in aggregate demand. Demand for tradable goods was satisfied by imports, while nontradable construction and service sectors raised their prices, unable to meet demand. Demand for labor increased faster than productivity, raising real wages but also reducing the competitiveness of domestic tradable nonoil industries. Concerns over deindustrialization and vulnerability to external shocks began to dominate macroeconomic policy debates.

The relatively small share of labor in hydrocarbon extraction, which was geographically removed from the main industrial and agricultural sites, meant that the sector hardly competed on the labor market with other sectors. At the same time, better access to international capital markets benefited all nonoil producers. Despite competition for skilled labor, nonoil sectors grew at least as fast as the nonoil exporting economies of the Commonwealth of Independent States (CIS) and the similarly defined nonoil sector of the Russian Federation. The difference in growth rate was due to faster accumulation of labor and capital in Kazakhstan than in the non-oil-exporting countries, while total factor productivity grew at roughly the same rate as in non-oil exporting countries, about 4% per year (IMF, 2005). Yet, the sectors that benefited from oil wealth most of all were construction and services, which did not have to compete with imports on the product market while benefiting from income and credit growth.

As Dutch disease models would predict, relatively slow growth has occurred in agriculture and manufacturing of tradable goods. Both sectors face fierce import competition. Agriculture has suffered as well from chronic underinvestment in rural infrastructure and an antiagricultural bias in economic development policy. Thus, Kazakhstan's agriculture employs vast numbers of low-skilled workers while its machinery is outdated and decrepit. Recent rural public programs have improved access to water, medical, and educational facilities, but the difference between rural and urban public services remains significant.

The land reform of 2005 introduced private land ownership and created a land market. In theory, land should have been allocated to the most efficient users, but privatization sparked little interest and proceeded more slowly than expected. The large majority of farmers were severely credit constrained, and so continued leasing their land from the government. Most importantly, privatization and restructuring procedures favored large agricultural enterprises over more efficient small and medium farms, partly offsetting the positive impact of land reform on agricultural productivity. However, an unambiguous outcome of the land reform has been to accelerate rural-urban migration.

Unlike agriculture, tradable goods manufacturing is relatively skill intensive, but had great difficulty competing with the oil and nontradable goods sectors for skilled labor. Egert and Leonard (2007) argue that nonpetroleum manufacturing has not been adversely affected by rising oil prices, largely rejecting the deindustrialization effect of oil wealth. However, they do not consider wage cost effects due to rising labor demand. Ter-Martirosyan (IMF, 2005) finds that manufacturing labor productivity grew more rapidly from 2000–2004 than in any other sector while wages grew more slowly. These patterns reflect competitive pressures and downsizing, and the manufacturing share in GDP has continued to decline throughout the current decade.

While labor demand has grown strongly since 2000, the vast contraction of both wages and employment in the 1990s has meant slack conditions, especially for unskilled labor. As conditions improved, many previously unemployed and self-employed entered formal employment, while the overall labor force participation rate (LFPR) increased, easing wage pressures. From 2000 to 2006, unemployment declined from 12.8 to 7.8%, LFPR rose from 66 to 70%, and self-employment declined from 43.5 to 34.8% of the labor force. Under such conditions, a naïve model would predict that wages would lag productivity; however this was not the case. Rather, demand for skills of the sort useful in a market economy (accounting, marketing, foreign languages) have soared, pushing up wages very rapidly in certain skilled submarkets, while unskilled wages remain low. Thus, a major feature of the current boom is rapidly rising income inequality.

5.6.2 *Fiscal and Budget Policy*

Rapid growth of oil-related revenues naturally affected fiscal policy. Budget deficits and declining revenues in the 1990s pressured GoK to strengthen tax administration and rationalize public expenditures, albeit with limited success. In the current decade these considerations have been superseded by concerns about longer-term management of oil revenues and fears of deindustrialization with the arrival of budget surpluses. Oil revenues eliminated the need for borrowing, and public debt declined, but this fortuitous experience resulted in unanticipated (if second-order) problems. The government bond market contracted sharply in terms of liquidity, variety, and volume of trade, and initially left the financial market without instruments around which the expectations could coalesce.

Not surprisingly, the efficiency of public expenditures suffered as public programs expanded. Increased efficiency in the provision of public services also promised to rein in government spending and aggregate demand growth. The rising inefficiency of public programs in 1990s stemmed largely from unwillingness to downsize, so that real wages rather than payroll numbers fell. GoK has since tried to reverse this process, but shortages of qualified educators, scientists and doctors, most of whom have changed occupations, retired, or emigrated, made the expansion of these sectors much more difficult than the contraction. With government services mismanaged and underfunded for a decade, it has proved difficult to effectively increase public services in response to improved funding.

In effect, the fiscal expansion, while understandable after the long night of decline and transition, ended up being strongly procyclical, further contributing to overheating of the economy, and contributing to inflation and real appreciation of tenge. Budgetary dependence on oil revenues increased vulnerability to external shocks, while in the very long run possible exhaustion of oil reserves may make the nonoil deficit unsustainable. In fact, Kazakhstani policymakers were aware of these issues and worked to devise fiscal policy rules targeted toward long-term objectives, and that would impose public spending discipline. In so doing, government took steps that would lessen Dutch disease effects.

Both the high volatility of oil prices and the possibly unsustainable nature of oil revenues called for a fiscal buffer between the revenue and the expenditure parts of the budget. Issuance of debt is possible but hardly an ideal buffer: debt financing becomes most difficult precisely when it is most needed, at the times of external shocks and revenue shortfalls. Large debt issuance actually may magnify adverse external shocks by requiring a country to make payments denominated in foreign currency when depreciation raises the cost of servicing sovereign debt. Furthermore, to be truly effective, government must be able to issue substantial quantities of debt. While Kazakhstan did obtain investment-grade bond ratings around 2002, it cannot issue nearly infinite amounts of debt at a fixed interest rate, in part because of the weaker fiscal positions and less responsible macro management of many other transition countries (with which Kazakhstan is somewhat unfairly associated). Therefore, GoK opted for a different fiscal buffer—an oil fund.

The National Fund of the Republic of Kazakhstan (NFRK) was created in 2001 with the express purpose of smoothing windfall budget revenues and saving oil revenues for future generations. These two tasks differed in the types of shocks they were designed to absorb, in terms of frequency, and in required fund size. On the one hand, unpredictable oil price fluctuations are a high frequency event, demanding flexibility and discretion in the use of the fund's resources. In contrast, oil reserve exhaustion is a one-time, predictable event, leading to the conservative goal of saving windfall revenues for future generations. The dual purpose of the fund was formalized in two revenue components: a "stabilization" part related to the excess of oil price over a US$19 threshold, and the "savings" part independent of oil price. NFRK has invested in a broad international index, excluding oil and oil-related companies. NBK and National Oil Fund reserves grew from barely US$2 billion at the end of 1999 to US$33.2 billion seven years later.

Establishment of the NFRK made the use of oil revenues more transparent and predictable. Being in effect a fiscal policy rule, it stimulated debates over the conduct of fiscal policy and compelled the fiscal authorities to make long-term fiscal projections. However, the rules were not explicitly integrated into fiscal policy and were rigidly biased toward meeting a savings objective that had neither been publicly debated nor even rationalized. Nor were the fund's revenue sources fully transparent (Bacon and Tordo, 2006). New NFRK rules adopted in 2006 represented an improvement in terms of better transparency and accountability, increased scope for parliament, and better integration with fiscal policy. However, the long-term savings goals remained arbitrary, which perhaps is not surprising, given the magnitude of oil price rises and GDP growth in recent years.

The new rules specified a list of state companies, mostly hydrocarbon producers, whose taxes formed the NFRK's noninterest revenues. Transfers to the Republican budget were determined as a sum of two components. One was to be set by parliament for several years, while the second was set in proportion to returns on fund assets in tenge terms. Because fund assets were invested in an index devoid of oil related companies, the return was expected to correlate negatively with oil prices. Finally, transfers from the NFRK were earmarked for "development purposes," an inherently discretionary component of the expenditures, rather than for meeting recurrent expenses.

During its first phase of the oil boom period, the GoK administration successfully resisted parliamentary pressure to increase spending. The NFRK contributed to a relatively restrained fiscal policy, slowing nominal and real appreciation of tenge, and dampening the effects of the Dutch disease. It remains to be seen whether this restraint can continue, especially in the face either of large negative shocks or of continued rapid growth.

5.6.3 Monetary policy

Following their abandonment of the crawling peg, Kazakhstan's monetary authorities appeared to target a trade-weighted real exchange rate in early 2000s, but in 2003 began to move toward gradual adoption of inflation targeting. The shift to inflation targeting was timely. An oil exporter itself, Russia experienced similar terms-of-trade shocks, making it possible for Kazakhstan's monetary authorities to target a REER dominated by Russia's ruble. But pegging to the ruble became less attractive given the declining share of Russian goods in Kazakhstan's international trade, and the authorities could no longer contain further real appreciation of tenge by monetary policy alone.

Foreign currency inflows increased the upward pressure on the REER and raised the relative costs of domestic production. The natural response of tradable-goods manufacturing and agricultural producers was to push for a weaker tenge. While it is unclear whether the NBK consciously acceded to their demands, it did continue to intervene in order to "smooth out fluctuations of the exchange rate." As a result, NBK foreign currency reserves increased from $2 billion in 2000 to $18 billion in 2006. Foreign exchange intervention was defended on the grounds that financial markets were unable to cover currency risks. In reality, NBK's interventions rendered provision of such financial services untenable, while exchange rate smoothing became increasingly difficult even for the NBK once foreign currency began to enter the country in the form of large chunky loans by commercial banks—more than $4 billion in the fourth quarter of 2005 alone.

Unwillingness to let tenge appreciate also stemmed from the NBK's prospective portfolio losses on holdings of foreign currency reserves and issues of tenge-denominated NBK notes, the main foreign exchange market instrument, given the dearth of other government paper. Appreciation would lower the value of foreign exchange reserves in tenge terms, while the rise of tenge-denominated debt removed the compensating benefit that would have occurred from dollar-denominated debt. By accumulating dollars and borrowing in tenge, the NBK was effectively shorting the national currency, so that appreciation meant inevitable losses.

These attempts to manage the REER appreciation compromised inflation targeting, the National Bank's main stated objective. CPI inflation consistently hovered just above the target, at 6–8%, while GDP deflator ranged from 15 to 20% during 2003–6. Yet, monetary policy did not tighten interest rates on government paper, which were declining, with the real interest rates being consistently negative during the last half decade.

Only in late 2006 did the NBK begin to tighten monetary policy. Its actions included raising the policy interest rate by 25 basis points, mopping up excess liquidity by issuing more NBK notes (which, given budgetary surpluses, had begun to replace Treasury bills), and allowing tenge to appreciate against the dollar from 153 in 2003 to 120 at the end of 2006. At the same time, financial regulators began to step up efforts to curb foreign capital inflows, with the approval of international agencies.

Ultimately, the NBK has multiple targets (exchange rate stability, domestic price stability, rapid real GDP growth) and fewer independent instruments. The trade-off it faces between exchange rate appreciation and inflation may be affected by financial regulators and fiscal authorities, who have additional instruments that will affect the real exchange rate in the medium term. Without further fiscal policy tightening, the NBK seems unlikely to shoulder the political costs of achieving low inflation.

5.6.4 The Financial Sector

The combined domestic assets of Kazakhstan's financial sector reached 65% of GDP in 2006. Banks, which dominate Kazakhstan's financial markets, were the main beneficiary of the oil boom, and were well positioned for rapid expansion by earlier restructuring and continued regulatory vigilance, which was enhanced with the Accumulative pension system reform. Financial deepening accelerated after the devaluation of 1999. Banking credit to the economy grew at an average rate of 45% per year, increasing from 7% of GDP in 1999 to 48% of GDP in 2006, an almost incredible rise, given the rapid increase in the denominator. Introduction of a deposit insurance program helped the banks to mobilize individual savings, which grew from a negligible level to exceed 30% of GDP by 2006. However, the main source of funds for banking expansion was foreign borrowing, which became increasingly attractive when banks' ratings came to reflect improvements in sovereign ratings. As noted above, banking has transformed since the mid-1990s. The number of banks shrank from 71 in 1998 to 34 in 2006 as consolidation continued. However, competition has increased despite consolidation. Smaller banks have expanded into new segments aggressively, squeezing margins, most likely at the cost of a worsening loan portfolio.

For the largest banks, syndicated loans and securitized bonds placed in European markets became the main source of rapid expansion in the early 2000s. External nongovernment debt reached US$28 billion, most of it acquired by banks. The relatively low cost of funds gave these banks the edge over smaller domestic banks and allowed them to expand into other CIS countries' financial markets. However, this international expansion indicated not only the favorable rating of Kazakhstan's banks (and hence low borrowing costs), but also lack of investment opportunities within Kazakhstan. Meanwhile, smaller banks competed for domestic deposits of small and medium businesses as well as household deposits; foreign banks, whose relative share has declined in recent years, kept their hold on profitable corporate clients. As low capitalization began to constrain further expansion, the leading banks began to acquire equity financing among European investors.

Rapid expansion of credit reduced the quality of the overall credit portfolio, even given the economic boom that should have resulted in substantial improvements.

The share of nonperforming loans increased to 2% (NBK-AFS, 2006). The sectoral composition of loans also reflected the changes characteristic of an economy experiencing real exchange rate appreciation, as well as the transition to a more consumer-oriented society with a burgeoning "middle class" (in reality, moderately wealthy professionals and businessmen near but not quite at the top of the income distribution) in major cities. The share of consumer credit, which did not exist in 2000, increased to 17% of total credit portfolio and began to attract even the most conservative banks, despite the risks involved. In 2005 credit to households for the first time exceeded their total deposits by households, causing further concern among regulators. Rapid financial deepening in part reflected the boom in the real estate (urban property prices quadrupled between 2000 and 2006)—and in part contributed to it, with the share of property-related loans increasing from a negligible amount to 34% (NBK, 2006). Increased exposure in the real estate and consumer credit made the banking system increasingly vulnerable to corrections in the real estate market and other extrinsic shocks.

Financial regulators responded to concerns over growing systemic risks in banking by tightening loss provisioning and raising reserve and capital adequacy requirements. Limits on external debt were imposed in response to growth of chunky external liabilities. Risk-weighted norms were introduced to internalize the systemic risks associated with foreign borrowing, portfolio currency mismatch, and property backed loans.

Beyond banking, pension funds were the only other relatively large financial institutions in Kazakhstan. Like banks, pension funds have grown rapidly since 1998, with total assets amounting to US$7.2 billion by the end of 2006 (figure 5.1). Unlike banks, their growth was largely a result of external factors, beyond the reach of pension fund managers. Individual mandatory contributions withheld at the source and equal to 10% of the wage bill were the dominant source of increased assets. As is inevitable in a nascent defined contribution system, investment income and account withdrawals remained insignificant. Indeed, during 2001–6, annual contributions equaled approximately 20% of base assets.

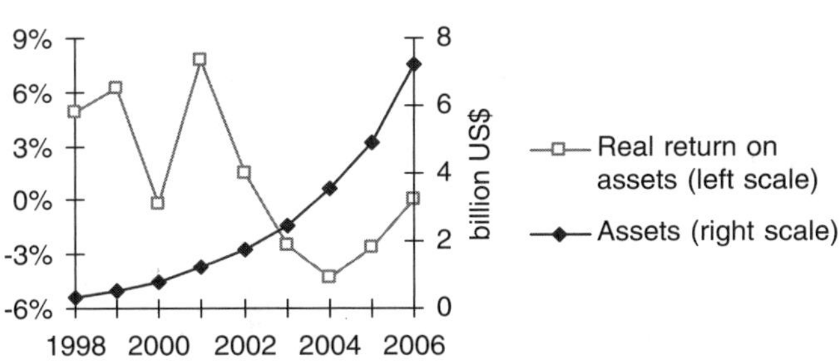

Figure 5.1 Performance of pension funds

Source: NBK, authors' computation

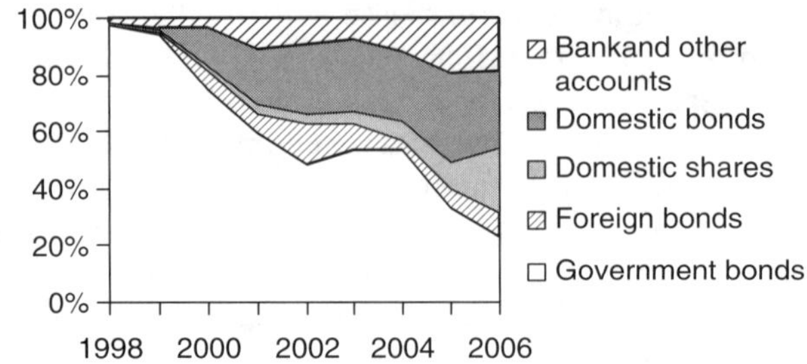

Figure 5.2 Composition of pension fund assets
Source: NBK

The huge contributions/pension asset ratio in part reflected the large gap between wage growth and the rate of return on pension funds' assets. In recent years, the pension funds have barely preserved the real value of pension savings while real wages grew at more than 10% per year on average.

However, the pension funds do not bear all of the blame for their poor performance. Pension fund investment guidelines cap their holdings of shares, requiring them to hold large numbers of low-yield government securities (and restricting competition among funds). On the other hand, international diversification, while initially restricted to 10% of assets, has steadily increased and is not a constraining factor. In general, fund guidelines were gradually relaxed as GoK found it did not need pension fund assets to finance budget deficits. Thus, the changes in the composition of pension assets in part reflect changes in investment caps (figure 5.2). Returns recovered somewhat in 2006, when the pension funds were given an opportunity to purchase more shares. However, slow development of the stock market also contributed to the low proportion of shares in pension fund portfolios. Losses in tenge terms also reflect the failure of most pension funds to anticipate the tenge's appreciation, or to hedge dollar-denominated assets. Other regulatory issues in the pension industry are described in Chapter 9.

5.6.5 *Industrial and Agricultural Policy*

Liberalization reforms decelerated in 2000s as the external and budgetary pressures on the government subsided. GoK has become increasingly assertive in its conduct of industrial policy and other interventions. Several state institutions were created to channel subsidized financial resources to industrial development projects. These policies, enabled by increased availability of fiscal resources, were justified by the need for further economic diversification and as a way to reduce vulnerability to external shocks. These policies did not find unequivocal support within the government or among the foreign investors and multilateral institutions. Industrial policies initiatives risk creating bloated, inefficient industries and suppressing more viable alternatives, and thereby ultimately increasing vulnerability to external shocks. However, industrial and import substitution policies are difficult to resist during a period of financial windfalls, though they were held in check somewhat by the obligations undertaken in preparation for WTO accession.

5.7 Conclusion

Throughout its 16-year independence, Kazakhstan's economy and macroeconomic policies have continually evolved in response to external shocks and liberalizing reforms—in effect, to internal shocks. Weaned off central planning and massive investments from Moscow, the economy collapsed in an environment of organizational turmoil and macroeconomic mismanagement. Following failed attempts to govern the economy by administrative fiat, GoK changed the course, committing itself to the development of modern institutions of market economic policy management and concurrently began irreversible privatization. The macroeconomic stabilization and structural reforms of 1995–99 paved the way for the rapid economic growth experienced since. While market-oriented government policies and supporting public institutions were in their infancy, the external shock of 1998 brought the economy to the brink of financial crisis. Ultimately, astute handling of the crisis by government economic policymakers turned the situation on its head, demonstrating competent management and boosting foreign investors' confidence. Since 1998, terms of trade have been steadily improving, contributing to a lasting economic boom and continuing inflow of foreign capital. Living standards have significantly improved in consequence, though improved terms of trade have reduced the competitiveness of domestic producers. As concerns over the Dutch disease began to dominate macroeconomic policy debates, calls to use oil wealth to finance industrialization policies have became increasingly insistent while the pace of economic liberalization has slowed down.

This brief history argues that successful macroeconomic stabilization was conditional on the development of modern market institutions governing both public and private sectors. Macroeconomic stabilization in 1994–96 successfully reversed the process of financial disintermediation and reduced the deficit, but also exposed the economy's structural flaws. Monetary and credit tightening in the early 1990s came under criticism when massive arrears, both among enterprises and to banks, arose because of the defunct payment system and soft budget constraints. Resulting liquidity injections to clear the arrears led to persistent inflation. Fiscal contraction reduced the budget deficit, but traditional budgeting practices led to pension and wage arrears. These problems were addressed by institutional reforms, including privatization and enterprise restructuring, tightening of banking regulation, development of a financial payments system, adoption of bankruptcy legislation, acceptance of modern accounting conventions, tax policy reform, and many other innovations. These reforms required concerted effort on the part of the government, but the payoff was worthwhile, as only after essential elements of market environment were securely in place did the economy stabilize and then achieve sustainable, rapid growth.

Successful execution of these reforms required building commitment and achieving consensus among major actors. In Kazakhstan, this was realized quickly in comparison with other transition nations. In part, policymakers recognized the bankruptcy of earlier governing paradigms and were willing to shift some of the administratively burdensome responsibilities to the private sector. When this was complemented by President Nazarbayev's support, the legislative changes quickly followed, paving the way for implementation. The rapid adoption of liberalizing reforms were helped as well by an absence of strong actors with competing visions, and in particular of entrenched business lobbies or consumer groups accustomed to government transfers. Thus, concentration of decision-making power was beneficial to the speed and the scope of reforms. While many were implemented hastily, resulting in haphazard preparation and subsequent modifications, the alternative was even less attractive. As the experience of a nation such as Ukraine shows, gradual liberalization can quickly become stalled indefinitely.

The recent oil boom offers a contrasting example of interaction between macro policy and structural adjustments. As Dutch disease symptoms arose, the calls for a weaker tenge policy became increasingly insistent. For several years, until late 2006, the monetary authorities resisted this pressure, though they did not clearly explain to the public (or even to the government) their decision to target inflation. The main danger in not communicating objectives clearly was not that the policy was put at risk, but rather lay in the NBK's failure to dispel the false perception that domestic competitiveness could be restored by accommodating exchange rate policy alone.

The extraordinary oil wealth has been a blessing, substantially reducing the harshness of tradeoffs faced by GoK (and, in particular, allowing for rapid growth in basic pension payments) and raising living standards. Yet, the blessing has been a mixed one, since the largesse invites reckless government spending and the dissipation of careful macroeconomic management. Proposals to subsidize manufacturing and agricultural production from the National Fund have become even more insistent, with support among the new industrial groups. If history is any guide, such policies are likely to be counterproductive. Similarly, government's restructuring of agricultural debt appears to have hindered productivity growth. By providing blanket debt forgiveness in 1998, the government gave unfair advantage to the less efficient farms that were linked to local administrations while more efficient farms had access only to market credit.

Today, the danger of squandering public resources on building negative incentives for productivity improvements is even more real because of the increased importance of large enterprises. Avoiding severe Dutch disease effects is best realized by curbing aggregate demand growth, especially in import-intensive sectors, and building up foreign exchange reserves via the National Fund. The temptation to tap these resources to subsidize nonoil, traded-goods sectors and to further increase transfers is likely to increase distortions and reduce aggregate productivity growth, while at the same time leading Kazakhstan down the boom-bust cycle characteristic of Latin American mineral exporting states. An independent central bank committed to inflation targeting and rigid fiscal policy rules provides a bulwark against such dangers. By depriving industrialization programs of the National Fund resources, macroeconomic institutions provide the first line of defense against the Dutch disease.

None of these comments should be taken to imply that Kazakhstan should not invest heavily in developing its human capital base (education and public health have suffered greatly since independence and have not recovered) or in its physical infrastructure, as these will promote long-run productivity growth. But even these measures must be conducted within a strict macroeconomic stabilization environment and accompanied by measures aimed at maximizing rational selection of projects, transparency, and accountability over expenditures—always a risk during a publicly funded construction boom.

6

Pension Benefits during the Transition Period

Shifting from a Solidarity PAYGO system to one based on individual accumulation accounts involves a long transition period. Those who already have many years of work history under the initial system cannot accumulate sufficient amounts under a new system, thereby necessitating a transition era during which those who contributed to the old system will continue to receive PAYGO support. This period is in principle a time of macroeconomic stress, since the state loses contributions (as individual payments are in large part directed to personal accounts) while continuing to have obligations. Consequently, the state's natural inclination is to keep strict control over the levels of Solidarity benefits paid, especially if one of the underlying reasons for system reform is to reduce overall commitments. These motives still operate in Kazakhstan, although rapid economic growth and surging tax revenues in the recent years have loosened constraints, enabling large increases in Solidarity pension benefits to those who retired prior to 2003.[1]

To understand eligibility for pension benefits and their size in the reformed system, along with the proportion of Solidarity and Accumulative components, it is necessary to distinguish beneficiaries by trigger event (retirement, disability, death of breadwinner), benefit formula, and period of assignment. We begin by presenting the MLSP beneficiaries' classification under alterative viewpoints.

6.1 Structure of Beneficiaries

Using 2005 definitions and numbers, figure 6.1 shows the structure of beneficiaries by trigger events, which are calculated by aggregating the MLSP beneficiaries' categories into four groups:

1. Old age retirees: those retired at standard pension age, both prior to and after 1998;
2. Pensioners who retired on privileged terms (including early retirees) prior to 1998, as well as a small number of post-1998 retirees;
3. Disabled and survivors, who comprise the most vulnerable population;

4. Noncivilian population under special pension provision, including retirees from the armed forces, Ministry of Internal Affairs, Ministry of Justice penitentiary officers, financial police, public firemen, and others given special ranks and subject to rules established under the Kazakhstan Law on Internal Affairs.

The largest category is regular LOS retirees, of whom there were 1.18 million, or 51.2% of total beneficiaries, at the end of 2005. The old-age-retiree share seems likely to rise, given the decreasing trend for those retiring on favorable terms. Nearly all of the pensioners on privileged terms (18.9% of the total) who retired prior to 1998 belong to pension categories that have since been eliminated.

The number of 2005 standard old-age pensioners was 23% less than the prereform level , implying abnormally low retirements during the first seven years of pension reform. Excluding emigration and new retiree mortality, which have fairly minor effects, we estimate that new old-age retirees from 1998 to 2005 were only 13% of the 2004 stock of all old-age retired persons. This low influx reflects massive early retirement during 1992–97, the small World War II cohort, an increased pension age, and cancellation of almost all favorable term pensions. After 1998, only two categories of favorable term pensioners were recognized: women with more than five children, and "citizens living in zones of extraordinary and maximal radiation risk," both of which were allowed early retirement.[2] As those retiring early and on favorable terms are disproportionately women, who have longer retirement lives, the stock of pensioners who retired on favorable terms decreased only 13.3% relative to 1997, a much smaller decrease than the total numbers who retired on standard terms.

The opposite tendency appears for social allowance recipients. Relative to 1997, 2005 disability allowance recipients were 16% greater, while the numbers receiving survivors' benefits increased by 1%. Thus, the social allowance beneficiaries' share in the total pensioner population (including the noncivilian contingent) rose from 21.7% in 1997 to 27.6% in 2005. Kazakhstan's figures are low in comparison with Uzbekistan, where this group made up 33% of all beneficiaries in 2001, but are comparable with Kyrgyzstan (19.1% in 1997) or Tajikistan (25.5% in 2003: Becker, Seitenova, and Urzhumova, 2006).

However, Seitenova and Becker (2008) describe some alarming patterns in disability by cause, most notably a rise in the numbers disabled from childhood and disability among children. In 1990, these groups comprised 9.3% and 6.7% of all disabled, respectively, while the 2005 shares were 23.8% and 11.8%. Conversely, the disabled population has a declining share (though not number) of those disabled due to general diseases, which decreased from 69% in 1990 to 57% in 2005. More striking still, the proportion disabled due to work-related injuries and occupational diseases declined from 9% to 3% during this period. Rather than reflecting dramatic occupational safety improvements, this decline reflects an artificial understatement of work-related incidents due to enterprises' unwillingness to report accidents in the post-Soviet environment. By law, materials from investigation of a workplace accident must be stored for 45 years at the enterprise where an accident has been recorded. Hence, firms that report an accident run a nearly

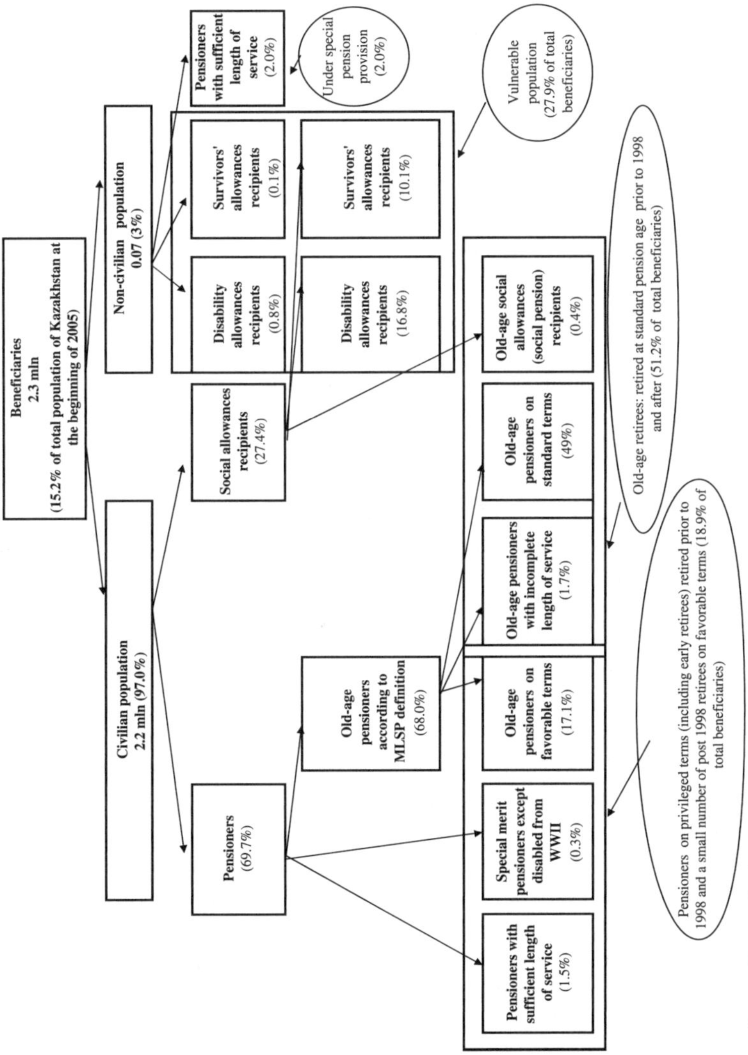

Source: Pragma database
(all figures in thousands and as % of total beneficiaries)

Figure 6.1 Structure of Kazakhstan's pension beneficiaries, 2005 (as % of total beneficiaries)

indefinite risk that current or former employees may file claims. To avoid this possibility, enterprises prefer to provide one-time compensation or privileges to actually or potentially harmed employees rather than reporting an incident. The enactment of Obligatory Social Insurance (OSI) and Employers' Obligatory Insurance laws in 2005 should lead to an increase in reporting accuracy, and hence in the numbers of disabled due to work-related injuries and occupational diseases, although there does not appear to have been an immediate effect.

Also noteworthy is the striking decrease in 2005 of the numbers receiving old-age social allowances and the corresponding growth in the number of old-age pensioners with incomplete LOS. These countervailing shifts reflect the introduction of a base, demogrant pension, which provides a strong incentive for erstwhile social allowance recipients to search for their work history certificates that verify at least one-half year of service before pension reform started or, alternatively, to open an Accumulative pension account just before retirement, as only in these cases can a retiree receive the base pension in addition to his or her Solidarity pension.

6.2 Benefit Levels

Individual pensions in Kazakhstan's reformed pension system consist of three components: base pension, Solidarity, and Accumulative. The *demogrant,* or government base pension, is paid to all citizens eligible for retirement benefits in accordance with Article 9 of the Pension Law and all who retired before January 1998, regardless of whether they receive Solidarity or Accumulative pensions or a disability allowance. The base pension is paid with no means testing. Recipients need only prove that they have attained retirement age. There is no requirement to satisfy income-level requirements, proof of dependents, or actual years of service worked in either the formal or the informal economy. At the same time, retirees with no service record can receive only one benefit: they are allowed to choose between a base pension and an old-age allowance. The size of the base pension is set annually, with the intention that it will gradually approach a genuine subsistence level. However, in 2005–7, its monthly size was maintained at 3,000 tenge (approximately US$22) and was smaller than the old-age allowance, the minimum pension for full LOS, and the subsistence level.

The *Solidarity Pension* is based on average pay for any three successive years, regardless of stoppage of work, and for LOS prior to January 1998. Men are entitled to 60% of average pay (income) after 25 years of service, with a further 1% for each additional year of service, up to a maximum of 75% of the three-year average pay. Thus, a man is entitled to an old-age Solidarity pension equal to 2.4% of average pay for each of the first 25 years of service, and 1% thereafter. Women are entitled to the 60% benefit after 20 years of service, thereby getting 3% of peak average pay for each of the first 20 years, and 1% thereafter. The 75% ceiling implies maximum credit of 40 years of work for men and 35 years for women. New Solidarity pensions also are capped at 15 Regulatory Calculation Indexes (RCI). The maximum Solidarity pension assigned prior to January 1998 for retirees (excluding World War II veterans and a few retirees on privileged terms) cannot exceed 18.75 RCIs (specifically, 75% of 25 RCIs).

Finally, contributing pensioners receive benefits from mandatory *pension accumulative accounts.* These can be paid in the form of a pension annuity from a life insurance company, directly from pension funds as scheduled withdrawals, or as a lump-sum amount, with permissible options depending on the of size of a contributor's Accumulative pension fund account. Restrictions on who is permitted to sign an annuity contract with an insurance company are determined by the monthly annuity, which, when calculated on the basis of individual accumulations, cannot be less than the monthly *minimum pension.* At present, annuities can be whole life or over a certain period, depending on contract terms. Although it is intended that annuities eventually will become mandatory for those with sufficient accumulations, retirees are not currently obligated to transfer accumulation fund balances to a life insurance company and purchase an annuity. For retirees who have an account balance of less than the official Individual Accumulation Threshold (in 2005–7, IAT = 100,000 tenge), a lump sum is paid from the APF; scheduled payments over several years are not allowed. All benefits formed on the basis of individual accumulations are paid upon attaining retirement age. However, for those whose accumulations are sufficient to pay a benefit of at least the minimum pension, pension accumulations may be claimed from age 55.

Table 6.1 describes in detail the procedures for calculating individual pensions, and shows how the components involved in calculating individual pensions are related to one another, depending on the LOS prior to 1998, individual income, and health status. In total, the classifications distinguish six subcategories of old-age retirees:

1. those who retired with complete LOS prior to January 1, 1998, and no work history in the reformed system;
2. those retired after January 1, 1998, having complete LOS in the PAYGO and the funded system together (LOS credits equal the sum of years of worked before and after January 1, 1998);
3. those retired after January 1, 1998, having incomplete LOS in the PAYGO and the funded system together (LOS credits equal the sum of years of worked before and after January 1, 1998);
4. those who retired with complete LOS in the funded system;
5. those who became permanently disabled (disability groups I and II); and
6. those who retired after January 1, 1998, with no work history.

In the near future, Solidarity payments will continue to be the largest component of pension payments. Therefore, it is not surprising that since the reform started, much of the debate has been on the levels of Solidarity payments, and to an extent perceived inequities within the structure of payments, rather than on the Accumulative component. Both the popular press and Urzhumova (2000) and Seitenova and Urzhumova (2003) criticized the use of RCIs to establish pension wage ceilings, as the RCI is not linked to standard indicators such as the subsistence level, minimum wage, or the average wage. Nevertheless, the 15 RCI measure was maintained during the reform's first decade, and when the ceiling was raised in 2008, it was increased to 25 RCIs.

Table 6.1 Individual monthly pensions in Kazakhstan's reformed system

Work history	*Base pension (BP)*(1)	*Solidarity pension (SP)*		*Funded pension (FP)*	*Combined pension income (PI)*
		Men	*Women*		
Complete length of service prior to Jan 1, 1998(2)	set annually in the Republican Budget Law; intended to gradually reach Subsistence Level	SP = [60% + 1.0% * min (YS > 25 prior to 01.01.98, 15)] * min (AMI, K* RCI)	SP = [60% + 1.0% * min (YS > 20 prior to 01.01.98, 15)] * min (AMI, K* RCI)	FP= Lump sum payment if IA < max {Q*MP,IAT)	PI = BP + max (SP, MP)
Complete length of service in both PAYGO and the funded system (sum of years of work before[3] and after Jan 1, 1998)		SP = [2.4% * (YS prior to 01.01.98) * min (AMI, K*RCI)	SP = [3% * (YS prior to 01.01.98) * min (AMI, K* RCI)	FP= Flexibly scheduled payouts (monthly, quarterly etc.) if IA is insufficient	PI = BP + max (SP+ FPm, MP)
Incomplete length of service considering the sum of years of work before and after Jan 1, 1998		SP = [2.4% * (YS prior to 01.01.98) * min (AMI, K*RCI)	SP = [3% * (YS prior to 01.01.98) * min (AMI, K*RCI)	FP= annuity on monthly, quarterly or other basis if IA is sufficient to purchase a minimum pension annuity	PI = BP + max (SP + FPm, DA)(4)

Permanently Disabled in groups I and II				PI = BP + FPm
Complete length of service in the funded system	0	0		
No work history	0	0	0	PI = OSA

(1) effective 01.06.05; (2) not less than 25 years for men and 20 years for women; (3) not less than one half year but less than 25 years for men and 20 years for women prior to Jan 1, 1998

(4) in case SP + FPm is less than the State social disability allowance (DA), the government pays the difference [DA – (SP + FPm)]

Abbreviations

RCI: Regulatory Calculation Index (minimalny raschetnyi pokazatel - MRP)
MP: minimum pension
AMI: Individual Average Monthly Income for any three consecutive working years
YS: years of service
IA: Individual Account pension accumulations
K = 15 before January 1, 2008; K = 25 thereafter
IAT: Individual Accumulation threshold (KZT 100,000 before 2008; KZT 250,000 thereafter)
FPm: funded pension on monthly basis
OSA: Old age state social allowance
DA: State social disability allowance
Q = 12 before 2008; Q = 30 thereafter

Thus, in the absence of regular increases (and, evidently, adjustments are infrequent and not mandatory), Solidarity caps will stagnate over time, leading to declines in replacement rates.

Alternative policies suggested by Becker, Seitenova and Urzhumova (2000a), Seitenova and Urzhumova (2003), and World Bank staff at various times (for a survey of the Bank's assessments, see Andrews 2005) did not lead to immediate responses. However, most likely in response to improved public finances, minimum pensions have been increased gradually, and ultimately a major change occurred in 2005. This was the base pension described earlier, adding a third pillar to the overall system. The base pension demogrant is consistent with World Bank recommendations and allows the nation to maintain minimum guarantees irrespective of funded system contributions and hence pension levels.

Other suggestions made include measures to equalize replacement coefficients in the Solidarity and Accumulative systems for men and a range of steps aimed at improving the pensions earned by women. Seitenova and Urzhumova (2003: 43) suggest indexing the basic pension to the nominal wage, thereby creating an automatic adjustment mechanism and also removing the need to regulate pension annuity payments, since pensions automatically would be higher than the minimum guarantee. However, an automatic adjustment procedure was not incorporated; instead, the revised law rather vaguely states that the base pension would be adjusted upward to "approach subsistence level on the step-by-step basis." It is difficult to predict how long it will take for the base pension to approach the official subsistence level (OSL), especially given that it has remained unchanged since its introduction. As a result, the fall in the ratio of base pension to OSL from 48% in the mid-2005 to 36% and 28% in 2006 and 2007, respectively, suggests that the demogrant may end up serving more as a supplement rather than a replacement for the minimum Solidarity pension, as originally intended.

These reforms do not address the thorny issue of annuities, which have been under discussion since 1999, if not earlier. In principle, the regulatory agencies would like pensioners to purchase life annuities.[3] In practice, annuities are risky products, since stable life tables cannot be calculated, and since accumulations will be too small for the vast majority of contributors to merit the fixed costs of purchasing an annuity product.[4] Thus, Seitenova and Urzhumova (2003) warn of slow pension annuity market development because of low individual accumulations. Insurance company expenses will be built into benefit calculation either explicitly or implicitly (through a lower interest rate assumed in annuity pricing).[5] As these costs will be prohibitive for most new retirees, pension annuities issued by insurance companies would be small in number for many years to come. Annuities are also especially risky to the insurance industry, since retirees with significant accumulations by definition come from high-income groups, and these groups have a high longevity risk from an insurer's perspective.

Table 6.2 provides a forecast of the prospective pensioner annuitant market through 2020. The numbers are tiny, reaching only 1% of new retirements in 2008. However, as LOS increases, and assuming economic growth is maintained, the eligible pool will begin to surge at the end of the next decade and, by 2020, will exceed

Table 6.2 Projections of retirees with Accumulative funds above KZT 1.5 million (US$ 12,000)

Year of retirement	*Projected numbers of pension fund contributors with accumulations over 1,500,000 tenge by year of retirement*			*Total number of pension fund contributors by year of retirement*	*Potential annuitants as % of all retirees by year of retirement*
	Male	*Female*	*Total*		
2005	54	45	99	55,311	0.2%
2006	129	145	274	61,092	0.4%
2007	148	173	321	66,662	0.5%
2008	349	415	764	70,928	1.1%
2009	899	793	1,692	82,505	2.1%
2010	1,930	984	2,914	97,265	3.0%
2011	1,959	909	2,867	97,468	2.9%
2012	2,279	1,568	3,847	104,429	3.7%
2013	3,895	2,777	6,672	107,127	6.2%
2014	5,598	4,096	9,694	108,905	8.9%
2015	7,487	4,953	12,440	111,183	11.2%
2016	7,500	4,929	12,429	112,093	11.1%
2017	7,995	5,139	13,134	115,383	11.4%
2018	7,985	9,198	17,182	118,252	14.5%
2019	10,787	13,223	24,010	116,297	20.6%
2020	14,024	16,985	31,009	114,894	27.0%

Source: Pragma Corporation 2005: 9

one-quarter of all new retirees. By any objective standard, this is an impressive achievement, but the goal of having all retirees purchase annuities remains an impractical objective for a middle-income country.

Information on actual Accumulative participant retirees is provided by the NBK's *Statistical Bulletin*, which is freely available online. Only a trivial number of retirees have bought any sort of annuity, even relative to the number retiring with sufficient accumulations. Evidently, people are exercising grace period options, as one might expect in an unsettled market. It is also clear that very few people participate in voluntary pension savings schemes; again, this is hardly surprising. However, the large and growing number of Accumulative system participants is impressive. The large majority of old-age retirees by now have some sort of Accumulative account—though, even after ten years of the new system, the average annual scheduled withdrawal per person is only US$587. Of course, this figure will increase rapidly as the system matures.

The one distressing signal from NBK published data is that large numbers continue to declare an intention to emigrate and then withdraw all assets from their accumulation accounts. This issue has received much attention in Kazakhstan, as there has been large net emigration. Loss of high income, skilled labor to Russia and elsewhere fluctuates according to attitudes toward titular minorities, while there is a new emphasis on the vast numbers of illegal immigrants into Kazakhstan from Central Asia proper.

6.3 Government Social Expenditures

Kazakhstan's pension reform is designed in part to limit the government's social obligations. In effect, the reform makes a large portion of society responsible for saving for retirement and provides savings incentives by tightly linking retirement benefits to individual contributions. In short, Accumulative pensions were to become the dominant component of retirement income. However, the evolution of Kazakhstan's pension reform during its first ten years indicates that the nation will retain a non-Accumulative component to a far greater extent than initially envisioned. The deviation from original design began in 1999, when net wage payments to the Solidarity system, that is, the 15% payroll contribution for pensions to the SCBP, together with all mandatory wage deductions, including wage bill deductions paid to the Mandatory Medical Insurance Fund (3%), the State Social Security Fund (1.5%), and State Employment Fund (2%), were replaced by a single social tax. This payroll social tax rate t was raised from 21% at the beginning of 1999 to 26% by the end of the year. In July 2001, the social payroll tax rate was again reduced to 21%.[6] This rate was maintained until January 1, 2004, when a new social tax collection system was introduced. Instead of a fixed percentage rate on all level of wages, a deliberately regressive social tax rate was introduced. The new rates varied from 20% to 7% depending on wage rate. The 20% payroll rate was applied to monthly incomes below 13,800 tenge (approximately US$100 at the time, now US$110), while lowest rate applied to incomes above 550,000 tenge (US$4,000). The primary motive for these changes was to reduce evasion by persons in high income brackets. Since social payments have strict caps as well, wealthy Kazakhstanis has complained about the lack of correspondence between their contributions and benefits and noted regressive payroll tax ceilings in other countries such as the United States.

With the introduction of a single social tax, benefit payments and social allowances started to be funded from the Republican budget. As can be expected during a period of transition from a PAYGO to an Accumulative system, the immediate impact of the various changes to Solidarity contribution rates is to transfer much of the burden for financing pension expenditures to the national government budget. This burden emerged most immediately because of the reduction in individual payroll contributions for the Solidarity system from 31% to 21%, as this tax was reduced in order to maintain the overall payroll rate, given that 10% was diverted to individual Accumulative system accounts. With rapid economic growth and surging government revenues along with slow growth in pension numbers, social welfare expenses steadily declined as a share of GDP and GoK expenses after the huge jump in 1999.

Given the 16.6% decrease of total number of beneficiaries in 2007 relative to 1997, one would indeed expect curtailed Solidarity expenditure growth. Yet, while both the numbers of pensioners and real Solidarity pension expenditures have fallen, the GDP share of government social welfare expenditures remains relatively high and comparable to the Soviet era. In the late Soviet era, Kazakhstan's pension and allowances' expenditures made up 4% to 5% of GDP (Becker and Urzhumova, 1998). By 1997, the total share exceeded 10% of GDP (most of which was not included in the central budget, although transfers from the Republican government budget to cover state pension fund arrears came to 3.5% of GDP), and the Republican government budget cost peaked at 7.9% of GDP in 1999. Even with dramatic GDP growth and curtailed social security expenditures in recent years, though, until recently GoK spent about 5% of GDP on Solidarity pensions and other social support payments. The 3.9% GDP share of social security expenditures in 2007 is the smallest during the reform era since the inception, and it remains to be seen whether this decline is permanent.

Solidarity pensions and social allowances are not the only social security expenditures. The third category of payments by Republican and local budgets includes a Special State Allowance (SSA), introduced on April 1, 1999 (in accordance with RK Law No 365-1), in lieu of previous payments from local government budgets to pay for communal services, fuel, and dwelling maintenance. SSA recipients include World War II veterans, families of deceased veterans, disabled persons, and families with many children. These supplements are sizeable. In particular, the additional SSA average monthly public social payments amounted to as much as 19% of average disability payments in some years. In general, the SSA plus similar types of social support make up about 20% of total government social welfare expenditure and, therefore, constitute an important if commonly neglected additional expenditure. Thus, simply relying on official public statistics that present only Solidarity pensions and government social allowances offers a misleading picture of total public expenditure commitments.

The presence of SSA payments may also help explain a striking divergence. There was a rising trend in real average Solidarity pensions during the period 2001–3 relative to 1997, while the real size of major government social allowances has grown much more slowly and in fact fell during the period 2001–4. It seems likely that the GoK maintained budgetary discipline by not fully indexing government social allowances to inflation and most likely maintaining subsistence levels of those who were extremely impoverished through SSA payments and other types of supplemental support. However, the situation changed markedly in 2006 when a new procedure of calculation of government social allowances replaced the RCI adjustment mechanism.

During 1998–2005, social allowance adjustments depended on the amount and frequency of RCI adjustments, rather than directly on inflation (appendix 6.1 provides state social allowances in terms of monthly RCI). The largest allowances were received by disabled veterans and the lowest by old-age pensioners with no work history. Adjustment kept pace with inflation only during the first two years of pension reform. The lag in RCI adjustments thereafter naturally reduced the real value of disability and survivorship benefits, the old-age social allowance, and special allowances, as these are all expressed in terms of RCIs. This factor in part offsets the benefit increases in terms of RCI mandated in 2002, 2003, and 2005.

According to the new method, the size of government social allowances introduced in 2006 is tied to the size of the official subsistence level.[7] The new practices are far more generous, as almost all categories of allowances, except mildly disabled (group III) and old-age allowances, exceed the official subsistence level (appendix 6.1). The low levels of these latter groups reflect public policy to restrict the distribution of contributions to noncontributors.

Solidarity pension indexation during the reform period is governed by the RK pension law (No. 136-1; notably Article 5, point 3) dated June 20, 1997, *On Pension Security in the Republic of Kazakhstan*, which merely affirms the right to annual indexing (from November 1999) and directs the government to design an indexation procedure (appendix 6.2). However, while there have been regular adjustments announced in various government decrees, the indexation method(s) used has not been revealed. In practice, GoK kept average monthly pensions near the subsistence level through 2001 and only as of 2003 provided substantial increases that raised most pensions above subsistence.[8]

Pensions jumped in 2003 due to an unscheduled recalculation for those who retired prior to January 1 of that year (in addition to the annual pension increase in accordance with Article 5 of the Pension Law). The recalculation was based on 2002 wages by economic sector and personal participation coefficients (calculated based on data maintained in SPPC pension files, with service years and preretirement wages as submitted on the date of retirement. This recalculation was of particular value to those whose earnings, and hence pensions, had been eroded by inflation. The result was a large jump in standard term and "privileged" old-age pensions. Made possible by economic recovery that filled government coffers, these boosts decreased the share of old-age pensioners receiving the minimum pension (in 2003, an amount almost exactly equal to Goskomstat's estimated OSL) from 58% in 2000 to 10% in 2003. This recalculation, together with the base pension demogrant in 2005, could have resulted in a very large rise in non-Accumulative pension commitments. GoK avoided this consequence by not fully indexing Solidarity pensions to inflation in 2004 and 2006, respectively. As a result, the average real monthly Solidarity pension decreased slowly during 2004–6, with the decline becoming substantial by 2006. However, the base pension more than offset the decline in 2005, though it, too, declined in 2006.

Given Kazakhstan's remarkable economic growth, these rising real benefits have not translated into increasing replacement rates (Figure 6.2) relative to current average wages, which more than doubled between 1998 and 2006. In fact, even the large 2003 pension increases, which raised the replacement rate for old retirees by 7.2 percentage points (0.2 points for new retirees) relative to 2002, still returned replacement rates for the stock of pensioners only to 1999 levels. Solidarity system replacement rates were highest at the time of reform and have been at their lowest points in the most recent years. This decline is not inadvertent: despite periodic increases that seem unavoidable, a core goal of the reform is to shed public sector responsibility for pensions.

In an ideal world, all pensioners and social allowances' recipients, and particularly disabled persons, would receive adequate payments. In practice, such social largesse is not easy to maintain in a middle-income country such as Kazakhstan, and virtually no nontransition nation at its level of development has pension expenditures as great. Reality (as reported in Palacios and Pallares-Miralles, 2000) is that no East and Southeast Asian developing and middle-income countries spend more than 3% of GDP on public pension provision, and most spend far less. Public pension spending ranges from 3.7% of GDP in Turkey to 4.2% in Jordan, to 1.4% in South Korea, 0.4% in Mexico. The only nontransition middle-income

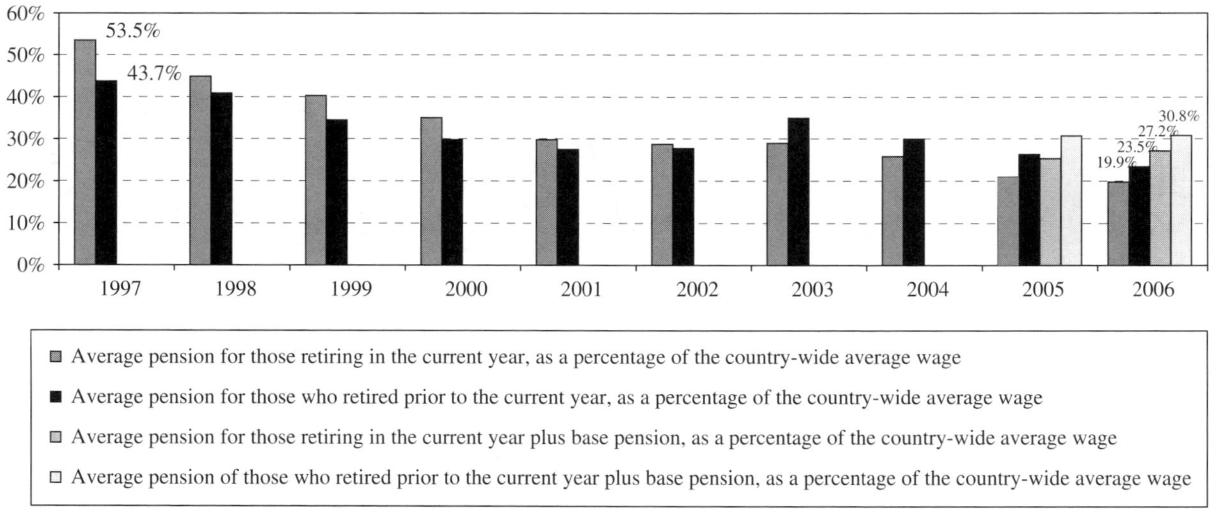

Source: Pragma database

Figure 6.2 Replacement rates for pensions assigned prior to and during the current year, 1997–2006

countries that exceed Kazakhstan's pension expenditure shares are Uruguay (15.0%), Argentina (6.2%), and Chile (5.8%)—and all three countries are struggling to contain these expenditures. In a competitive world, high payroll taxes and government spending pressures have serious effects on employment and economic growth, and it is difficult to argue for more liberal social expenditure policies. This is especially true for pension and social allowances in a nation such as Kazakhstan, which faces educational system deterioration and a need to recover public health services. From this perspective, Kazakhstan's pension effort in recent years has been considerable.

6.4 Labor Force Structure and Tax Compliance

We have focused thus far on pension and other social payments, but of obvious interest to the GoK is the pattern of social contributions, as these affect its capacity to increase social payments without borrowing or reducing other expenditures. In principle, pyramid schemes of all kinds—including PAYGO social welfare schemes involving intergenerational transfers, such as the Solidarity pension system—should fare especially well in periods of rapid growth. During such expansions, both formal sector employment and wage rates grow rapidly, and the contribution base expands for both those reasons. At the same time, increasing enterprise solvency increases compliance, while sustained employment reduces the pressure for early retirement due to dubious disabilities.

Figure 6.3 shows the structure of Kazakhstan's able-bodied population, defined as citizens aged 15–63 (males) and 15–58 (females). This labor force delineation details both the nature of employment and permits estimation of the number of social taxpayers. In 2003, effective contributors from large and medium enterprises made up approximately 94.7% and 96.7%, respectively, of the total number of employed in these enterprises. Only 80% of those employed in small-scale entities appear to be regular contributors. Overall, 83% of all hired labor (4.23 million workers) contributes social taxes; 12.9% of the 2.76 million self-employed also contribute. In total, 50.5% of the economically active population paid social taxes.

It would appear from figure 6.3 that major employers have high compliance rates, but somewhat more than half of the nation's labor force and employed populations are not actively contributing to the social tax system. Since the complying population is not static, it is likely that an even larger share—perhaps 60–70% of the labor force—will end up with insufficient years of service and correspondingly inadequate individual accumulation funds, should present trends continue. However, this should not be taken as strong criticism, since the levels of compliance achieved are impressive for a middle-income country. Recent data from Chile discussed in Chapter 11 suggest similar compliance rates and patterns across the range of firms from small to big. More detailed data on social tax contributions appear in table 6.3.

Solidarity system contributions are provided mainly by legal entities, that is, by all types of enterprises (including small-scale enterprises engaged in entrepreneurial activities) that submit reports to the Statistical Agency (SARK) of the Republic of Kazakhstan. Since noncontributing entities should want to avoid

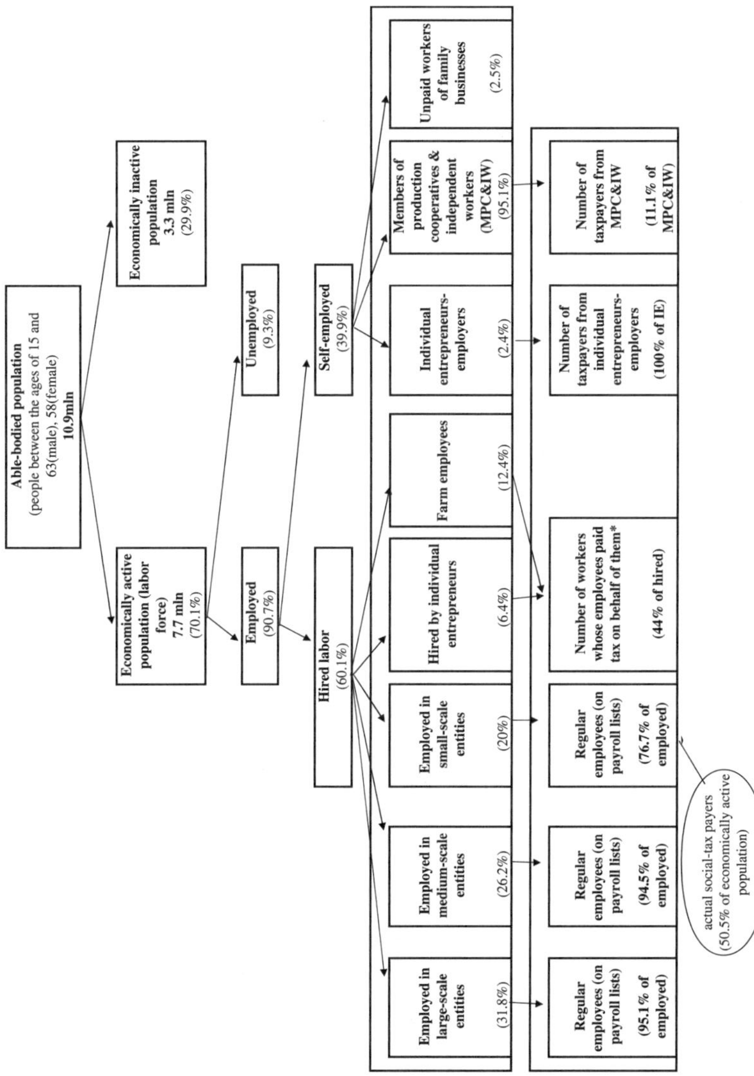

Source: Pragma database

Figure 6.3 Estimated social taxpaying population, Kazakhstan 2003

Table 6.3 Social tax collection indicators, 1997–2006

	1997	*1998*	*1999*	*2000*	*2001*	*2002*	*2003*	*2004*	*2005*	*2006*
Social tax, actual collection (1998: mandatory pension contributions to SPPC, the Solidarity system) in real terms, 1997=100	100.0	42.5	77.0	95.7	110.7	112.6	124.6	124.2	135.5	149.6
Share of enterprises submitting reports to SARK in social tax collection:										
large, medium and small enterprises **except** small-scale enterprises engaged in entrepreneurial activities, %	n/av	n/av	n/av	88.7	89.1	87.7	87.3	86.8	88.3	n/av
small-scale enterprises engaged in entrepreneurial activities, %	n/av	n/av	n/av	9.4	9.1	10.0	10.5	10.8	9.7	n/av
individual entrepreneurs, %	n/av	n/av	n/av	1.9	1.8	2.3	2.2	2.4	2.0	n/av
Total wage bill of enterprises submitting reports to SARK in real terms, 1997=100	100.0	91.3	87.5	97.4	114.2	133.3	150.5	180.0	213.3	249.6
Share of enterprises submitting reports to SARK in total wage bill:										
large, medium and small enterprises **except** small-scale enterprises engaged in entrepreneurial activities, %	95.8	94.1	92.7	91.2	90.4	89.5	88.0	87.7	86.3	85.5
small-scale enterprises engaged in entrepreneurial activities, %	4.2	5.9	7.3	8.8	9.6	10.5	12.0	12.3	13.7	14.5
Number of regular employees of large, medium and small enterprises submitting reports to SARK:										
Index, 1997=100	100.0	86.4	74.4	77.9	82.6	86.8	90.7	95.1	99.3	104.2
as % of Economically active population	45.4	41.4	35.6	37.0	37.3	39.6	40.0	41.0	42.4	43.8
as % of Employed population	52.2	47.6	41.2	42.4	41.6	43.7	43.9	44.7	46.2	47.5
Share of small-scale enterprises engaged in entrepreneurial activities in total number of employees submitting reports to SARK, %	6.0	8.0	10.8	12.9	13.8	14.6	15.2	15.9	15.9	15.8

Source: MLSP data & SARK online database

reporting their unmet tax liabilities, while those that do pay taxes in effect are reporting, there is essentially a one-to-one correspondence between reporting and social tax compliance. In practice, virtually all large- and medium-scale enterprises do provide reports. However, it is estimated that only 49% of small-scale enterprises submitted reports to SARK in 2002–3, with non-compliance especially great among those engaged in entrepreneurial activities. Noncollected taxes are a much smaller proportion of the potential total, as complying firms have larger workforces on average and pay higher wages. However, an offsetting problem of tax avoidance among active enterprises through understated wage bills or through underreporting the number of employees is widely known but has not been quantified.

Large- and medium-sized firms, and (compliant) small-scale firms *other than* those engaged in "entrepreneurial activities" account for the overwhelming share (85.5% in 2006) of the wage bill. Small-scale enterprises engaged in entrepreneurial activities accounted for 14.5%. To get a sense of overall compliance, it is first necessary to determine the plausible employment base. Given the low incomes and difficulty of collecting taxes, small-scale enterprises in entrepreneurial activities and self-employed are not regarded as being potential contributors unless they are registered with SARK. In Kazakhstan, it also makes sense to restrict the possible pool of regular tax contributors to full-time workers. Thus, the base chosen consists of workers in medium and large enterprises who are recorded as having a formal, strong attachment to their jobs (thereby excluding, for example, women on maternity leave, or on leave to take care of children; or "furloughed workers who left their posts at the initiative of management"). For small enterprises, it is most appropriate to use an estimate of the number of workers on regular assignment (excluding substitutes and other temporary workers) at each firm, and whose names have been submitted to the tax and statistical organs. On this basis, in 2005 there were some 3.4 million regular contributors of social taxes among legal entities. Of these, 2.6 million were employed by medium and large enterprises, plus small enterprises excluding those engaged in entrepreneurial activities; the remainder was employed in small-scale enterprises engaged in entrepreneurial activities. The numbers employed in small enterprises engaged in entrepreneurial activities almost doubled between 1997 and 2005, providing strong evidence of growing regularization of smaller firms. However, in tax compliance terms, progress has been slower: the small and medium enterprise (SME) share in social tax collection in 2005 was only 0.3 percentage points greater than in 2000.

Furthermore, while there has been progress in regularizing SMEs, only negligible increases in social tax payments by individual entrepreneurs have taken place. According to Kazakhstani legislation, self-employed entrepreneurs are "physical entities, engaged in entrepreneurial activities without formal legal registration, and in the absence of signs of being a legal entity." Prior to 2003, characteristics of the self-employed were virtually unknown. At that point, MinFin asked SARK to collect information on self-employed entrepreneurs and provide it to the MinFin's Tax Committee, with the intention of using this information for future tax inspections. However, this approach has proven rather naïve in its expectations about compliance. Out of 3.3 million of individual entrepreneurs in 2003, only 22.7% obeyed tax laws and, specifically, paid social taxes. Full tax compliance of the self-employed population amounted to only 13%. From the perspective of the GoK, these numbers seem small. Certainly, they imply massive current tax evasion, and also imply that in the future, large numbers of retirees will depend on base pensions (since those not paying social taxes almost certainly are not paying into Accumulative system accounts).

In spite of the fact that by 2006 the number of employed workers had increased by 13% and self-employed population had decreased by 5% in comparison with 2003, the structure of social taxpayers during this period indicated no significant improvement in tax compliance, though payments certainly did increase. While contributions were affected, the aggregate data indicate little impact from the regressive social tax structure introduced in January 2004 to improve compliance. GoK responded by further reducing the social tax rate on the lower bound of taxable income of legal entities from 20% to 13%, and concurrently reducing the social tax paid by individual entrepreneurs from three RCIs to two RCIs on his own behalf and from two RCIs to one RCI on behalf of employees, effective January 2008.[9] The GoK anticipates a considerable effect from this measure in the light of a simultaneous reduction in the value added tax from 14 to 13%. However, the extent to which new social tax rates improve incentives to reduce underreporting income and motivate the self-employed to comply with taxation regulations depends on the general economic situation, which in 2007–8 was one of slower economic growth.

In considering the sectoral composition of social tax contributors, recall that Kazakhstan has a dualistic economy similar to other middle-income, minerals-oriented economies. From the perspective of social and other tax collections, this dualism means that payments are highly concentrated. In particular, in the non-mining primary sectors, incomes and, correspondingly, contributions to the social tax fund are low. The first group consists of high-wage sectors, including the financial sector and mining. These two sectors account for only 1.5% and 6.0% of employment, respectively, but account for 3.6% and 11.9% of the total formal sector wage bill, and 4.3% and 14.9% of social tax payments. Correspondingly, the low- and mid-wage sectors account for 41.5% and 51.0% of employment, earn 52.8% and 31.7% of total wage payments, and make 55.5% and 25.3% of social tax payments. In contrast to the financial and mining sectors, agricultural workers comprise 6.1% of the regular active contributors but account for only 2.5% of the total wage bill and make only 1.2% of social tax payments. The question is not whether such inequalities exist, but whether they are large. In fact, by the standards of most middle-income and upper-middle-income countries, the extent of inequality is not surprising (even if one includes the self-employed, who are overwhelmingly in low-earnings activities). Relative to Latin American nations and poorer parts of the former Soviet Union (i.e., excluding Russia and the Baltic states), Kazakhstan has a large and highly compliant "medium wage branches" economy. It is also true that that compliance in the hardest-to-reach sectors is already nonnegligible and that Kazakhstan's tax authority's control is impressive by the standards of middle-income countries. In contrast, the extreme dualism of poor welfare states is avoided: in Kyrgyzstan, for example, Becker and Paltsev (2001) estimate that for every som contributed by rural inhabitants (2/3 of the population), 11 to 12 som are returned in pension and social payments.

In comparing 2003 with 1999, the year in which the general social tax was introduced, there was real wage increase in all branches as well as employment growth. During this first phase of Kazakhstan's rapid growth, employment declined in only a few areas (hotels and restaurants; power, gas, and water; agriculture; and fisheries) that together comprised only 11.4% of 2003 employment. Consequently, social tax collection in real terms increased in all branches except agriculture, hunting, forestry, and public administration.

The bottom line is that contributions for pension payments have grown to an extent that no one could have imagined in 1998. By 2007, social tax receipts in real terms were almost four times that of 1998; the increase in private pension fund accounts was greater still. Social tax contributions surged earlier, growing by 161% between 1998 and 2001, and "only" 52% during 2001–7. This slowdown in part reflects social tax rate decreases described earlier and is also likely explained in part by improvements in government administrative capacity in the early reform years. In contrast, the Accumulative system was met with initial skepticism and resistance, and contributions grew by only 49% between 1998 and 2001. In the following six years, however, growth was a phenomenal 235% reflecting both widespread acceptance of and growing confidence in the Accumulative system as well as continued improvements in monitoring and enforcement.

6.5 Mandatory Insurance

By 2005, Kazakhstan's financial sector also had developed to a degree hardly foreseen at the outset of the pension reform, though in many respects it was still a fledgling sector. As noted, policymakers used some of the state's windfall income to provide far more generous pension benefits than could have been imagined just a few years earlier. In so doing, they transformed a reform initially aimed at shrinking government and shifting responsibility for retirement savings to individuals to that of a system that ensures a significant welfare state. This comment is not critical: rather, one can view Kazakhstan as having used some of its oil, mining, and metallurgy proceeds to buy repairs for its historically large welfare system. There can be no doubt that the changes were popular and probably have contributed to much greater acceptance of the Accumulative system.

At the same time, policymakers' drives to deepen market-oriented reforms and to force-feed the nascent financial sector continued in two directions. First, 2005 witnessed enactment of two laws concerning obligatory social insurance and employers' obligatory insurance. These indicated government's intention to promote its new insurance market and to improve social protection of employees and occupational safety (tables 6.4 and 6.5).

During the first three years of existence of Obligatory Social Insurance Law, both employers (for all their employees) and self-employed individuals are required to acquire insurance that will provide unemployment and disability benefits, as well as

Table 6.4 Main features of obligatory social insurance (OSI): Social security tax rates

	Tax rates for employed persons: Payroll tax rate	*Tax rates for self-employed persons: Tax as percentage of minimum wage*	*Maximum taxable earnings base*
2005	1.5%	1.5%	10 × minimum wage
2006	2%	2%	10 × minimum wage
2007	3%	3%	10 × minimum wage

Table 6.5 Main features of obligatory social insurance (OSI): Benefits

	Monthly disability benefits	*Monthly survivorship benefits*	*Monthly unemployment benefits*
Eligibility	OSI taxpayers regardless of whether or not the person continues to work at the time of appeal for disability benefits	Dependents of OSI taxpayers	OSI taxpayers who have lost their jobs
Duration of payment	from the date of the claim until retirement age or rehabilitation date	from the date of the claim until the date when all dependents lose benefit eligibility	from 1 month to 4 months, depending on the length of contribution period
Benefit formula	= [average monthly income (subject to taxation) for the last 24 months – 0.8 × minimum wage] × Replacement Rate coefficient × the coefficient of participation in OSI		
Maximum income replacement rate	0.6	0.6	0.3

benefits to survivors. Moreover, as of 2008, the OSI law also extends coverage to pregnancy, childbirth, and maternity for employed women.

The employers' mandatory insurance law since requires all nongovernment employees to purchase workers' compensation insurance from an active, licensed nonlife insurance company. By the end of 2007, there were more than 25 general insurance companies licensed to insure employers' liability.

It is too early to assess the extent of compliance with the insurance mandated, though it seems likely that initial levels will be low but that rapid growth will follow. Broadly put, the law seems to precede the insurance industry's capacity, and underlying actuarial calculations are at best sketchy (for detailed analysis, see Pragma Corporation, 2005).

Rather than backing off, in late 2005 the FSA suggested creating a new State Annuity Company and quickly moved to charter it and provide 1 billion tenge in charter capital. This move demonstrates policymakers' seriousness of intent: if private insurance companies cannot provide the mandated products, then the public sector will. However, the intention is not to provide a new state entity but rather to encourage private insurers to enter once they see the potential for profitable business. However, that is unlikely to happen in the near future, in part because of cost uncertainty and in part because of regulations that make full cost recovery difficult (Pragma Corporation, 2005).

Ultimately, it is likely that many of the current problems facing both life and nonlife insurance companies will be solved. Thus, the second phase in using the pension reform to develop Kazakhstan's financial sector will continue to forge ahead. Both for pension funds and insurance companies, the next few years almost certainly will contain many problems associated with development. However, in terms of meeting citizens' pension and social payment needs, GoK has largely resolved the problem by using some of its growing revenue to provide base commitments.

Appendix 6.1

Disability allowance rules, in RCI

I. *Disability allowances* per disabled person

	Category	*1 Jan 98–1 Jan 02*	*1 Jan 02–1 Jan 03*	*1 Jan 03–1 Jan 05*	*1 Jan 05–1 Jan 06*	*1 Jan 06–present*
	Disabled due to general disease, work-related injuries and diseases; military disabled belonging to category (1)					
1	1 group (most severely and in principle permanently disabled)	6RCI	7RCI	7RCI	10RCI	1.36OSL
	2 group (moderately disabled)	4RCI	4.5RCI	5RCI	7.5RCI	1.06OSL
	3 group (lightly disabled; not prevented from working)	3RCI	3RCI	3RCI	5RCI	0.74OSL
2	Disabled children under age of 16	3RCI	4RCI	4RCI	7RCI	1.00OSL
3	Disabled children aged 16–18*:					
	1 group				10RCI	1.36OSL
	2 group				8RCI	1.11OSL
	3 group				6RCI	0.87OSL
4	Adults disabled from childhood:					
	1 group	6RCI	7RCI	7RCI	10RCI	1.36OSL
	2 group	4RCI	5RCI	5.5RCI	8RCI	1.11OSL
	3 group	3RCI	4RCI	4RCI	6RCI	0.87OSL
5	Disabled because of ecological disasters, including radiation impact; military disabled belonging to category (3):					

Appendix 6.1 *(continued)*

	Category	*1 Jan 98– 1 Jan 02*	*1 Jan 02– 1 Jan 03*	*1 Jan 03– 1 Jan 05*	*1 Jan 05– 1 Jan 06*	*1 Jan 06– present*
	1 group	8RCI	9RCI	9RCI	12RCI	1.61OSL
	2 group	6RCI	6.5RCI	7RCI	9.5RCI	1.30OSL
	3 group	5RCI	5RCI	5RCI	7RCI	1.00OSL
6	Military disabled belonging to category (2):					
	1 group	15RCI	16RCI	16RCI	16RCI	1.61OSL
	2 group	10RCI	10.5RCI	11RCI	11RCI	1.30OSL
	3 group	7RCI	7RCI	7RCI	7RCI	1.00OSL
II.	*Survivorship allowances*					

				Per dependent:		*Per all dependents*
1	1 dependent	4RCI	=”=	=”=	5RCI	0.66OSL
2	2 dependents	3.5RCI	=”=	=”=	4.3RCI	1.14OSL
3	3 dependents	3RCI	=”=	=”=	3.5RCI	1.41OSL
4	4 dependents	2.5RCI	=”=	=”=	2.8RCI	1.50OSL
5	5 dependents	2RCI	=”=	=”=	2.3RCI	1.55OSL
6	6+ dependents	10RCI divided among all dependents	=”=	=”=	12RCI divided among all dependents	1.61OSL divided among all dependents
III.	***Old age social allowance* per retired person**	3RCI	=”=	=”=	=”=	0.50OSL

(1) Disabled persons from the armed forces (excluding military personnel in temporary draft service), from the leadership and officers from the organs of internal affairs, and the former RK State Investigative Committee who were invalided as a result of accidents unconnected with the carrying out of duties of military service (or assigned duties), or illnesses unconnected with fulfillment of military and service obligations.

(2) Disabled persons from those on temporary duty in the Armed forces, disability for whom arose as a consequence of injury, contusion, maiming, or illness incurred during the course of military service; and individuals whose disability arose as a result of cleaning up residues from accidents at nuclear plants, either civilian or military, or as a result of accidents at nuclear plants.

(3) Disabled persons from the armed forces (excluding military personnel in temporary draft service), whose disability arose as the result of injury, contusion, maiming, or illness received during the course of military service; workers in the organs of internal affairs, and the former RK State Investigative Committee who were invalided as a result of accidents connected with the carrying out of assigned duties.

Appendix 6.2

Pension payments' indexation chronology, 1998–2004

Issue date	*Effective date*	*Legal documents*	*Type of pensions*	*Indexation*	
				Coefficient	*Minimum level*
2 Oct 98	1 Oct 98	RK Decree No. 990, dated October 2, 1998: *About pensions indexation from October 1, 1998*	minimum pension	2.3%	1999 min pension = 3000 tenge
3 Dec 99	1 Jan 00	RK Decree No. 1854, dated December 3, 1999: *About approval of rules for raising pensions paid by the SPPC.*	minimum pension	CPI accumulated from the last pension's indexation conducted on the October 1, 1998	2000 min pension = 3500 tenge
5 Mar 01	1 Jan 01	RK Decree No. 329 dated March 5, 2001: *About certain issues in raising pensions paid by the SPPC in 2001.*	all pensions < 10000 tenge	13% of 2000 min pension (2000 min pension = 3500 tenge, 13%*3500 = 455 tenge)	2001 min pension = 4000 tenge
11 Jan 02	1 Jan 02	RK Decree No. 31 dated January 11, 2002 No. 31: *About raising pensions paid by the SPPC as of January 1, 2002.*	All categories of pensions assigned before January 1, 1994	25%	2002 min pension = 4336 tenge
			All categories of pensions assigned before January 1, 1994, but which were recalculated on the base of higher wages for two years of working experience after initial pension assignment (in the case that a person kept working after retirement)	8.4%	

(Continued)

Appendix 6.2 (*Continued*)

Issue date	*Effective date*	*Legal documents*	*Type of pensions*	*Indexation*	
				Coefficient	*Minimum level*
			All categories of pensions assigned from January 1, 1994 through December 31, 1997	8.4%	
			All categories of pensions assigned from January 1, 1998 through December 31, 2001	8.4% of 2001 min pension (2001 min pension = 4000 tenge, 8.4% *4000 = 336 tenge)	
14 Jan 03	1 Jan 03	RK Decree No. 6 dated January 14, 2003: *About raising pensions paid by the SPPC as of January 1, 2003.*	All pensions assigned before January 1, 2003	12%	2003 min pension = 5250 tenge
29 Dec 03	1 Jan 04	RK Decree No. 1337 dated December 29, 2003: *About raising pensions paid by the SPPC as of January 1, 2004.*	All pensions assigned before January 1, 2004	5.4%	2004 min pension = 5800 tenge
21 Dec 04	1 Jan 05	RK Decree No. 1347 dated December 21, 2004: *About raising pensions paid by the SPPC as of January 1, 2005.*	All pensions assigned before January 1, 2005	7.7% 8.8%	2005 min pension = 6200 tenge
15 Dec 06	1 Jan 07	RK Decree No. 1212 dated December 15, 2006: *About raising pensions paid by the SPPC as of January 1, 2007.*	All pensions assigned before January 1, 2007	8.8%	2007 min pension = 7236 tenge

7

Performance of Pension Funds

7.1 Introduction

After ten years of collecting and investing 10% of the economy's wage income, Kazakhstani pension funds managed to accumulate an equivalent of 10% of GDP. This is second only to commercial banks, whose assets amounted to 90% of GDP by the end of 2007. However, if looked at as a source of old-age income, pension asset accumulations on their own have been insufficient. The chapter attempts to find explanations of why pension fund returns were underwhelming. The three 10s were produced by a combination of poor investment returns, pervasive tax evasion, and high wage growth. This chapter focuses on the first - investment returns.

As the subsequent analysis demonstrates, Kazakh pension funds were unable to channel their financial wealth into the economy. This chapter assesses performance of the pension funds over the last decade and attempts to explain why it was so poor. To some extent, performance reflects initial lack of scale economies, which in turn led to high costs as well as the consolidation of smaller funds (and migration of accounts).

Cost differences between the funds help explain the differences in their investment strategies and help understand the performance of the pension funds. Pension fund regulation also directly affected fund performance. However, other factors have played a far greater role in the pension funds' poor returns. These factors were of systemic nature and afflicted not only the pension funds but the rest of the economy as well. They include but are not limited to shallow and poorly developed capital markets as manifested by a dearth of investment instruments, the Dutch disease with its detrimental effects on competitiveness and rent seeking, shortage of experienced regulators and financial professionals, less than ideal corporate governance standards and low levels of disclosure, and an absence of shareholder activism focused on protecting investor rights.

7.2 Market Composition

By early 2008, pension assets reached 10% of GDP, or 1,208 billion tenge, or approximately US$10 billion. While the total assets of the pension system grew rapidly and steadily, some funds grew more rapidly than others. Figure 7.1.

illustrates the evolution of market organization since 1999 and reflects several secular patterns. Most critically, the share of the SAPF steadily declined. Many smaller funds merged or consolidated around the funds affiliated with large banks. In the last three years, the APFs owned by Bank Turan-Alem (BTA) and Halyk Bank continued to grow in relative importance, and the share of other non-government funds stabilized.

Usually, changes in market share can be explained by migration of the contributors to other funds and by faster wage growth of the contributors. Superior returns on assets explain the recent gain of the BTA fund. Appendix 7.1 provides timing details of the registration and consolidation process. The first six pension funds in Kazakhstan were created before January 1, 1998, the first day of the reform. Since that date, none of the funds have gone bankrupt, while two were taken over by other funds, one was liquidated because of the bankruptcy of the affiliated bank, and two corporate funds merged into an open fund.

Despite the SAPF's initial advantage, the contributors moved their accounts to other funds. The rise of private APFs reflects the emergence of confidence among Kazakhstan's labor force in the stability of the private funds, which in turn reflects growing confidence in the nation's private financial sector. However, concentration of assets remains high. In particular, as the SAPF's share of total pension fund assets has declined, the share held by Halyk Bank has risen almost commensurately. These two funds hold almost half of total pension assets.

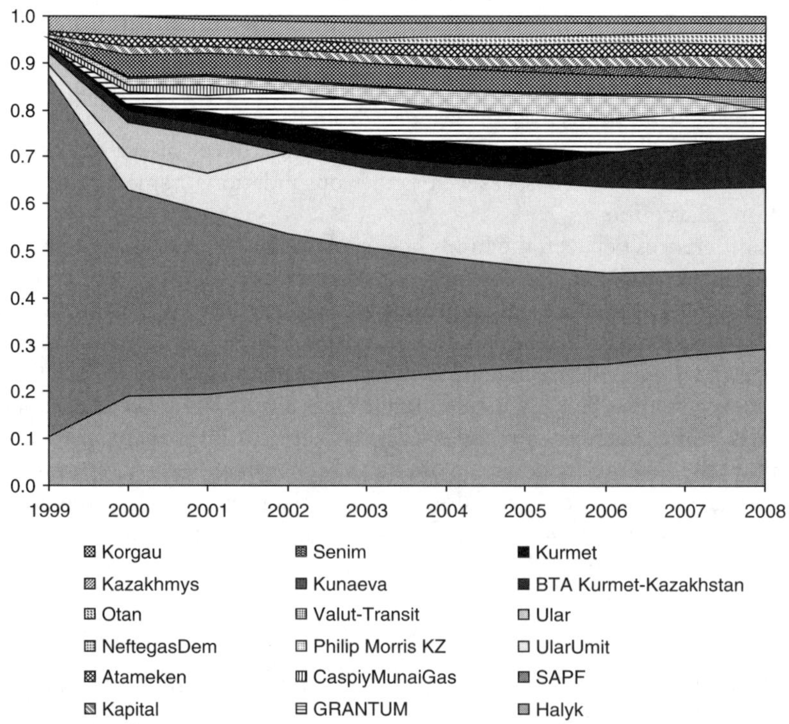

Figure 7.1 Evolution of market composition

7.3 Corporate versus Open Funds

One fact illustrates the difference in the economics of the two main types of funds better than anything else. The corporate funds had (and still have) much higher assets per account than the open funds yet did not become a viable alternative to open funds. The corporate pension fund of the multinational tobacco company Philip Morris accumulated some $5,000 per contributor after three years of operation. In twice as many years, the APF Kunaev, a small open fund, reached only a tenth of that number. Other corporate funds, such as those controlled by the multinational bank ABN-AMRO or the Caspian Oil and Gas company (KaspiyMunaiGas), had similar per account statistics. At the time, the tobacco sector paid the highest wages in the economy, four to five times the industrial average. Financial and mineral companies paid second highest wages, and also did so transparently, reporting payments to government authorities and making corresponding Accumulative account contributions.

Yet, despite higher per person contributions than most of Kazakhstan's contributions, corporate funds were still too small to break even. They had too few contributors and could not increase their numbers by accepting the contributors who migrated from other pension funds; they were limited on the revenue side by the limits on commission charges. As a result, most corporate funds consolidated or reorganized into open funds. Details are provided in Appendix 7.1.

7.4 Accumulative Fund Accounts: Descriptive Statistics

Unlike smaller companies, those companies that set up corporate pension funds pay wages regularly, do not pay wages in kind, do not have idle accounts, and do not have difficulties identifying individual account holders. The accounts of corporate pension funds receive regular contributions. Moreover, the turnover of the labor force in these companies is low. Only those workers who leave the company are able to transfer their pension accounts to other funds. Since few workers leave these companies, most accounts have been active since the first day of the or from the time that an employee joins the firm. At the same time, many accounts in open funds are dormant, either because the worker is no longer paying contributions or because the worker has opened a second account in the same or in a separate fund. The number of such dormant accounts remained surprisingly large at 39% in 2003. Pension funds often report the number of accounts instead of the number of contributors. The number of the taxpayers paying social tax in 2003 was equal to 3.87 million, very close to the number of APF contributors, 3.81 million. This is not a coincidence, because social tax payers are required to contribute to pension funds as well. The number of accounts exceeded the number of active contributors by 60% in 2003. The presence of these dormant accounts suggests that the number of pension fund contributors in any given year stands at approximately a half of total labor force, not four-fifth as the official statistics suggest. Table 7.1 provides a detailed picture of contributor accounts at the various APFs for the end of 2002, five years after the start of the reform.

Open funds also serve workers of different sectors and different regions, which leads to strong variation in sizes of pension accounts. Data from the SPPC on income distribution of the contributors in 2001 are used to compile table 7.1 and the other values reported here.

The contributions themselves come irregularly. Only 29% of all contributions in 2003 were made on a monthly basis, and 73% of the accounts had contributions made from 4 to 12 times a year. Some irregular payments may simply be late payments. Since the penalties for late payment are not large relative to the cost of funds, employers are clearly motivated to delay payments. Late wage payments are another factor of irregularity.

As expected, almost all accounts in corporate funds are active. The number of inactive accounts is the greatest among the funds that were started in 1998 when SICs were still assigned haphazardly.

The SAPF has the largest proportion of inactive accounts simply because it was the largest fund in the inaugural year of the reform, when a large number of wrong SICs were assigned to the SAPF by default (Chapter 3 describes the motivation for the default assignment). These blank accounts stayed with the SAPF while many functioning accounts eventually transferred to other funds. The SAPF continues to clean up the accounts of nonexisting people and to merge duplicate accounts. In 2003, only 0.7 million such unassigned accounts remained, down from 1.7 million in 1999. The remaining ones are harder to find.

Table 7.1 Share of total assets and total accounts, Accumulative Pension Funds, end of 2002

Fund	*Share of assets, %*	*Number of accounts (000)*	*Share of total accounts (%)*	*Share of voluntary accounts, %*	*Investment income/ pension Assets*	*Average size of pension account (US$)*
Capital	0.2	20.1	0.4%	7.2%	3%	31.1
Philip Morris Kazakhstan	0.2	1.2	0.0%	0.3%	13%	547.5
Kunaev	0.3	30.4	0.6	0.1	32	27.0
Otan	1.0	28.5	0.5	0.0	5	91.0
Korgau	1.5	65.0	1.2	0.0	15	60.3
Narodny	1.9	138.1	2.5	0.1	26	36.7
NefteGas-Dem	2.4	123.5	2.3	0.1	27	52.0
Kazakhstan	2.7	90:2	1.7	0.0	29	81.3
Valut-Transit	2.9	292.6	5.4	0.0	21	26.9
Kazakhmys	3.3	92.1	1.7	0.0	39	96.0
Kurmet	4.1	244.7	4.5	0.0	21	45.6
Senim	4.7	148.7	2.7	13.0	26	85.7
ABN AMRO-KaspiMunayGas	7.0	123.6	2.3	0.0	24	153.0
UlarUmit	17.2	811.6	15.0	0.4	29	57.1
Narodny Bank	22.5	914.7	16.9	0.0	28	66.5
SAPF	28.0	2,299.4	42.4	0.0	50	32.9
	100.0	**5,424.4**	**100.0**	**0.5**	**33**	**49.7**

Source: Authors' calculations

As would be expected, the distribution of pension fund contributors reflected the distribution of income in the population, with few high-income contributors and many low-income workers. For example, the average size of pension contributions collected in 2002 per active account came to US$117.6 and estimated average monthly contributor's income (EAMCI) was equal to US$98 per month. This 22% deviation of EAMCI from the average monthly income in all sectors of the economy in 2002 (US$126) most likely reflected the presence of a sizeable number of low-income, sporadically-contributing entrepreneurs. In 2002, self-employed workers constituted 13% of Kazakhstan's labor force, while among the self-employed, some 61% were SAPF customers. This ensured the small size of average yearly contributions (US$71–89) and the EAMCI of the SAPF (US$52–74) compared with most of the non-state APFs. In particular, low- and middle-income pension fund participants (especially those from rural areas) were far less susceptible to the non-state APFs' campaigns to attract new customers; for that matter, the private APFs had little interest in attracting customers from remote areas and with small contributions. In contrast, the SAPF was a ubiquitous and trusted institution, and therefore it retained the bulk of lower-income Accumulative fund participants.

On the whole, the data suggest that almost all of the hired (non-self-employed) population (which in 2002 numbered 4.03 million) were customers of some pension fund but that only 82% of them were effective contributors. Taking into consideration that out of all self-employed population, about one hundred and fifty thousand people were nominal customers and three hundred and fifty thousand were effective, it is reasonable to conclude that about one million accounts could be considered passive or duplicate on the basis of 2002 data. Those account holders do not contribute to their accounts either because they had emigrated without having closed their accounts, or because they had lost their jobs or had joined that portion of the self-employed population that prefers to evade taxes.

Thus, as our calculations of the percentage of effective contributors from hired labor (82%) and self-employed population (13%) are reasonably consistent with the estimates of social tax effective contributors in 2003 in Chapter 6, it is nearly certain that the potential for drawing new pension fund customers in Kazakhstan is far from ended. Indeed, were GoK to design an effective inducement for self-employed workers to pay contributions, about 2 million additional workers conceivably could become participants of the Accumulative pension system.

7.5 Costs and Revenues

During the first two years of operations almost all funds except for the SAPF and Halyk Bank APF lost money. The fact that APFs in their start-up period were loss making should not be surprising. Moreover, the fact that some of them reached break-even points or even started to make profits is almost startling, given that the fee rates established at the beginning of the reform were low in comparison with most other countries.

Initially, pension funds' charges were limited at 1% of contributions plus 10% of investment returns (IR; for details see Chapter 9). This fee structure was in place for four years, which turned out to be the favorable period of time in terms of investment returns of funds. In 2003, the 1% of contributions commission was replaced by .05% of commissions on assets. Commissions on investment incomes were raised from 10% to 15%. As a result, the total amount of commission fees slightly decreased compared with the preceding year. Evidently, the decline in base commissions on the entire account was greater than the rise in commissions on investment returns. This was not foreseen by the regulatory authorities, but rather stemmed from declining investment returns.

Low unit start-up costs can be attributed to the economies of scale in the larger APFs (e.g., SAPF, Halyk Bank APF). Without rejecting this hypothesis, it bears mention that with all similarities and differences in establishing the new pension system in Kazakhstan compared with other countries, there were conditions peculiar to Kazakhstani pension funds during their start-up period, namely, the association of many with concurrently developing financial institutions. These conditions laid the foundations for the classification of pension funds of Kazakhstan by their association with commercial banks.

The rationale for categorizing APFs in this manner arises from the historical evidence that the pension funds having a commercial bank with substantial retail operations as founder or major shareholder had advantages over the funds associated with corporate commercial banks, while the latter funds had advantages over APFs with no bank association. This situation in Kazakhstani pension funds is explained by a simple fact that banks, especially those associated with an APF, supported pension funds by using their broad agent networks and general corporate advertising and visibility to attract contributors. Moreover, in practice, the choice between one APF or another depends mostly on the relationship between managers of firms and the banks that are founders or shareholders of a particular APF. Thus, if an enterprise had a banking relationship with a particular bank, it would be highly likely to adopt that bank's affiliated APF for its Accumulative payments. While individuals could later change pension funds, this initial linkage inevitably gave a home field advantage to the incumbent APF. Consequently, it is reasonable to divide Kazakhstan's APFs into three following categories: (1) pension funds whose founders or major shareholders are linked with commercial banks with substantial retail operations, (2) pension funds whose founders or major shareholders are linked with corporate commercial banks, and (3) pension funds with no bank association.

In the light of our classification, it is possible to explain why the Kunaev pension fund could not take advantage of being one of the first APFs to enter the pension fund market, and was left behind by younger funds such as Korgau, Capital, and Otan that entered the market three or four years later. Lack of strong founders during the whole period of Kunaev's operations and the absence of its association with a commercial bank was, in our opinion, a critical reason for its inability to afford the number of contributors necessary to break even, by attracting 150,000–200,000 customers. We can make the same conclusions regarding APF Korgau and NefteGaz-Dem, which also belong to the third category of funds according to our classification. Conditions are different for the remaining two funds in that category. These two, the corporate funds of Philip Morris and the copper smelting giant Kazakkhmys, have small numbers because of their restrictive purview, though their captive market, absence of advertising, and high levels of steady contributions translate into far lower administrative costs than other funds. In general, it will be difficult for unaffiliated APFs to survive a period of recessionary economic conditions or tightening of prudential norms.

APFs included in the second category have a much better safety margin. Yet all of them, possibly excluding APF Otan, suffer from having a contributor base below the level necessary to break even. As for Otan, the reason behind its immaturity is its late market entry. In general, all funds that belong to this category can be characterized as funds that cover corresponding labor market segments as they are under the patronage of medium-sized banks or a particular kind of financial group.

The first category superficially may appear miscellaneous because it covers all groups of asset intervals; in other words, it includes both small-, medium-, and large-sized APFs. Nevertheless, there is a sense to consider them in one category because of the features several common features.

From the beginning, APF Narodny Bank had more favorable conditions than other nonstate APFs owing to the brand name of "people's bank" and the availability of the wide regional network of its major founder, Narodny Bank of Kazakhstan (later changed to Halyk Bank: Halyk is the Kazakh and Narodny the Russian word for "People's"). Starting its activity by opening offices in all regions of Kazakhstan, which were authorized to conclude pension agreements on behalf of the fund, it could attract significant number of contributors throughout the nation. Having also significant number of contributors employed at major blue chip enterprises such as the state railroad, Kazakhstan Temir Zholy, NNK Kazakhoil, NKTN Kaztransoil, and joint company KEGOC, APF Narodny Bank became a leading contender among nonstate APFs capable of competing with SAPF. Certainly, the competent and stable management of this APF has played a big role in its achievement of such considerable results throughout its operating history.

Unlike APF Narodny Bank, Ular-Umit has been created as a merger of three APFs, Ular, Umit, and Trade Unions. However, the merger did not live upto expectations. Before merging, Ular and Umit had together almost the same number of contributors as APF Narodny/Halyk Bank. But after merging, the gap between UlarUmit and Narodny/Halyk began to widen rapidly. However, UlarUmit enjoys the support of a large bank, just as APF of Halyk Bank does, which has helped UlarUmit to hold on to its market share.

Two medium-sized funds, namely, Kurmet and Kazakhstan, have the same major shareholder, TuranAlem Bank. One would expect them to merge, and they eventually did so in 2004. The youngest APF, Capital, which entered into the market later than others, dared to compete with the established pension funds most likely because of Bank Center Credit's (BCC) assistance in financing its promotion costs and the strategy of attracting new members through BCC's services on preferential terms.

The goal of this discussion is to show that the essential component of pension funds' activities in drawing new customers and establishing their operations during the start-up period was the shareholder's structure and, particularly, commercial banks' presence among them. However, it seems likely that, after the start-up period, the most critical determinant of a given pension fund's results was the cost of drawing new customers and advertising. Available data allow us to compare costs attributed to these purposes to estimate pension fund account growth for each APF, as well as for account transfers from one APF to another. From this comparison, it is clear that the funds that enjoyed the biggest growth in their customer numbers in 2002–3 also had largest amounts of administration costs and costs of drawing new customers, including advertising costs. Thus, APFs faced the choice between pursuing a low administrative expense but low growth strategy versus a high cost/high growth approach. The likely Nash equilibrium in such an environment is that of one or a few large APFs, possibly along with a number of small niche players.

7.6 Portfolio Composition

Pension funds in almost all emerging markets that embarked on pension privatization reforms have been hard-pressed to construct a balanced and well-diversified portfolio in a financial environment with limited liquidity and pervasive opaqueness. Kazakhstan has not been an exception. Initially, the portfolio of the funds was filled with GoK bonds of short maturity. This practice gave way to more widespread use of long-term GoK bonds, until the government sharply reduced their supply during 2002–3. Since its peak, the proportion of GoK bonds in APF portfolios has declined by 30 percentage points. Eventually, as the funds were allowed to hold more corporate paper, the share of corporate bonds increased to 25% and the share of equity to 15%. The shares and the bonds today have become a stable presence in the portfolio of every fund. In the interim, the gap was filled by the short-term NBK bonds, which are highly liquid and with very low average yield. Figure 7.2 demonstrated the changes in the portfolio composition of an average fund.

7.7 Effect of Currency Appreciation on Returns

In the beginning of 2003, the Kazakh currency unexpectedly started to appreciate versus the U.S dollar. The tenge's appreciation reflected rising oil and minerals' prices, but despite the fairly transparent cause, few if any bankers, economists, or public officials in Kazakhstan ever envisioned a strong tenge/weak dollar era. Needless to say, although pension funds' liabilities were in tenge and many assets were dollar-denominated, none had hedged against their currency exposure. Since most securities in the portfolios of pension funds were denominated in U.S. dollars, the return on pension assets started to decline rapidly. As a result, almost all APFs showed negative real rates of return in 2004 and have had weak performances since then as well. The unexpected event affected the performance of all funds, providing a stress test for the system, since it is challenging to adjust the portfolios with a lack of liquid assets. Subsequently, some funds began to use hedge exchange rate risks, but the share of foreign investments has never reached the same level since.

The greatest losses from tenge appreciation were experienced by the funds that failed to convert dollar-denominated securities to tenge. Moreover, it is necessary to emphasize that in the middle of 2003, a transition to a new methodology of estimation of pension assets occurred in connection with the transition of APFs and AMCs to international standards of financial reporting. According to older

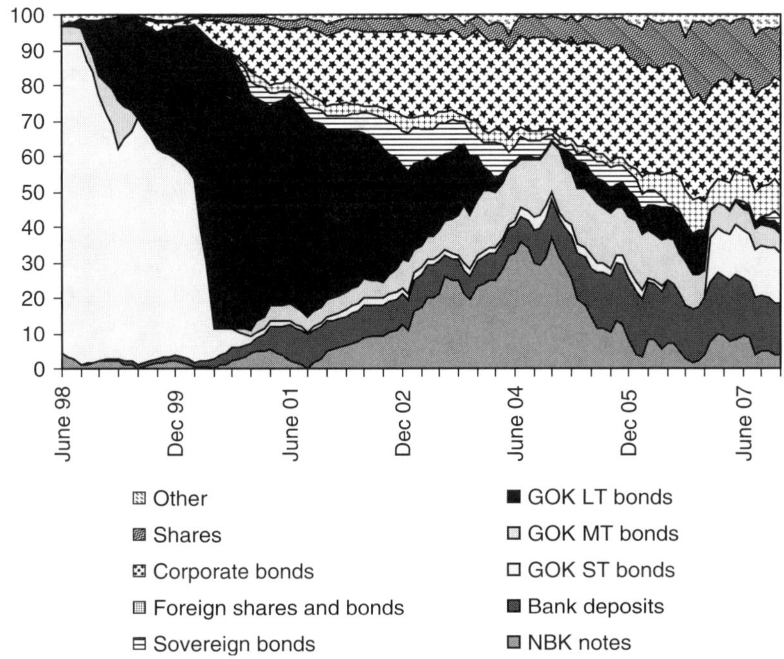

Figure 7.2 Portfolio of pension funds

accounting standards, securities were valued at the face value or at cost of purchase. This failure to 'mark-to-market' tended to overstate the returns on pension assets.

Tenge appreciation caused asset losses in all firms and at the same time suppressed returns, since APFs were accustomed to benefiting in tenge terms from appreciation of foreign-currency denominated assets, and this gain vanished. The impact of marking to market was a bit more ambiguous. While in a few APFs there was a "positive reassessment" that showed that investment portfolios of these funds were underestimated, the majority of APFs have received a negative assessment. That is, net assets were revalued downward, and the losses contributed further to decreases in net investment income as a percentage of pension assets during the reassessment years (2003–4) in comparison with prior years.

Also contributing to the decline in the APFs' net investment returns and related to the tenge's appreciation was the decline in real returns on GoK and NBK securities, where a majority of pension funds assets were invested during 2002–4. Rising petroleum and other raw material export prices meant increased GoK royalties and tax revenues, hence reduced need for debt finance, and hence reduced interest rates—especially in real terms, since demand pressures have gradually translated into rising inflation. Reduced GoK financing needs and debt yields translated into a decline in attractive high-return, low-risk investment opportunities for pension fund assets. Regulations governing AMCs' investments exacerbated matters, as in 2002–3, not less than 35% of pension assets were required to be invested in government securities. Indeed, during 2003—4, the budgetary deficit was negligible

Table 7.2 Real return (%) on assets, Accumulative Pension Funds, 1998–2004

	To previous year					
	Dec 1998–Dec 1999	*Dec 1999–Dec 2000*	*Dec 2000–Dec 2001*	*Dec 2001–Dec 2002*	*Dec 2002–Dec 2003*	*Dec 2003–Dec 2004*
Valut-Transit		5.36	7.54	5.42	−0.53	−1.88
Kunaev		5.79	7.56	4.94	−2.05	−1.75
Narodny	46.54	7.63	8.48	5.50	0.69	−0.03
Kazakhstan		6.29	9.53	6.26	−1.36	0.33
Narodny Bank	47.47	6.63	8.10	5.73	0.54	−3.78
Kazakhmys	51.10	7.75	7.96	6.02	−3.19	−0.43
UlarUmit	45.52	7.25	7.38	5.98	−0.88	−1.83
NefteGasDem	46.23	-	8.82	6.12	−1.16	−1.60
Kurmet		5.22	9.53	6.26	−1.50	−1.83
ABN AMRO-KaspiMunaiGas	44.30	5.25	7.62	5.67	0.56	−1.88
Senim		6.61	8.57	5.92	−0.01	−2.40
Korgau			8.57	4.47	−1.05	−3.73
Philip Morris Kazakhstan				4.52	0.34	x
Otan				3.07	0.10	0.18
Capital				-	−0.26	−1.56
SAPF	29.13	4.50	8.87	7.69	1.87	−4.92

Source: Authors' calculation

(1% in 2003 and 0.3% in 2004) and budgetary surpluses were achieved in 2002 (0.03%) and 2005 (0.6%). In spite of the fact that there was no need for domestic borrowing, MinFin issued securities solely in order to support pension funds—in effect, amounting to a subsidy to the APFs from the government of Kazakhstan.

In fact, the pension funds' negative real rates of return became a source of great anxiety in 2004–6 not only for the pension funds and AMCs themselves but also for the GoK. This is evidenced by the fact that in the beginning of July 2006, Prime Minister Danial Akhmetov, charged the MLSP to develop with evolving a strategy for the development of measures to help raise real rates of return of pension funds. Earlier still, in response to an order from the president (Order no. 3274, dated August 12, 2004), Prime Minister Akhmetov set forth a *Program of Development of the Accumulative Pension System* (Order no. 281-p of the prime minister) aimed at stabilizing and improving the Accumulative system. Important projects included introducing government guarantees of pension fund deposits, efforts to increase the share of long-term financial instruments available to funds, introduction of systematic hedging of foreign currency risk by the funds, issuance of long-term, inflation-indexed government securities, and the development of project finance opportunities and the development of new securities' and stock-market options for the pension funds.

Of course, all of these measures could not immediately take effect to increase real pension returns. Therefore, in order to mitigate public dissatisfaction with pension assets' yields, since April 2005, the Financial Supervisory Agency (FSA) ceased publishing annual estimates of returns on pension assets, and instead now published three-year weighted average rate of return data. While doing so is not strictly inappropriate, especially as pension funds are intended to be making long-term investment decisions and should not be unduly concerned about short-term financial fluctuations, the data-smoothing exercise is obfuscatory, and at the same time seems unlikely to bolster confidence in the soundness of pension fund investments.

As of December 2006, 16.90% of assets of the pension funds were invested in short-term, medium-term, and long-term securities of the MinFin, 1.44% were in NBK notes, and 50.51% were held in stocks and bonds of nongovernment securities issued by domestic issuers. Putting a positive spin on the remarkable shift in pension fund assets, the reduction of the share of investment in state securities from 95% in 1998 to 17% in 2004 and a corresponding rise of the share of investments in corporate bonds can be regarded as a major step toward pension funds' participation in investment in Kazakhstan's real sector. This shift out of funding of public sector debt—a major objective of Accumulative reformers that is rarely realized—has been achieved in Kazakhstan to a degree that could not possibly have been foreseen at the outset of the reform. In effect, the reform has created a pool of funds quite unusual in middle-income countries. Pension funds' assets are not greatly needed by government, nor are they of use to the truly massive oil and raw materials' investments underway, as these rely on global funding. Thus, the pension funds provide a pool for medium-sized industries, local governments' securities, and for securitized bundles of smaller debts.

7.8 Conclusion

Poor performance of the pension funds should be seen in context. If their returns are measured against the wage growth, which makes sense for evaluating the advantages of a fully funded system over PAYGO, then their performance falls far short of their original promise as a social security institution. If pension funds' performance is measured in terms of real returns, it appears barely adequate at 1%. However, if the performance is understood in the context of the many factors that tended to limit portfolio choices of the funds and suppress the returns on assets, then the funds appear to have lived up to their potential. What the pension system needs now is not criticism of the funds, but an attempt to understand the underlying causes of their poor performance in order to develop effective policy. Continued regulatory improvements, discussed in Chapter 9, are critical, as is improved transparency. Addressing Dutch disease effects is also important, but none are so policy relevant as the regulatory effects on the performance of pension funds.

Appendix 7.1

APF: Date of establishment, number of licenses, and evolution

N		*Type*	*1997–1998*	*1999*	*2000*	*2001*	*2002*	*2004*	*2005–2007*
1	UlarUmit (until Mar 2001 –APF Umit)	OC	No. 1, 27 Nov 1997		Umit merged with Trade Unions on 29 Oct 2000	Umit merged with Ular into UlarUmit on 3 Sep 2001			
2	Valut-Transit	OC	No. 2, 27 Nov 97						Liquidated in Summer 2007
3	Kunaev	OC	No. 3, 10 Dec 97	Zhardem joined to Kunaev on 1999					
4	Atameken (until April, 2006 – Narodny APF)	OC	No. 4, 24 Dec 1997						Narodny Renamed Atameken on 6 Apr 2005
5	SAPF	OC	No. 6, 29 Dec 1997						
6	BTA Kurmet - Kazakhstan (until 9. 2004 – Kazakhstan)	OC	No. 7, 02.02.98					Kazakhstan merged Kurmet on 9 Nov 2004	

7	Narodny Bank	OC	No. 8, 2 Feb 1998 (No. 22 since Nov2003)						
8	NefteGas-Dem	OC	No. 12, 8 May 1998						
9	Grantum (until April 6, 2006 - ABN AMRO-KaspiMunaiGas)	OC				No. 19, 16 Feb 2001		Philip Morris Kazakhstan joined to ABN AMRO-KaspiMunai-Gas on 25 Oct 2004	ABN AMRO KaspiMunai-Gas is renamed Grantum 6 Apr 2006 -
10	Senim	OC		No. 16, 8 Jul 1999					
11	Korgau	OC		No. 17, 17 Nov 1999					
12	Capital	OC					No. 21, 23 Jan. 2002		
13	Otan	OC				No. 20, 1 Nov. 2001	-"-		
14	Kazakhmys	OC	No. 9, 11 Feb. 1998						

(*Continued*)

Appendix 7.1 (*Continued*)

N	*Type*	*1997–1998*	*1999*	*2000*	*2001*	*2002*	*2004*	*2005–2007*
APFs that have closed as the result of mergers with other APFs:								
Zhardem	OC	No. 5, 26 Dec 1997	___1999 joined to Kunaev	closed				
Trade Unions	OC		No. 14, 3 Feb 1999	joined to Umit 29 Oct 2000	closed			
Ular	OC	No. 10, 20 Mar 1998		3-Sep-01 merged with Umit into UlarUmit	closed			
ABN AMRO	OC		No. 15, 22 Feb 1999		merged with KaspiMunaiGas into ABN AMRO-KaspiMunaiGas on 1 Mar 2001	closed		
KaspiMunaiGas	OC	No. 11, 17 Apr 1998	No. 11, 16 Apr 1999		merged with ABN AMRO into ABN AMRO-KaspiMunaiGas on 1 Mar 2001	closed		

Philip Morris Kazakhstan	OC			No. 18, 01 Feb 2001	joined to ABN AMRO-KaspiMunai-Gas on 25 Oct 2004	closed
Kurmet	OC	No. 13, 16 Nov 1998			merged with Kazakhstan 9 Nov 2004	closed

OC - open fund, CC - corporate fund

8

Legal Aspects of the Accumulative Pension System

Substantial pressure on legal institutions has been an important feature of Kazakhstan's pension reform. While the entire legal system began undergoing intensive change with independence in 1991, the most intensive of these changes undoubtedly occurred during the period 1996–2000 when different types of institutional investors emerged.

Maintaining the traditional, Soviet-era legal doctrine could not effectively establish the legal status of assets or financial instruments in a manner consistent with the normal activity of modern financial markets. The limitations that arose concerned foremost the fundamental provisions of the right of ownership but to some extent also involved other similar property-right statuses known as proprietary rights under Kazakhstan's continental law. Initial changes to the legal base did not affect its fundamentals, as they were aimed mainly at filling in the law with new economic and political ideas characteristic of the market economy and did not address legal methodology. The result was a situation in which accelerating institutional change was retarded by traditional views regarding property rights, while the swiftness of asset ownership changes realized in the financial market collided with the conservative approach to these issues in the Civil Code.

As financial assets do not contain specific, distinguishing features, it is impossible to identify the owner of a particular property when these assets are under control of an institutional investor. However, bankruptcy and general creditors' suits demand a clear-cut definition of the monetary assets' and financial instruments' owners. The need to assign ownership does not cause problems elsewhere under the common law system, which permits the creation of trusts. However, the issue was a major problem in Kazakhstan, with its basic legal doctrine demanding definition of the property owner at any time and in any place. The impossibility of determining the property owner provides a basis for recognition of an asset as ownerless, with the implication that ownership should revert to the state.[1] However, even when the property owner was known, another danger existed in that the creditors, including those of the institution holding the property, could take recourse against the property. This naturally caused risks for the institutional investors and those who transferred money to financial institutions. These risks adversely affected public confidence in the new type of the institutional investors, namely, the APFs that were established to ensure the material well-being of elderly and disabled people, thereby fulfilling a key right enshrined in the national constitution.

The lack of preparation of Kazakhstan's legal base and its rapid reform implementation generated an extreme situation for the law—an attempt to impose completely new ideas on the basis of old legislation structure and concepts. The rush to undertake reforms was driven by economic forces outlined in earlier chapters, and the need to reduce budgetary pressures did not allow time to carefully prepare a new legal base. In this context, Kazakhstan's experience in reforming its pension system differs sharply from that in pre-existing market economies, as new economic institutions were imposed despite initial conflict with the existing legal tradition. The following sections address in greater detail some of the legal aspects of Kazakhstan's Accumulative pension system that required careful attention during the process of the reforms, and which even today keeps experts busy in making further modifications to the nation's legal code.

8.1 Development of the Legal Structure

8.1.1 The Legal Structure and Development of Kazakhstan's Accumulative Pension System

A three-pillar social security system with a core mandatory, individual account, funded, defined-contribution Accumulative pension system has been implemented over the course of the past decade, with APFs at the center of this system. Other elements of the system include pension asset management companies (AMCs) and custodian banks (CBs). After obtaining a license to carry out investment activity, an APF also acquires the right to invest pension assets independently, that is, without involvement of an AMC, but many funds continue to rely on AMCs. Relationships between the elements of the pension system are built as follows: (1) a pension fund, an AMC, and a CB enter into a contract governing the terms and conditions of pension assets' custody; (2) the pension fund and the AMC sign a contract establishing conditions for the investment management of pension assets; and (3) if a pension fund carries out investment activity independently, then it simply enters into contractual relations with a CB.

The relationships of the contributors with these various elements of the pension system and the Accumulative pension system as a whole are subject to common rules and are based on a pension contract that a contributor signs with an APF. Each contributor's obligation to sign a pension contract is mandated by the Pension Law. Direct obligations set forth in the law put the system's mandatory nature into practice, while contributors' choices are restricted to the freedom to choose whichever pension fund he or she prefers. Thus, the Pension Law activated the new system but did so as a mandatory, top-down initiative from the government. While this approach was necessitated by the nation's deteriorating public finances, it may also have affected the underlying attitude of state regulations, and it seems fair to characterize the pension system as one in which the authorized state agency (now the FSA), rather than competitive market forces, plays the leading role.

The remainder of this section emphasizes the pension system's legal dynamics. These legal system changes did not involve major innovations but, rather, largely adopted the Chilean practices. In accordance with legal requirements, contributors need to choose a pension fund and sign a contract therewith. The contract used is a model contract and is standardized across all APFs. The authorized state regulatory agency controls the compliance of actual pension contracts with a model contract. Once a contract is signed, a contributor is obliged to pay contributions as soon as he or she earns income.

There are a number of technical differences involving when and how contributions are paid. If a contributor has an employer, then the employer pays contributions on behalf of the contributor, thereby acting as an agent with regard to transfer of the contributor's money to APF. Otherwise, the contributor is responsible for making direct payments. Once payments are made, the chosen APF is licensed to accept these contributions and will accumulate, account, and invest them either independently or through an AMC. Legislation further specifies the types of financial instruments in which pension assets may be invested and also delineates investment limits for each instrument. Earned investment income is then distributed among the APF contributors prorated according to their accumulated savings in the individual pension accounts, less commission charges of the APF, and, if present, the AMC.

When conditions for payouts as specified in the Pension Law are met, pensions are paid to the recipients provided that they have submitted documents confirming their rights to receive their pension assets. The list of such documents is determined by special instructions issued by the current state supervisory agency. However, the main criterion for payout is the fact that a contributor has reached the legally specified retirement age (63 years for men and 58 for women).

All pension monies and financial instruments bought with pension fund deposits are kept in CBs, and a special regime is applied to ensure against the possibility of mixing the custodial bank's money with these pension assets. Moreover, a bank planning to carry out custodial activity must obtain a special license that requires it to meet supplemental criteria to ensure that it is a reliable financial institution.

An unusual feature of Kazakhstan's pension system model is that money from the contributors or transferring agent does not go directly to a CB. Instead, it first enters the transitional accounts of a special government organization, the SPPC. The SPPC keeps records of the contribution transfers to the pension system, keeps information about the transactions, and assigns SICs that identify the contributors and recipients within the system. The SPPC also ensures the security of the system by maintaining backup databases that record all payments by pension contributors to their APFs. In addition, the SPPC supports the public Solidarity system by paying state pensions.

Broadly speaking, limited attention to the legal framework during the period of preparation for the reforms left several unresolved issues in the Accumulative system's legal model. The new pension model was first announced in a Concept document regarding pension system reform approved by the government in March 1997. This Concept was not a final bill, but rather anticipated the model would be discussed and possibly amended, much as would be a bill presented from the government to its parliament. However, the traditional (from the Soviet era and earlier) and still prevailing practice was to accept the government's declarations as the *only* possible approach, thereby restricting all but modest deviations from the structure proposed in the Concept. The core element—creation of Accumulative pension funds—did not receive a thorough review to determine its legal status, or the rights to assets the APFs attracted from contributors. It was taken for granted that the APF was a legal entity that accumulated pension contributions and paid out pensions. Nobody raised the questions of exactly *who* owned the assets accumulated by APFs and what would happen to these assets if the APF creditors were to take recourse against them. Indeed, it appears that the government did not perform any legal modeling during the process of preparation for the reform. In April 1997, USAID-funded experts suggested a variant of the Pension Law, in which emphasis was made on the establishment of the pension trusts with a view to ensure the pension assets' protection against APF creditors; and the then valid Article 156 of the Civil Code of Kazakhstan that could be used as a bridge between the Anglo-Saxon trust concept and continental law.

Subsequently, though, this bridging article was excluded from the Civil Code, as leading local legal scholars declared it problematic as it involved mixing different legal approaches. Their basis for this rejection was that the brief mentioning of trust operations in the Civil Code was not supported by further disclosure and regulation, either in the Civil Code or in any other legislative acts. They further argued that the concept of a legal trust itself contradicted both the continental doctrine and the existing Kazakhstani principles that determined the right of ownership as a "triad" consisting of the right of ownership, right of use, and right of disposal. More fundamentally, the draft law outlined in the Concept failed to win the support of the local legal establishment because its structure and mentality did not coincide with existing legal language used in Kazakhstan and, in particular, did not make use of statement stylistics reminiscent of the Soviet era.

Further rejection of the trust concept was dictated as well by the nation's conservative legal establishment. Those government lawyers who regularly advised prominent local civil lawyers refused flatly to use the trust and instead declared it an institution not inherent in the local legislation. An alternative would have been to use the so-called *fiducia* as a substitute for trusts, as it appears to be more acceptable under Kazakhstan's continental law, but insufficient knowledge and experience prevented it from being adapted. While it has appeared in some legal systems, notably Canada's Québec province, the fiducia as a legal institution was not sustained by a significant number of examples from international practice. An absence of experts familiar with the fiducia system also appears to have prevented it from being suggested as an alternative during the period of preparation for the reform.

The structure whereby the SPPC serves as an agent for pension contribution transfer also came under criticism. The first draft of the Pension Law did not specify that SPPC would serve in this capacity; rather, it was specified as the mandatory transfer agent in GoK Decree No. 1733. This decree was in fact implemented over the objections of many expatriate consultants and APF representatives, who felt that it contradicted the Pension Law and introduced an additional, unnecessary link in the chain of the contribution flow to APFs. Of particular concern was the decree's failure to stipulate any responsibility on the part of the SPPC for making prompt contribution transfers to CBs or impose any penalties for failing to do so. There was also concern that the SPPC would use pension contributions to APFs to pay benefits to the PAYGO pensioners (as appears to be happening at present in China). These suspicions were mainly based on the persistent unwillingness of the government to incorporate into the legislation penalties for the SPPC in the event of delays in contribution transfers. As events have unfolded, these fears have proven unwarranted, but that does not mean that they were wrong *ex ante*. A similar reform implemented in a country with less fiscally sound macro policy and poorer export earnings could easily result in pilferage of private contributions to meet public obligations. As of today the Pension Law contains the earlier-mentioned penalties.

8.1.2 A Financial Institution or an Institution of Social Security?

During the period in which Kazakhstan's Accumulative system model came into being and related fundamental legal principles were formed, the issue arose as to whether pension funds should be seen primarily as financial entities or as social security institutions. This issue was widely discussed in government, parliament, and mass media and in turn involved debate over government's objectives with respect to pension funds as well as the extent of public regulation. The government control doctrine that has emerged in Kazakhstan now regards pension funds and other financial institutions as private bodies subject to regulation by a special governmental authority.

The intention has been to ensure efficient government regulatory management under a single agency. However, in practice, areas exist in which two or more state authorities have some jurisdiction, reducing efficiency and leading to more bureaucracy and conflict. There are also spheres in which a regulatory "duopoly" has appeared due to overlapping characteristics of particular sectors. For example, the activity of Kazakhstan's sole credit bureau is regulated by one agency in the area of disclosure and information and by another agency with responsibility for financial markets and financial organizations. The former regulates general aspects of the information-collecting process in the country and existed prior to the appearance of the credit bureau; the latter regulates activities of the credit bureau as an organization that serves the banking sector. Both agencies issue normative legal acts, and perfect administrative consistency would require efforts to ensure that these acts do not contradict one another, and hence that there should be a mechanism to assess and remove conflicts. However, apart from information services, which were provided by various companies before the credit bureau was formed, the pension services of private funds in effect were an institutional innovation. Thus, as the Accumulative pension model was developed from scratch, from the outset there was a chance to determine the nature of the APF as a financial body, a social security institution, or a specific entity regulated by special legislation. Doing so would have provided the foundation for establishment of the unified state regulatory body; by failing to do so, the result has been multiple regulators for the first several years of the reforms.

Indeed, as we detail elsewhere, the pension system has had a remarkable history of changing regulatory bodies. During the first years of the new pension system, APFs were regulated by the National Pension Agency, which in turn was accountable to the MLSP, while the AMCs were regulated by the National Securities Commission. Thereafter, both the APFs and AMCs were regulated by the NBK. While government control has since been unified under the new FSA combining supervision on all financial institutes, APF regulation remains a sensitive issue: the problem has been solved from the practical point of view, but potential conflicts still remain because APFs play a social as well as a financial role, while they are regulated by a state body that has extpertise only in the regulation of financial sector institutions.

Furthermore, as regulations are gradually designed and implemented, the problem of setting priorities need to be addressed on an ongoing basis. The latest amendments to the Pension Law concerning the limits of the APF liabilities can be taken as an example. Currently, APFs are liable to their contributors for an amount equal to all received contributions, with due adjustment for inflation.[2] Moreover, the GoK guarantees safety of all APF assets. These regulations thus imply a social security priority.

However, other government regulations give priority to financial aspects, such as the absence in the earlier-mentioned regulations of any limits to APF liabilities, or the understanding of accumulated pension savings only as the funds kept in the contributors' individual accounts. We address these issues in more detail later, and simply note here that under such approaches, one could regard an APF as having fulfilled its liabilities to the contributor, even if it ultimately paid out a sum that is only a tiny fraction of the amount of pension contributions paid in. To see how this apparent contradiction emerges, one has to appreciate narrow legal nuances. The Pension Law charges the APFs with responsibility to pay out pension savings to the contributors; and as "pension savings," the law meant the funds actually available in a contributor's individual pension account. The inconsistency stems from the fact that the idea of the governmental guarantees to pension recipients came from the MLSP, which was responsible for further development of the social sphere, while representatives of the NBK tended to understand the Accumulative pension system primarily as a financial institution. These conflicting forces may have been greater in Kazakhstan than elsewhere, since virtually nowhere else was an Accumulative system reform used to jump-start an entire financial sector. However, in Kazakhstan, the reform model was transformed with the simultaneous, competing pressures of two institutions, namely, the MLSP and NBK. Although there is now a single regulator, both of these bodies (and other agencies) continue to seek to influence regulation of the Accumulative system.

It is not important from the pensioners' perspective which ministry is in charge of pension security. However, in order to understand the gravity of this problem, one should consider Kazakhstani legal doctrine and tradition. With the gradual strengthening of the executive power within the government, and hence the growing importance of the branch ministries and committees, the choice of regulatory ministry or agency acquires increasing significance. Furthermore, with maturation of the executive power structure, increased differentiation of effort is taking place. Each ministry and committee acquires a narrow specialization, and hence their spheres of influence and focus are increasingly divergent. The result is the emergence of differences of interests and conflicts among various ministries, as each is interested in having as much power as possible and answers to different interest groups.

Thus, the existence of two regulating governmental authorities in one system is fraught with power struggles. At the same time, it is unrealistic to recognize pension funds solely as either financial or social security institutions. The Accumulative pension system in Kazakhstan is now mandatory and eventually will overshadow. With this ultimate transfer of responsibilities, the government has imposed the function of the pension security of its citizens, for which previously it was completely responsible, on private pension funds, implying that one cannot regard these funds only as financial organizations. Article 28 of the Constitution of the Republic of Kazakhstan contains an absolute statement of the governmental guarantee of a minimum pension. At the same time, the financial nature of the APF makes it impossible to consider it as a pure social security institution, so that regulation must satisfy both social and financial considerations. In practice, the lack of effective compromise may manifest itself in diametrically opposite trends in the process of law making, as exemplified by the conflicting implications of limits to APF liabilities and governmental guarantees with regard to the private pension funds' liability to their contributors.

In developed market counties, this sort of conflict is avoided. Private Accumulative pension funds are regarded as a strictly financial business and have a fiduciary responsibility to seek to earn high income on pension assets, while the public sector is charged with ensuring minimal well-being of the elderly. In contrast, key objectives of Kazakhstan's pension reform included reducing pressures on the state budget and improving the private investment climate; it is likely that in the difficult times of 1996–98, improvements in social security were seen as a secondary objective after economic recovery. However, the pace of growth has vastly exceeded expectations, resulting in rising expectations of and demands for a stronger "social" component to the nation's pension system. With rapid economic growth since 2000 and a greatly strengthened GoK fiscal position, it appears that the conflict is being resolved along the lines of developed market economies, with government shouldering responsibility for ensuring minimal well-being of its retired and disabled citizens.

8.2 Problems in the Evolution of Pension Legislation

We have noted already that during the introduction of the new pension model, both lawyers and nonlawyers debated options caused by the attempt to adapt the new legal concepts to the old conservative underpinnings of local legislation. Below, some of the most significant of these issues are discussed in detail.

8.2.1 Who Owns Pension Assets?

The issue of how well pension assets are protected against the endeavors of other entities is connected directly with another issue pertaining to ownership and legal status of pension assets. Kazakhstan's legal doctrine states that the owner is held liable for all of his or her property, and hence, if one cares about the safety of the pension assets, it is critical to know to whom they belong and whose liability risks may endanger their safety.

The initial draft of the Pension Law adopted in 1997 delicately parried this question as the drafters faced a situation that was complex and poorly understood by parliamentarians and most of local legal experts. The Civil Code understands the right of ownership as the sum (known in Russian legal terminology as a *triad prav*, or triad of rights) of three elements: the right to own, the right to use, and the right to dispose. The right to own means the right to possess something; the right to use means to derive its useful properties; and the right to dispose means having a possibility to decide its "destiny," that is, to transfer or sell an asset. These concepts date without revision from Roman private law. The delicate silence of the Pension Law drafters with regard to this issue had two consequences. First, money does not possess any distinguishing features. Thus, when a contributor transfers money to the APF, he or she loses the right of ownership to this money, as it is supposed that the contributor eventually will reclaim not the money that he or she has transferred to the fund before but rather its equivalent. If one then supposes that the APF or the CB that keeps the contributor's money becomes its owner, the doctrinal premise about the owner being liable for all the property would apply also to the pension assets. Clearly, this interpretation has a potentially disastrous consequence, but at the same time it was equally dangerous to regard the contributor as the owner. Under the latter approach, a creditor could take recourse against the contributor's pension assets if the contributor was in debt; in the former case, creditors can seek to attach the assets if the APF or the CB has a liability. In principle, this problem easily could have been resolved, as it reflected the absence of legislation governing the establishment of trusts in the form understood in common law systems. Just the idea of introducing the trust in its genuine meaning into the local legislation was strongly opposed by prominent Kazakhstani legal scholars, who argued that both equity law and a set of cases that further established legal practice were prerequisite.

A compromise was needed between the conservative approach of the local legislation fundamentals and the dictates of the time. Specifically, a status was needed that would allow the APFs to treat pension assets as their own assets, but at the same time ensure that the APF would not be the owner, in order to exclude the possibility that these assets could be seized by creditors in the event of a pension fund's liability. Russia faced similar problems when drafting its Pension Law and made an imperfectly successful but undoubtedly more challenging attempt to solve these problems. The Russian draft stated, "The Fund contributor shall have the right of ownership to the pension accumulations prior the occurrence of the pension security, unless otherwise is provided by the contract." As distinct from Kazakhstan, the Russian law thus did not ignore the problem, though it has not been solved completely. This wording had the positive effect of providing the opportunity to determine the specific status of given pension assets in the fund-contributor contract. While the extent of freedom in forming contracts may have been excessive, the Russian law did overcome the conservatism of the underlying legislation and also made new legislation less immediately critical. The specific reference to the possibility of "another approach" enabled a regime under which neither contributor nor pension fund was the pension assets' owner, that is, the Russian law created something similar to Quebec fiducia or "autonomous ownership." This approach thereby made possible an arrangement that separated an individual's pension assets from the mass of other invested funds and removed them from liabilities faced by an APF toward its creditors.

8.2.2 The Need for Trust Arrangements

The risk of pension assets' loss due to absence of the trust concept in Kazakhstan was noted by foreign experts for the first time in the spring of 1997 when the new Pension Law was being drafted. One draft followed another, but none of them clarified the status of pension assets. Pension asset safety measures included (a) governmental guarantees to the SAPF that insured their pension savings, (b) licensing requirements governing APF, AMC, and CB activity; and (c) requirements concerning reputability of the APF and AMC top management. However, these measures referred only to certain administrative aspects. This lack of resolution reflected an understandable focus on quickly enacting the Pension Law, and thereby avoiding detailed discussions that would have uncovered shortcomings and necessary supplemental legislation, which in turn would have delayed implementation.

In March 1998, experts working under the USAID and World Bank projects again attempt to draw the GoK's attention to the fact that pension assets lacked legal protection but were rebuffed by government authorities who argued that it would be politically incorrect to amend a law that had been just adopted. Perhaps more accurately, a flurry of Pension Law amendments would have revealed its drawbacks, thereby tarnishing the image of the law and its drafters while adversely affecting the well-publicized advertising campaign. Thus, given the fiscal pressures of the time, the government's strategy was appropriate and defensible, but the lack of clarity over property rights was disconcerting.

Those arguing that the Pension Law should have been quickly amended implicitly regarded Kazakhstan's civil law doctrine as in fact providing for the possibility of setting up trust relations. As noted, only a trust or its continental fiducia analog can establish a regime under which the pension assets would be protected from the claims of the creditors of both the contributors and APFs. While similar to the property owner in terms of authority to possess, use, and dispose of a property, the trustee has one clear distinction: he or she does not bear liability to debtors of the property held under the trust. The same is true with regard to a person who has assigned his or her property under the trust, in that this property is excluded from trust's liabilities.

While the principle has not been formally established, the triad of property concepts, which are also contained in the majority of continental law systems, almost certainly could have been construed to allow incorporation of notions similar to a trust, and would have been sufficient to preserve pension assets. As noted, existing international practice provided examples of the trust idea implementation into the continental systems in the form of the fiducia. The 1994 Quebec Civil Code put into practice a new term, "autonomous property." In Quebec, continental law principles merged with trust concepts and thus were implemented through written legal provisions. Under this scheme, the founder assigns the property to a specific property pool for a certain purpose, with the pool managed by another person. A fiduciary pool is an independent and autonomous property to which neither a founder nor a trustee has a property right (articles 1260 and 1261 of the Civil Code of Quebec). This scheme thus meets the aims of a trust even in the absence of a law regarding equities.

Mikheeva (1999) and many other Russian scholars have argued that countries with continental law may and should establish a trust-like concept and that "management of the outsider's property in the interests of the third parties has become common under continental law a long time ago." A simple, standard example of a natural fiducia in the continental law arises when an estate owner dies while the designated heir has not yet been born or come of legal age so that the estate is managed by a specially appointed person who is not the estate owner. By analogy, it should be possible to establish artificially, on the basis of existing law, such a regime in which there is no owner of pension assets while these assets are circulating within the pension system and until a pensioner receives pension savings.

Despite past and ongoing criticism of such approaches leveled by many prominent legal scholars from both Kazakhstan and Russia, it appears that division of the right of property into three triad components of ownership, use, and disposal in the continental law systems (paragraphs 1 and 2 of Article 188 of the Civil Code of the Republic of Kazakhstan) in fact does allow for so-called property splitting. In turn, this division should enable distribution of ownership authority between the trustee (owner of record) and beneficiary (legal owner or persons assigned by the legal owner). Even those who disagree with this view appear to accept that the trust in its current form is based exactly on such splitting.

As a general rule, when a trust is established, its trustee may be assigned various combinations of elements of the triad of property rights. However, as a rule, the entire triad is transferred, as the trustee needs the right to own in order to hold a property, while he or she needs the right to dispose in order to act quickly, without any additional instruction on the side of the trust's founder in each case. As far as the right to use is concerned, two opinion strains may be traced in Russian and Kazakhstani legal literature. Some legal experts think that benefits and profit belong to the beneficiary. The other opinion, held by those opposed to introduction of the trust concept, suggests that the trustee's award consists partially of the benefits due to use of the property under the trust, meaning that the trustee also derives benefits from the property, in line with legal usufructory rights. This second opinion appears to more accurately reflect current reality.

Further, trust opponents argue, the key right is that of disposal: simply assigning disposal rights is sufficient to transfer material property from the ownership of the trust founder, since a trustee having the right to dispose of an estate could assign it to the ownership of a third party. If ownership rights encompass all three elements, then when this triad is assigned to another person, the right of property is transferred as well, as no differences between the legal owners and the owner of record are delineated. Thus, it would appear that two identical statuses are denoted by two different terms, which seems illogical. The result is removal of the possibility of understanding a trust as having a separate status, and it will be impossible to speak about a trust as an independent type of legal entity. Hence, introduction of the term "autonomous property" as used in Quebec would not be successful in Kazakhstan, as it is not in harmony with the legal terminology traditionally used.

In order to avoid confusion or unconventional terminology, expatriate advisors suggested using one of the Civil Code's doctrinal provisions that presupposes dividing all civil rights into demand and holding rights. Specifically, Article 115 of the RK Civil Code divides property rights into direct benefits and ownership rights. The concept of direct benefits pertains to a situation in which a property is structured in such a way that it is possible to own or derive other useful properties without requiring any additional actions on the part of other persons. Ownership rights refer to a situation when a person does not have an absolute power over an asset, and possession of the property or extraction of any useful properties thereof necessitates additional actions on the part of the owner. Thus, it is possible to associate direct benefits with the rights to receive a benefit stream from an asset and to associate ownership rights with the law of obligation or rights of demand as it is used in the traditional terminology. Compared to other persons possessing property rights, the owner has final or absolute authority and has a multitude of advantages and opportunities with respect to the property. Based on this status, the right of property has been referred to as having full rights to an asset.

Moreover, the RK Civil Code sets a hierarchy of the rights to a property. Following Article 195, the right of property ownership is at the very top, with all other rights to an asset being secondary. Moreover, paragraph 2 of Article 195 states directly that the types of the rights to a property not specified elsewhere in the article may be determined in other laws and that these laws may establish the regimes for those rights to the asset in question that are different from other asset rights. In particular, it then becomes possible to distinguish in another law how rights to ownership of an asset will differ from rights to receive benefits from an asset. Hence, in the Pension Law setting, it would have been possible to have a pension assets regime that would differ from conventional property rights by the fact that the pension assets would not be included into the general liability of any APF, AMC, CB, or individual contributor to its creditors. Inclusion into a potential total liability pool would have been obligatory only if pension assets were regarded as being included in that property at risk in actions against any of earlier-mentioned entities. Thus, a legal ground was found to separate the pension assets from other assets of APF, AMC, CB, and contributors, making it possible to establish statutorily an institute of law similar to that in Quebec. In other words, placing pension assets' management and holding rights under the category of special rights, and specifically different from property ownership rights, made it possible to avoid the conservatism of the right of property that negatively affected the pension assets' safety, removing access to them by the creditors of APFs, AMCs, CBs, and individual contributors.

This interpretation rests on an intermediary point of interest, as an example, that the Roman triad of property law is not ideal regardless of how it is interpreted and needs to be reconsidered with the transition to a modern market economy. In 1998, the Civil Code added a new institution called an "estate beneficial ownership" (EBO). This institution was born as a result of attempts to incorporate a trust analog into Kazakhstani legislation, but the EBO proved unacceptable for the pension system, as bankruptcy by the founder of a beneficial ownership asset entailed the inclusion of its property under the trust into the bankruptcy assets. However, this institute did allow assigning the triad of asset rights to other persons while preserving the former owner.

Following the logic of dividing property rights into three components, it seems reasonable to assume that with the assignment of all triad aspects to another person, full asset property rights also will be assigned to this person. However, in practice there are many cases when asset ownership does not change with transfer of the three types of rights. For instance, in continental law there are types of contracts when the owner assigns the full authority over an entity to another person remaining, however, the owner according to the title and in fact able to prove his or her right to the property by availability of a registered title. Cases also arise where the title cannot be assigned, but a person states that he or she is the owner because when the person transferred the triad of rights to another entity, he or she did not intend to transfer the right of property ownership. In Kazakhstan, Article 188(1) of the Civil Code formalizes property rights, and while it is commonly understood to cover only three aspects, the separation of formal ownership means that property rights actually contain four elements. While this distinction surely seems trivial to those not interested in legal bases of social security systems, the implication is in fact important: a plausible interpretation of the legal base inherited by Kazakhstan and other transition countries is that it would have permitted trust-like entities.

Thus, Article 188(1) of the RK Civil Code states, "The right of property is the right of a subject, recognized and protected by the legislative acts, *ad libitum* to possess, use and dispose the property *belonging* to it" (emphasis added). Paragraph 2 of this article then explains that the rights to own, use, and dispose belong to the owner, thus listing only three components. However, from paragraph 1 it is clear that in addition to the standard three components, the right of property will take place when the property is not only under ownership, use, and disposal of a particular person, but also belongs to said that particular person, thereby implicitly defining a fourth "belonging" component. Provision of paragraph 3 of Article 188 also implies the existence of this fourth component, according to which the owner may remain as such even if he or she has assigned all three components. In essence, "belonging" is the most fundamental component of all, and thereby takes precedence over the other property right components.

In the case of a nonmonetary, physical asset, it is clear that the owner of a title has no problems establishing himself or herself as the asset's owner, even if he or she has assigned all other rights to another person. In contrast, money and other assets that have neither such a title nor any individual characteristics may easily be assimilated with the trustee's property unless they have been assigned a special legal status.

As a rule, when money is transferred to another person, a transfer of property rights takes place, and a creditor instead acquires the right to claim the execution of liabilities; that is, the right to get back the analog of the money lent. Today in Kazakhstan, there is still a need to enact legislation that provides more and clearer details on the fundamentals of property rights. A possible option is to incorporate into the Civil Code a concept of "documented owner," with proper understanding of the document as not a separate certificate of the right of property but, in fact, as the contract or letter of attorney under which an asset is transferred. However, considering a trust solely from the point of view of identifying who is the estate owner, then in order to prove a property right, one may refer to a contract for the property's trust management, in which the property owner is indicated. But considering a trust from the point of view of protection, that is, of the entrusted property in the event of claims by third parties (such as creditors of a contributor or pension fund), then the most important issue is to segregate the entrusted property from the trustee's assets and assets of the trust's founder. In order to exclude pension assets from the total pension fund pool, it would be necessary to determine their status.

A simple declaration in the Pension Law that pension assets are not included into bankruptcy assets in case of the bankruptcy will be insufficient to offer adequate protection. While an asset owner may transfer property to another person and in so doing surrenders a variety of rights, there is some risk of attachment, unless the Quebec autonomous property scheme is employed. Safety of pension assets demands their complete isolation from the claims of any creditors during that time when pension assets are inside the pension system, and if these assets are not assigned a special status, it is possible that they will be lost. Even if the assets are not explicitly referred to as the APF property, they may be considered as the object of somebody's property rights and thus be referred to as somebody's property and be subject to the creditor's claims. Ideal principles include the following:

- clear-cut delineation of the right of property ownership from other asset rights, and in particular to the right of the property trust management;
- segregation of the pension property, under status similar to that of a trust, from the total property mass of a subject; and
- introduction into the Civil Code of a regulation that would allow establishing of trust management regimes in other laws, and stipulation that under this regime the bankruptcy of the trust management founder does not entail inclusion of the assets it has assigned under management into its bankruptcy assets.

These principles were advanced by the expatriate consultancies and their Kazakhstani lawyers who created the draft of the trust analogy conception for the legislation of Kazakhstan based on the principals of the continental law system in 1997 (Ivlev, 1997). Ultimately, GoK rejected these appeals to create trust analogs. The rejection was a matter of strategy, and not a backdoor way of reducing the security of pension assets. On the contrary, despite their opposition, senior NPA and MLSP officials, along with some members of parliament, showed great understanding and appreciation of the issues.

Such was the nature of deliberations at the time of review of the legal project both by the GoK and others involved. It is important to note the understanding and acceptance of pressures from various sides by the senior directors of all government departments involved in pension reform. All those participating realized that they needed to formulate the notion of a trust in terms of local legal language, avoiding terminology that would be nontraditional in the Kazakhstani context and, more generally, avoiding creating any new concepts or destroying commonly accepted higher doctrinal norms of the Civil Code.

8.2.3 *What are the Alternatives to a Trust?*

Kazakhstani adherents of the Anglo-Saxon type of trust strongly opposed the idea of a trust in Kazakhstan. Nevertheless, the very first version of the Civil Code (1994) included a special article stating the possibility of having trust operations. However, by the time pension reform started, this article already had been excluded from the code. Of course, a useful legal idea cannot be restricted to only one country or legal system. In order to understand the notion of a trust and its importance, it is necessary to turn away from purely positivistic understanding of the law as a collection of the regulations written by particular individuals at specific points in time, or as the subjective opinions of local legal scholars. Instead, it is useful to consider the trust as having symbolic importance in terms of convincing the public of the safety of their assets: once regarded as important for this purpose, it can be put into acceptable wording compatible with the national legal system. Conversely, it seems risky to neglect the international practice of wide use of trusts and instead refer only to the peculiarities of the local laws. At the time of the initial pension reform, nobody had any arguments to object to the counterargument that the purpose of the trust was to have an owner of record, while its analogs had been widely used for a long time in the local law.

Ultimately, implementation of the trust concept may be reached by different ways, including the usage of the continental law principles so as to maintain ties to the underlying legal base. So it eventually happened in Kazakhstan. It was necessary to find a compromise that would implement key ideas without contradicting existing legislation. Changing the existing interpretation of property right concepts, as noted above, was impossible in light of strong opposition by those who took a traditional approach to ownership rights. It was therefore necessary to find in existing legislation an institution similar to that of ownership rights but excluding the aspect that owners' potential liability includes all of their property. The only institution close to that of trusts, namely that of trust managers, could not solve the pension asset safety issue in case of the bankruptcy of the trust management founders.

The solution reached emerged suddenly following a review of the Pension Law at the end of 1998. Article 195 of the RK Civil Code states that, in addition to the right of property, other rights pertaining to an asset may exist and that the status of these rights may be defined in other laws. The current Pension Law now uses a provision of Civil Code Article 195 and declares a special status for pension assets, making it neither the *de jure* property of the APF, nor of the contributor, nor the AMC, nor the CB. This provision enables all of these bodies to avoid including pension assets among the resources that can be attached if they have debt liability, while applying to these pension assets all other provisions of property law. Thus, the difference of a special status from the right of property lies in the fact that the special status assets cannot be attached, while in normal cases such a liability is prescribed for the owner. This idea emerged after it became apparent that the Civil Code would not be changed and that the government would not exclude property under trust management from the liability of its founder.

8.2.4 Limiting APF Liabilities

In the course of drafting the Pension Law, serious discussion was held around the limits of APF liabilities. According to the first version of the Pension Law adopted in 1997, the APF was held liable to the contributors up to the amount of money contributed and credited to their individual pension accounts (IPA), as the term "pension savings" meant money held in IPAs (Article 1 of the Pension Law). The APFs had no other liability to the contributors except the amount of pension savings contributed. Thus, even if the contributor's pension savings decreased significantly (that is, if the IPA account value plunged), the APF would be viewed legally as a bona fide executor of the liabilities to the contributor.

Moreover, a double standard existed in understanding the AMC's liability to the contributor. Kazakhstan civil law specifies liabilities arising as the joint consequence of legislative acts and regulations, binding contracts, and established facts pertaining to damage. Hence, if pension savings decreased because of the poor performance of the AMC, a contributor could not sue the AMC as he or she did not have a direct contract with AMC and there was no indication of the AMC liability to the contributor under the Pension Law, which stated that the AMC is liable to the APF. However, this interpretation was not the only one to be made: given the vagueness of the law's wording, some felt that it regarded as damage any reduction in the pension savings compared with their highest value during the whole period of the contributor's participation in the APF, implying that the contributor could sue the entity at fault, namely the AMC. While an attractive interpretation from the perspective of contributors (essentially offering a one-way bet on returns), the possibility for contributors to recover the difference in the pension asset value compared to its peak value would have affected the viability of the whole pension system.

The Pension Law *did* in fact include a phrase concerning the AMC's responsibility to act with due diligence, but such phrase under continental law either has no meaning or is at most a nonimperative declaration. Nor are the words "diligence" and "good faith" clearly defined at any point. This sort of broad statement therefore carried no substantive meaning, especially in the absence of a lengthy stream of precedents and detailed equity law that serve as sources of guidance.

While the law had difficulty defining the term "inappropriate management," and did so with little detail, it provided an exhaustive description of the concept of "harm." Its definition covers any decrease in the property's value (i.e., in the IPA). If there is no clear indication of the specific liabilities for which each of the APF and AMC can be held responsible, then, as noted, in principle they could risk any decrement from the maximum. Paradoxically, this could lead to a situation in which potential liabilities for pension funds would be greater under a defined contribution system than when liabilities are predetermined in defined benefit schemes.

Broadly speaking, two sorts of viewpoints were expressed during the early days of operation of the Accumulative system. The first perspective was that the law should not specify APF liabilities at all. The underlying logic was as follows:

The right of the contributor to his or her pension savings is a property right, in fact, it is the axiomatic right of the contributor to claim a certain amount from the funds, and Civil Code Article 115(2) already defines these property rights;

- At the time t_1 the contributor has the right to the pension savings *X1*; at the time $t_2 > t_1$ the contributor has the right to the pension savings *X2*;
- Let $X2 < X1$. Then the difference as initially stated is defined as the "harm" caused by the APF, regardless of whether the reduction in asset value is because of APF's operational errors or AMC's poor (or because of unanticipated public policy decisions or genuinely random macro shocks). Formally, harm is the decrease of property as a result of the material right violation, and material rights are absolute: everybody has the right that none of their rights are violated by others (RK Civil Code Article 8);
- According to Articles 7 917 of the RK Civil Code, if harm is caused, this fact may serve as grounds for securing compensation *in full.*

This approach provides contributors the opportunity to bring suits against APFs or AMCs, but has problems as well. If harm is caused through an APF's fault, then the burden on the APF will be more substantial, as in this case the losses are understood as compensation for reduced pension savings, in an amount up to their highest value for the total period of the contributor's participation in the fund. In such a case, the highest value of pension savings (total contributions, possibly adjusted for inflation) also will be used as a base to determine the amount of compensation to be paid by a potentially liable AMC, and the legal system will not be interested in exact pension contributions. Confusion and an absence of uniform understanding of damage also threaten to result in the lack of the uniform judicial practice, creating potential for judicial corruption. Moreover, the possibility for the contributor to file a suit against the AMC could release the APF from responsibility for selecting a particular AMC.

An alternative viewpoint started from the premise that the Pension Law did need to state that APFs are obliged to compensate pension savings losses if they become less than actual contributions and if accumulations were reduced due to an act or omission for which the APF and AMC should be held responsible. Compared to the previous position, the concept of responsibility is changed. In the first approach, *harm* is grounds for determining liability, while under the second approach, potential compensation for reduced pension savings up to the amount of *actual paid-in contributions* appears to be an APF's obligation arising from the law (Article 7 of the RK Civil Code). Liability caused by harm or damage is always wider, as the concept of damage means decrease of property, while responsibility for nonexecution of liabilities is restricted by further limits of that liability. In case of nonexecution, a liability arises only in cases in which the difference between the amount of actual contributions and amount of funds in the IPA is positive. Apparent management failure, as in the case of an abnormal decline in returns to accumulated assets, will not be considered as loss as long as (nominal or real, depending on interpretation) returns remain nonnegative. This second approach implies a significantly lower risk to the pension funds. However, the protection offered to pension funds may be excessive: APFs avoid responsibility for incompetence or malfeasance as long as nominal returns are nonnegative.

Kazakhstan's international advisors took a middle road suggesting that APFs should be held liable if the amount of the actually paid contributions adjusted for average returns. However, when amendments were made to the Pension Law in 2002, the Ministry of Labor's position was accepted, which insisted that adjustments should be made for the inflation rate and not for the average return. Subsequent amendments and additions to the Pension Law (specifically, Article 6(1)) also were adopted that provided a GoK guarantee of the safety of pension savings. This was critically important in protecting APF contributors and recipients but, at the same time, created additional liabilities for the state budget—and escaping these liabilities was an initial impetus to the Accumulative system reform. The difference, of course, is that with rising oil prices and government budget surpluses, Kazakhstan, by 2002, was able to extend the coverage of its welfare state.

Today, in accordance with the Article 6 of the Pension Law, government guarantees the safety of the pension savings in the amount of the mandatory pension contributions paid in by contributors, including full adjustments for inflation, with the amount payable at the time a recipient becomes eligible for the benefit payments. Procedures for such compensation payments must be in compliance with the procedure specified by RK law, *On the Budgetary System*, and provisions of the Pension Law, and may be specified in these or other laws. This open-ended guarantee naturally unnerves government economists interested in maintaining macroeconomic balances; in principle, it also encourages abnormally risky behavior by APFs and AMFs. In practice, these entities are highly constrained by other restrictions on portfolios, and from a political perspective, the guarantee is an extension of state commitment, which is both expected and a measure that adds to public confidence.

8.3 Challenges to Further Development of the Pension Legal Structure

The Chilean pension model has set the pace for subsequent social security system reforms in a number of countries. However, it is inaccurate to regard the Chilean model as the principal benchmark for current views concerning pension security development. Approaches to pension reforms are driven by different macroeconomic and demographic indicators and are much broader than a particular model in a particular country. In general, developments in a social security system should be aimed at reduction of the risks facing both the nation at large and its individual citizens. These risks in turn can be classified into general risks related to the problems of legal underpinnings; risks related to protection of pension assets that are internal to the system; and risks related to pension assets that lie outside the system itself.

8.3.1 The Risks of Hurried Legislation

The first group of risks includes problems caused by the imperfections of local legislation. An effective system is impossible when its rules are inconsistent, unclear, or allow multiple interpretations. Lack of uniform understanding of the legal standard content creates uncertainty among system participants, as contributors' rights and APF and AMCs' liabilities are not well defined. Indeed, even if a specific interpretation is currently accepted, there may be doubt as to the permanence of that interpretation. Policy consistency and the credibility of a last-resort government commitment are both essential to establish and maintain confidence. This is particularly the case with respect to social security policy, which lies at the core of government's guarantees to its citizens.

Social reforms are initiated by governments and must be preceded by enabling legislation. For social security, these laws and regulations are factors of paramount importance. While in civil law one finds situations in which new regulations overlap with or even follow naturally developing public policy practices, as a rule, social security policy shifts arise only after the government has adopted an enabling directive or regulatory act. In consequence, legal norms merit priority in social security reforms, and improving the legislative process is an essential ongoing task. Deficiencies in a country's legal system may be offset in many areas by customary practices and the development of practices based on analogs to strong legal underpinnings, including sound civil society, a high level of business ethics, and adherence to existing practices that may be upheld in court. However, in the social security arena, such a parallel approach is problematic, as from the very outset practices must follow legislative will. If a legislative rule serves as the impulse for relations to arise, then only improved rules will generate better practices. In the case of Kazakhstan, even at this stage there remain areas that invite improved legal structure.

How should the law-making process be organized? Logically, efficiency of the legislative rules should be a key criterion, as these rules should set legal relations, regulating them without any difficulty in their understanding, without inviting inconsistent interpretation, and without excessive formalism. In short, good law should address rather than create problems. Both the Pension Law and, more broadly, Kazakhstan's Civil Code fall short of this ideal. Indeed, this situation is hardly surprising in that a vast array of new economic relations have descended upon a legal environment not aimed at a market-based society, and which has responded either quickly but inconsistently or slowly and hence incompletely.

That problems should exist a decade or two after independence is inevitable. Of greater frustration to the legal community (though hardly unique to Kazakhstan) is that legislative rules often become more rather than less difficult and intricate. Article 36(2) of the Pension Law in its 1st edition that was valid from 1997 until 2003 serves as a classic example:

> During the period of the Accumulative pension fund establishment, no person has the right to own, dispose or manage, directly or indirectly, more than 25 percent of the shares that provide the voting right in said Accumulative pension fund.

This sentence superficially seems clear, but in fact may have two different meanings. If at that time the Accumulative pension funds issued two types of shares—ordinary and preferred—then it is possible to base this restriction as applying to 25 percent of ordinary shares, as only these shares enjoy voting rights. Alternatively, it might be possible that APF shareholders are restricted to holding less than 25 percent of ordinary and preferred shares together (thereby making it possible for a single shareholder to hold far more than 25 percent of voting shares). Nor is this point merely academic: cases already have arisen in which attempts were made to suspend the licenses of some APFs on the basis that they were established with violations of this legislation.

This passage illustrates the consequences of hurried legislation aimed at achieving macro stability quickly. There is no surprise that inconsistencies and vagueness resulted, and pointing these out should not be taken as criticism of the work done under great time pressure. However, a more valid criticism is that today, with the crisis period well past, there is no systematic effort to review the enacted legislation and regulation.

Ideally, such a review would clarify the rights to hold, use, and dispose of assets; it would also define both what actually constitutes property and what would specify the liabilities of different legal entities. Even more broadly, an effort might be made to define government obligations and, hence, to formally define social protection and social security. The development of modern law requires deviating from purely positivistic views and also involves philosophic consideration of matters associated with the law. If a judge regards the rules of law or the law itself in his or her own way and interprets them too liberally (expansively) or conservatively (narrowly), the result is a ruling inconsistency with the basis on which the law is founded. This misinterpretation then leads either to revision of the law or to continued inconsistency. The former is important and needs to be formalized through a legislative review panel in Kazakhstan and other middle-income countries. As discussed earlier, the alternative—tolerating inconsistencies—inevitably invites both corruption and injustice.

The present lack of philosophical underpinnings and consistency in Kazakhstani law reflects both the pace of change and the absence of a legal school. Clearly, it is impossible to describe and cover all possible aspects of the human activities by means of legislative rules. Further, different people inevitably will understand the same statement or event differently. Finally, there are many deep aspects that cannot be detected in the wording of the law, as they arise from the mentality, traditions, or logical framework. These points together demonstrate the importance of explaining and interpreting the law and, hence, building a base of historic precedents; doing so requires uniform concepts, understanding, and perception. As a legislative base cannot prescribe rules *ex ante* that will cover all eventualities, establishing a philosophy is critical. In the case of transition and rapidly developing countries, the luxury of a vast set of precedents is absent; the only viable alternative is to devote substantial resources to careful legal development at the present and to establish procedural rules to minimize inconsistencies.

8.3.2 Risks Due to Imperfect Separation of Pension Assets

The second set of risks will be minimized by separation of the APF-, AMC-, and CB-owned assets from those of pension system participants. This objective implies further development of the legislation aimed at strengthening administrative provisions that regulate the current activity of the pension system's financial institutions. Ideally, government also will mandate concurrent upgrading of qualifications of key personnel in these organizations. Ongoing monitoring of both accounting and reporting procedures is necessary as well, in part to detect both progress and problems in the legislation.

8.3.3 Risks Due to Asset Composition Rules

The third type of risk is currently the most urgent and reflects problems related to preservation of the assets that already have been invested in financial instruments. These include the problem of defaults by issuers of securities bought with pension assets, and other causes of reduction of the portfolio yield. For example, the absence of bank trusts gives rise to the risk of loss of the pension assets invested in bank deposits because as soon as pension assets are transferred from the pension system to the banking system, their special status ceases and they become the property of the bank. This status transfer means that, in the event of a bank's bankruptcy, these pension assets will be included into the bank's bankruptcy estate! At the same time, it should be noted that recent changes to the pension legislation have strengthened administrative requirements for the procedures governing the investment of pension assets. Moreover, requirements regarding the professional qualifications and responsibilities of AMC managing staff also have been raised.

The third group of risks also includes the risk of unavailability of an adequate number of the corporate financial instruments in the market, which prevents establishment of an effective system of risk rating and fair assessment of financial instrument cost. The existing assessment of financial instruments carried out under the aegis of the authorized body (currently, the FSA) is affected by the nascent development of the financial market and absence of nonstate market makers. Consequently, the assessments that do emerge cannot meet international standards. In this respect, the recent development of securitization and project finance is vital, as it will allow more low-risk financial instruments and opportunities to invest pension assets in major sectors of the economy. The recently enacted securitization law stipulates creation of financial instruments whose liabilities are secured by the right of claim and which represents an asset unmixed either with the assets of the debtor of these rights of claim or with the assets of a special vehicle that issues these instruments.

The methodology of the law is partly based on Italian practice, which prescribes unmixed assets.

Once again, departure from the traditional fundamentals of the right of ownership and development of fiduciary provisions creates an immediate problem. The method of separation of assets in the pension system serves as a practical experience for addressing the securitization problem. In practice, other than pensions, there is currently no inheritance law in Kazakhstan. In the process of creating the draft law on securitization, theoretical problems arose that were analogous to those involving the distribution of pension funds' shares.

The core problem today concerns limitations in the law rather than economic deficiencies. Since 2000, Kazakhstan has enjoyed outstanding economic progress, but the development of its legal base has lagged. The conservative approach now retards economic growth, specifically by making it impossible to create efficient securitization legislation, and hence development of different forms of project finance. As discussed, the traditional approach toward property rights does not allow establishment of types of shares or property that do not belong to a specific individual or legal entity, which means that any sort of property or shares can be confiscated by creditors. Formation of a pool with special nonconfiscatory status (for example, originated and securitized credit assets) is essential in order to reduce investors' risks.

A closely related problem regarding asset composition is that at present, Kazakhstani legislation does not allow investing of the pension assets into risky financial instruments or creating any special high-risk funds. The list of permitted financial instruments as of early 2006 is given below. For comparative purposes, pension asset investment rules from October 2006 until early 2008 are then presented. Permitted pension asset investments as of early 2006 included:

(1) GoK securities (including those issued in accordance with the legislation of other nations or international financial [IFIs]), excluding those issued by the local government bodies. The APFs or AMCs must place at least 25 percent of assets into these securities.
(2) GoK securities issued by local authorities (including those issued in accordance with the legislation of other nations), provided that these securities are allowed for circulation in the trading systems of the auction organizers, and permitted by the NSA to be purchased with pension assets. Holdings of these assets cannot exceed 5 percent of the total.
(3) Deposits in the NBK and second-tier banks specified according to Pension Law appendix 2, with limitations specified in appendices 5 and 6.[3] Holdings of these assets cannot exceed 15 percent of the total.
(4) Securities of foreign nations that comply with the terms of appendix 2, nongovernmental securities of foreign issuers, investment fund shares that comply with the terms of appendix 4 of the Pension Law, and securities issued by IFIs specified in appendix 1. Holdings of these assets cannot exceed 40 percent of the total, and include:
    (a) securities of foreign nations that comply with the terms of the paragraph (2) of appendix 3, and nongovernmental securities of the foreign issuers and investment fund shares that comply with the terms of

paragraphs (3) and (4) of appendix 4. These holdings cannot exceed 30 percent of all pension fund/AMC assets.

(b) securities of foreign nations that comply with the terms of the paragraph (3) of appendix 3, and nongovernmental securities of the foreign issuers and investment fund shares that comply with the terms of paragraphs (5) and (6) of appendix 4, which limit legal options to highly rated assets. These holdings cannot exceed 20 percent of all pension fund/AMC assets.

(c) securities of foreign nations that comply with the terms of the paragraph (4) of appendix 3, and nongovernmental securities of the foreign issuers that comply with the terms of paragraphs (7) and (8) of appendix 4. These holdings cannot exceed 10 percent of all pension fund/AMC assets;

(5) Mortgage bonds issued by organizations of the Republic of Kazakhstan that are included in the official list of the auction organizers. These holdings cannot exceed 20 percent of all pension fund/AMC assets;

(6) Other nongovernmental securities, in addition to mortgage bonds, included in the official "A" listing of the auction organizers that are issued by the organizations of the Republic of Kazakhstan, in accordance with legislation of Kazakhstan and other nations. These holdings cannot exceed 50 percent of all pension fund/AMC assets (with restrictions imposed by appendix 5).

(7) Bonds issued by the CJSC Development Bank of Kazakhstan. These holdings cannot exceed 50 percent of all pension fund/AMC assets.

(8) Precious metals that meet the international quality standards adopted by the London Bullion Market Association (LBMA) and marked as London good delivery standard in the documents of the LBMA. These holdings cannot exceed 5 percent of all pension fund/AMC assets.

By October 2006, the guidelines had increased considerably both in terms of liberalization and sophistication. The complexity is apparent:

1. The following items comprise financial instruments that AMCs and AMFs with pension funds under investment management were allowed to purchase. Restrictions imposed are noted as well.

No.	Financial instrument name
1.	State securities of the Republic of Kazakhstan (including those issued in accordance with legislation of other countries), issued by the MinFin and the NBK as well as other securities guaranteed by the GoK.
2.	Securities issued by RK local government bodies, providing these securities are allowed to circulate in the trading system of the auction organizer and are allowed by the authorized body to be purchased using pension assets.

3. Deposits at the NBK.
4. Deposits at second-tier banks within the Republic of Kazakhstan, providing that as of the placement date, these banks: have a long-term international credit rating, not lower than BB- on the Standard & Poor (S&P) international scale or kzBBB on the S&P national scale, or similar level rating of any other rating agency; or that these banks are subsidiary of a resident bank, with the parent nonresident bank having long-term credit rating not lower than BBB- on the S&P international scale, or similar level rating of any other rating agencies; or they are banks in which shares have been included into official list of auction organizers at the highest category of listing.
5. Securities issued by the following IFIs:
   International Bank of Reconstruction and Development;
   European Bank of Reconstruction and Development;
   Inter-American Development Bank;
   Bank for International Settlements;
   Asian Development Bank;
   African Development Bank;
   International Finance Corporation;
   Islamic Development Bank;
   European Investment Bank.
6. Securities issued by the central governments of foreign states, and having a sovereign rating not lower than BBB- on the S&P international scale, or the equivalent by another rating agency.
7. Nonstate securities or shares issued by foreign organizations: with a sovereign rating not lower than BBB- on the S&P international scale, or the equivalent by another rating agency.
8. Investment fund shares with an S&P property stability fund rating not lower than BBBm- or an S&P fund credit quality rating not lower than BBBf-.
9. Nonstate securities issued by organizations of the Republic of Kazakhstan in accordance with the legislation of the Republic of Kazakhstan and other states:
   (1) stocks with a rating not lower than BB- on the S&P international scale or kzBBB on the S&P national scale, or the equivalent from another agency;
   (2) debt securities with a rating not lower than BB- on the S&P international scale or kzBBB on the S&P national scale, or the equivalent from another agency;
   (3) infrastructure bonds of legal entities of the Republic of Kazakhstan;
   (4) debt securities issued by Kazakhstan Mortgage Company;
   (5) mortgage bonds of legal entities of the Republic of Kazakhstan;

(6) debt securities issued by the Kazakhstan Development Bank and securities guaranteed by the Kazakhstan Development Bank;
(7) those stocks and debt securities of domestic legal entities officially designated in the highest category of listing;
(8) those stocks and debt securities of domestic legal entities officially designated in the second highest listing group;
(9) Investment fund time shares, when the management company is directed by a resident of Kazakhstan, and providing that these funds are included on official traded asset lists, but excluding those listed at the Regional Financial Center in Almaty.

10. Refined precious metals, meeting international standards of quality, adopted by the LBMA and designated as meeting the "London good delivery" standard, including those metals held at foreign banks' subsidiaries in Kazakhstan, if those banks have a rating for the preceding 12 months not lower than AA on the S&P international scale, or its equivalent.

11. Principal protected notes, issued by the organizations possessing rating score not lower than BBB- on the S&P international rating scale or its equivalent, and having an insurance by the debt issuer to ensure full repayment of the debt principal.

12. Derivative securities: depository receipts, with the base including stocks indicated in the list below, with derivatives including, futures, option, swap, and forward contracts with the base asset including financial instruments, allowed to be purchased at the expense of pension assets in foreign currency. Derivatives may be based on the following calculation indices:

    1. MICEX (Moscow Interbank Currency Exchange Index)
    2. DAX (Deutscher Aktienindex)
    3. CAC 40 (Compagnie des Agents de Change 40 Index)
    4. NIKKEI-225 (NIKKEI-225 Index)
    5. TOPIX (Tokyo Price Index)
    6. HSI (Hang Seng Index)
    7. ENXT 100 (Euronext 100)
    8. RTSI (Russian Trade System Index)
    9. DJIA (Dow Jones Industrial Average)
    10. S&P 500 (Standard and Poor's 500 Index)
    11. FT-SE 100 (Financial Times Stock Exchange 100 Index)
    12. KASE-Shares (Kazakhstan Stock Exchange-Shares)
    13. MSCI World Index (Morgan Stanley Capital International World Index)

13. Debt securities that have passed the listing procedure and are registered at the Almaty Regional Financial Center;

14. Foreign currency of countries rated not lower than BBB- on the S&P international rating scale, or its equivalent, as well as foreign currency of countries that have no rating scores.

2. Investments in any of the following financial instruments should not exceed 5 percent of pension assets of an individual APF:

1. Debt securities of legal entities of Kazakhstan with a rating not lower than BB- on the S&P international scale or kzBBB on the S&P national scale, or those who do not have a rating score, provided that these securities are on the official list of the auction organizer, and are included in at least the second highest listing category.
2. Investment fund time shares, when the management company is directed by a resident of Kazakhstan, provided that these funds are on the official list of the auction organizer, and are included in at least the second highest listing category.
3. Debt securities that passed the listing procedure at the Almaty Regiunal Financial Center, with a rating not lower than BB- on the S&P international scale or kzBBB on the S&P national scale, or their equivalents, or those who do not have a rating score.
4. Futures, options, swaps, and forward trades involving base assets that are included in caterogies 1–3 above.

Finally, the volume of an APF's pension assets invested in officially rated financial instruments has been restricted by the creation of lower bounds. In January 2007 no less than 30 percent of a pension fund's assets were required to be invested in rated financial instruments. This minimum was increased to 40 percent in July, 50 percent in January 2008, and 70 percent as of July 2008.:

These guidelines ensure a moderately diversified but conservative asset allocation on the part of any particular fund—though the exceptionally high proportion of assets that may be held internationally is remarkable and is critically important for overall portfolio diversification. However, to make the Accumulative pension system better contribute to Kazakhstan's total development and to the extension of investments outside a limited number of raw materials and energy areas, a mechanism must be found that will enable securities or bonds of smaller and riskier firms to be acquired. Indeed, this has been a key focus in the past some years, for government and private financial institutions both, to find the possibilities to extend a number of permitted financial instruments to invest pension money. As is implied by the new investment rules, there is new attention to the development of collective risk reduction schemes, and notions of bundling, and securitization, and hedging have entered the local financial jargon.

Yet, effective bundling and securitization are predicated upon both revitalization of Kazakhstan's investment climate as well as finding compromises between the expansion of investment activity and asset preservation. Any investment activity is connected with a risk-return tradeoff. But this need not mean that all risky assets should be avoided. At present, requirements to ensure the safety of pension assets' investments restrain them from working for under-funded portions of raw materials processing and manufacturing sectors of the economy (since the only low risk investments are on a truly vast scale and are funded mainly via international FDI: see Moody, 2005), which is where capital investments would be most helpful.

Furthermore, funding for small- and medium-scale enterprise investments outside the energy, metallurgy, and mining sectors needs to be long term. This makes pension fund investments all the more critical, as the funds by definition receive long-term deposits and thus can make long-term commitments.

A collective Self-Regulating Organization (SRO) or contract to which several funds are party might be used as a mechanism to reduce overall risk, if the participants commit to compensating one another when losses above a certain trigger occur or to pool risks in some other manner. In such a case, making a risky investment transaction would require a preliminary consent of the participants of an SRO or parties to a contract as a prerequisite of their future liability if that investment transaction results in losses. Such a mechanism is similar in nature to the U.S. Securities Investor Protection Corporation (SIPC).

In Kazakhstan, the idea of creating such an SRO came up in 2001 at the initiative of the SAPF and senior pension fund regulators. However, the idea was limited to internal discussions among market participants, and serious research into the possibilities of such a direction never occurred. In the United States, the SIPC was formed in 1970. Although it is a government regulatory body, it is fully financed by securities market participants. By law, all members of national stock markets and the majority of NASDAQ members are required to be SIPC members as well; dues are assessed according to the value of their securities' transactions. The SIPC has since founded a special trust fund in case the assets of bankrupt entities are insufficient to satisfy their debts to creditors.

Another related concern lies in the imprecise definition of the term "inappropriate investing," which is a term used but never formally defined in the Pension Law. A local analog of the SIPC for investing in pension assets could ease the process of qualifying the notion of inappropriate investment activity.

Having studied the dynamics of the pension legislation, it is evident that the various changes to date have addressed mainly the aspects related to ensuring APF safety and improvement of the administrative provisions. However, neither the latest Pension Law changes strengthening APF asset safety nor the state guarantee of APF liabilities to their contributors, nor the establishment of the FSA as a unified regulatory body have fully created conditions that would allow APFs to realize higher returns.

A country's choice of pension system normally is driven by issues related to demographic structure, macroeconomic and public finance constraints, and the nature of labor markets. Efficiency gains due to improvement of the pension system administration are only a secondary concern. If the returns to contributions fall well below returns to other assets in an economy, which is characteristic of the Solidarity systems in low-income economies, the system requires constant budgetary support, especially in societies with nearly rectangular population pyramids. The efficiency gain from moving to an individual Accumulative account system is potentially substantial (though not inevitably: see Brown, 1997), but that will not be true if pension funds cannot invest in high-expected yield assets. Given prudential norms, it is essential to create legislation and regulations that further increase effective diversification. Diversity may be reached through development of voluntary insurance products, which in turn implies development of the insurance industry as a strategically important direction.

By implication, current trends in development of Kazakhstan's pension system are connected crucially with improved risk management. If the collective responsibility of the pension assets investors in the form of an SRO or contract is inherently limited by the degree of financial market soundness, and hence can only modestly reduce the riskiness, then a multipillar system may be used to provide broader risk reduction through diversification between the two parts of the pension systems, public and private. Continuance of either a guaranteed minimum pension or a more elaborate Solidarity system implies *overall* risk reduction. The implication of this for financial regulation is important. As economic growth in Kazakhstan continues and minimum payments to elderly and disabled pensioners are regularly increased, it is appropriate for the FSA to steadily reduce the stringency of asset allocation requirements.

8.4 Next Steps

It is common for actuaries and economists to focus on demographic structure, compliance, financial, micro and macroeconomic conditions in assessing a pension system's performance and needed changes. Unfortunately, legal structure is often overlooked. General confidence in the system, returns on pension fund assets, and government-contingent liabilities, all depend on the nature and clarity of governing laws and regulations.

Kazakhstan faces many tasks in the next few years, including improving general legal methodology to remove inconsistencies, creating uniform legal terminology and concepts, and forming a set of principles determining the direction of legislation development and regulating the Accumulative pension system. A second task is to further amend and clarify traditional provisions of the right of ownership and develop fiduciary provisions. This in turn leads to the need to develop formal trusts and related trust law. The fourth task is to establish a legal basis for securitization and project finance that allow issuing new moderate- and low-risk financial instruments that can be purchased by pension assets. A related fifth measure is to create a legal framework for development of the schemes for collective reduction of risks for the pension asset investors. As discussed elsewhere, regulation of mandated annuity insurance forms a sixth task. Finally, it is critical for Kazakhstan to determine the extent to which it will provide minimum payments to the elderly and disabled—and, ultimately, to build in these commitments statutorily.

That much remains to be done a decade after introduction of a radically new pension system should not be taken as a criticism. On the contrary, many of the tasks at hand reflect successful growth. However, the list should also serve as a warning to other countries considering radical pension reform. Especially for formerly socialist countries, implementation of such a reform is not easy. On the contrary, it requires vast and ongoing efforts. From the standpoint of legislation and regulation, an ongoing commitment to improve institutional development is needed.

9

Regulation of Pension Funds

9.1 Approaches to Regulation

The emergence of pension funds required that the Kazakhstani government take a series of new regulatory policy decisions, formulate regulatory policy, and set up a regulatory authority. The GoK took a stepwise approach, addressing the issues as they arose, rather than presenting a well-defined structure from the outset. Given the haste with which the Accumulative system was introduced, this stepwise approach was inevitable. While it resulted in many lurches in terms of administrative structure, there was surprising consistency in terms of regulatory practice. This consistency reflected a determination to maintain a moderately liberal but highly transparent system and to borrow best practices from abroad.

Kazakhstan's new pension industry has been tightly regulated from the outset, reflecting the financial and social instability of the time. The regulations also reflected the extent to which the components of the reform were consistent with existing government regulatory practices. As the GoK discovered, regulation was more complex than establishing imperatives for the participants of the system under regulation. As a complex system management function, effective regulation needed to be consistent with basic principles of management and financial theory.

These management and financial control principles emphasize the interrelatedness of seemingly distant actions and the inappropriateness of government control actions taken without full consideration of their broader impacts. This invites both a systems management approach and a recognition that an emerging industry may need a modified version of conventional management and external control structures, to some extent internally, but almost certainly on the part of government regulators. For the GoK, the challenge was to go from fiat regulation over nonmarket financial institutions to a looser but still bounded regulation of competing, market-oriented, private financial institutions in such a way that competition would be encouraged, while fiduciary responsibilities to asset owners were still guaranteed. Accordingly, GoK's pension system regulation today, as type of management, consists of continuous development of new strategies and practices in response to its own evolution.

Contemporary management science derives behavioral rules from principles of complex system evolution, and in particular the properties of self-organization. As applied here, the kernel may be seen in the fact that the Accumulative pension system continually creates new tasks, forcing regulators to respond constantly and, if the system is to work well, quickly.[1] In other words, the state's authoritative function in the broader pension system will depend on the challenges that naturally appear from other agents in the system itself. Here, we emphasize the initial regulatory system and the regulations that actually occurred, without focusing closely on the reasons for those changes. In nearly all cases, regulatory changes were adopted on the basis of consistency with international practice and of being quick and simple to implement. Proactive, anticipatory regulatory change did occur, but for the most part the extraordinary pace of institutional development and economic change put regulatory bodies in a reactive mode.

The effectiveness of Kazakhstan's regulatory efforts can be evaluated on the basis of what is commonly regarded as efficient regulatory management. This includes

- determination of long-term objectives and prospects (strategy);
- determination and analysis of system risks, challenges, and external and internal initial system conditions (or "threats," in SWOT jargon);
- realistic forecasting that adjusts to changing external and internal conditions;
- a direct relationship between the management body and objects under management;
- absence of parallel managing structures with similar functions;
- clear understanding by both the manager and a managed agent of decision-making algorithms, along with understanding of decision notification and implementation practices, and information collection procedures;
- ongoing monitoring of managed agents and of external conditions, and application of the knowledge obtained in the course of management activity;
- availability of procedures for detection and elimination of the conflicts between the managerial body and managed agents;
- creation of a consistent planning procedure that meets the aims and objectives of regulated agents (assuming that the agents' environment frequently changes, the planning procedure needs to have a flexible adjustment mechanism);
- Availability of a human resource development program in the regulatory body to ensure that it has the necessary skilled manpower to carry out its assignments. Correspondingly, it needs to mandate capacity development on the part of the industry to ensure that it has the capacity to follow mandated regulations.

With these principles in mind, we turn to the evolution of GoK's regulatory system in practice. In the initial environment as described in previous chapters, although the GoK did not consistently meet all of these objectives, it came surprisingly close to doing so.

9.2 Kazakhstan's Regulatory Model

Before considering regulatory practice, it is useful to diagram the formal model of the state regulation of Kazakhstan's Accumulative pension system. The following figures reflect objectives formally declared in the various regulatory acts governing the Accumulative pension system. Figure 9.1 provides the objectives of pension regulation and supervision that were announced in the initial documents that set forth a supervisory structure and regulations for the new pension industry (IMCC, 1997b). From the very beginning, a set of core principles governed the regulatory and supervisory system. (figure 9.2).

We refer to these generally applicable purposes and principles in order to show the extent of their realization. These principles translated into a large number of measures for ensuring pension asset safety as established by Article 6 of the 1998 Pension Law, which in its turn set the framework for the reformed pension system (appendix 9.1). These measures were aimed at the achievement of the enunciated objectives (figure 9.1) and principles (figure 9.2). Appendix 9.3 also references the corresponding regulations developed during initial decade of pension reform to ensure that these measures would be realized. Despite the considerable list, only those regulations in force as of December 2007 are listed, and superseded interim regulations are not given. Indeed, a host of new regulations and procedures flowing from these regulations were developed at the initial stage of preparation for the reform and were issued hurriedly by the several ministries and government agencies that shared responsibility for regulation of the Accumulative pension system before the FSA was established.

In principle, the general regulatory aspects of Kazakhstan's pension system follow well-established standards of international practice. At the outset of the

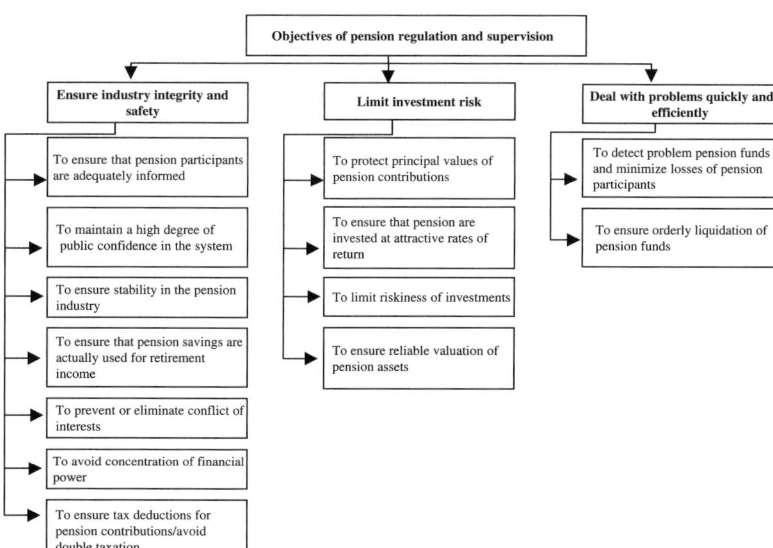

Figure 9.1 Accumulative system pension regulation and supervision objectives

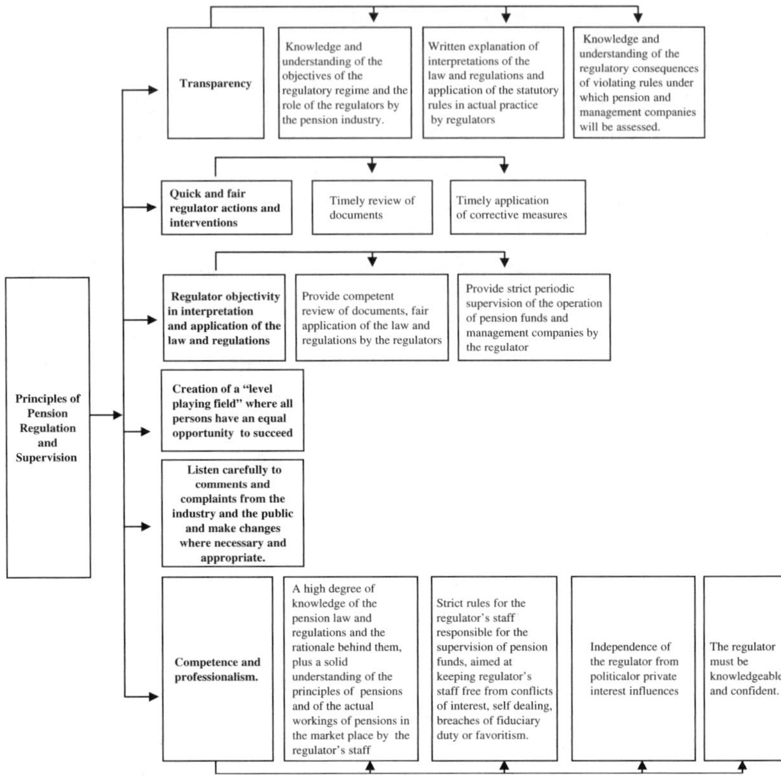

Figure 9.2 Principles of pension regulation and supervision

reform, the main regulatory emphasis was on ensuring the safety of pension savings—a reasonable focus, since there was little public confidence in the system. Licensing is the first step in the regulatory oversight of a private pension system and is especially critical in transition countries. It is difficult to remember today, after a period of financial stability and rapid growth, that Kazakhstan embarked on its new pension system and a financial development program in an almost poisoned atmosphere, with huge credibility gaps due to the public's recent experience of pyramid schemes and bank failures. Thus, it is not surprising that the Pension Law regarded licensing of pension funds and of companies that manage pension assets and bank custodians as key to ensuring the security of pension fund assets. In order to eliminate past mistakes and establish confidence in the new industry, licensing procedures were necessarily highly comprehensive and stringent.

The main components of the Accumulative pension system regulation in appendix 9.2. This table follows the rules for handling pension assets from the initial licensing of an Accumulative pension fund to the point at which an account is liquidated at an asset-holder's retirement.

Appendix 9.1 describes the details of licensing requirements faced by founders and summarizes ownership rights and capital requirements for licensed pension funds, AMCs, and custodian banks. The requirements shown are those in place since 2003. Compared with the initial 1998 rules, some of these requirements reflect a softening of policy. For example, at the beginning of the reform, only a resident of Kazakhstan could be a pension fund founder. This restriction has since been modified to allow nonresident legal entities to become founders or shareholders of an open APF, provided that they had been assigned a rating by one of the approved rating agencies. In this case, entities founding an open APF were barred only if they were commercial organizations registered in offshore zones or if their charter capital included participation from entities registered in offshore zones, either directly or through affiliated entities. The pension regulatory body itself determines the list of relevant "offshore zones." Nonresidents were allowed to be executive officers of the funds in 2006. The requirements on AMCs were eased as well. Licensing requirements for custodian banks have remained unchanged since the beginning of the reform, including capital requirement set at 1 billion tenge.

Initial business plans represent another strictly regulated component of the license application. These must cover all core elements of the pension business development strategy including marketing, organizational structure, human resources, capital sufficiency, and investment policy. The central requirement is that the plan should demonstrate viability of the proposed pension operation. Kazakhstani regulators also expect the plan to project future results for at least three years, although forecasting techniques remain rudimentary. It is further expected that all data sources will be clearly identified and projection assumptions and methodologies fully described. In addition to reviewing an applicant's business plan, the regulators often exercise their right to interview the applicants.

9.3 Evolution of Regulations

In reviewing the regulations as described earlier and in appendix 9.1, it is apparent that the main shortcoming was a failure to incorporate long-term planning as a key principle. Thus, after reforming the old Solidarity system, there were no general principles invoked to serve as the regulatory basis for the new Accumulative system. Actual policy in this area was limited to the postulates set forth in the Concept of the reform adopted in March 1997, before the Pension Law came into force and pension funds started operating. The Accumulative pension system received subsequent mention in various government programs, but a specific document devoted to the long-term strategy of the Accumulative system's development was never developed. The March 1997 pension reform Concept was oriented only at reforming of the old system, and with implementation of the new system, its declarations lost relevance, while no strategic directives for the further development of the system emerged. The closest measure to a strategic vision occurred in 2000, when the MLSP drafted an initiative document that attempted to work out the government's vision of the Accumulative system's development through 2005. The draft was not generally accepted and did not become policy.

The Accumulative system's regulations as enacted were highly reasonable, although it is also obvious that there were considerable policy changes during this period. These changes were not vast and can be regarded as virtually inevitable during the early years of a new system introduced in a *tabula rasa* setting. Moreover, the initial legislation did establish a comprehensive monitoring structure, with both regular and periodic detailed reporting requirements for all subjects of the Accumulative pension system under regulation.

Rather, the major limitation proved to be the system's development and regulation in the absence of longer-term vision of sector development. This meant that many of the requirements could not possibly be met by the pension industry in its early years. Monitoring and supervision were limited because of shortage of staff and capacity limitations. Nor did the various GoK regulatory agencies have the necessary analytical capacity. One cannot say that there was no monitoring at all; it would be more appropriate to say that the monitoring did not have a large impact on practices. The actual practical experiences of pension fund firms were monitored and their experiences generalized, but for statistical purposes rather than for making management decisions. Inertia prevented the government regulatory bodies from rapidly responding to the results of actual practices and accounting for these results when correcting forecasts and preparing legislation.

The economic objectives of the Accumulative pension system evolved over time in Kazakhstan, and these changes in turn were reflected in modifications to the GoK's prudential regulation. Appendix 9.4 charts the evolution of APF prudential norms of APF. Unlike prudential norms for pension funds, those developed for AMCs have been quite steady. However, there have been considerable changes in the distribution of assets that AMCs are authorized to hold (appendix 9.4), with increased liberalization occurring over time.

9.4 Evolution of the Regulatory Authority

Not only did regulations and the regulatory bodies' duties change frequently, there were also numerous metamorphoses of the regulator itself. There were five stages on the path toward a single regulatory body, which finally emerged in January 2004. In the first stage, the regulatory and supervisory duties were shared by the NPA, the NSC, and the NBK. Despite this multiplicity of responsibilities, during its existence the NPA served in the lead role as the authorized body responsible for the regulation of pension funds. In compliance with its major objectives, the NPA implemented a large number of requirements and detailed the functions and the responsibilities for various participants. During its fairly brief existence, the NPA established an enormous groundwork for the sector. Many of its regulations were untouched or only slightly modified by the four succeeding regulatory bodies. However, the regulatory objectives did change significantly.

The first management change was undertaken in April 1999, when the NPA was reorganized and renamed the Committee on Regulation of Pension Funds Activity (CRPFA) but continued to be under the MLSP. The NPA's main objectives was the initiation of means to obtain stated goals, while the CRFPA's objectives were somewhat more abstract and involved choosing goals themselves. This shift reflected evolution beyond an initial crash implementation phase and represented a positive step toward increased responsibility and scope of activity for the regulatory body. Under this new charge, the CRFPA's professional staff began to view the many mandatory requirements as the tools of pension system maintenance, the guarantors of its stability, and the means of protecting the interests of the beneficiaries, rather than simply rules to be enforced.

In practice, this shift in emphasis meant a large difference in Kazakhstan's regulatory environment. Agencies traditionally enforced existing regulations but did not design regulations themselves with the aim of achieving larger policy objectives. Devolution of responsibility and authority has been an important feature of postindependence Kazakhstan and has been especially pronounced in the areas of pension and financial sector supervision.

A similar approach relating to the broader financial market is expressed in the first two goals of the FSA, established at the beginning of 2004 after its Regulatory and Supervision Department was separated from the NBK. Moreover, prior to separation, the former NBK Regulatory and Supervision Department gradually had absorbed the NSC in August 2001, and the MLSP's CRFPA in June 2002.

The FSA's third charge included establishment of equal conditions for competing financial organizations aimed at maintenance of fair competition in the financial market, and meeting that objective necessitated an integrated supervision and regulatory body, rather than having several different regulators. However, the real motive behind the consolidation of regulatory institutions was the anticipation of improved efficiency. As Rocha et al. (1999) write,

> An integrated agency can achieve much greater efficiency at supervision at a much lower cost (for both the supervisor and the supervised institutions), due to a number of factors, including: economies of scale and scope, a sharp reduction in the duplication of reporting requirements, more consistency in the treatment of different sectors, more capacity to solve conflicts, more accountability, and much more capacity to implement a risk-based supervision model (through which resources are allocated to the areas that place the highest risk).

Having the NBK serve as the sole regulatory body ostensibly met the efficient management criteria, as it was a unified body regulating both APFs and all issues related to pension asset investment. However, it is important to ask whether the advantages of a unified system—guidance, direct connection between the regulator and the regulated body, and quick responses when making policy decisions—would be achieved when the unified regulator also has regulatory responsibilities beyond the Accumulative pension system. In Kazakhstan's early reform years, the NBK also was in charge of the banking sector, insurance industry, and the securities market. Advocates of regulating the entire financial sector through the National Bank emphasized that banks, insurance companies, and pension funds were the institutional investors attracting the citizens' money and hence that the activities were interconnected. When the GoK considered the ideal regulatory body structure, a wide range of options received consideration, including establishment of a unified body regulating the Accumulative pension system only and not regulating banks, insurance companies, and securities market participants.

Ultimately, it decided to go with a single financial regulator, and that decision appears to be stable—that is, the period of regulatory transition is likely over.

During periods of rapid institutional and economic development, sectoral growth rates and policymakers' priorities can shift rapidly. At present, Kazakhstan's pension funds are the main holders of long-term money and, therefore, represent critical national investors outside the petrochemical sector. However, it is possible that in coming years, other parts of the financial market, such as the insurance industry or investment funds, will develop with the same intensity. The emergence of new industries can lead to conflict: in the financial sector example, all of the industries noted are institutional investors that attract citizens' funds and are interested in capturing certain capital markets. In a perfectly competitive environment, all firms throughout the financial sector would compete freely for funds. In the more restricted environment and nearly all middle-income countries, success depends in part on rulings and set-asides by regulators that favor a particular firm or industry within the financial sector.

In Kazakhstan, the FSA now serves as a sole regulator of all financial organizations and financial markets. The positive aspect lies in the fact that, in principle, the FSA has no preference in regulating any particular industry within the financial sector, though some risks remain. As the FSA gains multifunctional status, its regulatory effects may be adequate and timely in one industry while inadequate and less effective in another industry, inducing the agency to copy the style and methods of regulation from successful or familiar industries and apply them to new industries, or those with less successful experiences.

Recent practice has already demonstrated some of the negative aspects of such an approach. Specifically, as they developed pension system regulations, FSA specialists drew on their more substantial experience in bank supervision and, at times, approached the pension funds with a bank regulation mentality and style. Application of bank style requirements to pension funds is one such example. Another is the application of minimum return guarantees, which, although inherited from the Chilean prototype, does not represent the best practice in defined benefit schemes.

Banks, which are liable to provide the liquidity on demand and at fixed interest rate, need to hold much more capital to satisfy the claims on their assets under the most adverse conditions. Bank capital also provides a cushion against deterioration of asset quality. The opportunity cost of holding capital and liquid reserves increases the interest margin and suppresses deposit rates. Depositors are willing to reward the shareholders of a bank because they enjoy the luxury of withdrawing on demand. Unlike commercial banks, pension funds do not need to hold much capital because their liabilities are very different from those of a bank. Banks do not know when any given account will be closed until after the event, but they know the interest rate that a bank is liable to pay on deposit at the time the account is opened. Pension funds do not know what the actual return on pension assets will be until the account is closed, but know decades in advance when any given account will mature. Pension funds as investment funds in general pay on a predetermined date in some distant future whatever the value of the account happens to be at the day of retirement. Many and in some circumstances all risks are borne by the contributors.

It would be natural to expect that pension assets should earn a double premium for this double benefit, referred to as the equity premium and the liquidity premium, that pension funds have over deposits. However, given rigidly conservative regulation, the pension funds cannot afford to pay a liquidity premium because they need to pay for costly capital to sit idle. Nor can pension funds afford to pay the equity premium. No matter how well they diversify, pension funds need to purchase a costly insurance against poor returns, priced not unlike an exchange-traded put option contract. This pushes down the return on pension assets to a level slightly above the rate paid on bank deposits, with none of the advantages. This example illustrates how well-meant regulation may produce counterproductive results.

Funds and managing companies are more sophisticated now than they were a decade ago. The regulator has evolved too. However, the lapses into command style of regulation still happen. Recent developments indicate that in achieving the stated objectives FSA regulators continue to rely on brute force and use their legislative-shaping power to obtain desired results. Although the market participants are limited in their access to informational resources and technical expertise, they are in part organized and coordinated by the Association of Financiers of Kazakhstan (AFK). The AFK has full-time but entirely non-analytical staff that solicits the opinion of the market participants to better formulate and present their unified position. The AFK monitors the regulatory developments at the early stage and alerts the fund to any encroachment on their interests. This has proved a productive and beneficial venue for discussion of regulatory developments before they reached the point of no return, but the proposal and the discussions from both sides still suffer from being reactive and myopic rather than proactive and visionary.

One obvious remedy would be to institute a dispute settlement procedure between the regulator and the various bodies under its regulation. While at present it is possible to appeal any management decision made in accordance with the current legislation in court, legal proceedings are more appropriate for extreme conflicts than for relatively minor disputes occurring during the course of normal system operation. More appropriate would be a mandatory pretrial adjudication with the FSA's involvement. This would allow a regulated body to have the opportunity to apply to the regulator, while the latter is constrained by current rules in a manner that permits the regulated entity to state its arguments and the regulator to agree or reject these arguments. Documents used for such a procedure also can be used in court at a later date when the need arises to prove existence or absence of bona fide behavior of the contestant parties.

At present, a weak point in Kazakhstan's public management system is the extreme difficulty of proving unfairness or inappropriate action on the part of a state body that exerts regulatory authority over a nonstate entity. In lodging a claim before a government body, a claimant may state his arguments, but the government body may ignore these arguments when responding thereto and is not required to address issues specifically raised. Nor is the government body subject to punishment for an incomplete response, since acceptance of the initial and subsequent petitions depends completely on the wish of an official working for the petitioned government body. The prevailing practice is for a government body to respond to a claim and then for a dissatisfied claimant to bring the case to court—hardly the optimal policy in a country undergoing substantial change in its judicial system and in which few citizens or enterprises have substantial experience with the court system. Availability of a pretrial system would provide an opportunity to have a regulated discussion of questions at issue and of course would be quicker than a lawsuit. Furthermore, it would enable documentation of officials' actions, thereby controlling unduly arbitrary behavior with regard to the regulated body. It should be apparent as well that such a pretrial system would be appropriate for virtually all other countries currently considering social security system reforms, as few if any have more developed judicial systems than Kazakhstan.

Yet another problem is that, in accordance with Kazakhstani legislation, no other body may interpret the laws adopted by the parliament, while an authorized body may interpret those legislative acts it adopts. In effect, then, it is impossible to block a broad interpretation by an authorized body, such as the various pension industry regulators, of any legal norm it has issued. Again, an institutionalized claims adjudication system that brought parties together prior to a courtroom resolution almost certainly would improve efficiency and equity and could rapidly build a set of precedents.

On a more positive note, as far as the qualification requirements to the employees of the authorized state body are concerned, the requirements set by the current legislation appear to be comprehensive. Moreover, regular attestations and a range of possibilities for acquiring new expertise from different training courses speak well for the high professional level of the employees of the state regulatory bodies.

At the same time, many of the regulatory standards issued are questionable and fail to meet industry-specific goals and needs. This criticism is not surprising and reflects the regulators' inexperience—but note that the absence of checks and balances and the frequent reorganization of regulatory authority exacerbate the problem. Thus, it is not difficult to give examples of regulatory instructions full of inconsistencies and vague language.

9.5 Lessons from a Crash Course in Pension System Administration

The reader who has doggedly followed this chapter and its appendices to the end is likely to emerge dazed by the evolving nature of administration of Kazakhstan's Accumulative pension system and sobered by the vast number of complex issues the regulatory agencies had to address in a short time period. To summarize the process we emphasize that

- during the Accumulative system's initial phase, state regulation focused on ensuring safety of pension savings and fulfillment by the pension funds of their liabilities to the contributors. This summary follows from the description of regulatory requirements, guarantees, licensing aspects, and prudential requirements aimed at ensuring safety of pension accumulations.

- state regulation did not pay sufficient attention to monitoring and forecasting of the system. To provide an extreme example, pension legislation did not mandate the regulator to perform actuarial studies.
- in recent years, state regulation has generally improved as the result of removing parallel regulatory structures and institution of a unified regulatory body.

Regulatory improvements notwithstanding, the regulatory structure has been hindered by ongoing methodological problems. These have reduced overall regulatory effectiveness and equity. Key shortcomings include

- the absence of a unified methodological approach to development of the normative legal acts regulating the Accumulative pension system;
- the absence of a mechanism for efficient cooperation of pension system regulators with the Ministry of Justice for the assessment of the regulators' normative legal acts;
- the absence of an institutionalized pretrial procedure for conflict resolution between the regulatory bodies and its regulated subjects; and
- the absence of a proper mechanism for testing and raising the professional level of regulatory agency personnel.

A matter not addressed thus far concerns control over regulatory management expenses. System costs not only include direct financial outlays, but also time and labor costs. Ideal administrative practice would be to optimize system structure, with returns gained from clarity and effectiveness of system administration offset by various costs that accrue both to the regulatory agency and to those regulated. The system is far from being ready for such formal benefit-cost analysis, although instituting some simple net benefit rules could lead to easy improvements. Indeed, the changes advocated above all fall under the category of Pareto improvements—though without doubt there are still some costly reforms that would add to efficiency, and cost savings that could be realized with little if any loss in regulatory effectiveness. However, we believe that these savings are largely of a secondary order of magnitude: the regulatory agencies are reasonably but not lavishly funded, while Pareto efficiency gains already realized are fairly large. These suggestions also envision harmonization of regulations, both with each other and with prior normative legal acts. Building consistency among the many regulations will add to the Accumulative system's clarity and improve public confidence in it. In that case, it will be perceived as a stable organism rather than as an applied institution whose rules depend upon many random factors and current subjective interests.

One might also question the need for the strictness of regulatory control that has emerged in Kazakhstan's Accumulative system. However, the rationale for strict control is clear. Firm control was necessary to build public confidence in the system: more laissez faire treatment would have compounded already great skepticism. In addition, the early days of the Accumulative system were not propitious for competition. Those who did not choose a pension fund were given to the State Accumulation Pension Fund (SAPF) by default, and thus the SAPF started out with a large majority of the market. The regulatory agencies in turn encouraged the development of private APFs and hence the emergence of a more competitive environment. A strong regulatory presence was further justified by restricted choices of pension funds faced by contributors, in part because enterprise managers often strongly encouraged a specific fund and in part because of private APFs' limited presence in much of the country, especially rural areas. To this can be added limited awareness of their options on the part of many if not most contributors. In this setting, the regulatory agencies had no choice but to play a highly active rather than passive role, since the system's success depended on their ability to increase competition and information flows.

Ideally, Kazakhstan's antimonopoly legislation should determine criteria that characterize a dominant market position with regard to the pension system. Such legislation also should contain measures to restrict monopoly power, if shown to be harmful to the interests of contributors and recipients. In practice, issues of market power in the Accumulative pension industry have not been touched by antimonopoly legislation, perhaps in large part because the dominant firm has been publicly owned and also because effective competition has been growing. Nonetheless, it is important that the FSA delineate concepts of fair and unfair competition with regard to specifics of the Accumulative system and develop an effective mechanism to redress harmed parties in the event of unfair competition or collusive behavior. To date, regulatory policies have been driven by concerns over APF financial stability and security of pension payments to contributors, and with ensuring nonnegative real returns on accumulated pension savings. One could easily imagine how such objectives would lead to regulatory practices that encourage the development of a cozy oligopolistic situation, with a few large funds operating profitably while offering modest returns and a small number of pension products.

These tasks confront the FSA over the next few years. By global standards, Kazakhstan's pension funds do not offer a rich array of asset choices that would enhance competition and provide better effective service to contributors. While this limited choice to some extent reflects the system's lack of maturity and lack of experience by APF managers, it is also the case that regulatory bodies have hardly encouraged creativity and innovation. Together with improved regulatory coherence and mechanisms for dispute resolution, and continued surveillance over the industry's financial practices, the challenge for regulators is to encourage creative behavior within the industry in areas ranging from hedging against currency risk to offering a wider range of portfolios to contributors.

Appendix 9.1

Licensing Requirements

For Open Pension Funds

Founders and shareholders. Founders and shareholders *may be* residents of Kazakhstan, legal entities and individuals, that satisfy the requirements and nonresident legal entities, if rated by a rating agency accepted by the regulator. Legal entities registered in offshore zones, or affiliated to legal entities registered in offshore zones, and public enterprises *may not be* founders or shareholders.

Ownership rights. No entity shall have the right to own directly or indirectly, dispose or manage more than 25 percent of the total number of voting shares of any given APF, except when permitted by the regulator.

Executive positions. A person who lacks higher education, executive experience, or has a tarnished reputation *may not* hold an executive position. A person who was a chief executive or a chief financial officer of a financial entity that has been closed down for reasons of mandatory share redemption, license cancellation, liquidation, or bankruptcy declaration within last 12 months *may not* hold an executive position. A person who was recalled from an executive position of a financial entity by the regulator within last 12 months *may not* hold an executive position.

Capital restrictions. The regulator determines the minimum charter capital, procedure of its formation, and its composition.

For Corporate Pension Funds

Licensing requirements are similar to open funds, except for two positions. *Founders and shareholders* may be only legal entities of Kazakhstan. No *ownership restrictions* apply to corporate funds.

For AMCs

Founders and shareholders. Founders and shareholders may be resident and nonresident legal entities and individuals that meet the requirements of the regulator and that are rated by the rating agencies accepted by the regulator. Legal entities registered in offshore zones or affiliated to legal entities registered in offshore zones, and public enterprises may not be founders or shareholders.

Ownership rights. Own capital of an AMC with nonresident participation may not exceed 50 percent of total capital of all companies managing pension assets in Kazakhstan.

Executive positions Same as for an APF, except that the executive of an AMC does not need to pass a qualification exam and does not have to be a citizen of Kazakhstan.

For Custodian Banks

Founders and shareholders. Only those banks approved by the Board of the NBK may own, dispose of and manage shares in an APF or AMC directly or indirectly. State banks may not be the founders or shareholders of pension funds, except in cases permitted by the authorized body.

Ownership rights. A custodian bank may not directly or indirectly own, dispose or manage more than 25% of voting shares of an APF, except in cases permitted by the regulator. A bank may not acquire shares of the company if the bank is a custodian bank for a pension fund that carries out its activities through the company in question. A custodian bank may acquire shares of a pension fund provided that such participation does not exceed 10% of the bank's equity.

Appendix 9.2

Evolution of Prudential Norms for APFs until 2004

			Version of regulation				
	Constraint	*Target of the constraint*	*27 Aug 1997*	*22 May 1998*	*21 Apr 2003*	*4 Aug 2003*	*27 Dec 2004*
1	K1 Capital adequacy	Open APF	x	x	≥ (15 LogPVPAx LnPVPA+250) x 10^6	=	≥ (LA - L)/MREC, where MREC = 0.15 × 3-year AGI
2	K2 Assets to equity ratio	Open APF Corporate APF SAPF	≤0.5 ≤0.2 ≤0.5	≤0.3 =”= ≤0.3	≤0.4 ≤0.2 x	x x x	x x x
2	K2 Highy liquid assets ratio	APF	x	x	x	x	K2 = HLA/(MREC × 0.3)
3	K3 reserve capital	APF	x	x	≥ (8 LogPVPAx LnPVPA)x10^6	x	x
4	Investments at the cost of owned assets (book value)	Open APF	x	x	≥K3 (daily)	x	x
5	One party exposure in investment portfolio	securities and deposits issued by a commercial bank	x	x	≤.10 FE and ≤.25 BE [1]	≤.10 FA and ≤.25 BE	≤.10FA and ≤ .25 BE[2]
		securities and deposits of a commercial bank and affiliated persons			≤10%FA	=	=

			Version of regulation							
		securities of a non-financial organization					≤10% FA and ≤ min[IC/4 VB/4]		≤10%FA and ≤ min[IC/4, or VB/4]	
		5.4. shares of issuer that is not a 2nd-tier bank					≤10% FA and ≤10% IC		a) ≤15%FA and b) ≤10% IC	
		Type of APF	27 Aug 1997	22 May 1998	31 Jan 2000 2000	GOK Decree #1547 17 Oct-2003	NBK Decree #96 21 Mar 13 Jan 2003	RK Law N 369-II 13 Jan 2003	Decree GOK #2 8 Dec 2004	Decree GOK #1287
6	**Minimum capital**	Open APF	≥ 55mT	≥ 90mT	≥180mT	=	≥ 250mT (≥ 500mT for APF with AMC)			
		SAPF	10mT			180mT				
		Corporate APF	≥ 10mT	≥ 20mT	≥ 50mT		≥ 100mT (≥ 300mT for APF with AMC)			
7	**Limits on commission charge**	APF	≤1%PC and ≤ 10% IR					≤.05% PA plus ≤ 15% IR	≤.02%PA plus ≤ 15% IR	≤.05% PA plus ≤ 15% IR

Notes:

1. Including pension assets and own assets of the APF in voting stock of a bank.
2. No greater than 35% of the own capital of a bank (excluding purchases of state-backed financial assets and mortgage securities). If bonds issued by a bank are rated below S&P BB- or Moody's Ba3, investments are limited to 50% of own capital.
3. With the exclusion of financial agencies' securities, mortgage securities, and securities issues with the guarantee of the GOK or FSA.

Appendix 9.3

Main characteristics of state regulatory components

	Pension Law Article 31, item 4	APFs are required to compensate the contributors the difference beween the properly defined minimum return and the actual return of an APF.
Minimum charter capital and prudential norms	Pension Law Article 47, item 2	The minimum charter capital of APF, procedure of its formation, and composition shall be determined by the authorized body.
	Prudential norms for the APF	Equity adequacy requirement
		Limits on one party concentrations, including corporate securities, bank deposits, equity shares
Regulations on costs	Pension Law Article 25, item 2-1	Pension assets of the accumulation pension fund may be used for the following purposes only: (1) investment in financial instruments, the list of which is determined by the authorized body; (2) pension payouts in accordance with the legislation of the Republic of Kazakhstan; (3) transfer of pension accumulations to another accumulation pension fund or insurance company under a pension annuity contract in the manner stipulated by RK legislation; (4) payback of erroneously credited pension contributions and other erroneously credited money; (5) reimbursement of expenses related to making pension payouts and transfers of pension acccumlations in accordance with RK legislation.
	Pension Law Article 48, item 1	APF's commissions are no greater than 15% of annual investment income plus 0.05% of monthly assets
APF liquidation	Pension Law Article 45, items 1 and 8	An APF is liquidated by the general meeting of its shareholders, and executed by the liquidation commission set by the regulator and according to the procedure established by the regulator.
APF reorganization	Pension Law Article 43, item 1	Reorganization of an APF takes form of a merger, split-off, or changing the legal form of the APF from a corporate to an open fund by a general meeting of shareholders and with the approval of the regulatory body.
	Regulation	Content
Licensing	Pension Law Article 39	Activity regarding the attraction of pension contributions and payment of *pension* benefits is licensed by the authorized body according to the rules established by the legislation of the Republic of Kazakhstan.
	Pension Law Article 58	The *pension assets of pension funds investment management* is licensed by the authorized body according to the rules established by the legislation of the Republic of Kazakhstan.

Appendix 9.3 (*Continued*)

Governance rules	Article 64 of the law "On Joint Stock Companies"	Defines 'an affiliated person'.
Asset segregation rules	Pension Law Article 25, Point 1-1	Rights of the legal entities and individuals to the pension assets refer to the proprietary right. By implication, legal entities and individuals have the right to pension assets.
	Pension Law Article 6, item 7	Separate accounting of the pension fund's own assets and pension assets of the contributors and control over their purposeful placement.
	Pension Law Article 49, point 1	APFs must keep accounting and submit separate reporting for their own assets and pension assets in the manner established by RK legislation.
	Kazakhstan Civil Code Suppoint 4, point 2 of Artilce 195	In the absense of a concept of a fiduciary, the amendment to the Civil Law codified the basic principles of property rights distinct from full ownership. This enabled the Pension Law to define pension accounts as assets immune to the claims of the creditors.
Independent custodian	Pension Law Article 6, point 5	Pension assets are protected by the requirement to keep them on an account held in a custodian bank not affiliated with an APF or its AMC.
External audit/ actuary	Pension Law Article 6, item 11	Requirement of annual audit of APF and its AMC
	Pension Law Article 49-1	Audit of an APF is to be carried out by a licensed auditor
		Audit disclosure is required.
		Includes inspection of compliance with the prudential norms and the accounting standards and, in case of APF managing its own assets, inspection of investment and portfolio requirements.
Disclosure Requirements	Pension Law Article 41, points 3 and 8	The accumulation pension funds shall: Inform a contributor about the status of his pension account at least once a year and at his request free of charge. Provide access, including electronic, to information regarding a client's pension account.
		Publish APF's financial statements and other information about APF's activity.
Investment regulation	Pension Law Article 51–59	Asset management of pension funds is performed by an external asset managing company or by an APF itself, provided the APF has been appropriately licensed.
Guarantees	Pension Law Article 6, item 1	The Government guarantees the recipients safety of their mandatory pension savings in the amount of actually paid contributions adjusted for inflation.

Appendix 9.4

Evolution of prudential norms for AMCs

N	*Regulation version number*	*1*	*3*	*4*	*5*
	Effective date / *Prudential norm*	*9 Sep 1997 (Regulation)*	*1 Jan 2001*	*14 Dec 2001*	*1 Apr 2005*
1	Adequacy of owned capital (K1)[1]	1. κ1≥ 0.02 if PA ≤ 5bT 2. κ1 ≥ 0.015 if 5bT ≤ PA ≤ 10 bT 3. κ1 ≥ 0.01 if PA ≥ 10bT	no change	1. κ1 ≥ 0.02 if PVPA ≤ 5bT 2. κ1 ≥ 0.015 if 5bT<=PVPA ≤ 10bT 3. κ1 ≥ 0.01 if 10B ≤ PVPA ≤ 30B 4. κ1 ≥ minK1=0.01*0.95^ n, Where n=(PVPA-25)/5 if 30B ≤ PVPA ≤ 50B 5. κ1 ≥ minK1=0.0086*0.96^ n, where n=(PVPA-25)/5 if PVPA ≥ 50B	K1 ≥ 1 daily
2	Real rate of return of pension assets (K3) for each APF	K3 ≥ min{0.5K3av; K3av-2%}	no change	No change	
	Nominal rate of return of pension assets (K2) for each APF				devK2 ≥ 30%K2av

3	Ratio of investments of own funds in fixed assets and other intangible assets to equity (K4)	K4 < 0.25	no change	no change	
	High liquidity assets adequacy requirement (K4)				K4 = HLA / (MREC × 0.3) ≥ 1
4	Reserve capital	MRC ≥ 0.25%PA if PA ≤ 5B MRC ≥ 0.20%PA if 5B ≤ PA ≤ 35B MRC ≥ 0.15%PA if 35B<=PA ≤ 50B MRC ≥ 0.10%PA if PA ≥ 50B ARC ≥ PA*(K3-max{50%K3av; K3av-2%})	MRC ≥ 0.25%PA if PVPA ≤ 5B MRC ≥ 0.20%PA if 5B ≤ PVPA ≤ 10B MRC ≥ 0.10%PA if PVPA ≥ 10B ARC ≥ PA*(K3-max{50%K3av;K3av-2%})	no change	deleted
5	Investments at the cost of owned assets	Not set	BVIca ≥ permissible min (MRC+ARC)	no change	deleted

[1] **k1 = (E_AMO – LA)/(A_AMO + PVPA)**. This formula was valid from January 1, 2001 to April 1, 2005; since April 1, 2005 **k1** is calculated as follows: **k1 = (LA – L)/MREC E_AMO**: AMO equity
LA: Accounts receivable of affiliated entities and other AMO assets required to be listed
A_AMO: AMO own assets
PVPA: Pension assets under management
HLA: Highly liquidity Assets
MREC: minimum required equity capital
K3av: Period Average Real rate of return of pension assets
K2av: Period Average Nominal rate of return of pension assets
devK2: K2 deviation for each APF.
LA: liquid assets
L: liability

(Continued)

Appendix 9.4 (*Continued*)

	Regulation version number	*12*	*4*	*5*	*6*		
	Effective date Prudential norm	*9 Sep 9 1997 (Regulation)*	*22 Sep 1999 (regulation)*	*14 Dec 2001*	*16 Jun 2003*	*22 Sep 2003*	*1 Apr 2005*
6	Investments in non-state securities of one emitent; restrictions on deposits in any one second-tier bank, and cash balances.	**1. Deposits at, bonds, and shares of second-tier banks**	**1. Deposits at and securities issued by any given second-tier bank**	**1. Deposits at and securities issued by any given second-tier bank**	**1. Deposits at and securities issued by any given second-tier bank**	**1. Deposits at and securities issued by any given second-tier bank**	**1. Deposits at and securities issued by any given second-tier bank**
		I $\leq$ min{100% BC; 10% PA}	Ipa $\leq$ 10% of PA of each APF separately	no change	no change	Ipa $\leq$ 10%of PA of each APF separately if Ipa to voting stocks $\leq$ 10% voting stocks of Bank	no change
			Ioc $\leq$ 10% OA			Ioc $\leq$ 10% OA	no change
			Ipa+Ioc $\leq$ 25% BC			Ipa+Ioc $\leq$ 25% BC	Ipa+Ioc $\leq$ 35% BC Ipa+Ioc $\leq$ 50% BC on condition (1)
		2. Bonds of issuers included in KASE listing A	**2. Bonds of issuer that is not a second-tier bank**	**2. Bonds of issuer that is not a second-tier bank**	**2. Bonds of issuer that is not a second-tier bank**	no change	**2. Bonds of issuer that is not a second-tier bank**
		I $\leq$ min{50% IC; 5% PA; 15% of a particular bond issue}	Ipa $\leq$ 5% of PA of each APF separately	no change	Ipa $\leq$ 10% of PA of each APF separately		

		Ioc ≤ 5% CA		Ioc_f ≤ 10% CA_f		
		Ipa+Ioc ≤ min{25% IC, 25% of a volume of bonds of particular bond issue}	Ipa+Ioc ≤ min{25% of a volume of bonds of particular bond issue, 25% IC}	Ipa+Ioc_f ≤ min{25% of a volume of bonds of particular bond issue, 25% IC}		
	3. Stocks of issuers included in KASE listing A	**3. Stocks of issuer that is not a second-tier bank**	no change	**3. Stocks of issuer that is not a second-tier bank**	no change	**3. Stocks of issuer that is not a second-tier bank**
	I ≤ min{5% of volume of shares of stock; 5% PA}	Ipa≤ 5% of PA of each APF separately		Ipa ≤ 10% of PA of each APF separately		Ipa ≤ 15% of PA of each APF separately
		Ioc ≤ 5% CA		Ioc ≤ 10% CA		Ioc ≤ 15% CA
		Ipa+Ioc ≤ 5% of a volume of shares of particular stock issue		Ipa+Ioc ≤ 10% of a volume of shares of particular stock issue		no change

Abbreviations:
PA: pension assets
OA: AMC's own assets
CA_f: Organization with AMC license's own assets
BC: Bank Capital
IC: Issuers's own capital
Ipa: Investments if pension assets invested
Ioa: Investments if owned assets invested
ARC: additional reserved capital
BVIoc: book value of own asset investments
KASE: Kazakhstan Stock Exchange
K3av: Average real income
PVPA: pension assets addmitted by company in investment management
MRC: main reserve capital

(1) In the case that debt paper issued by a bank has a rating value not lower than "BB-" (according to rating classifications of Standard & Poor's or Fitch) or "Ba3" (according to the rating classification of Moody's Investors Service.

10

Actuarial Forecasts: The Reform's Distributional Consequences

A key issue that is often downplayed concerns the distributional impact of moving from a Solidarity system to an Accumulative system. Perhaps this is not surprising: the initial focus tends to be survival-oriented, identifying forces and problems that could cause the new system to crash, and making sure that the potential fiscal burden during transition is not overwhelming. Nor were distributional issues important in the initial wave of Accumulative system adoptions in Latin America for the simple reason that countries like Chile were not welfare states to begin with. In these countries, there was neither an initial commitment to ensure adequate standards for the poor in general, nor a particular commitment to the elderly, disabled, and rural poor. Thus, the individual account system was something of a bonus (that one paid for) rather than the replacement of a birthright.

In formerly socialist countries, and especially in former USSR, much higher expectations existed. A reform that worsens expected conditions for a large share of the population will not be regarded as being successful, even if it achieves the goals of macroeconomic balance, financial market development, and increased savings. Thus, distributional issues have been important almost from the start, with assessments of poverty consequences emerging within two years of the reform, and public debate focusing on distributional aspects from the very beginning.

This chapter addresses the distributional aspects. Although there are many actuarial simulations from which to draw, most of the analysis is based on and reports simulations from Dina Urzhumova and Ai-Gul Seitenova's KAZAK2 model, and specifically from their unpublished World Bank report (Seitenova and Urzhumova, 2003), which is the source for all figures not elsewhere attributed. Their work supersedes earlier, even more pessimistic analysis (Becker, Seitenova, and Urzhumova, 2000). The KAZAK2 results incorporate more sophisticated modeling and quite different assumptions about the growth environment that we now know seem to be well justified. Before turning to this analysis, section 10.1 raises issues as to what sort of assumptions are appropriate in a country with exceptionally high variance in its growth. It also discusses those forces that determine poverty risk in an Accumulative system: expected retirement duration, earnings inequality, labor market participation and employment in retirement system compliant "formal sector" firms. The following section presents known characteristics of contributors, and also briefly mentions government rules that govern minimum payments. Section 10.3 then presents forecasts from the waning Solidarity system, while section 10.4 offers simulations of several alternative scenarios, ranging from a pure Accumulative system (with a gradually diminishing Solidarity component) to a system with substantial public transfers. It also discusses effective risks in light of the GoK's commitment to provide a demogrant. The following section addresses labor market problems, ranging from years of service to household structure to noncompliance by employers. Finally, Section 10.6 turns to some other difficult issues, including geographic distributional effects, public social spending in Kazakhstan, annuity payouts, and the cost of different social security options to GoK.

10.1 Growth and Distributional Modeling in a Minerals-based Economy

By definition, the value of an individual's accumulated savings equals the sum of past contributions C_t made during period t ($t = t_0, \ldots t_R$, where t_0 is the age at which one starts work and t_R is retirement age), increasing at rate of return r. Contributions in turn equal the payroll contribution rate c (whether paid by employer or employee) times an individual's wage w times hours worked h per year (or the labor force participation rate at an aggregate level), times the compliance rate fs (or the likelihood of being employed in a formal sector job at an aggregate level). Thus,

$$V(t_R)=\sum_{t-t_0}^{t_R}[C_t(1+r)^{t_R-t}]=\sum_{t-t_0}^{t_R}(c_t w_t h_t fs_t)(1+r)^{t_R-t} \tag{10.1}$$

The amount of accumulations will therefore depend on these underlying parameters, and hence on their growth rates. A given accumulation value V will then translate into an annual expected retirement income (AERI) according to the duration of expected retirement, $t_T - t_R$, the rate of return on assets held after retirement, r_A (which can reflect either the return on formal annuity assets, or on assets gradually withdrawn from a bank), and on government transfers GT—residual Solidarity system payments, supplemental minimum allowances, or a demogrant. Thus, the forces that determine expected retirement income stream are (with signs given underneath, and time indicators dropped, so that variables such as w represent a vector of earnings in different years):

$$AERI = f(\underset{+}{c}, \underset{+}{w}, \underset{+}{h}, \underset{+}{f_S}, \underset{+}{r}, \underset{+}{r_A}, \underset{-}{t_T - t_R}, \underset{+}{t_R - t_0}, \underset{+}{GT}) \tag{10.2}$$

The sections that follow focus on several of these factors in detail. To the extent that particular forces are understood by policymakers to be important and potentially variable, it is desirable that they be the subject of actuarial modelers' sensitivity analysis, and must not be overshadowed by benchmark values chosen for other terms, especially if there is considerable uncertainty over these variables' values. This point seems obvious, but in reality, modelers have a very large number of parameters for which to choose values, and cannot explore the sensitivity of results to every possible factor, especially when interaction effects are critical. The preferred strategy is to generate (by assumption or statistical analysis) distributions of future values of all major parameter inputs, and then generate a distribution of possible outcomes, both for the economy/social security system, and for individuals. This can be done via Monte Carlo simulations, and is in fact standard practice for sophisticated models in advanced countries (Lee and Teljapurkar 1998, Holmes 2003, Lee 2004). However, it is not standard practice in actuarial simulations for transition and other middle-income countries; to our knowledge, Becker and Paltsev's (2006) initial work on a simple model of Kyrgyzstan is the sole exception. The reason for this absence is a mix of pressure to produce results quickly and an absence of data from a long, structurally stable time series. Thus, modelers tend to offer a small range of scenarios ("baseline, optimistic, and pessimistic") based on variation in one or a few parameters judged to be key, and treat other terms as stable.

This approach is hardly ideal for the purposes of macroactuarial modeling in which one is concerned with matters such as future government liabilities and total social welfare spending as a share of GDP. It is more problematic still when examining projections for individuals. In the macro setting, many results are obvious: the budgetary effects of previously committed social transfers become unimportant in an environment of rapid economic growth. Moreover, many variables may exhibit far less uncertainty at the aggregate than at the individual level. For example, it is fairly easy to trend the share of wages in GDP for macro modeling purposes, but this information is likely to be of lesser value in projecting wages for a given cohort of workers, much less for individual workers.

While these issues are general problems in social security modeling, they are felt even more acutely in modeling outcomes in a nation such as Kazakhstan, where oil and other minerals' revenues amplify structural uncertainty. In the absence of a credible time series, long-run forecasts will be inherently subjective. Nonetheless, choices must be made, and the uncertainty that exists does not completely invalidate actuarial modeling exercises—though it limits the information provided.

To learn from the modeling exercises, we start with a general principle and then explain several patterns from a large number of sensitivity analyses, thereby providing a guide to the results that follow. The principle is simple: actuarial forecasters, when forced to make choices under very restricted information, should exhibit a somewhat conservative bias, taking decisions less likely to generate high AERI values. Our rationale for this is that risk-averse individuals will care more about ensuring a minimum standard of living in old age or while disabled than they will about having a high expected standard of living.[1] From the state's perspective, there is an implicit obligation to care for destitute elderly and disabled persons, again making an upper bound of extreme poverty risk more important than a best guess at expected pension incomes. There is also a common-sense explanation: if the economy performs well for a long period, pensioner poverty will no longer be a critical social problem, whether addressed via individual savings or state transfers. Instead, actuarial forecasts are of greatest importance in the event that rosy situations do not emerge, as constraints will be more binding.

The impact of rapid economic growth (with wages following apace, or lagging slightly) obviously will be raised AERI. In an Accumulative system, rapid growth has the superficially counterintuitive result of lowering replacement rates, when those rates *RR* are defined as AERI divided by a person's wage over a near-retirement period, or by the average economy-wide wage at retirement. The reason is in fact simple: accumulated assets will have been built during years when wages were lower, but are being compared with recent, high wages. The extent to which this is problematic depends on how one views individuals' preferences: if absolute standard of living is what matters, then a high growth world with larger pensions but lower replacement rates is still a good deal, and distributional analysis should focus on estimates of absolute poverty or relative replacement rates across different groups. On the other hand, if people get disutility from invidious comparisons of their own living standards with those of others (that is, if pensioners are irritated by their children's wealth), then absolute replacement rates matter.

In most economic growth models (exogenous to actuarial models), wage growth and the rate of return to assets are closely linked. In a two-factor model with Cobb-Douglas technology, $w' = r + K' - L'$, where the prime denotes the growth rate. If, in addition, the capital: labor ratio is constant, then wage growth will equal the return to assets—nullifying the result reported above, and implying stable replacement rates.

Contemporary Kazakhstan does not evoke such a simple growth model. Massive inflows of foreign capital have funded minerals and petrochemical development and generated a healthy public sector budgetary picture, rapid growth in expenditures notwithstanding. This expansion and the associated minerals' and oil price boom have increased employment and real wages, in turn leading to a rise in domestic savings from several sources. Skilled labor markets have been especially tight, while the huge difference in living standards between Kazakhstan and its southern neighbors has meant large-scale illegal immigration, thereby depressing wage growth in the already fairly slack unskilled labor market. But those workers who have active Accumulative system accounts are disproportionately skilled, and since the introduction of pension reform have had substantial real wage increases. While demand for investment funds has grown substantially—for mortgages, small businesses, and some larger firms' investments—savings and capital accumulation have grown more rapidly, especially given the decline in government borrowing. The upshot is that real interest rates are quite low, and $w' > r$ seems likely to be a long-term characteristic of the Kazakhstani economy. As discussed in Chapter 4, this pattern is embedded in the KAZAK2 simulations, while reverse assumptions of an extremely slack labor market and high interest rates because of government borrowing needs were made in KAZAK1.

The difference in modeling assumptions reflects the very pessimistic view of Kazakhstan's economic prospects in KAZAK1. Long-run labor force participation and compliance parameters are also more optimistic in KAZAK2, and these imply higher replacement rates. Yet the underlying assumptions remain fairly conservative, and for this reason may understate eventual accumulations. On the other hand, labor supply models suggest it is possible (though not certain) that rapid economic recovery will lead to a decline in labor force participation among women, especially as birth rates recover, leading to overly optimistic accumulation forecasts for women. The final nonpolicy term in section 10.2, expected retirement duration, is driven by life expectancy and disability risk. Substantial recovery in age-specific mortality rates are assumed, though these rates remain high by global standards. Unfortunately, the evidence thus far suggests that the mortality assumptions in both KAZAK1 and KAZAK2 are "conservative" in that they imply longer retirement life expectancies than recent data warrant.

In the next five to ten years, it will be possible to conduct meaningful study of the actual distribution of accumulations, along the lines just now being done for Chile. Until then, assessments of the adequacy of individual accumulations must be based on illustrative work, since we do not even know the long-run wage distribution of contributors, much less long-run compliance and labor force participation rates—which almost certainly will vary across gender and wage group.

Still, even before turning to formal actuarial calculations, we can identify four characteristics that greatly increase the risk of having inadequate savings. Most obviously, *women* are at greater risk than men, as they have lower wages, lower h, and higher retirement life expectancies. *Rural workers* also will have lower accumulations, with dramatically lower w and fs. Indeed, it is difficult to imagine that the Accumulative system will provide meaningful retirement income to more than a handful of rural Kazakhstanis. To a lesser extent, those living in *smaller cities and towns* also are at a disadvantage, with lower w, fs, and likely h, with the last term reflecting greater unemployment. Finally, *unskilled workers* have lower fs, h, and w; in addition, elastic labor supplies from neighboring countries implies that skilled: unskilled wage gaps in Kazakhstan are likely to grow. Those with several unfavorable characteristics for the most part will remain outside the Accumulative system, and will be almost completely dependent on public transfers for disability and retirement incomes. Thus, the analysis that follows is aimed mainly at those in larger cities who do expect to have substantial contributing work histories.

How large is this group? Data from 2002 indicate that one-quarter of the potential labor force or 36% of the economically active population participated in the Accumulative system. This is actually a very large number for a middle-income country, though it also represents something of an upper bound, since many of those who contribute will be sporadic rather than regular contributors, and will not amass significant funds. However, as Chapter 5 discussed, the formal sector's employment share continues to grow with the oil sector boom, and may offset the positive bias noted above.

10.2 Minimum Payment Rules and Contributor Characteristics

The simulations that follow reflect rules in place and the contributor structure of 2002–03. Data are available with roughly a one-year lag, and rules change with considerable frequency, so that any given forecast becomes dated quickly, but so do subsequent simulations. The projections generated are therefore best viewed in a relative light, rather than as forecasts of the future.

In these simulations, the retirement age for men is 63, and for women, 58. As has often been pointed out, the state does not do women a favor by expecting them to retire early if it also expects them to save for their own retirement. Nevertheless, there has been no serious discussion of equalizing retirement ages.

Throughout the pension reform process, the GoK has consistently recognized some obligation to take care of those with inadequate personal accumulations. In addition to maintaining a commitment to those who contributed to the Solidarity system, with that commitment diminishing as years of participation decline, it has recognized a variety of disability and survivorship rights, as well as minimum pension payments (prior to mid-2005) or demogrants (since 2005).

Calculation of these minimum payments prior to the demogrant was needlessly complex. A holdover from the very high inflation days that immediately followed independence, a so-called Regulatory Calculation Index (RCI) was used to formulate different system parameters (and is used in the forecasts reported here). These include the wage ceiling for old-age Solidarity pensions, disability and survivorship benefits, old-age social allowances, and various special allowances. While current law does not set rules for automatic RCI value increases, in practice there has been almost full inflation indexation. The RCI has no economic meaning, and indeed obscures the relationship of various benefits to standard social indicators such as the minimum subsistence level, the minimum wage, and the average wage, all of which also feature in the Kazakhstan government's social policy analysis.

Further, linking the full array of public pension payments to the RCI has prevented them from being tied formally to more obvious measures. Since near hyperinflation and economic crisis in the 1990s made near-retirement wages a meaningless basis for calculation of Solidarity payments (including old-age pensions, disability, and survivor benefits) to formerly contributing (social tax-paying) retirees, a reasonable approach is to make payments based on current average wages (by occupation, industry, or education), with demogrants tied either to average wages or the poverty line. In contrast, noncontributor benefits (disability allowances for impaired children and the nonparticipating population, as well as old-age welfare benefits) would best be linked to social indicators such as group-specific subsistence levels. In recent years, payments to both groups have been adjusted along the lines suggested, but these adjustments have been ad hoc, and further increases are not guaranteed. Nor is the absence of indexation a feature restricted to various minimum pensions: general old-age Solidarity pension indexation also remains unspecified. It, too, has been addressed in a sporadic, ad hoc fashion.

Rather than endogenize nonmandated government responses, the simulations below do not assume further adjustment. The problem with this is that payments quickly decline in relative terms: relative to average wage, the minimum pension (by 2003 rules) falls from 23.3% in 2003 to 15.4% in 2010, and ultimately 3.4% by 2050 (Seitenova and Urzhumova, 2003:40). The wage ceiling (cap on social payments) declines from 55.3% in 2003 to 36.6% in 2010 and then 8.1% in 2050, while social allowances fall from 11.1% in 2003 to 7.3% in 2010, and only 1.6% in 2050. Furthermore, while there are social payment ceilings, there is no comparable cap on social tax payments, which remain proportionate to wages. This inconsistency was not a major issue when wage ceilings were introduced in 1997 (as equal to 6.9 minimum wages; later restated to equal 15 RCIs), since the ceiling was 72% above the average wage. But the restatement, inflation, and rising real wages have combined to make the ceiling an issue within a decade.

Adding further to both complexity and unequal treatment of comparable individuals, old-age pension calculations have dealt (until recent reforms) somewhat clumsily both with the system transition and the crisis years. The Pension Law requires a new retiree to submit a wage certificate for any three years from January 1, 1995 to the date of retirement. Reported wages for years after January 1, 1998 are accepted for pension benefit calculation only if a retiree submits proof of 10% mandatory contributions to the funded system for the same period. If a retiree does not provide an acceptable wage certificate, his or her pension is calculated based on the minimum wage and employment history (service years) as certified by the labor book records (or other documents such as labor contracts). All retirees laid off prior to 1995 but not retiring until after January 1, 1995, are given the minimum pension even if they worked a complete number of years while making Solidarity contributions, and even if they can demonstrate high wages prior to 1995. In fact, almost no one can do so, since payments are based on an individual's three highest wage years, but until recently without adjustment for inflation. The consequence of these various rules has been that more than 50% of male and 60% of female new retirees after 1995 received minimum Solidarity pensions—saving the system expenses, but also undermining confidence.

Unfortunately, no easy solution exists. Even though wage certificates for years prior to 1995 are accepted, obtaining such certificates would be rare, both because many firms were liquidated and because others did not keep accurate wage records for the crisis years. If pensions are instead assigned based on labor book records (without proof of individual wages) and on the average wage for the respective branch of the economy, there is great potential for falsification. The compromise solution has been to wait many years before taking this latter step.

The Solidarity system parameters and adjustment procedures as described generate significant mismatch of individual contributions and pension benefits. Although of decreasing importance for those whose benefits will come from the Accumulative system, that group will not be a majority for several decades. From the standpoint of the KAZAK2 projections that follow, this mismatch implies low replacement rates, and modest government expenditures.

Of course, GoK will not let the situation deteriorate along lines suggested by the forecasts if it has the means to prevent it, which it now does. Thus, in mid-2003, government raised the minimum pension by roughly 40% to 5500 tenge and increased pensions for those who retired prior to 2003 based on personal participation coefficients and 2002 wages by branches of the economy. Further increases occurred in 2004, and a demogrant was introduced in 2005, though these are not captured in the forecasts reported. Offsetting these rises has been continued rapid wage growth. Thus, the ad hoc adjustment process is likely to mean continual lags in government pension payments, and hence in a permanent diminution of replacement rates—but not the dramatic declines generated by forecasts with no political responses.

10.3 Providing a Solidarity Safety Net

We have seen in Chapter 4 that the gradual decline in Solidarity pension commitments prior to the introduction of a demogrant would reduce GoK expenditures as envisioned. From the perspective of individual pension recipients, what did this withdrawal mean? What were the distributional implications? Most critically, what happens to new pensioners when there is a radical shift from a traditional public PAYGO single pillar system to one with multiple pillars in which the primary form of accumulation comes from individual accounts?

What actually happened in Kazakhstan was not the only possible outcome, and at the time of the reform, it was not even a remotely likely one. However, the history of what happened to the Solidarity safety net is instructive, as it seems highly likely to be repeated elsewhere. Briefly, as we discuss below, Solidarity payments were made in accordance to (lagged) government capacity. Replacement rates initially fell, stabilized, and then fell again as wages began rising rapidly. Real pension payments began rising rapidly once the GoK recognized that its fiscal problems were diminishing. Indeed, a dispassionate analysis of Kazakhstan's public expenditures since 2000 would likely conclude that public pension expenditures rose too rapidly relative to other social needs, notably education and public health.

However, as a point of departure, it is important to recognize that PAYGO systems do not simply disappear. At the end of the year before the Accumulative reform was implemented, there were 2,061,873 old-age retirees in Kazakhstan, of whom only 88,862 (4.3%) retired during that year. Five years later, new retirees accounted for only 2.4% of the old-age retirement population, which had declined to 1,664,568. This decline of nearly 400,000 retirees reflects a combination of high mortality and small new retirement populations coming from the war-time birth cohort. Since post-war baby-boom retirements began as early as 2001 and will continue for roughly two decades, the retirement population is forecast to stagnate during the current decade, and then to begin rising sharply, by about 12% between 2010 and 2015, and by another 32% by 2025, more than doubling the present retirement population by 2040. While numbers with fewer than full length of service will fall sharply, this will not take place during the current decade. Moreover, because a large number of "favorable terms" pensions were granted during the early 1990s, the proportion of pensioners on favorable terms actually rose between 1997 and 2002, even though the number of new favorable pensions dried up with the reforms (falling to only 6.1% of all new pensioners in 2002 vs. 24.5% of the stock), reflecting higher mortality of regular pensioners. Thus, the old Solidarity system is destined to very gradually fade away rather than disappearing abruptly, and pension payments will be dominated by Solidarity payments for many years to come. Specifically, the KAZAK2 actuarial forecasts predict that Accumulative contributors will not be a majority of all new retirees until 2012 or 2013, and will not be a majority of the stock of retirees until after

2025—and, of course, many of those who contributed also will have some Solidarity entitlements.

This fact had two implications during the early years of the reform. First, pensioners and middle-aged workers cared far more about policies related to Solidarity pension payments than they did to the new Accumulative system's potential. Second, there was great skepticism at the outset with regard to the Accumulative contributions: few expected the accumulations to be substantial or the funds to be secure, and hence did not initially see their payments as a guarantor of financial well-being in old age. While the pension funds have not been without problems, their generally smooth history devoid of scandal has altered these early perceptions.

Yet, it was true that PAYGO contributions from government would be the main source of social security for the first two decades. It is also apparent in retrospect that GoK's policy was to maintain pension payments in real terms (Seitenova and Urzhumova, 2003:12 show considerable stability in real pension payments from 1997–2002) while reducing both the numbers of new favorable pensions granted and the variance of pension payments. As Seitenova and Urzhumova document (p. 13), there were virtually annual adjustments to the pension indexation rules, and while the details are of little interest, the outcomes are worth noting. Minimum pensions rose in real terms, and did so more rapidly than average pensions, so that inequality among pension payments declined. Since Solidarity pensions had been linked to prior earnings, in effect the partially notional defined contribution (NDC) component greatly diminished, and payments became increasingly like a demogrant. Thus, while in 1999 (and earlier) the distribution of pension payments was bimodal, by 2002 it was unimodal, with over 62% of pensioners receiving the equivalent of US$ 30 to 40 per month.

As we have seen in Chapter 5, wages began rising with the first signs of real recovery, even in the face of massive unemployment. Stable real pensions therefore meant falling replacement rates, and so it did, from an average of 0.52 in 1997 to 0.29 in 2002. The driving force in this was a 58% real wage rise over this period (figure 10.1), though declining real Solidarity pension caps and the maximum wage used in calculating pension incomes (the wage ceiling) also contributed to the average pension decline.

Forecasts for future Solidarity pensions are inherently arbitrary, since the NDC link is now small and will become increasingly unimportant in the future (as wages earned in the PAYGO system in the years prior to the reform decline relative to current wages, even if the latter are adjusted upward in real terms). Thus, what matters are GoK decisions regarding the demogrant—minimum pensions payable to all. If the GoK were to maintain its current rules for Solidarity pensioners, indexed the minimum pension to 85% of the subsistence level (keeping it constant in real terms), set social allowances to equal three (arbitrary but vaguely linked to subsistence) RCI values, and set the wage ceiling at 15 RCIs, then Seitenova and Urzhumova (2003:69) forecast a collapse in replacement rates from about 35% in 2003 to 5% in 2048—even for those with full years of service. However, this forecast is not a prediction of disaster for the elderly, but merely an indication of what would happen if pensions were kept constant in real terms while wages progressively grew.

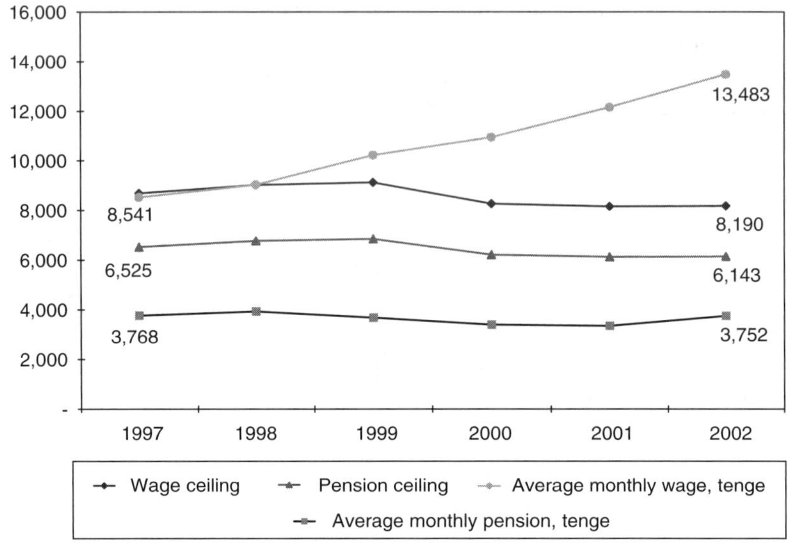

Figure 10.1 Average monthly wages and pensions vs. maximum wage and pension ceilings, 1997 prices

10.4 Individual Account Forecasts

The issue at the heart of the Accumulative reforms is whether the individual accounts would generate adequate savings to provide for old-age retirement (and, ideally, insurance in the event of premature retirement caused by disability). Conceptually, the issue can be divided into two parts—whether those fairly high-wage, regular contributors will have adequate accumulations and whether those with lower incomes and more sporadic participation will have substantial savings as well. The answers depend on earnings trajectories, participation rates, compliance rates, returns on assets, administrative costs, life expectancies, and income distribution. We discuss the assumptions underlying the macroactuarial simulations in KAZAK2 and then turn to results.

Kazakhstan has enjoyed exceptional real wage and GDP growth, but it remains a highly unequal society in terms of income distribution. Based on data from the early 2000s, Seitenova and Urzhumova (2003: 51) estimate a Gini coefficient of 0.52 for near-retirement-age persons (women aged 55–57; men aged 60–62). Even though it is a more homogeneous group, they also find a surprisingly wide distribution of earnings among Accumulative system contributors (figure 10.2).

Focusing first on male contributors, two striking patterns emerge. First, the log wage distribution of contributors is remarkably uniform: there are nearly equal shares of contributors earning no more than the minimum wage, one–two minimum wages, two–four, four—eight, and more than eight minimum wages. Second, this pattern is highly stable across age groups for those 25 years and older. This dispersion makes it difficult to talk of a "typical contributor."

Among women, the pattern is much less even. Women are far more prevalent among zero—four minimum wage group earners. At the same time, while 40% of

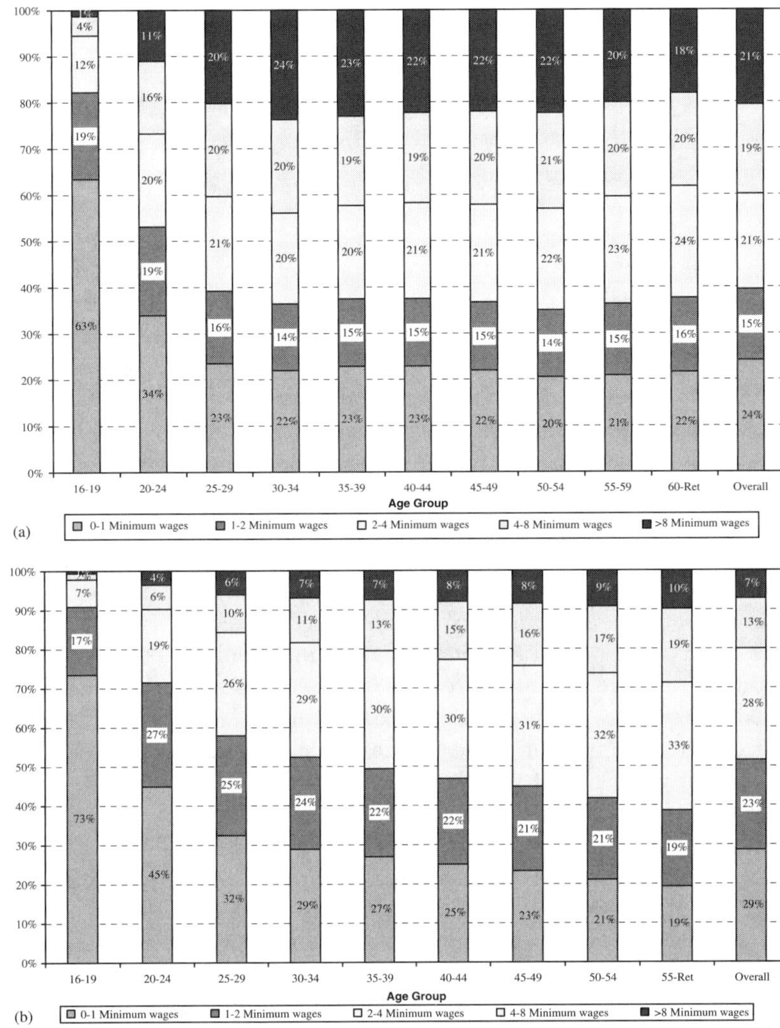

Source: Seitenova and Urzhumova, 2003:50, Figures 2.2.5 and 2.2.6

Figure 10.2 (a) Income distribution of Accumulative system contributors by age, 2001—men
(b) Income distribution of Accumulative system contributors by age, 2001—women

male contributors earn more than 4 minimum wages, only 20% of women do. The distribution of earnings among women ultimately is more important than that of men, for the simple reason that they constitute a large majority of total retirees (about 70% in 2007) and a smaller but still substantial majority of contributor retirees (about 59% in 2007). Because of the earlier age at which women retire, together with increased numbers of contributing workers, KAZAK2 forecasts project that the proportion of women among Accumulative system retirees will actually increase, peaking at over 68% in 2010, and falling slightly but constituting two-thirds of all Accumulative pensioners in 2050. This high long-run share of women in the retirement population also reflects the much higher life expectancy among women.

Thus, even without proceeding to actuarial simulations, the demographic patterns reveal likely social issues. Low accumulations will be a far greater problem for women than men, since only a small proportion of women are likely to have high pension accumulations, and since they have to spread these savings over a much longer retirement period.

A more positive perspective emerges when one examines patterns of social contributions by economic sector. In 1998, 5.4% of formal sector workers were employed in high wage activities (notably mining and finance), accounting for 11.4% of the wage bill, and 20.8% of social taxes paid. In contrast, low-wage branches (public administration, education, public health and social services, trade, repair of vehicles and home appliances, fishing, agriculture, hunting, and forestry) accounted for 50.6% of formal employment, 35.1% of the wage bill, but only 8.5% of social taxes. Four years later, these patterns were far less skewed. Although high-wage employment and its wage bill rose to 7.6 and 15.6%, respectively, the share of social taxes actually declined to 16.2%. Among low-wage activities, the employment share was virtually unchanged and the wage share actually fell to 31.9%, but social tax collection rose to 23.0% of the total. This pattern attests to the growing effectiveness of GoK administration as economic recovery proceeded, as well as diminished financial disruption that made it easier for enterprises to comply with tax obligations.

Creating sensible long-run macro-actuarial assumptions is extremely difficult in Kazakhstan's environment of rapid change. Sharp declining and then rising trends rather than a stable time series means that the modeler will be making forecasts about vastly out-of-sample values without the comfort of any historical continuity. Historic data are used for the first years. Moderating patterns are assumed thereafter, with input from the Ministry of Finance. Although inflation and wages and GDP growth thus far all have been much higher than projected, the conservative assumptions are prudent for reasons outlined above.

The relative efficiency of an Accumulative system relative to a PAYGO alternative will depend on the rate of return on investment relative to the rate of growth of wages plus the rate of growth of the contributing labor force. At the time the Accumulative system was introduced, the effective labor force was shrinking and real wages were falling, threatening a system meltdown. These patterns have been reversed during the boom, and to some extent that is captured in the model. Wage growth exceeds the rate of return on capital. This return is even lower during the decumulation stage, when pensioners are drawing down assets, as these are assumed to be conservatively invested and indexed to inflation. As is discussed below, effective employment growth is also rapid. Guessing at the rate of return on capital is hazardous indeed, and the figures used here are deliberately conservative. This conservatism also reflects the fairly narrow choice of investment options within Kazakhstan (restricted investment demand is a broad economic problem that the Accumulative system cannot address); at least in recent years, an appreciating tenge has lowered returns on assets held abroad as well.

The surge in mortality during the early years of independence eventually abated, with slight recovery occurring in the late 1990s (Becker and Urzhumova, 2005).

Life expectancy at birth for males peaked at about 65 years in the late 1980s, fell to 58 years in the mid 1990s, recovered to 60–61 years by 1999 and has stagnated since. For women, life expectancy at birth fell from its 1990 peak of 75 years to 69 in 1995, and has since recovered to about 72. The KAZAK2 modelers find it difficult to believe that Soviet-era life expectancy peaks will never be recovered, especially as life expectancy, both at birth and at retirement ages, continues to enjoy secular growth in most middle-and high-income-countries. It is therefore assumed that Soviet-peak life expectancy returns between 2015 and 2025, with eventual rises in life expectancy by 2050 to 73 years for men and 81 years for women. Note that these increases are not fiscally favorable either for the GoK or for individuals: infant mortality in Kazakhstan is low, so that the gains are realized more at older ages, implying increasing old-age dependency ratios.

Along with rising mortality and, as is discussed below, declining marriage, birth rates also plummeted with the collapse of the Soviet Union. In Kazakhstan, the total fertility rate (TFR, expected live births per woman who survives her entire fecund period) had gradually declined with modernization from 4.50 around 1960 to 3.16 in 1989. A fall of the same magnitude, to a subreplacement 1.76, was recorded in a single decade, with the TFR bottoming out in 1999. Yet, as Becker and Seitenova (2007) explain, birth rates in Kazakhstan are very sensitive to expectations of prosperity, and by 2003 the TFR had recovered to 2.03. This recovery is captured in the KAZAK2 simulations, but the modelers do not anticipate positive long-run population growth from births. Marriage rates seem to have permanently declined from their near universal levels in the late Soviet era, and, even though nonmarital birth rates have risen, it seems unlikely that fertility will ever come close to returning to Soviet levels. In retrospect, the replacement-level TFR assumption may have been somewhat conservative, but it also has the advantage of being neutral in the sense of favoring neither a defined-benefit PAYGO system (which would be the case if population and ultimately labor force were to grow rapidly) or the Accumulative system (which is favored when population and labor force are shrinking). Remember, though, that the Accumulative reforms were undertaken when marriage and birth rates were collapsing, ensuring low labor force growth or actual declines in future generations.

Population also grows or declines according to net international migration. Throughout the 1990s, there was a very large population loss in Kazakhstan due to net emigration: on net, 13.0% of the urban population and 8.7% of the rural population emigrated between 1990 and 1999 (Becker et al., 2005). This net emigration slowed to a trickle after the Russian crisis, and more recently has been reversed. Today, Kazakhstan is a major destination of international migrants from Central Asia, many of whom are undocumented (and never will be part of the national social welfare system). This surge was difficult to forecast even a few years ago, and its continuation is heavily dependent upon continuation of the boom. Once again, the KAZAK2 modelers elected to be conservative, assuming that net emigration would cease by 2015 and remain zero thereafter.

Both for GoK Solidarity budget purposes and for individual accumulations, labor market assumptions are among the most critical of all, comparable to wage growth assumptions and dominating demographic and macroeconomic assumptions.

Of the three key parameters, the least critical concerns unemployment. The values assumed, a stable 8% for men and 11% for women, are moderately high but hardly extreme by the standards of upper-middle-income countries. They reflect a decline from the late 1990s' peak but not a return to full employment. The high unemployment assumption can be justified on two grounds. First, for many older workers there is a skills mismatch between current market needs and training provided during the Soviet and early independence eras. Second, there is now a large influx of unskilled immigrants and rural migrants heading to Kazakhstan's cities. These workers are poorly trained and, while too poor to survive without working at all, are likely to have high turnover rates and therefore high average unemployment rates.

The second set of assumptions concerns overall labor force participation rates. These are set at 76% for males and 65% for females for the entire period and for all age groups, except for at ages close to retirement, to adjust for early retirees. These assumptions are slight, non-critical simplifications. Far more important would be any trends, but the evidence is too unclear at this point to justify assuming a rise or fall. The data on disability do not support secularly improving trends (Seitenova and Becker, 2008) and, while GoK has moved to curtail disability retirements, it seems unlikely that further decreases are in order. Stable fertility is consistent with stable labor force participation. The decline in marriage rates, especially for the cohort born between 1965 and 1985, may translate into a wave of higher female labor force participation rates, but this second-order effect is not captured in the KAZAK2 model.

The final assumption is that of a rise in overall compliance, including both participation in the Accumulative system and contributing to the PAYGO public fund. Although this increase, reflecting the relative growth of the formal sector, was not certain even as recently as 2003 when Seitenova and Urzhumova wrote, the experience since then indicates that this assumption was indeed appropriate. They assume that the share of employed persons contributing will rise from 43% in 2003 to 56% in 2015 and will ultimately level off at 58%.

Rising social security participation has a powerful impact. From the perspective of government revenues needed to finance the Solidarity system, it means roughly an extra 2% of revenue each year between 2003 and 2015. Since this is a period of high labor force entry anyway because those entering the labor force did so before birth rates collapsed, and as retirements are small because of small wartime cohorts, the outcome is a boom in the number of effective contributors from 3.00 million in 2003 to 4.29 million in 2015, an annual growth rate of 3.04%. To repeat a point made previously, PAYGO systems in middle-income countries are great during boom periods, as the base of the pyramid surges. The surge is not permanent, though: the contributor base grows at a rate of only 0.18% annually between 2015 and 2050, when it reaches 4.57 million workers.

The demographic and labor market assumptions together imply trends in the ratio of the working-age adult and, alternately, social security contributing populations relative to the retirement age population. These are termed the system (effective) support ratios (ESR), but it should be recognized that they omit disabled persons and other early pensioners. However, from the perspective of capturing trends, this omission is unimportant. The current era is a demographic/labor "gift" period, with the ESR rising from 1.8 in 2003 to 2.3 in 2015. This rise reflects improved aggregate compliance and working age population growth. Thereafter, the ESR slowly declines until it reaches 1.1 in 2050.

In reality, an ESR as low as 1.1 is unlikely, since it implies very high taxes (to cover those with inadequate accumulations), very low replacement rates, or both. As is discussed below, a nearly inevitable reform is an increase in the retirement age for women to parity with men. If this does not happen, women who retire at age 58 in the 2040s will have retirement-age life expectancies of up to 25 years, for which they could not possibly save adequately during their working lives. Even a gradual rise in women's retirement age to 63 keeps ESRs above 2.0 until the mid-2030s, at which point it seems likely that further increases in retirement age will be necessary for both men and women.

The average replacement rates generated by the Accumulative system parameters and Kazakhstan's demo-financial-economic environment are shown in figure 10.4. Replacement rates rise steadily as average years of participation in the system increase until about 2028 for women and 2033 for men, at which point all participants will have the opportunity to qualify for full years of service. When the system is mature, the average replacement rate for men is about 24%, a considerable level, but below the 35 to 40% that is generally recognized as a target (and which was realized by the USSR pension system). The sensitivity of the replacement rates to rate of return on accumulated savings is demonstrated as well: if returns fall to 4.0%, then the replacement rate plateaus at about 18% for men.

For women, the pure Accumulative system is even less favorable, as replacement rates plateau at about 13%, even with 5% returns on savings. The situation improves somewhat, with replacement rates rising to 17%, if retirement ages for women are increased to 63. Mandating unisex life tables in calculating annuities raises female retirement rates by roughly an additional 1%; conversely, male replacement rates decline.

To achieve an average replacement rate of 40% in a pure Solidarity system, without considering additional contributions to cover the disabled population, will require a payroll tax averaging about 20% between 2003 and 2025 (Seitenova and Urzhumova, 2003: 62). Thereafter, the required payroll tax increases, reaching 35% by 2050. If female retirement ages are increased to parity with that of male, then the required payroll tax rates do not reach 20% until 2033 and are only about 28% in 2050. Smaller replacement rates will require proportionately smaller taxes.

The demogrant implemented in 2005 is similar in spirit to this proposal (except that it provides an unnecessary transfer to high income/high accumulation individuals). A demogrant that provides a 20% overall replacement rate engenders costs that could be met by an 8% or 9% payroll tax today, though that level will double by mid-century. At present, most of the cost is met by the existing payroll tax, but that will not continue indefinitely without raising tax rates. Taken together with the Accumulative system, the demogrant seems likely (though its level is not guaranteed to future generations) to generate adequate average replacements in the 35% to 45% range.

Those uncomfortable with statistics may find it confusing that the low replacement rates forecast for the Accumulative system actually reflect assumptions of strong (though not extraordinary) economic growth. In such an environment, wages rise rapidly, as has been the case in Kazakhstan in the preceding decade. If the value of savings does not rise as rapidly, then the ratio of accumulated asset value to final year wage will decline in this setting. However, since lifetime wage income exceeds lifetime income from assets for the vast majority of the population, most people would prefer a setting in which wages grew at 8% and the return on savings was only 2% to the converse (a point made only stronger by discounting and mandatory saving). This point is reinforced by the fact that some wage income will be spent on investments in physical assets, notably housing and consumer durables that yield utility well into retirement.

Thus, the low replacement rate makes the Accumulative system look unduly bad. If wage stagnation were assumed, replacement rates would be much higher, yet welfare would be lower. This point is illustrated by table 10.1, which shows KAZAK2 projected constant price average wage and Accumulative pension increases.

Sustained economic growth makes for high real wages in the distant future and hence low replacement rates. But, comparing expected pensions to wages earned during one's working career (that is, examining "lagged replacement" rates), then accumulations are far more impressive, at least for men. The current structure ensures a tremendous gender disparity that must be addressed. We return to this theme in section 10.5.

The average Accumulative pension annuities will be augmented by a minimum pension or more, if prior years of service entitle one to a higher Solidarity pension. While it is impossible to tell the amount that GoK will commit in future

Table 10.1 Average Accumulative system pension monthly annuities and replacement rates (for contributors retiring after 1/1/2003, constant 2003 tenge)

		2003	*2015*	*2025*	*2035*	*2050*
Average monthly wage, 2003 tenge	Men	28,772	57,315	83,477	119,632	196,109
	Women	17,769	35,396	51,554	73,882	121,110
Current replacement rate (average Accumulative pension/ average wage at date of retirement),%	Men	3.3	7.4	11.4	15.0	18.0
	Women	2.0	4.2	5.8	7.2	8.3
Lagged replacement rate I (average Accumulative pension/ average wage from previous period – e.g., 2035 pension/2025 wage),%	Men		14.7	16.6	21.5	29.5
	Women		8.3	8.4	10.3	13.6
Lagged replacement rate II (average Accumulative pension/ average wage from base period – e.g., 2035 pension/2003 wage),%	Men		14.7	33.1	62.4	122.7
	Women		8.3	16.8	29.9	56.6
Average monthly Accumulative pension, 2003 tenge	Men	949	4,251	9,516	17,945	35,300
	Women	355	1,469	2,990	5,320	10,052

Source: Calculated from data given in Seitenova and Urzhumova, 2003, Volume II, *Summary Tables*, pp. 7, 15

years, one can forecast how much certain packages would cost. To get a sense of this, we contrast a no further reform (NFR) environment (that, however, builds in mandated minimum pension and minimum wage increases in 2003 and 2004) with three alternate scenarios simulated by Seitenova and Urzhumova via KAZAK2.

Scenario A (a) recalculates pensions for those who retired prior to 2003 based on 1997 wages by branch or, lacking such information, the national average, and indexes these to account for inflation between 1997 and 2003; (b) sets the new PAYGO pension as the maximum of the old pension, the recalculated pension, and the minimum pension, subject to a Solidarity maximum of 15 RCI; (c) indexes all payments to inflation in all years; (d) raises in 2004 this "old-age state allowance" to be the maximum of its 2003 value and 20% of the official subsistence level; (e) raises it in 2005 to be the maximum of its 2004 value and 40% of the official subsistence level; and finally (f) sets it thereafter to be the maximum of its 2005 value and 65% of the official subsistence level. This scenario was formulated as an option by the GoK and, while not legally binding, is in effect the demogrant option.

Scenario B (a) indexes the minimum pension to prior year nominal wage growth as of 2004, thereby fixing the minimum pension at 24% of average wages forever; (b) sets the social allowance—available to all retired persons regardless of length of service, if they do not qualify for regular pensions—at 12% of the average wage; (c) increases the wage ceiling used in Solidarity calculations to 4 minimum wages as of 2004; (d) recalculates pensions for those who retired prior to 2004 based on 2003 wages and personal participation coefficients, with a maximum Solidarity pension of 3 minimum wages; (e) indexes all future pensions to past year inflation; and (f) raises the female pension age by six months per year, starting in 2004, until parity with males is achieved in 2013. This scenario greatly increases the bases for Solidarity pension commitments, but also reduces Solidarity obligations to women.

Scenario C incorporates the changes in B, and also adds a minimum pension guarantee, comparing the Solidarity pension for retirees who contributed to the Accumulative system for at least 75% of their eligible period (from 1998 until retirement). If their prorated Solidarity pension is below the minimum pension, then the minimum pension (now 24% of average wage) is paid as a demogrant, regardless of entitlements from the Accumulative system. In effect, this is the most expensive option, combining both improved Solidarity conditions and a (more expensive) demogrant.

A comparison of these scenarios appears in table 10.2. Beyond the trivial (if GoK spends more money on pensions, replacement rates will increase), several lessons emerge. First, without some sort of demogrant, replacement rates will simply be too low (say, below 25%), and will fall very quickly. Second, while a demogrant similar to that currently in place will suffice for the coming decade or so, it will not be adequate in the long run unless minimum values are linked to average wages, as in scenarios B and C. Third, when benefits are tied to average wages, replacement rates are reasonable even in the absence of a demogrant; with a demogrant component, replacement rates are stable or slightly rising. Fourth, scenario C is not cheap, especially in the long run, when the fiscal benefits of further

Table 10.2 Government expenditure commitments and average replacement rates (RR), various demogrant and Solidarity scenarios (replacement rates for contributors retiring after 1/1/2003, constant 2003 tenge)

			2003	*2015*	*2025*	*2035*	*2050*
No further reform	Government expenditures, % of GDP		**3.2**	**1.8**	**1.2**	**0.7**	**0.3**
	Government expenditures, % of effective contributor wage bill		**16.7**	**6.5**	**4.4**	**2.6**	**1.1**
	Men	Solidarity RR	33.9	16.3	8.8	4.1	0.5
		Accumulative RR	3.3	7.4	11.4	15.0	18.0
		Total replacement rate	**37.2**	**23.7**	**20.2**	**19.1**	**18.5**
	Women	Solidarity RR	33.7	16.2	9.0	4.7	1.1
		Accumulative RR	2.0	4.2	5.8	7.2	8.3
		Total replacement rate	**35.7**	**20.4**	**14.9**	**11.8**	**9.4**
Scenario A: Basic demogrant	Government expenditures, % of GDP		**3.5**	**3.0**	**2.2**	**1.4**	**0.7**
	Government expenditures, % of effective contributor wage bill		**18.3**	**10.7**	**7.7**	**4.9**	**2.7**
	Men	Solidarity RR	33.9	25.2	14.9	8.3	3.0
		Accumulative RR	3.3	7.4	11.4	15.0	18.0
		Total replacement rate	**37.2**	**32.6**	**26.3**	**23.3**	**21.0**
	Women	Solidarity RR	33.7	25.0	14.9	8.4	3.3
		Accumulative RR	2.0	4.2	5.8	7.2	8.3
		Total replacement rate	**35.7**	**29.2**	**20.7**	**15.6**	**11.6**
Scenario B: Improved bases for Solidarity calculations + increased female retirement age	Government expenditures, % of GDP		**3.2**	**2.4**	**2.9**	**2.6**	**2.7**
	Government expenditures, % of effective contributor wage bill		**16.7**	**8.3**	**9.8**	**8.9**	**9.3**
	Men	Solidarity RR	33.9	39.5	31.9	22.5	12.7
		Accumulative RR	3.3	7.5	11.5	15.7	18.4
		Total replacement rate	**37.2**	**47.0**	**43.4**	**37.8**	**31.1**
	Women	Solidarity RR	33.7	38.2	30.0	20.4	15.1
		Accumulative RR	2.2	5.4	8.3	11.2	14.8
		Total replacement rate	**35.9**	**43.6**	**38.3**	**31.6**	**29.9**
Scenario C: Improved bases for Solidarity calculations + increased female retirement age + demogrant	Government expenditures, % of GDP		**3.2**	**2.4**	**2.9**	**3.0**	**3.9**
	Government expenditures, % of effective contributor wage bill		**16.7**	**8.3**	**10.0**	**10.1**	**13.5**
	Men	Solidarity RR	33.9	40.0	32.8	25.4	24.6
		Accumulative RR	3.3	7.5	11.5	15.2	18.4
		Total replacement rate	**37.2**	**47.5**	**44.3**	**40.6**	**43.0**
	Women	Solidarity RR	33.7	38.7	30.7	24.9	24.6
		Accumulative RR	2.2	5.4	8.3	11.2	14.8
		Total replacement rate	**35.9**	**44.1**	**39.0**	**36.1**	**39.4**

Source: Calculated from data given in Seitenova and Urzhumova, 2003, Volume II, *Summary Tables*, pp. 9, 15

raising the retirement age for women are limited to shorter retirement lives, and do not include a reduction in new retirements.

Ultimately, it seems likely that the coming decades will witness a compromise between scenarios A and C that costs the government 2.0 to 3.0% of GDP. However, while Table 10.2 is informative, it is not sufficient for making informed policy choices. Because of the high degree of inequality, average real pensions and replacement rates omit a critical part of the story. Addressing inequality is essential to achieve a sustainable system and a reasonably equitable outcome for all pensioners.

10.5 Labor Market Problems, Income Distribution, and Gender Inequities

A very large number of parameter values are necessary for the simulations in this chapter, and for many the database is weak, not in the sense that current values are unknown, but rather that there is vast uncertainty over future trends. Although this uncertainty certainly pertains to overall economic conditions, financial variables, and demographic forces, the most critical uncertainty concerns labor market conditions. This is not a peculiarity of Kazakhstan, but rather reflects a shift common in middle-income countries from informal or unregistered to formal, registered employment, with employers making contributions to individual Accumulative accounts and paying taxes to cover public social security expenditures.

From the perspective of macroactuarial forecasting, three sets of parameters are affected by overall labor market conditions. The first concerns years of service in aggregate, and the age- and gender-specific LFPR times the employment rate (or, one minus the group-specific unemployment rate). This set is important in Kazakhstan, but less so than in historically market-oriented economies (HMOEs), especially in Latin America. HMOEs have had much lower LFPRs and higher unemployment rates, meaning that there is more room for growth in contributing labor force than in successful transition economies like Kazakhstan or the Baltic states.

A second set of parameters involves the relative size of the registered, formal sector. Under Soviet socialism, nearly the entire legal economy was in the formal sector, but with the dissolution of the USSR, registered employment plummeted. With Kazakhstan's recent rapid growth, the informal sector's share of employment is dwindling rapidly, but clearly will not disappear. As we have noted, the projected continuation of relative growth of formal sector employment creates a one-time "gift era" for the PAYGO system, and indeed for Kazakhstan's tax coffers more broadly. This structural shift is well underway in Kazakhstan, and the parameters assumed in the model seem remarkably prescient.

In HMOEs, there is much more uncertainty about the evolution of formal sector employment. Certainly, an increase of the sort anticipated for Kazakhstan would be extremely optimistic. Most middle-income HMOEs do not have a comparably strong social and tax information database; most have less educated labor forces; most also have higher unemployment and underemployment, and loose labor market conditions with low levels of human capital create pressures that result in growth of an informal sector. Slower growth of registered employment also seems likely in transition states in the Caucasus and Central Asia that are poorer, and have suffered more disruption. This is especially true in a nation such as Azerbaijan, which combines rapid growth in the petrochemical sector with a lagging hinterland, and the burden of a population of whom nearly 10% are refugees. For such countries, the gift era of a surging PAYGO pyramid base will be correspondingly smaller.

The third set of parameters relate to compliance of registered firms. This overall rate depends in turn on the size distribution of firms (large enterprises are more compliant than small), on the sector, and on general economic conditions. Seitenova and Urzhumova (2003: 32–36) provide a discussion and data underlying these points, and find that only 28% of the working-age population actually paid social taxes (and a similar number made Accumulative contributions). More striking still, while virtually all large- and medium-size enterprises submitted reports to the National Statistical Agency (and hence to the tax authorities), only 54% of *registered* small enterprises submitted reports. That number is also likely to rise, and is assumed to rise in the KAZAK2 simulations, though compliance will remain an important issue for all developing and middle-income countries. In general, compliance will be greater in countries with a high ratio of employment in large enterprises relative to small firms; again, Kazakhstan is unusually fortunate in this regard.

While these factors are important for system-wide forecasting of government deficits and average replacement rates, assessing system adequacy also requires knowledge of the distribution of earnings, how earnings change as one ages (that is, one needs to know the distribution of age-earnings profiles, both at present and likely future patterns), and how sector of employment, employer compliance, and LFPRs relate to the distribution of earnings. The data available for Kazakhstan are remarkably detailed, and include age-specific distributional information (figure 10.2). Age-earnings profiles that control for cohort effects do not exist, nor do forecasts, but plausible assumptions can be made. The primary limitation is that panel data do not exist, so that it is impossible to estimate transition probabilities from one earnings class to another, other than by linking movement to age.

When KAZAK2 is simulated for specific income groups, a clear moral emerges: average replacement rates matter little in any reasonable assessment of Accumulative pension system adequacy. The reason for this is apparent from figures 10.3 and 10.4 replacement rates vary enormously according to both contributor income class and gender.

For moderate income men, Accumulative system replacement rates (RR) for those with a full career in the system will be slightly more than 22% (given a 5% rate of return on assets, and about 17% with a 4% return). Expressed as a ratio of the economy-wide average wage, these rates are even lower. Not surprisingly, those men with incomes less than two minimum wages (MWs) have even lower RRs in the 10–15% range. For low income women, the situation is even worse: RRs range from 15 to 20% for those earning two to four MWs, and 13–18% for those earning less than two MWs. None of these rates is likely to provide an adequate pension income, especially as the rate is expressed as a percentage of a low wage.

The situation is dramatically different for higher-income groups, especially men. Assuming a 5% rate of return, men earning 8+ MWs (group 4) can anticipate a

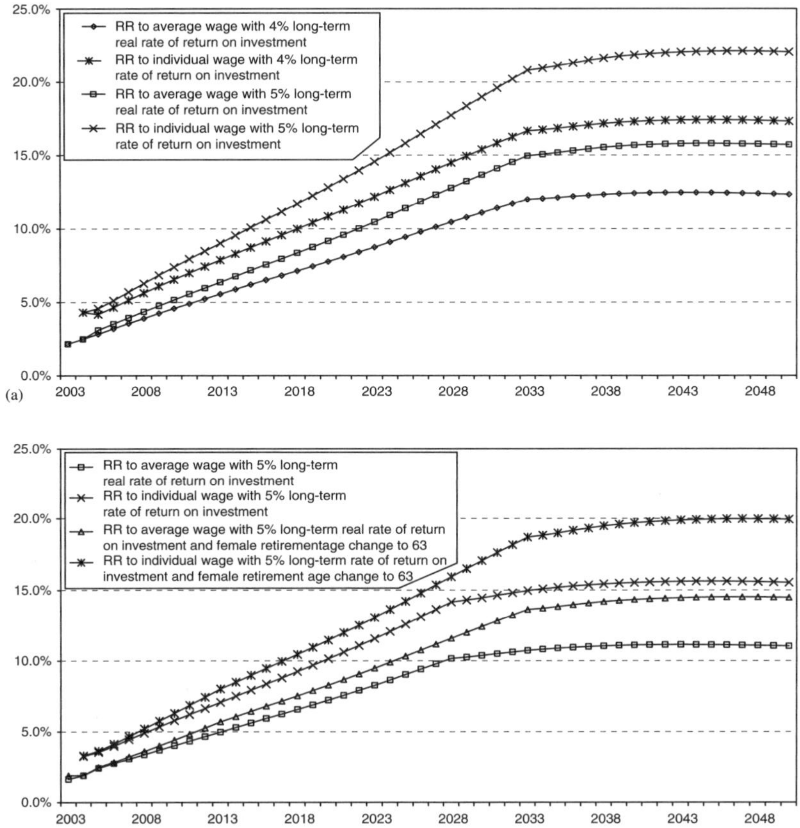

Source: Seitnova and Urzhumova, 2003:76–77, Figures 2.4.11 and 2.4.12

Figure 10.3 (a) Accumulative system replacement rates for new male contributor retirees earning 2–4 minimum wages
(b) Accumulative system replacement rates for new female contributor retirees earning 2–4 minimum wages

replacement rate relative to the average wage from the Accumulative system of over 70%! Even those in the four to eight MW category (group 3) will accumulate savings that give a replacement rate of about 27%. Comparable RRs for women in groups 4 and 3 are 62% and 24%, respectively.

Pulling these figures together, men (women) earning 8+ MWs can expect retirement incomes about 4.5 (5.2) times greater than those earning 2–4 MWs, and 2.8 (2.6) times retirement income for those in the 4–8 MW range. Much of this difference simply reflects higher lifetime earnings of high-income groups. However, Accumulative savings are less equal than earnings during working lives, since those in lower-income groups have lower labor force participation rates, higher unemployment rates, a lower likelihood of working for a registered enterprise, and lower compliance rates if they do work for a registered enterprise. To summarize, the Accumulative system does far better at ensuring adequate retirement incomes for upper-middle-and high-income workers than for those in

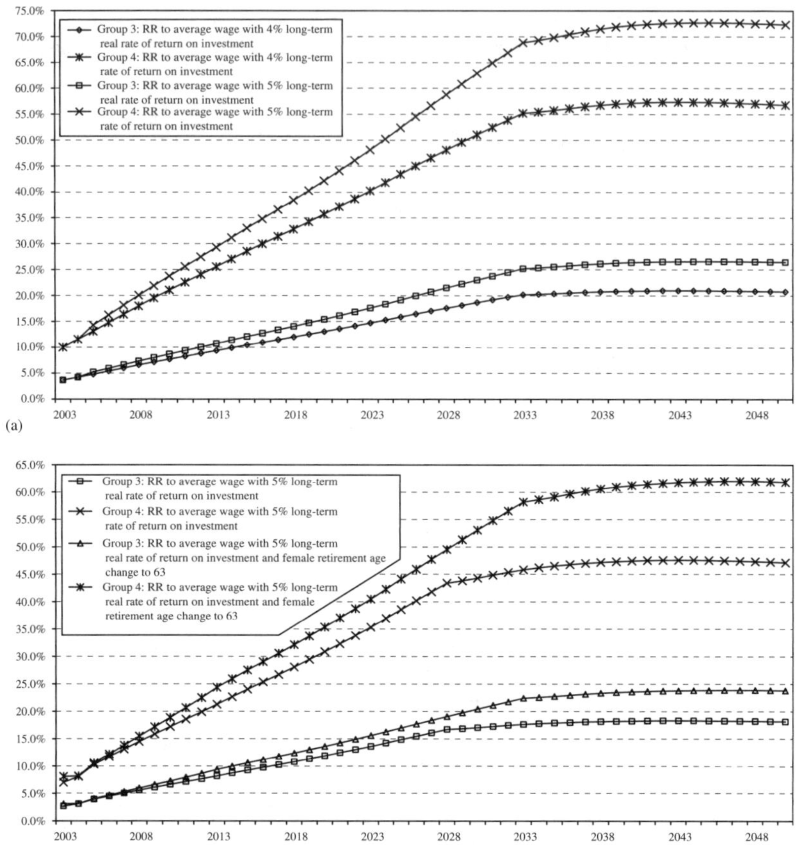

Source: Seitenova and Urzhumova, 2003:78, Figures 2.4.14 and 2.4.15

Figure 10.4 (a) Accumulative system replacement rates for new male contributor retirees earning 4–8 and 8+ minimum wages
(b) Accumulative replacement rates for new female contributor retirees earning 4–8 and 8+ minimum wages

lower-income groups. The risk of elderly poverty is especially great for women, who have shorter working lives and have lower earnings, on average.

10.6 Thorny Issues: Family Structure, Retirement Age, Geographic Distribution, and Annuities

10.6.1 Family Structure

The fact that low-income workers, especially those with interruptions in contributions, will have inadequate Accumulative system savings means that some sort of old-age support outside the Accumulative system is virtually inevitable. However, while inequality generated by the Accumulative system is considerable, it also may be overstated by the simulations of the previous section. The reason is simple: these simulations show individual retirement incomes, not expected incomes of pensioners. Since pensioners live in households, actual income will depend not only on the individual's pension savings, but also on the incomes and consumption demands of others in the household.

Simulation models such as KAZAK2 do not map individual pension income flows into retirement consumption, as doing so would require a distribution of household types and nonpension incomes for each possible pension asset group. However, Becker and Seitenova (2007) argue that household structure at retirement is likely to differ vastly according to whether or not sustained economic growth continues, and is accompanied by recoveries in marriage rates. If year 2000 age-specific marriage, divorce, and mortality rates are maintained, then by 2035 only 26% of women at retirement age will be living with a husband. However, if from 2005 onward, age-specific marriage rates recover to 1990 levels (of women 2.5 years older to allow for a permanent increase in age of first marriage), if divorce rates decline by one-third, and if male mortality declines to 1990 levels, then in 2035 some 58% of all women will be married when they retire.

The implication is simple. With sustained economic growth, there will be far more intrahousehold income redistribution than if economic conditions deteriorate and social patterns continue to exhibit the decay of the 1990s. In this latter scenario, poverty among one-person, female-headed households will be a severe social problem. Redistribution along the lines of scenario C (table 10.2) will be important to combat severe elderly poverty. With sustained economic growth and social recovery, better-targeted and less costly public transfers likely will suffice.

10.6.2 Women's Retirement Age

In effect, the shift from a pure PAYGO to an Accumulative system carries with it the commitment to raise the retirement age for women to parity with men. In some countries, that would be true in part because of cost factors, but in Kazakhstan, projected social security costs to the government are sustainable even without this increase. Rather, the difference in individual account savings, especially when spread out over anticipated retirement life span, is so much lower for women than men that measures must be taken to raise women's replacement rates if the Accumulative pillar is to be meaningful for more than a handful of high earners.

As noted above, Seitenova and Urzhumova (2003) find that the most obvious step, moving to unisex mortality rates for the purposes of pension calculation, has only a small effect on the replacement rate disparity. The reason is simple: the large majority of the retired population consists of women, and mainly women with low and moderate wages, with considerable spells outside the registered labor force, during their working lives. Having a significant impact on the replacement rate necessitates raising something more dramatic that will both raise accumulations and lower significantly the period over which those funds are spread.

Raising women's retirement age from 58 to 63 years will increase average funded pension replacement rates by about five points. Its impact is far greater than a modest demogrant, which (unless increased) is worth about two points for women. Indeed, the nearly inevitable conclusion to be drawn is that raising women's retirement ages to parity with men *and* improving the bases used for calculating demogrant and other PAYGO transfers cannot be avoided if Kazakhstan is not to have a major social problem involving large numbers of poor, elderly women. While intrafamily transfers will mitigate this problem considerably (especially within the ethnically Kazakh population, which has stronger family ties, larger families, and fewer family members abroad than ethnically European extended families), the problem will not be fully resolved. As we have seen, a large cohort of women who will never marry already exists, and marriage rates, while recovering, are unlikely to return to Soviet-era levels.

Raising retirement age is politically unpopular, usually extremely so. A unilateral increase, while reasonable to economists, actuaries, and demographers, is a most unlikely move for a government not facing a fiscal crisis. It is difficult to imaging that Kazakhstani political figures would countenance a formal retirement age increase during the current era of high growth and healthy government budgets.

A way out of the resulting conundrum is not to mandate a retirement age increase, but rather to grant the right to delay retirement. This can be phrased in a gender-neutral fashion, if all citizens are allowed the right to work until age 65. Expressed as a positive right, rather than a requirement, the increase is likely to draw far less criticism, especially if it were accompanied by a right to remain employed on a part-time (say, 20-hour/week) basis, health permitting, for citizens between ages 63 and either 67 or 70. There is ample precedent: in the United States, for example, while some jobs (notably, high stress positions in the public sector) have early mandatory retirement, it is decreasingly common in the private sector, and there are millions of older workers. Productivity does fall off, and a high proportion of elderly workers are part-time—but they are valuable to firms, which find them useful, especially in periods of tight labor markets. There is an obvious parallel with Kazakhstan, which has lost a large share of its skilled labor force, and which will have small cohorts of young workers entering the labor force during the era 2010–25. Facing labor shortages, Kazakhstani employers will benefit from the effective increase in the labor force, and at the same time will enable workers to increase accumulation accounts to levels that will support adequate retirements.

In moving from a predominately PAYGO to a mainly Accumulative system, the notion of retirement age also should change from being a public standard to a matter of individual choice. Critical issues become ensuring adequate health and disability insurance—nascent issues in Kazakhstan, though coverage that policymakers with considerable prescience are trying to make widespread (and, in principle, mandatory). With adequate insurance, workers can choose retirement date according to their work capacity, financial considerations, and individual preferences, rather than working out of financial pressure until incapacitated or until a legally mandated retirement date.

10.6.3 Geographic Distribution of Pension Contributions

Thus far, we have regarded Kazakhstan as a single entity. This is wildly inaccurate, since general level of economic development and the pace of recent growth both are highly concentrated. While the data available are for Solidarity system payments and receipts in 2002, there is no reason to believe that the regional patterns for Accumulative system contributions would differ substantially. Regional differences also are likely to be persistent over time.

On the basis of Solidarity payments and receipts data, it is possible to divide Kazakhstan into three groupings. The first grouping consists of five oblasts that are heavily rural (rural pensioners account for 49–73% of the total), poor (high wage branches account to 0–9% of social tax payments; low-wage branches account for 50–61%), and largely outside the formal sector, which accounts for 22–43% of the employed population, while in each oblast more than 40% of workers are self-employed. Per capita social tax payments are low, ranging from 3,083 tenge in South Kazakhstan to 5,559 tenge in Akmolinskaya oblast. Those oblasts in this group located in the southern part of the country have a small (less than 10%) share of pensioners in the population, while the proportion is much higher in the northern oblasts. Effective support ratios (ESRs) are very low (1.1 to 1.7) while replacement rates are high, ranging from 36% to 45%. While we do not have regional accounts, it is obvious that these regions will be net deficit oblasts for the PAYGO system.

At the other extreme, accounting for roughly one-fifth of all pensioners, are the high income areas of Almaty, Astana, and the oil-producing regions. ESRs are high (1.8 to 4.5), low-wage branches are small (9–40% of social taxes), the self employed are less than one-fifth of the labor force, save for in West Kazakhstan, and social tax collections are five to ten times as high as in the first group. However, PAYGO replacement rates are low, ranging from 14% to 25%. These are large surplus regions.

In between these two groups lies about half of the country, with intermediate level ESRs, self-employment shares, social tax payments, shares of low and high branches of production, and replacement rates. Much of the intermediate groups consist of the old industrial heartland and regions with now-booming metals processing and mining industries. Other than the two largest cities in the second category, this group is the least rural of all. The oblast averages shown themselves mask enormous intraoblast inequality.

This regional pattern matters for choice of pension structure. The old Solidarity system in effect represented a vast transfer from dynamic cities and oil-producing areas to rural areas and regions with stricken smaller cities that had lost key industrial plants (a point made earlier by Becker and Paltsev, 2001, with respect to neighboring Kyrgyzstan). If the PAYGO system were to be closed down, then large interregional transfers from wealthy to poor areas would cease—and, without doubt, such a move would be opposed by parliamentarians from net recipient regions. On the other hand, development of an Accumulative system will reduce the current inequity in replacement rates, since individual accumulations will not be transferred from wealthy to poor regions.

To summarize, Solidarity systems that provide little variation in individual payments (that is, those without NDC components, as is pretty much the case in Kazakhstan) involve considerable resource transfers from rich to poor areas, and generate impressive replacement rates in the latter. An Accumulative system does not involve these transfers, and hence reduces inequality in replacement rates, but at the same time has no mechanism for taking care of the poor in stagnant regions. The fact that Solidarity payments do not account for regional differences in cost of living accentuates the contrast: rural pensioners now live fairly well in Kazakhstan, while those in big cities struggle, despite increases in minimum pensions. The two-pillar system that has emerged once again seems like a natural response, and it is difficult at this point to imagine either part disappearing without substantial protest from a natural regional constituency.

10.6.4 Annuity Payments

Thus far, we have assumed that accumulated savings magically turn into actuarially fair payments to pensioners. In reality, this is not an effortless event. As it has been addressed elsewhere in detail (Seitenova and Urzhumova, 2003; Sipos, 2003; Moody, 2005) and the basic points are well known, we limit remarks here to a brief summary.

Purchasing an annuity involves a one-time fixed cost to the issuer, a monthly administrative cost, and a cost proportionate to the size of the annuity to compensate for longevity risk, assuming that a whole-life annuity is being considered. If the amount accumulated is small, these costs overwhelm returns on the assets, and it makes no sense to require conversion of the fund into an annuity. Rather, it is best to permit a lump sum or scheduled withdrawal of the savings over a fixed period. Kazakhstani law recognizes this, and requires pensioners to purchase an annuity only if the monthly payout exceeds a legally specified minimum (or, in effect equivalently, that the amount saved does, though this will vary by gender).

In 2003, this amount translated into accumulations of 900,000 tenge for men and 1,250,000 for women; Seitenova and Urzhumova (2003) estimated that only 145 men and 46 women would reach this hurdle. While the numbers who will be able to purchase an annuity is forecast to grow rapidly to 3,164 newly retired men and 729 women by 2010, these numbers amount to only 11 and 1% of newly retiring men and women respectively. While projections further out are extremely speculative, there can be no doubt that, even in the very long run, substantial numbers of retirees will not be able to purchase whole life annuities.

With the commitment to institute a demogrant, the potential political issue of the mandated annuity was largely defused. The slow growth in the numbers of annuity purchasers is actually somewhat advantageous for prospective insurers, who at present have little idea of the longevity risk of the insured population. Indeed, given the vast swings in population mortality, even projecting life expectancy at retirement age for the entire population involves vast uncertainties. If insurance companies offer large numbers of policies based on life expectancy estimates based on little information, they risk bankruptcy if pensioners live "too long." On the other hand, if insurers offer policies that compensate for this risk, thereby assuming improved longevity, in effect they will extract large profits from the elderly—and will further reduce the number who must buy policies in the first place. While large international insurers could offer annuities with a trivial impact on overall risk, they are unlikely to do so for tiny numbers, unless they are assured of preferential access to the market in the future as the number of prospective annuitants increases.

One might reasonably ask why annuities are legally mandated at all, when a system of scheduled (or unscheduled) withdrawals would be much simpler, would involve no creation of risk for insurers, and would not effectively confiscate a high proportion of accumulations for those retirees in bad health. The answer appears to be that GoK is intent on using the Accumulative pension system to develop the nation's financial sector. If large numbers of prospective annuitants opt out, a critical mass may never be reached that allows those who want annuities to opt in. Moreover, the risk from annuity insurance will be negatively correlated with life and disability insurance risk: if age-specific mortality proves higher than expected, insurers benefit from the annuity products they provide, but suffer added costs for other insurance products. Thus, advocates of a policy that strengthens financial sector development overall tend to see annuities as an important piece of the puzzle.

If accumulations prove adequate, a simple way of resolving the payout issues raised is to spread out payments over a large number of years (say, five years beyond retirement age life expectancy), with a lump sum payment at the end. If the recipient dies before the term annuity ends, then the present value of remaining payments can be made to the estate. This structure eliminates uncertainty of payment value. However, it also requires (in principle) a larger overall accumulated fund than a whole life annuity, as the expected payout period in this latter case may be shorter, and there is no balloon payment at the end.

With the emergence of supplemental demogrant funding for retirement, it is also reasonable to ask whether there are alternative uses to which individual savings could be put. Two possibilities, both of which have precedents in the United States, jump out. One would be to enable early withdrawals for educational purposes for oneself or, more likely, for one's children. This would have the effect, using U.S. counterpart terms, of combining a mandatory 401(K) plan with a 529-education savings plan (ESP). A second possibility would be to allow withdrawals for specified health needs, in effect adding (again in U.S. terminology) the analog of a Health Savings Account (HAS) component. Both HSAs and 529 ESPs have quickly grown in popularity in the United States, and it seems likely that they would be even more valuable in a middle-income country such as Kazakhstan. In particular, health insurance is limited, and a catastrophic illness or accident is likely to entail large out-of-pocket expenses. While HSAs are intended in the United States to supplement health insurance, in Kazakhstan they could play an equal or even primary role. Were these uses to be added, the option to voluntarily increase individual contributions might also be appropriate.

Considering annuity payout options and alternative uses for accumulated funds remain to be fully resolved in Kazakhstan. Because there are few retirees thus far with substantial accumulations, these issues are academic rather than critical. Resolving them will occur during the next phase of the reform.

11

Lessons for Future Reformers

There is by now a vast literature on social security reform throughout the world.[1] This chapter does not seek to repeat (or worse, repeat and add to) the long list of universal lessons repeatedly prescribed. Nor do we close by presenting and taking sides in the passionate and often entertaining debate over the merits of traditional PAYGO, unfunded public systems (with the extent of the NDC component also a matter of debate) versus fully funded, defined contribution systems versus alternative constructs such as the Kotlikoff-Sachs Personal Security System (Kotlikoff, 1999).

Our reason for sidestepping these debates and avoiding presenting general lessons emanates from our belief, applicable to much public policy and certainly to social policy, that quality and flexibility of administration are central to a reform's success. These characteristics are far more important than whether or not the initial design was or was not optimal, given the initial conditions prevailing at the time. The value of a detailed case study is that it gives the reader a sense of how rapidly circumstances change in a transition setting, and how many unanticipated surprises greeted pension system administrators. Kazakhstan's success to date reflects a fortunate coincidence: the shocks received have been positive ones, in general, and administration has been professional, transparent, and creative. It is also noteworthy that the system as it now appears to be emerging is quite different from that envisioned at the outset.

What if any implementation lessons can be learned from Kazakhstan for those still to undertake serious reform? After all, large Accumulative (funded, individual account, defined contribution) reforms began in Chile and elsewhere in Latin America well before they occurred in Kazakhstan, and there is a large pile of evidence from a range of reformers in Latin America and Eastern Europe. However, Kazakhstan is unique in that it undertook reforms in the absence of more than a rudimentary financial system and in fact intentionally used the pension reform as a means to jump-start its financial sector. Kazakhstan is also exceptionally well documented, making it easy to identify both successes and problems. Indeed, the transparency that has characterized the entire reform process is rare if not unprecedented for a developing or transition country. This openness extends as well to the statistical information, especially on the finance sector, and legal information (virtually all laws are available for free online at www.zakon.kz). Thus, the reform process that has been documented in the preceding chapters may not differ enormously from that in other countries with a coherent social security policy vision and competent administration: the difference is that in Kazakhstan it is fully documented. Finally, the Kazakhstani experience is not well known, even though it is both radical and occupies a unique position among the reformers.[2]

Thus, what one learns from the Kazakhstan case study is likely to be quite different from a set of general principles. Abstract debates mean little to administrators facing an untenable current situation, and trying to decide where to go next. Their questions are likely to be more along the lines of: If we implement a particular reform, will the system that emerges be sustainable? And when problems with the reform appear, will they be easy to address? The study of Kazakhstan's Accumulative reform does suggest sustainability, at least in certain circumstances, and with caveats to follow below. Recounting the issues that arose and GoK's responses may forewarn prospective future reformers, helping them address their second question as well.

A key moral already has been asserted: likelihood of success of any reform depends on administrative capacity and political will. It is also obvious that both NDC and Accumulative reforms are far more complex than measures that revise Solidarity PAYGO parameters, and we believe that sophisticated systems should not be implemented until administrative (and information technology [IT]) capacity is in place. There are several deeper and more subtle lessons as well, but these await description, in the following two sections, of several different types of prospective reformers, and a brief mention of some of the other social security reforms undertaken.

11.1 Upcoming Reformers: The Cautious, the Paralyzed, the Bold, the Complex

While major pension reforms are under way across middle-income countries throughout the world, there are many countries that have not yet determined a path or that have been plagued by tentative, inconsistent, or false starts. It is impractical to offer lessons from Kazakhstan, either alone or relative to other reformers, to all countries whose social security strategies are not firmly set, and we do not have the expertise to do so in any case. Rather, the comments that follow are intended to be relevant to one or more of three important and representative countries. China is by far the most important and complex ongoing reformer. In view of the range of programs it has adopted already, the description that follows is terse, and interested readers are directed to the references for detail. Ukraine is of interest because of its political paralysis and delayed economic recovery, making it a bystander while most of its neighbors made major reforms. Azerbaijan also delayed its reforms, but was careful to build a world-class information database that will serve it well in its upcoming plans that, in light of rapid economic growth occasioned by rising oil prices, are now under way.

Of the three countries, pension reform is most urgent in Ukraine. Its population is rapidly aging, fertility is below replacement, a notable share of the productive labor force has emigrated, and a large share works for the informal sector or in noncontributing enterprises. As of 2005, an extraordinary 15.3% of GDP was devoted to pension expenditures (World Bank, 2006), far higher than in Kazakhstan or the CIS average, far above the Baltic states (which range from 5.3% in Lithuania to 9.8% in Latvia), and even well above the levels in formerly socialist Eastern Europe, which tend to be demographically older. To address this large burden, the Ukrainian government enacted a mandatory second fully funded pillar and a third, voluntary private funded pillar in 2003 (for a detailed description in Ukrainian, see http://www.pension.kiev.ua/). However, it was never implemented, beyond unimportant voluntary pension funds (World Bank, 2007), and as of June 2007 the official national website was still announcing a pilot program in a raion in Lviv oblast.

This failure reflected domestic political conflict and, quite likely, constraints imposed by relatively slow economic progress. Nor is it certain that Ukrainian political leaders fully grasped the seriousness of the situation. The most recent announcement from the Ministry of Labor regarding pensions concerned increases to the Solidarity payments rather than imminent multipillar reforms (Utro.ua, 2008). However, it is clear that both the World Bank (World Bank, 2007) and USAID (which has funded many pension projects, including the national pension website referenced above) have been highly concerned and almost certainly frustrated by the slow domestic progress. Indeed, USAID has funded the financial sector reforms that were intended to accompany pension reform and these, it appears, are moving along fairly well.

The reform in Azerbaijan has proceeded quite differently than elsewhere. Azerbaijan experienced a short but disastrous war with Armenia following independence that left the nation without about one-fifth of its territory and nearly 1 million refugees. Independence and the war were economically traumatic, and while there were significant international investments in the oil sector, prices were generally low in the 1990s. Social security reform inevitably was a secondary issue in this environment, and primary emphasis was on maintaining a PAYGO Solidarity social safety net.

Yet, while Ukraine and Azerbaijan started out from a similar position economically, their approach to pension reform varied markedly. Azerbaijan made steady progress in terms of planning reforms and, while unprepared financially to undertake a major reform, built administrative capacity. In 2001, a Concept paper was put forth, followed shortly thereafter by a law *On the Personification of Accounts in the System of State Social Insurance* (SSPF, n.d.). With international assistance, a massive computerization program both at the national level and in the raion centers was undertaken. Between 2004 and 2006, 80% of all pensioners were issued plastic withdrawal cards, enabling them to receive pension and allowance payments from post offices and ATMs throughout the country. SSPF now has a database, coordinated with the Tax Ministry, on all contributors as well as payment recipients (Tsyganov and Mejidov, 2007). Thus, implementation of reform stages will be quick once a plan is finalized.

At present, the Azerbaijan government (GoA) envisions a reform fairly similar to that in Russia, described below. However, there has not been a firm commitment to a particular design, although GoA does hope to have both a mandatory NDC and a mandatory "Real Fund" defined contribution, fully funded component as part of a second pillar. A final decision is likely to take place in 2009.

The complex situation in China reflects the great range in levels of economic development of its regions, both across provinces and between rural and urban areas. The Chinese social security developed along the lines of that in the USSR (for a detailed history of the system and reforms, see Chen, 2005; Leckie and Pai, 2005; and Salditt et al., 2007). However, since until the economy opened up a quarter century ago to private and autonomous cooperative enterprises, and began an export-oriented approach, China was far poorer than the Soviet Union. Thus, its initial social security efforts were limited to disaster relief and to pensions for civil servants and workers in state enterprises. As China also was overwhelmingly rural prior to 1980, this meant that that the vast majority of the population had no formal pension system.

As in the USSR, China had and continues to maintain an internal passport (*propiska* in Russian; *houkou* in Chinese) system that specifies a city, town, or rural area of authorized residence. Public schooling, medical services, and other social goods are available (in principle) only at one's authorized residence. As we have seen, legislation in the late Soviet era unified pensions across republics and, within them, oblasts; pensions also were extended to rural collective farm households (though contributions from these collective farms were tiny and continue to be very small in all newly independent states of which we are aware, relative to authorized pensions). Payments in early post-Soviet pension systems were still the responsibility of oblast or even raion (district) regional offices, which meant that impoverished areas with few contributions ended up seriously in arrears or making payments in kind (or both) during the economic contraction of the early and mid-1990s. Thus, one of the key initial reforms in nearly all post-Soviet republics was to ensure Republican (national) government responsibility for pension payments.

The unification of pension rights and payments that occurred in the USSR and its successor states has not taken place in China. With a few minor exceptions, the elderly and disabled in rural areas are supposed to be taken care of by the cooperative farms to which they are assigned, or by local governments. Voluntary private pension funds for rural workers (to be supplemented with contributions from collective farms) have been established, but given the continued poverty of most rural areas, these have not proven viable. Rodriguez (2005) reports that about 12% of China's 500 million rural workers had participated, with an average fund balance of US$311. However, these figures are for 1998–2000, and since then rural reforms have largely collapsed.

Large enterprises originally were responsible for their workers' pensions. However, many of these enterprises have closed or have been taken over by entities that managed to avoid assuming pension and other liabilities, leaving large numbers of workers uncovered (Rodriguez, 2005). China's shift to a market economy thus left a pension system far worse off than in the former USSR and Eastern Europe, with only a small fraction of the population likely to receive adequate transfers to cover living costs in their non-working years. Added to this was an inevitable consequence of China's one-child policy: its boom in the young adult population between 1980 and 2005 is destined to be replaced by a shrinking labor force in the future. Taking the ratio of population aged 20–59 to that over age 60 as a measure of old-age demographic support capacity, China's capacity was forecast to fall from 5.6 in 2000 to 2.0 in 2040 (World Bank, 1997), a far more dramatic decline than that forecast for Kazakhstan (from 4.3 to 2.9), for example. To add to the stress, Chinese nominal retirement rates have remained at 60 for men and 55 for women despite very large gains in life expectancy at retirement age. The World Bank's (1997) actuarial projections warned vividly of looming social security system deficits or untenably large payroll charges to cover necessary costs of the current system. More recent simulations by the prominent Chinese demographer Zeng Yi (2005) again point to the necessity of raising retirement ages.

As one would expect, the Chinese government's concern rose as it became aware of these problems, starting as early as 1991 (Chen, 2005), and both the World Bank and Asian Development Bank actively pushed a reform agenda, with initial studies (notably, World Bank, 1997c) highlighting the extent of the problem. A three-pillar scheme was embarked upon, with the core goals of unifying pension obligations across enterprises (state and private), thereby achieving portability (a new issue in China, since, historically, few workers changed employers). A National Social Security Fund (NSSF) was established, operating in effect as an NDC system with limited funding (Rodriguez, 2005; Zhao and Xu, 2002). A social pool comprises the first pillar. Although the NSSF is now a gigantic fund, the system has experienced imperfect compliance, especially in its early years, and there is vast regional variation in compliance, coverage, and administrative quality (for a general discussion of these issues, see Ramia et al., 2008 and Chen, 2005). Thus, NSSF collects funds from a variety of national government sources, and makes transfers as needed to provincial governments. There has also been imperfect separation between the general social pool and individual pools, with funds from the latter at times used to supplement shortfalls in the former.

As Chen (2005) details, even intraprovincial pooling of urban pensions has largely failed. She attributes the failure foremost to massive debt overhang: vast, unfunded liabilities from the prior system remain (and there has been no effort to recover unfunded obligations from enterprises, nor would doing so be practical). Areas experiencing high growth are able to run surpluses, but more slowly growing areas are simply overwhelmed by current funding requirements. Thus, many provinces face deficits rather than investible surpluses. Moreover, even when local government accumulates surpluses, there are inadequate investment opportunities, and rates of return on the main vehicle—government debt—are low. Thus, by the early 2000s, only Beijing, Shanghai, Tianjin city provinces, and Shangxi province had achieved full pooling (Chen, 2005), and only 45% of urban workers nationwide were participating in provincial pooling as of 2002. A third critical problem is the very high replacement rate (averaging more than 75% in the state sector and often exceeding 100% for some categories of workers: Chen, 2005: 22), a problem noted earlier by the World Bank (1997c).

As Chen (2005: 23–25) emphasizes, the other side of pooling vast unfunded liabilities is free rider and moral hazard problems. System pensions are based on salaries a short period before retirement. However, while firms rather than the state set these wages, the provincial system pays the resulting pensions. Of course, this is true not only in China, but a key difference is that wages have risen at such precipitous rates that the difference between contribution and defined benefit streams is much greater. Naturally, this reward structure encourages implicit contracts in which wages are highest shortly prior to retirement. Eventually, NDC rules will lessen the inappropriate incentive, but that period is still a long way off. The municipality-based system of collecting contributions, which are then pooled at the provincial level, creates a compounding moral hazard problem: local units face little penalty for collection shortfalls and, especially in regions where many enterprises are struggling, will face great social pressure not to collect all obligations.

Provinces have been encouraged to experiment with their own social security reforms, and some, most notably Liaoning in China's northeast rust belt, have done so. Liaoning was especially appropriate, since it was among the provinces hit hardest by contraction in the state enterprise sector. As Salditt et al. (2007) note, although in 2004 Liaoning province accounted for only 3.2% of China's population, it contained 7.2% of the nation's state-owned enterprise (SOE) retirees.

The Liaoning reforms began in 2002, with ADB support. It is telling that the ADB support was intended to explore the possibility of establishing a provincewide IT system to manage accounts and collect contributions. A national, unique SIC system covering all Chinese workers, rural and urban—a necessary condition for an effective second pillar—remains on the horizon. The Liaoning experiment involved segregating individual accounts from social pooled funds, along with a large basic benefit incentive provided to workers who contribute for more than 15 years (Chen, 2005:18); for those who worked 32 years, a social pool pension equal to 30% of current average urban pay was to be provided. The experiment lowered the required individual account NDC contribution from 11 to 8%, and thereby lowered the projected replacement rate from 38.5 to 28%—but in effect kept the target total replacement rate at around 58%. These moves reflected concerns about low compliance. In addition, enterprises were encouraged to contribute to a third pillar with actual individual funded accounts, termed "enterprise annuities" (Leckie and Pai, 2005). While the reforms are viewed as somewhat successful, compliance problems have remained. Moreover, the NDC fund at retirement is to be paid off as a scheduled withdrawal over 120 months, which is about 50% less than the retirement age life expectancy. Thereafter, the provincial government absorbs the liability and continues to pay the monthly amount as long as the recipient lives (Leckie and Pai, 2005).

Although the experiment required massive central government support, the pilot project expanded to Jilin and Heliongjiang provinces in 2004 and 2005, respectively, and then in 2006 to Henan, Hebei, Hunan, Shandong, Shanghai, Shangxi, Tianjin, and Xinjiang provinces. Salditt et al. (2007) report general success in setting up individual accounts, but huge reliance on both central and local governments for financial support, with, in the case of Heliongjiang (also a rust-belt region), government funds accounting for 80% of individual account deposits.

The outcome is that, nationally, only about 40% of China's 200 million urban workers in 2000 were covered by any pension system (Rodriguez, 2005); as of 2006 the proportion was still below 50% (Salditt et al., 2007). Clearly, financial solvency is a distant prospect. More positively, Zhao and Xu (2002) report an increase in participation/compliance from urban public and private enterprise employees from 50.4% in 1998 to 63.4% in 2000. However, even with further increases, vast problems remain. These include funds' misuse and theft (with the most striking public example of misappropriation occurring in the otherwise successful Shanghai pension fund: Salditt et al., 2007). While inconclusive, estimates of the impact of pension transfers on reducing poverty are also disturbing: Salditt et al. (2007: 38) conclude that "it seems likely . . . that the Chinese pension system does very little to reduce overall income inequality, and certainly less than in any OECD country." To this, one could also add that it does less than in any Eastern European or USSR successor state.

A good sense of the problems with which China's policymakers must grapple is given by the example of Hebei, a largely rural and moderately poor area near Beijing (IMR, 2008), and where the reforms have had a rural focus. Data from a recent (apparently 2005 or 2006) 1% population survey show that pensions and all other allowances and transfers account for barely 6% of the income of the rural elderly (IMR, 2008). Family support accounts for 59%, and labor income (33%) accounts for nearly all of the remainder. In short, the welfare state does not go far beyond the big cities. Many of Hebei's rural citizens—about 3 million in 159 counties—participated in the 1990s' rural pension insurance pilot projects. However, the accumulation fund peaked at renminbi (RMB) 470 million in 1999, falling to only 397 million the following year (during which the State Council declared that rural social insurance was a premature concept: IMR, 2008). Activities remained moribund until late 2005, when the provincial government enacted a new rural old-age insurance program for "peasants whose land had been requisitioned" (IMR, 2008). By the end of 2006, this fund involved 2.3 million people in 11 cities and 141 counties, with a total fund of RMB 565 million. The rules of this fund do not appear to be constant across counties: in a few areas, townships and enterprises made large contributions; elsewhere, they made little or none. In 2007, Qianan city (which contains rural areas) announced a new rural old-age pension scheme that has considerably more public support (notably, the collective fund covers 40% of the premium, which in turn is set at 28% of the "basic contribution wage," which in turn equals 50% of the average 2005 wage in Hebei province). Nearly 72% of those eligible to participate have done so, an order of magnitude greater than the somewhat more than 8% who participate (as of 2006) across the province (IMR, 2008).

Despite these considerable efforts, the pension system remains problematic. Out of nearly 28 million rural working age adults in rural Heibei, only 2.3 million participated in the schemes as of the end of 2006. Some 2.4 million were employed outside the province; if they made any pension contributions elsewhere, at best they can get individual account lump sum refunds upon leaving. Within Hebei, local governments often were in arrears with respect to their obligated contributions, and returns on bonds in which the assets were invested was only 2.5%, essentially ensuring a tiny replacement rate.

To a considerable degree, China's exceptional economic growth has eclipsed its social security system failings. Rapidly rising real wages mean improved living standards that were difficult to contemplate only a few years ago, and as most people effectively own their housing, personal saving for retirement is not unduly difficult. Where the system fails is not with the average urban worker, but with those in need of a social safety net—the disabled, the childless (who have social obligations to support their parents in old age, but will not have children of their own to provide support), the unemployed living in decaying rust-belt towns rather than in booming areas, the unskilled, and, above all, those still in the countryside, along with "floating" migrant workers in the cities, many of whom have few rights. Unfortunately, in China these categories still comprise a large majority of the adult population.

In reality, China need not face a pension crisis. Although its young adult population is set to shrink, its productivity-adjusted labor force will continue to grow as the population shifts from rural to urban areas, and as productivity generally rises. Thus, a nationally unified benefit or defined contributions system, notional or otherwise, will be sustainable for decades to come, since the base of the pyramid will grow rapidly. This conclusion is stronger still if China were to adopt more realistic retirement ages. It is no surprise that these recommendations, along with using proceeds from SOE privatization to meet social security commitments, were at the heart of the World Bank (1997c) recommendations. Nor does China have a particularly unmanageable pension burden at present: Salditt et al. (2007) estimate that social security transfers of all kinds only summed to about 3% of GDP in 2005 (albeit a substantial rise over the less than 1% figure in 1990). The real burden is in terms of future rather than present obligations, and central government transfers, while large, are not at present a huge burden.

Why has China not moved more vigorously to reform its social security system? While we can only speculate, several possibilities seem likely. The first is that regional differences are vast: a system appropriate for Shanghai is likely to be ill-suited for impoverished Guizhou. China is a huge nation that for the purposes of social policy may be better regarded as a collection of individual countries, and its policymakers may have decided to do just that. A second reason is more pragmatic: a nationally unified system with consistently enforced contributions would force overt recognition of the bankruptcy of many SOEs; as Chen (2005) suggests, there are strong political reasons to protect them. Perhaps most pragmatic reason of all is that the bill for past liabilities is just beginning to come due, and current political leaders may find it easier to defer hard solutions to the future—especially when there are even more pressing social problems, such as the deterioration of the state health system, and when both SOEs and private enterprises resist paying social taxes. In the meantime, as virtually all authors cited above emphasize, the confidence of ordinary citizens in the social security system is very low.

11.2 Competing Alternatives: The NDC Paradigm and Mixed Systems

The main alternative to the fully funded, mandatory defined contribution programs (that normally include a minimum pension provided by the state through a first Solidarity pillar) is a reformed PAYGO system. The structure to emerge is one in which individual virtual accounts are created and prior contributions are recorded, with payments reflecting the extent of past contributions—in other words, an NDC system. First pioneered in Sweden, it has a large number of adherents, both in prospective reforming countries and in the international aid and financial agencies that proffer advice.

The first NDC reformer in the former USSR was Latvia, which introduced its current system in 1996 (Natali, 2004; for a background on the three reforms, see Schiff, et al., 2000). Resembling Sweden's system, the core pillar is an NDC PAYGO, and covers both those who retired before 1996 and those who did so after 1996. Augmenting this since July 2001 is a second pillar, the State Mandatory Funded Pension Scheme. The initial contribution rate to this scheme was a 2% payroll tax, but it is slated to gradually increase and reach 10% of wage by 2010. The mandatory component was compulsory (as of 2001) for those under 30 years of age and optional for those aged 31–49; those over 50 were not included. Around 43.5% of all working age population participated in this scheme in 2004. The average age of participants was 31.5 years. A voluntary private pension third tier also was set up in 1998. Its size is small but gradually growing, with about 2.7% of the working age population participating as of the end of 2004.

Estonia's three-pillar system was introduced in 1998–2002 (Fultz, 2004). As in Latvia, the reforms moved from the Soviet system to a clearer NDC paradigm; pension ages also were equalized for men and women. Estonia's public pension system has an average replacement rate of about 40% and has managed to keep the majority of pensioners above the poverty line. A second pillar covers only old age and does not provide support for the risk of disability and survivorship. Participation is compulsory for new entrants to the labor force beginning in 2002 and voluntary for those already in the labor market before 2002. Participation requires contribution from employees of 2% of the wage rate. In addition to that the state adds four percentage points from the pension-earmarked part of the social tax. At about 70% of the labor force in 2004, Estonia's second pillar participation rate is perhaps the highest among transition nations. A third, voluntary pillar takes two forms: pension insurance policies offered by licensed private insurance companies and units of pension funds managed by private fund managers. By October 2004, over 10% of all employed had pension contracts with life insurance companies and around 1% of employed participated in voluntary pension funds.

Lithuania's pension reform started in 1990 with the establishment of an autonomous National Social Insurance Fund (SODRA); reforms followed that related pension benefits more closely to previously earned income (Fultz, 2004). Like Latvia, full-term replacement rates were maintained at about 40% during the transition period. Retirement ages for women and men are 60 and 62.5 years, respectively. A third reform phase involving partial privatization was implemented in 2003, transferring a portion of social insurance contributions to private funds. The current system, based on 2002 legislation, consists of a Solidarity minimum plus NDC public pension system and a voluntary individual account system. Regardless of age, all persons paying contributions to the public pension system were given the option of remaining solely in the social system or joining the new private pillar. Every year during an open season people can switch to the new mixed system; however, the law prohibits returning from the mixed system to the solely public system. By July 2004, 47.6% of those insured by the full public pension system had decided to join the mixed one. Thus, Lithuania's and Kazakhstan's pension systems to some extent have converged in recent years.

Compared with other reformers, the Baltic states are distinguished by several common features. All experienced mortality increases during the early years of independence, but recovered by the late 1990s. All also experienced considerable economic dislocation at independence as well, but are now well ahead of Soviet era peaks in terms of per capita income. Extreme inflation and lack of confidence in the banking system have long disappeared. Perhaps most fundamentally, the entire region has below replacement fertility and high demographic old-age burdens. As Schiff et al. (2000) document, the ratio of pensioners to employed population rose between 1990 and 1999 from 45 to 64% in Estonia, from 43 to 63% in Latvia, and from 47 to 65% (1998) in Lithuania. The share of disability pensioners also rose in all three countries, especially Estonia, where disability pensioners as a share of all pensioners rose during this period from 10.8 to 17.5%. To contrast them with Kazakhstan, economic deterioration was much less, but heavier demographic burdens certainly compensated in terms of putting pressure on the social security system.

Relative to the Baltic states and Kazakhstan, Russia was a late reformer. As Sycheva and Mikhailov (2006) and Williamson et al. (2006) detail, the financial crisis of 1998 forced it to reconsider its very large social security expenditures, but the first laws on reforming the pension system were not passed until the Putin administration in 2001. Unfavorable demographics also were a major motivating force (Baskakov, 2006). Based on the standard three-pillar scheme, the reformed pension structure contains a publicly funded PAYGO pillar designed to ensure that all pensioners receive at least subsistence level income. Through this pillar, a flat pension is available to all workers with at least five years in the workforce. The mandatory second "insurance" pillar is an unfunded NDC system, with accumulations inflation-adjusted, credited with additional interest as of 2013 (!), and disbursed over a fixed retirement period (Lim, 2005). In general, the rules of the second pillar are stacked against both high replacement rates and a high degree of inequality in payments (Baskakov, 2006), despite the stated intent. The distribution of payroll contributions dedicated to this second tier and a third funded Accumulative portion depend on the worker's age. Within the funded portion, workers can choose between private AMCs or a state-managed fund. Currently, most Russians are choosing the government-managed provident fund account option. On top of this is a voluntary DC supplemental insurance pillar. These pensions are controlled by non-state pension funds supervised by the Ministry of Labor; as in other transition countries, this segment is not economically important. The reforms were accompanied by (highly unpopular) reductions in subsidies for pensioners' health care, transport, and utilities. The increases in pensions did not cover the entire loss of value of subsidies, and, following protests, the Russian government relented to some extent in 2005–06. Overall, Baskakov (2006) forecasts a decline in the average replacement rates from all pension sources from slightly more than 30% in the early 2000s to 2050 rates of 25% (based on 2002 rules) or even 15% (based on 2005 rules).

Russia's pension reform appears to win the prize for complexity. Sycheva and Mikhailov (2006) present the reform in great detail and note that the size of the mandatory funded contribution (a 4% payroll tax scheduled to rise to 6% in 2008) is far below that established elsewhere, thereby assuring relatively high administrative costs (also a feature of the small voluntary funds) and low replacement rates. Nor is the issue of increased retirement age addressed.

11.3 Old and New Accumulative System Reformers

Relative to Kazakhstan and other formerly socialist countries, the early Accumulative system reformers in Latin America built on weak welfare states (with the exception of Uruguay) and strong market financial institutions. The weak welfare state was a blessing for the pension reformers, if not the population, since transition costs were low.

During the past quarter century, pension coverage and other social benefits have expanded in Latin America. However, the actual shrinking of the formal sector in many countries, associated with liberal reforms, has greatly retarded this expansion (Mesa-Lago, 2007). Mesa-Lago (2007) estimates that only 53% of Latin America's population is covered by general social insurance, putting the region as a whole well behind Kazakhstan and other prosperous formerly socialist nations.

By far the most prominent reformer is Chile, whose military dictatorship replaced the troubled public social insurance system in 1981 with competing, private retirement account (PRA) funds known as AFPs.[3] Yet, while the Pinochet regime instituted the reform without debate, previous centrist and left-wing governments had sought, albeit unsuccessfully, to implement major reforms as well (Arenas de Mesa et al., 2008). Prior to the AFP reforms, Chile had a fragmented structure with a large number of different, largely unfunded "funds" whose coverage of workers overall declined dramatically during the Allende era, and which ran deficits in the 1970s of 1 to more than 3% of GDP (Arenas de Mesa et al., 2008: 26–28).

Membership in the AFP system was mandatory for all workers entering the labor force from 1983 onward, save for the self-employed and members of the armed forces. Those currently in the labor force had the option of joining or remaining in the state pension system; Pinera (2004) reports that 95% jointed the personal retirement account reformed system. Individuals were required to make a 10% payroll contribution to the AFPs, augmented by a charge (averaging about 3%) for administrative costs, and with an optional supplemental deduction of up to 10%. Payments could be taken as an annuity with prescribed survivor benefits, as a scheduled withdrawal, or as a combination. The reformed system included a public minimum pension guarantee for AFP participants with more than 20 years of contributions along with a means-tested, noncontributory public system aimed at the indigent (Arenas de Mesa et al., 2008: 29). At the other end, the system also provides some tax benefits for those who wish to supplement the minimum 10% contribution with additional amounts. In essence, the Chilean reform was the model for the World Bank's three-pillar plan some 13 years before *Averting the Old Age Crisis* was published.

The success of the Chilean reform continues to be fiercely debated. The economy grew rapidly, and savings surged. Whether this growth spurred development of the pension funds, or vice versa, or both, remains unclear. As is discussed below, time series evidence today suggests that the pension funds did spur financial deepening. Among the reasons for the almost immediate deepening is that workers who joined the PRA system were given "recognition bonds" equal to the value of their implicit (now explicit) "rights" accumulated in the old PAYGO system (Pinera, 2004: 195). These bonds carried a 4% real interest rate, matured upon retirement age, and were tradable assets.

However, they also were troubled in many dimensions. Administrative costs were very high and heavily devoted to competitive advertising to win a portion of what was ultimately a zero-sum game. Many workers remained uncovered: 15 years into the reform, Charlton and McKinnon (2001: 79) report that about one-third of the labor force remained outside the system; data from Acuña and Iglesias (2001) indicate a very slow rise in the first two decades from an almost immediate 53% coverage to 70% coverage. Many more did not contribute regularly.

Thanks to a remarkable longitudinal database, the Chilean Social Protection Survey (SPS), it is possible to gain new insight into the nature of accumulation funds and contributors.[4] Data from 2002 and 2004 suggest that men contribute to APF accounts during about half of the months in which they are eligible, and women contribute about one-third of the time. Very few contribute when they are self-employed, unemployed, or outside the labor market (for example, while raising children), but about 90% of wage workers contribute, indicating a very high rate of legal compliance and coverage within the formal sector.

The SPS also reveals considerable ignorance over APF rules, entitlements, and account values. Those who claim to know their account values make fairly accurate estimates (when checked against administrative records), but only about 40% of respondents provided an estimate. Median accumulations from this respondent group were about US$5,600; the median APF for all accumulation accounts from the SPS survey was half as much (Arenas de Mesa et al., 2008).

Lower wages, a five-year earlier retirement date, and fewer contributing years create the same gender gap in replacement rate forecasts from the SPS in Chile as emerged from the KAZAK2 simulations in Chapter 10. Women with average labor force experience can expect a replacement rate, including PAYGO residuals, of only about 23% at retirement age (60); men who contribute 80% of eligible months will have a replacement rate of about 58% (Arenas de Mesa et al., 2008: 40).

As of the mid-1990s, pension fund holdings were poorly diversified, with stocks accounting for less than 30% of APF portfolios and government bonds accounting for more than 40%. Since creating private pension funds that buy only government debt, which in turn is increased by the diversion of contributions from public coffers to pension funds, amounts to a "shell game" in Kotlikoff's (1999: 16) scathing words, this portion of the system is a mirage. However, data from Arenas de Mesa et al. (2008) indicate that by 2003, just under one quarter of APF assets were invested in government debt (though indirect holdings might be higher, since another 26% of assets were placed in financial institutions). Another 24% were invested in foreign assets (a rise from virtually none in 1995), as Kotlikoff would have recommended. However, since the Chilean peso has appreciated from over 700 per U.S. dollar in 2003 to 462 as of April 2008, it is likely that Chilean pension funds as well as their Kazakhstani counterparts have experienced losses on that account.

The intention was that the 10% contribution would generate a 70% replacement rate (Pinera, 2004), which seems astonishingly optimistic. Or perhaps not: as Pinera (2004: 197) reports, over the first 21 years, the real rate of return averaged 10.7%, and average replacement rates after 15 years of 78%. However, the data tables from Acuña and Iglesias (2001) indicate that initial returns to system assets were far above prevailing interest rates, suggesting that the Chilean government may have provided implicit subsidies to the funds, given the high share of government debt in total assets. If true, then one reason the Kazakhstani Accumulative system appears to be less successful in terms of generating high returns than its Chilean counterpart is that it is less protected (another reason is that stock markets throughout the world did much better from 1981 to 2001 than from 1998 to 2008).

Yet another, very recent Accumulative system reformer is Turkey, which implemented a two-pillar reform in 1999, followed by a general health insurance reform in 2006. These reforms are described in Elveren (2008), whose simulations also document a gender gap even worse than in Kazakhstan. Women are very unlikely to be actively covered by the social security system (only 16%), and there are substantial wage and employment duration disadvantages as well. However, women are far more likely to be married in Turkey than in transition nations. Unusually, Turkey also has committed itself to eventual retirement parity between men and women. Beyond gender inequity, many of the problems Kazakhstan faced (most notably, PAYGO deficits) motivated the reform; compliance (at about 50%) appears to be lower than in Kazakhstan. The Turkish example is of interest, as it suggests that level of overall development rather than transition nation status is the defining characteristic that generates many of the distributional features of an Accumulative system. However, with a much weaker welfare state to support those at risk, elderly Turks will be far more dependent on immediate and extended families than Kazakhstanis will.

11.4 The Lessons

A glance at the list of reformers and the policies they adopted should suffice to convince even the most naïve that noneconomic considerations played an important role in virtually all pension reforms. Williamson et al. (2006: 166) bluntly attribute Russia's adoption of a complex three-pillar system to "(1) . . . social policy related cultural-diffusion operating through the international networks of social security experts associated with major financial institutions such as the World Bank and the International Monetary Fund . . . (2) the desire for international legitimacy in a world dominated by neo-liberal institutions." This claim is an overstatement, if only because the World Bank and IMF often disagreed with one another, as we have seen, and also disagreed with other agencies such as the ADB, USAID, and the EU's TACIS. There was also substantial disagreement within the World Bank, though not initially. Nor did Russia increase pension age, which is a consistent theme across different international institutions' experts.

However, a weaker form of these claims—that reformers did seek advice and often chose from the set offered on the basis of friendships rather than dispassionate analysis, and were cognizant of the legitimization benefits conferred by choosing a broadly recommended course of action—does seem plausible. So, too, does the claim by Charlton and McKinnon (2001) in their well-documented historical analysis of the evolution of alternative pension reform schemes that ideology played an unduly important role in the recommendations from World Bank and other advisers. The sheer complexity of pension reform makes selection difficult: policy choice should depend on administrative ease, capacity (especially with regard to IT systems) and costs, effectiveness of the social safety net, demographic factors, financial returns, the underlying legal framework, government financial sector regulatory capacity, spillovers to other sectors, and macroeconomic and government budgetary implications. Few individuals have this perspective, especially for many alternative structures. In consequence, they tend to recommend the familiar and are disinclined to engage in objective assessments of a comprehensive set of alternatives.

This political choice argument also might help explain why Baltic states emphasized NDC reforms. As their demographic structures were unfavorable to a PAYGO system, they seemed well suited for a fully funded DC system, while geographical location and anticipated admission to the EU would have raised the rewards from jump-starting their financial sectors (though, in fairness, they may have believed such help from social security reforms to be unnecessary). The NDC measures also may have been seen as more politically palatable, since by establishing rates of return, the system in effect creates an individual-specific defined benefit that would be highly attractive to risk-averse people. Yet, these rates can be manipulated arbitrarily, and there is no reason to suspect that electorates did not perceive that. The NDC reforms also may have been perceived as more egalitarian (though perhaps quite inaccurately so) and, with a clear state guarantee, less risky. A cynic might also wonder whether Russia was determined not to copy Kazakhstan and in so doing committed to what would be a far inferior strategy. Not only ideological factors, but also political and administrative ones play a major role in the choice of the pension system. In case of Kazakhstan, an unfamiliar system had the benefit of looking easier to implement than struggling further with a system that, to date, had proven too difficult to fully repair.

Future reformers will benefit from an awareness of the political pressures and a commitment to build internal analytical capacity. Emphasis should be on effectiveness of targeting assistance to the poor, meeting general needs of the elderly in a simple and transparent manner (which would seem to work against having both NDC and mandatory funded components), and designing a system that is complementary with both other sectoral development goals and general macrobudgetary constraints.

Future reformers also will gain from understanding the motives of different external agents, as well as the demands of political interest groups in their own countries. They need as well to understand the difference between transitory and permanent events. In the late 1990s, for example, a key concern in Accumulative fund reforms was that of funding transition costs. This is now a lesser concern for countries such as China and Azerbaijan, as both have vast reserves or borrowing capacity. Yet, while many of the concerns are different today, several of the core messages enunciated by Charlton and McKinnon (2001) bear repeating.

> Ensuring sustainable income flows, within a government's capacity, to the poor elderly and disabled who cannot work is a central priority.
> Funded Accumulative systems will be of no relevance to the large majority of citizens in very poor countries (and in very poor regions or for very poor groups within middle-income countries).
> The assertions that a private Accumulative system increases savings rates, or that it generates higher returns after administrative costs than would a publicly managed system, remain without conclusive empirical support.
> Administrative simplicity is important in countries with limited administrative capacity.

At the same time, we emphasize the importance of controlling burgeoning public welfare costs and note the impressive externalities from using an Accumulative system to develop a transparent, competitive financial sector. Having made these general comments, we now turn to several specific issues.

11.4.1 Do demographics matter?

The inescapable conclusion from poring over actuarial simulations is that demographic factors are absolutely critical. Age-specific death, disability, and migration rates matter because they have immediate implications for the size of both the pensioner population and the contributor population. Birth rates have a longer run impact on labor force growth (and on pensioner population, but with an even greater lag); more immediately, they affect female labor force participation rates. Nuptiality, the rate of family formation, affects birth rates, and in the longer run affects family composition at retirement age, which in turn influences poverty rates and distribution. Divorce and spousal abandonment rates influence the same factors, but with an opposite effect.

The more interesting question is whether or not demographic factors are neutral with respect to pension system choice. The answer is that they are not neutral, but apparently do not weigh in the minds of the policymakers as much as they should. Since any PAYGO structure, NDC or a simpler Solidarity system, is in essence a pyramid scheme, its viability is critically dependent on the growth of the pyramid's base. This can come from productivity gains that raise workers' pay, from migration into the base of contributors (whether from actual immigration, as in Russia, or from internal migration from rural areas, as in China, or from growth of formal sector employment and improved compliance, as in Kazakhstan) or from natural labor force growth. Defined contribution schemes do not have this direct dependence on demographics.

The lack of correspondence between system choice and demographic prospects is striking. Sweden appears to have a relatively favorable demographic structure, at least by European standards, making its early choice of an NDC structure plausible. However, Poland and the Baltic states, all of which followed Sweden to some degree, appear to have done so with little reference growth of the working-age population, and hence to dependency rates. With entry into the EU, all of these countries have witnessed considerable emigration; meanwhile, fertility rates are below replacement, even in relatively high fertility Poland. Taking all of these factors into account, Matysiak and Nowok (2007) forecast that Poland's old-age dependency ratio will rise from 21% in 2005 to 42% in 2030 and 64% in 2050. This is hardly the structure for a thriving NDC system.

While demographics are even less favorable in China, the implications are less clear. A central reason for this is that China is a far less open economy than any of the other countries under discussion in this book. For small, open economies, the Accumulative system option allows pension funds to invest internationally—indeed, as Kotlikoff (1999) and others have suggested, the optimal strategy is to purchase a global index. For large economies such as China, while it is true that the NSSF has been directed to invest some of its assets abroad, full international diversification is implausible. Thus, rising labor shortages may not only depress payroll contributions to PAYGO schemes, they also may depress returns to capital, making Accumulative systems less attractive as well. As Brown (1997) emphasizes in his classic paper, in a closed system the resources available for consumption by pensioners is equal to the surplus produced by the working-age population, and this is not affected by the choice of pension system.

11.4.2 Does economic structure matter?

Throughout this volume, we have emphasized that growth of contributors in middle-income countries depends on growth of the formal sector. This is true for both PAYGO and funded individual account systems, at least in a country like Kazakhstan, where compliance with social tax obligation goes hand in hand with contributions to Accumulative accounts. Thus, a key factor in any reform's success is structural transformation, with relatively rapid growth of employment in medium and large registered, compliant enterprises.

Whether or not such a transformation occurs and the pace at which it does both depend on underlying economic structure and policies. Much of Kazakhstan's industrial sector—at least that in mining and metallurgy—survived transition and has grown since, providing a growing pension system contributor base. Strict and centralized tax administration plus rapid economic growth contributed to growth of the "registered" sector as well. In contrast, China is far more rural, and its social tax administration system far more decentralized and less effectively administered. Thus, while its formal sector is growing rapidly, there are significant collection problems.

However, the real contrast lies with countries that have not experienced rapid growth or growth of the modern sector share. This stagnation is harmful to pension contributions of all sorts. However, it is especially damaging to Accumulative reformers, since it limits system coverage. Worse yet, as many workers will move from the informal to the formal sector and back, a high informal sector share is likely to mean large numbers of small accumulation accounts, implying high administrative costs and low replacement rates. Indeed, the system can act as a deterrent to development of the formal sector, as it will discourage compliance and registration.

For a country like Ukraine, which has committed to paying a large minimum pension, and which has a large informal sector, expansion to include an Accumulative system may be premature. Small, urbanized economies with a core number of large, stable employers will find it easier to adopt an Accumulative system than large, heavily rural economies with considerable employment instability and large informal sectors. Countries with high degrees of interregional inequality also may find that an Accumulative system has little relevance to large areas—a problem even for Kazakhstan, as Chapter 10 showed. Thus, the natural Accumulative adopter would be a small, flourishing Baltic country (and, to a lesser degree, a minerals-based economy like Kazakhstan). Perhaps it is no accident that Lithuanians have taken so enthusiastically to personal funded accounts, making their system largely Accumulative de facto.

11.4.3 Retirement age

The forecasts in Chapter 10 point to the critical role of retirement age in a pension system, regardless of type. Retirement age affects the old-age dependency ratio in the long run. It also gives a one-time transition boost, as raising the retirement age creates a period of small retirement cohorts. This gives some breathing room to stressed ministries of finance that are finding it difficult to finance transition costs, especially with the adoption of an Accumulative system.

In the long run, there is no substitute for choosing a retirement age that balances contribution flows with needs for a reasonable standard of living in retirement. A country such as China, which still has a large labor "surplus" in rural areas along with rapidly growing urban wages, can temporarily delay increasing pension age without threatening government budgets in the short run. However, young retirement ages add to unfunded future liabilities in a PAYGO system, and China's modest current account government deficits do not reflect the rapid growth of subsequent obligations.

In an unfunded system, early retirements simply imply transfers from future to current generations, or inflation that reduces the real value of pensions. In an Accumulative system, debts cannot be reduced via inflation. Instead, as we saw in Chapter 10, too few working years for each year in retirement simply means very low replacement rates. This is a particular problem for women, who have lower wages, lower average labor force participation rates, longer life expectancies, and, in most transition nations, lower retirement ages. For women to have reasonable pension savings, retirement ages must be increased at least to parity with men. To reiterate a point made earlier in this book, to adopt a funded, individual Accumulative system is to equalize retirement ages for men and women, barring massive compensatory public transfers.

To actuaries, demographers, and economists, these points seem trivially obvious. Yet, as we note above, there is great political resistance to raising retirement ages, and not only in reforming or developing middle-income countries but also in advanced market societies. Indeed, many governments seem interested in alternative pension structures as a means of avoiding coming to grips with a burgeoning pensioner population, whether from unsustainably early retirement or from lax practices regarding disability. This may have been particularly true in the 1990s, when asset prices rose rapidly, encouraging policymakers to believe that high rates of return on capital would be sufficient. However, these returns have not been sustained, and, as the Kazakhstani experience shows, many pension funds in recent years have been experiencing negative returns rather than double-digit earnings.

Of course, there is a possible trade-off. If a society with an Accumulative pension system really wants to provide long, opulent retirements for its members, such a system can be designed. However, that design, which involves very high contribution rates (and hence low consumption) during working years, is not likely to be attractive. On the contrary, a major problem of Accumulative systems in practice is that mandatory contribution rates have been set at implausibly low levels. Perhaps it is not surprising that countries with long retirement periods tend to have large PAYGO components, as some of the costs are then transferred to the future.

11.4.4 Can an Accumulative pillar stand alone?

The traditional objective of a pension system is to provide security in old age and disability. This is usually taken to mean encouraging profitable savings by those able to earn incomes sufficient to support adequate accumulation, along with public support at a socially acceptable level to those unable to provide for themselves. Thus, this question can be reinterpreted as asking whether all people are capable of accumulating for themselves, given proper incentives, and also whether the Accumulative pillar provides proper incentives for all.

Quite clearly, defined contribution, funded individual accounts will not cover the entire range of humanity in any society, and certainly not in middle-income countries. A small but significant share of the population is disabled at birth or prior to having the opportunity to accumulate adequately. Disability insurance markets could help with this, but in practice they are quite limited, even in highly developed countries. The disabled will require public support, and virtually all transition countries recognize this.

It is also indisputable that large numbers of able-bodied people in middle-income countries will never enjoy adequate retirement savings through an Accumulative system. This is true even in Kazakhstan or Chile, with high formal sector employment and compliance rates, and rapid economic growth. While the labor force proportions of different groups analyzed in Chapter 10 cannot be determined accurately, it seems unlikely that more than a modest minority—perhaps one-quarter of the labor force, and surely less than one-half—will be able to save adequately by themselves even under good conditions. If returns on assets remain negative, or if the economy falters, the proportion will decline further.

As both the KAZAK2 simulations and the Chilean estimates from the SPS database have shown, women are especially unlikely to generate adequate replacement rates via an Accumulative system. Indeed, using household survey data from Argentina, Chile, and Mexico, James et al. (2003) find that women generate annuities only 30–40% of those accumulated by men. However, in these countries improved targeting of revised publicly funded base pension pillars have an offsetting effect, as do restrictions such as joint annuity requirements for a married couple. Thus, James et al. (2003: 181) conclude that "low-earning married women are among the biggest gainers" from the Accumulative reforms as enacted. However, while this finding is highly relevant for Turkey, it is less relevant for Eastern European and former Soviet transition economies that have much lower marriage rates (at least for the immediate posttransition cohort) and far higher premature male mortality. It is also of less relevance to very poor countries in which a large portion of the labor force remains outside the formal sector.

The fact that an Accumulative system does not provide a universal safety net even for labor force participants is not a reason to discard it. If a sizable share of the population can save for its retirement needs, and another sizable share can contribute to partly meet those needs, then governments with limited fiscal capacity can devote their scarce resources to assisting those unable to provide adequately for themselves. Countries such as Azerbaijan and, especially, Ukraine, with bloated welfare systems that are poorly targeted, are likely to find that a deliberate paring down of general commitments is consistent with poverty reduction. Part of this paring down may mean forcing able individuals to save for themselves. Of course, this will only happen if the savings in reduced commitments exceed reduced revenues, which is possible but not inevitable.

For an oil-rich state such as Azerbaijan, which is suddenly experiencing exceptional inflows into public coffers, the choice of pension system is tied to the nature of society envisioned. It is fairly easy for petro-states, from Saudi Arabia to Venezuela, to provide a substantial base transfer to all citizens expressing need. The environment also invites infant industry protectionism, corruption, inefficiency, and disincentives to work. This "curse of riches" ultimately can stifle economic growth: Latin America, the Middle East, and Africa have many examples to offer in this regard. A nation that wants to spark an innovative and entrepreneurial culture may deliberately choose to trim its welfare state, in which case mandatory individual savings for retirement and strict means testing before transfers are provided may be part of a considered growth strategy.

11.4.5 Complementarities and extreme solutions

At this point, the reader may be waiting with growing impatience for this volume to settle conclusively on a preferred pension system. Sadly, a clear resolution will not be offered.

The reason is that initial conditions dictate the appropriate strategy, and since many factors interact, there are few simple rules. The Kazakhstani case provides a good example of this. At the outset of the reform, Kazakhstan's demographic structure did not point to the need for an Accumulative system, but its shrinking formal sector, low compliance, and pension expenditures all made it a plausible choice. As we have emphasized in earlier chapters, GoK badly wanted to shed spending commitments and restore fiscal order. In principle, it could have done this within the Solidarity structure, and without international loans to finance the transition costs, Kazakhstan might well never have undertaken the Accumulative reform. Yet, with the loan, the commitment to future fiscal rectitude clearly was more credible by adopting an Accumulative system.

Had Kazakhstan's economy continued to struggle, the Accumulative system would at least have provided a small number of workers with reasonable pensions, saving scarce resources for a minimum pension for others (as net commitments clearly declined). Had the economy grown moderately, then the combination of effective macroeconomic policy, financial sector regulation, and low financial sector corruption and scandals might have sufficed to make the pension reform have its anticipated impact on financial sector development.

As events turned out, explosive growth made the pension-financial system complementarities stronger than could be imagined. Surging government revenues meant that debt issues were curtailed, forcing the pension funds to seek private assets. In contrast to Latin American countries, Kazakhstan's funds diversified extremely rapidly—not by choice, but by necessity. Rapid growth also meant a large increase in the formal sector's share of the workforce, and in compliance, so that the Accumulative system deepened rapidly. It was highly successful, except that the same forces that led to rapid growth also resulted in collapsing real interest rates, and hence in returns to pension fund assets. These returns were further worsened by the tenge's appreciation, which meant that unhedged pension funds, with dollar-denominated assets and tenge-denominated liabilities, lost heavily. This is a temporary rather than a permanent phenomenon, but it helps indicate the sensitivity of system choice to a range of external factors.

Indeed, the growth that resulted in the Accumulation system's deepening would have been even more favorable to simple PAYGO system reforms, since the pyramid base expanded so rapidly. However, US$140/barrel oil was not on the horizon in 1997, when system choices were made, and to have chosen reforms in anticipation of a rapid expansion of the PAYGO base would have been recklessly optimistic. To summarize, Kazakhstan's Accumulative system's success has been dampened somewhat by the nation's general good economic fortune. From a macro policy perspective, this is not bad, since the boom makes it possible to renew and expand PAYGO commitments—in effect, policymakers hold a somewhat diversified portfolio of strategies whose returns are negatively correlated.

The Accumulative system's successes in Kazakhstan also depended on many complementary conditions that are not present in all prospective reforming countries. A poorly supervised and highly corrupt financial system is not a good foundation on which to build a new structure that will pour in funds. These issues in China and other prospective reformers must be resolved before a funded individual account system is installed; otherwise, much of the savings may be stolen or appropriated by regional governments. Likewise, unstable macro policy adds systemic risk to assets: countries should not attempt Accumulative reforms until solid macroeconomic management practices are in place.

Finally, it should be noted that, even discounting the positive oil shocks it received, Kazakhstan did not present the best of all possible worlds for an Accumulative system. Rather, it has been consistently hampered by limited investment demand outside the oil, mining, and metallurgy sectors, none of which needed or sought domestic funds for expansion. Limited investment demand has been a cause of low returns on pension assets, the system's Achilles' heel. However, the NBK, the FSA, and the Ministry of Finance are unable to influence investment demand greatly—although, by creating a national credit bureau, creating a housing mortgage market and a system of collateral registration, they have done far more than most counterparts elsewhere. Nonetheless, had national economic policy spurred small and medium enterprise investment demand, the reform's success would have been greater still.

11.4.6 Meeting the needs of the poor

A clear lesson from the KAZAK2 actuarial simulations is that an Accumulative system will not meet the needs of the poor when they retire either prematurely because of ill health or later due to old age. The obvious implication seems to be that minimum old-age pensions, survivors' benefits, and disability allowances are critical to meet the needs of members of society unable to take care of themselves. This can be handled either via a demogrant (minimum pension) to all citizens, or via specific need-based transfers to those with inadequate pensions, either because of insufficient Accumulative or NDC accumulations, insufficient years of service in a standard PAYGO system, or because of an uninsured disability.

In reality, the choice of appropriate strategy is not so obvious. Demogrants do not involve marginal distortions and, in particular, do not remove the incentive for low- and middle-income workers to accumulate, which is the case in a system that offers a guaranteed minimum pension by meeting the difference between an individual's accumulated fund and the amount needed for a minimum monthly payment. In this latter case (for example, in Russia: see Lim, 2005), a large class of modest-income workers faces an effective 100% tax on their contributions. However, demogrants have the disadvantage of providing PAYGO transfers that are not targeted to need. Since these expenditures have an opportunity cost, one could easily imagine a combination Accumulative system plus targeted transfers that reduces poverty more than an ostensibly "progressive" but crude PAYGO system.

The poor targeting of social safety net programs in transition nations is well documented (in particular, see Fox, 2003). In part, this is not surprising, since poverty in transition nations appears to be highly transient (Fox, 2003: 6), or at least it was until sustained recovery was well under way. Even in Russia, where targeting is relatively good, Clément (2007), using Russian Longitudinal Monitoring Survey panel data, finds that only 41% of those who were persistently poor in terms of nontransfer incomes are moved out of chronic poverty by government transfers, and only 20% experiencing transitory poverty are moved to a nonpoor state. To summarize crudely, Russia's vast social welfare system (absorbing 16.4% of GDP in 1998) is effective if not efficient at protecting against the risk of becoming poor, but is fairly ineffective at helping households escape from poverty. Nonetheless, the importance of general social programs that benefit many nonpoor households and individuals, and the far greater attention and funds committed to the elderly than to poor children (upon whom the nations will in part depend to pay taxes in the future) are salient features of transition nations.

This conclusion certainly holds for Azerbaijan, a far poorer country than Russia, and with a very large population of internally displaced persons. Habibov and Fan (2007) use the 2004 Azerbaijan Household Budget Survey to examine the impact of social transfers on household consumption. Even given the large share of oil revenues and hence government revenue in GDP, along with low levels of economic activity outside the oil sector and the capital city, their findings are staggering. Social transfers account for 48% of all households' consumption, with the figure rising to more than 81% for poor households (and 38% for the nonpoor). Thus, despite following a pro-private sector development strategy since the collapse of the USSR, Azerbaijan in some respects remains a socialist country, with the citizenry's welfare heavily dependent on the state.

Given the huge transfer share in household consumption, it is hardly surprising that the transfers have a huge effect on reducing poverty, cutting the incidence in half (Habibov and Fan, 2007: 57) and virtually eliminating extreme poverty. Yet, transfers are poorly targeted: 70% of nonpoor households receive transfers from social security programs (versus 82% of poor households), and nonpoor households receive 61% of all transfers by value (and 64% of old-age pension payments). That is, transfers do reach the poorest, but they also reach nearly three-quarters of the entire population. Despite their importance in household budgets, until recent increases (notably, a doubling of minimum pensions in 2007), average payments were too small to eliminate poverty and, for half of the poor, merely reduced the intensity. In short, given current economic conditions, Azerbaijan's social transfers are critical, yet extremely inefficient.

Indeed, Fox (2003: 12) and others cited in her paper have been critical of "overspending on pensions," especially relative to means-tested transfers. Thus, the shrinking of the pension side of the welfare state may well be an egalitarian move—though still a politically unpopular one. The moral for late reformers is not to be too generous with first-pillar benefits, and to make policy commitments before budgetary improvements make cuts in Solidarity payments politically infeasible.

11.4.7 Corequisites for financial sector development

For more than a decade, a debate has raged over the extent to which pension reforms can spur capital market development. The debate is almost inherently speculative, given the long lags involved, and the myriad of possible impacts. Focusing on Argentina, Chile, and Peru, Walker and Lefort (2002) find from both time series and a 33-country panel analysis that the creation of an Accumulative system with privately managed pension funds is consistent with reduced cost of capital, higher traded volumes of securities, and lower securities' price volatility. These findings are hardly universal, and the mechanisms are not obvious: after all, small, open economies in principle can delink investment level from domestic savings. Thus, at least in a simple model, increased pension savings might well just replace other sources of savings. Furthermore, as Walker and Lefort note, pension and other reforms tend to be undertaken concurrently, so that attributing events to pension reform is not straightforward. Nonetheless, when they tease out pension reform–specific effects, the reforms do appear to matter independently. The precise mechanism whereby the reform matters cannot be determined, but several possibilities arise. These include complementary development of a more transparent reporting system (pushed by the emergence of a domestic interest group with a much larger constituency than others, and that requires improved disclosure, accounting, and auditing procedures), demand for long-term assets (securities and stocks) that leads to growing securitization, and improved shareholder oversight and hence better corporate governance. Walker and Lefort also argue that private pension funds stimulate financial innovation, and that certainly has been true in countries with underdeveloped financial sectors. Catalán (2004) concludes that pension reforms do lead to stock market development, but cannot identify the extent to which this is attributable to improved corporate governance.

While a formal analysis of this sort has not been conducted for Kazakhstan, it seems reasonable to posit that the effect should be much larger than in Latin America. Given the virtual absence of a capital market at the outset, potential benefits were much larger (sectors outside of oil and mining did not have access to unlimited foreign capital or domestic savings) in the Kazakhstani setting. The reform also spurred the creation of a remarkable set of pro-transparency regulations, as well as ancillary bodies from a national credit bureau to a thriving (until recently) mortgage credit market. The Latin American data reported by Catalán (2004) also indirectly reflect on Kazakhstan's success: outside of Chile (where pension fund assets as a share of GDP equaled 53.3% in 2001) and Bolivia (31.6%), all of the other early Latin American reformers had fund asset to GDP ratios in the 6 to 8% range in 2001, and equity plus mutual finds held by private pension funds as a share of total stock market capitalization in the 2 to 8% range, with Chile at the upper end (7.9%). By these standards, Kazakhstan's pension funds have grown rapidly both in terms of total assets and importance in the domestic financial sector.

A key lesson from Kazakhstan reiterates a point made by Walker and Lefort (2002): there are many necessary conditions for these effects to operate. Corequisite conditions first of all include sound macroeconomic management, and as we have seen, Kazakhstan had a highly effective central bank that was exceptionally independent during the formative years of the Accumulative system; it also had a Finance Ministry committed to fiscal rectitude. Walker and Lefort further list capital control liberalization, strong and consistent regulation of the financial sector and pension funds, competition among private firms in both areas, clear property rights, bankruptcy legislation, and investor protection—all of which emerged in Kazakhstan during the reform period. The Walker-Lefort list additionally includes privatization of state-owned enterprises, which did not occur as quickly as many had hoped for in Kazakhstan; moreover, given the large size of the nation's main SOEs, the pension funds were not destined to be important players in the privatizations that did occur. Nor have tax incentives played an important role in the development of the pension industry or in capital market development. Indeed, the conclusion to be drawn from the Kazakhstan case study is that these last two conditions may not be particularly important, at least when rapid economic growth leads to other outlets for funds, and contributions to pension funds are legally mandated.

Given the presence of strong time trends and short time series, plus many concurrent events, conclusions from econometric studies are highly tentative at best, even when modern time series techniques are employed. Walker and Lefort suggest that the cost of capital (as reflected in stock price-to-book value ratios) declined with pension fund investments in Chile but not in Argentina or Peru. Stock price volatility also declines with pension fund investments in all three countries. Panel regressions for 33 countries confirm both of these findings.

What Walker and Lefort do not assert directly is that funded pension system reforms directly raise national savings rates. This is a controversial point (for a skeptical view, see the review of the Chilean experience in Charlton and McKinnon, 2001:116), and although it is often taken to be an important reason for Accumulative system reforms, in our view it misses the point. Small, open economies of the sort capable of having viable funded pension systems are not generally starved for capital (except for when they default on international obligations). However, those flows do not go everywhere, and some segments of prospective investment demand are most unlikely to receive international investments, at least at the outset. Home mortgages are the most obvious examples in Kazakhstan, but in fact there are many other sectors that, especially when small long-term loans are bundled and securitized, are likely to especially benefit from the growth of pension funds.

11.4.8 Epilogue: Can creeping entitlements be avoided?

From the perspective of political leaders, publicly provided pensions are seductive. Commitments made today, if credible, bring popular approval and hence popularity. But most of these commitments pertain to future liabilities, and since public systems are almost never fully funded (as that would spoil the popularity boost), the costs are borne largely by future generations. Hence, future political leaders will have to design mechanisms to cover the cost of past commitments or will have to renege to some degree on past generosity, a thankless task in either case.

Given this natural tendency to overcommit, astute economic advisers interested in achieving optimal policy have incentives both to overreact during periodic purges of welfare state commitments and to promote systems that constrain future fits of unfunded public generosity by parliaments and governments. This natural restraining force is probably the true advantage of a defined contribution, fully funded, individual account Accumulative system, as it takes a large portion of transfers from the working population (in this case, people during their working years) to nonworkers (the same people when retired) out of the hands of the state. Notional defined contribution systems do not put contributions at arms length, and the temptation to meddle remains. In the most egregious cases, as in China, funds headed to individual accounts can be diverted to meet basic Solidarity pension commitments. More subtly, policymakers can court popularity by promising to increase the real return notionally credited to individual accounts.

A middle-income nation that wants to utilize its resources to achieve improved living standards must aim to achieve high rates of labor force participation, investment, and skills accumulation (education). Crowding out and disincentive effects of high taxes means that these goals will be difficult to achieve alongside very high social transfers, as in Ukraine (or Russia, though the oil boom temporarily makes these transfers affordable). The combination of a base pension plus an NDC system almost certainly invites a higher rate of gradual improvement of terms—creeping entitlements—than does an Accumulative system, giving the latter a dynamic efficiency advantage at the economy-wide level.

Realization of this positive feature almost certainly was in the minds of Kazakhstan's pension reformers in 1996 and 1997. Although the Solidarity system was officially planned to be dismantled (and expatriate advisers and even domestic observers appeared to believe that it would be), all key players in the reform understood that publicly funded minimum pensions would not disappear, barring total economic disaster. They also realized that base pensions would increase in real value with economic recovery, as in fact has been the case. In reality, the reformers' goal was to curb the welfare state—to ensure that pension transfers never reached 15% of GDP—not to dismantle it.

The extent of their success remains uncertain. The Accumulative pension system certainly has grown as much as could possibly be hoped for, to about US$10.5 billion as of February 2008, or 10% of GDP (NBK, 2008). There are slightly more than 9 million accounts (in a country of 15 million people, a large number of accounts must be inactive; otherwise, the entire labor force would be participating), with an average account balance of about US$1,050. The assets are highly diversified: Kazakhstan government securities and NBK notes together account for only 25.2% of assets; foreign holdings make up 14.3% of Accumulative fund portfolios.[5] Even given the low returns and fund losses in recent years, these figures are impressive.

Still, the Accumulative system is not a perfect barrier to creeping entitlements. While the natural tendency of social payments as a share of government expenditures should be downward (since Solidarity system pensioners are dying off and are being replaced by pensioners with a mix of Solidarity and Accumulative pensions), this is not taking place. Rather, according to the Ministry of Finance database (www.minfin.kz), social transfers accounted for 15.9% of consolidated Republican and local government expenditures in 2006, 14.8% in 2007, and 16.3% in the first quarter of 2008 (Republican figures alone are much higher, but with the same trend).

The bottom line is that it is difficult for any system to resist pressures to increase social transfers. As in recent years, when government is flush with revenue, it is difficult to argue against increasing transfers to a segment of the population that, while not destitute, is fairly poor. The problem is that there is an opportunity cost to these expenditures. The real test of the Accumulative system will be whether it, along with non-Accumulative pension payments by government, manages to provide reasonable retirement incomes in the coming decades and at the same time allows growing shares to be devoted to health and education, both of which are in dire need of greater attention.

Notes

Chapter 1

1. Specifically, Fitch (2002: 1) states:

   > A further support to the ratings is provided by the pension reforms started in 1998. Pension reform has reaped benefits by limiting the fiscal implications of the previous system, stimulating growth in domestic capital markets and (for the time being) providing a near-captive market for government paper. Pension funds hold nearly half of the outstanding stock of sovereign eurobonds, and demand for new government paper remains strong, providing the authorities with a relatively easy means of debt refinancing, at lower costs than might otherwise be the case.

2. As the Fitch report (2002) notes and Eicher (2004) analyzes in detail, Kazakhstan's banking system until recently was heavily dollarized, with about 60% of all domestic deposits denominated in U.S. dollars. Pension funds assets are also heavily invested in dollar-denominated assets, while their obligations are in national currency—a position that has yielded considerable losses since mid-2003.

Chapter 2

1. This pattern is also noted by Palmer (2007: 6) in his survey of the pre-reform Solidarity system. As he wryly puts it, "contributions were negotiable at the margin."
2. Prior to the reform, while the Ministry of Labor and Social Protection (MLSP) had responsibility for Solidarity system administration, the system in practice was extremely decentralized. Each *raion* (county) office had responsibility for collecting contributions and paying benefits. While *raions* were supposed to send 30% of proceeds to the national MLSP for redistribution, in practice redistributive efforts lagged, since there was no incentive for surplus regions to make an effort to collect contributions at the margin (Andrews, 2000; Palmer, 2007). As a result, payments in poorer regions were often made in kind, and were less than in richer regions.
3. In fact, during the 1980s, insurance contribution rates varied across different branches of the economy. The maximum rate was 14% for workers in sectors such as civil aviation or machine building; the minimum of 4.4% was set for workers in agricultural enterprises. These low Soviet-era replacement rates are reported in Anderson, et al. (1997: table 11) also.
4. There is also a major inconsistency in official data for 1993. MLSP data do not match the official data, and do not yield figures consistent with the recorded level of pension expenditures to GDP, namely, 4.1%. In 1993, according to MLSP data, the total amount of monthly pensions comprised 343.9 million tenge, while the average yearly number

of pensioners was equal to 2.8294 million. Thus, average monthly pension was equal to 124.7 tenge. Since the recorded average wage was 127.5 tenge, the replacement rate was 97.5%. The implied share of pension expenditures in GDP is then an implausible 14%. Given the data problems for 1993, we worked backward to infer the overall dependency ratio from GDP share data. The data problems are due mainly to the fact that all 1993 statistical data were recorded in the new national currency, the *tenge*, which was not put into circulation until November 1993. Given the high inflation that occurred for both the rouble and the tenge, it is inevitable that many effective calculation errors occurred.

5. Becker and Seitenova (2006) discuss fertility and marriage patterns in Kazakhstan. The TFR declined from 3.2 at independence to around 1.8 in 1999–2001, but recovered to 2.03 in 2003.
6. These data are based on reasonably careful forecasts following relative stabilization of vital rates. At the time of the reform, rougher and simpler projections were used. The reform was based on these numbers, which projected a rise in Kazakhstan's old-age pension population by more than 17% between 2000 and 2010 (and by 32% between 2000 and 2015). See Anderson et al. (1997: table 15).
7. The extent to which KAZAK1 favored the Accumulative reforms over continuation of the Solidarity system can be seen from Andrews (2000:10, Chart 1, which is derived from these projections). Under the reform, pension payments (presumably from GoK, and including disability payments, continued Solidarity obligations, and other non-old-age pensions) as a share of GDP declines fairly smoothly from near 7% of GDP in 1998 to about 2.5% in the 2040s. In contrast, a maintained Solidarity system is projected to experience a decline to slightly less than 5% of GDP from the 7% initial value during the period 1998—2007, but then rises and hits 9% by midcentury.
8. The World Bank identified social security budgetary problems in Kazakhstan as early as 1994 (Palmer, 2007:15; Andrews, 2000). While the World Bank was not the primary mover in initiating Kazakhstan's pension reform (as Palmer (p. 31) in his review of the Bank's performance puts it, "the Bank was apparently dormant in the initial design discussions"), it did support moving to individual financial account schemes (either notional or regular defined contribution). The bank also emerged as a strong advocate of a minimum basic "demogrant" pension (Palmer, 2007; Andrews, 2000).

Chapter 3

1. The legislation consisted of two laws, *On State Pensions in the USSR*, April 28, 1990; and *On Pension Provision in the USSR*, May 15, 1990.
2. For example, see the law *On Pension Provision in Kazakh SSR*, June 17, 1991. In addition to these, there were various decrees and edicts concerning ad hoc pension increases and more detailed descriptions of GoK's occupation-specific pension liabilities.
3. Cabinet of Ministers, Decree #300, *On the Pension Fund of the Republic of Kazakhstan*, April 14, 1993.
4. Cabinet of Ministers, Decree #1120, *Rules of Collecting, Accounting for, Transferring, and Expending of the Funds of the Pension Fund of the Republic of Kazakhstan*, October 6, 1994; amended on May 27, 1997.
5. Cabinet of Ministers, Decree #1329, *On Some Issues Concerning Operations of the Pension Fund of the Republic of Kazakhstan*, November 30, 1994.
6. Cabinet of Ministers, Decree #177, *About Additional Measures for Provision of Timely Payments of Wages and Pensions*, February 20, 1995.

7. GoK, Decree #1306, *About Serious Shortcomings and Additional Measures on the Pension Fund of the Republic of Kazakhstan Accounts*, October 1995.
8. Cabinet of Ministers, Decree #771, *The Rules of Transfer to and Uses of Fines by the Pension Fund of the Republic of Kazakhstan*, June 2 1995.
9. GoK, Decree #1600, *On Measures for Improved Collection of Contributions to the Pension Fund of the Republic of Kazakhstan and for Enforcement of Pensions*, November 1995.
10. GoK, Decree #133, *On Pardoning the Penalties for Late Payment of Pension Contributions to the Pension Fund of the Republic of Kazakhstan*, January 31, 1997.
11. GoK Decree #1600, *On Measures for Improved Collection of Contributions to the Pension Fund of the Republic of Kazakhstan and for Enforcement of Pensions*, Article 2, paragraph 5, November 1995.
12. Presidential Edict #2629, *On Initiatives to Improve Living Standards of the Population of the Republic of Kazakhstan*, December 19, 1995.
13. Originally, the prime minister singled out Ministry of Social Protection for reform proposal development, while all three ministries (MSP, MinFin, and Ministry of Labor) were held mutually responsible for the pension arrears.
14. The Russian law remains in force today, even though a more substantial pension reform in Russia is underway. The more cautious Russian approach is also found in the lengthy hiatus between the date of its acceptance of the principle of a multipillar pension reform (May 1998) and the date when it actually commenced (January, 2002).
15. A representative of the voluntary pension funds was a member of the GoK Working Group assembled in January 1997, which replaced the Inter-Ministerial Working Group and developed the *Pension Reform Concept*, published in March 1997.
16. Regulation of voluntary pension funds was drafted by a DAI and USAID team of Mario Abuhadba and Marcela Ruiz-Tagle during the summer of 1996. However, these documents did not raise the issue of corporate structure of the pension funds that would ensure proper fiduciary standards within Kazakhstan's legal environment. These issues were raised only seven months later during preparation of the pension reform.
17. For example, DAI (1996a) recommended against tax voluntary pension contributions at all, rather than deferring taxes.
18. Orenstein (2000) argues that relatively low implicit pension debt at the beginning of the reform explains Kazakhstan's relatively radical pension reform compared with those undertaken by Poland or Hungary.
19. The World Bank's attitude toward Kazakhstan's pension reform eventually changed when the first Bank mission dedicated to social security came to Kazakhstan in May 1997, ready to share the experiences of earlier reformers. However, by the time the mission arrived, it was too late to offer advice on the pension law, as it was already being debated in parliament. Since then, the World Bank has strongly supported Kazakhstan's pension reform by providing technical assistance and a US$300 million loan to finance the cost of fiscal transition.
20. *Government Decree #1716*, December 31, 1996; amended by *Decrees N 936* (June 6, 1997); *N 979* (June 17, 1997); *N 1094* (July 10, 1997); *N 1810* (December 19, 1997); *N 253* (March 23, 1998); *N 685* (July 22, 1998); *N 693* (July 24, 1998); *N 10* (January 7, 1999), and eventually repealed.
21. *Order of the Prime Minister #385-p*, August 13, 1996; appended by *Order of the Prime Minister #458-p*, September 30, 1996.
22. *Presidential Edict #3168*, October 29, 1996, merged the Ministry of Labor and the Ministry of Social Protection into a single Ministry of Labor and Social Protection (MLSP) as part of government reduction program. This brought three of the four

funds, the Pension Fund, the Social Insurance Fund, and the Employment Assistance Fund, under the MLSP. Members of the new working group included NBK Chairman Jandosov, Minister of Labor and Social Protection Natalia Korzhova, NSC Chairman Marchenko, Chairman of the Senate Budget and Finance Committee Sembaev, the head of the presidential administration, two deputy prime ministers, and the deputy ministers of Justice and Economy, as well as others. The new working group was smaller but more influential. Notable is the disappearance of the USAID pension reform advisor.

23. *Kazakhstanskaya Pravda*, "The Conception of Pension Reform," Almaty, March 20, 1997.
24. *Regarding the Non-Acceptability of Government Version of Pension Reform*, statement of the joint conference of the political movements Pokolenie, Azamat, and the *Coordinated Meetings of Political Associations "Republic,"* Almaty, April 12, 1997.
25. Technical assistance in the development of the Commercial Law was provided by the University of Maryland's Institute for Research on the Informal Sector (IRIS), also funded by USAID.
26. Orenstein (2000) acknowledges each of the four points that follow in the text, but ultimately appears to conclude that "authoritarian political institutions" (p. 16, p. 20) was the decisive factor that distinguished Kazakhstan from more pluralistic Hungary and Poland. Yet, this conclusion is not obvious even from Orenstein's own analysis, since he documents public opposition to the reforms in the press, in parliament, and from various senior officials (pp. 22–24). His paper also suggests that opposition may have been muted since the strongest interest group—existing pensioners—was most interested in a commitment to remove arrears and increase payments in the current Solidarity system, and was less concerned about proposed changes that would affect future retirees, but not themselves. Orenstein, while emphasizing that the demographic pressures for reform were greater in Hungary and Poland, seems to neglect the fact that the macroeconomic crisis was far more severe in Kazakhstan. Had there not been a crisis, it seems unlikely that pension reform could have been implemented at anything close to the pace at which it occurred.
27. Declines in fertility and increase in mortality during the early and mid-1990s had halted by the end of the decade. Modest improvements in life expectancy have been recorded, while marriage and fertility have definitely rebounded with the economic boom (for analysis of mortality, see Becker and Urzhumova, 2005, and Becker and Seitenova, 2006, discuss marriage and fertility in Kazakhstan).
28. A somewhat secondary but still important contribution to the successful and rapid implementation of the reform came from the willingness of both IMWG members and expatriate advisors to appear at symposia, give press interviews, and meet with opposition groups. While the outcome was not uncritical acceptance of the reform, hostility was somewhat diminished, and the proponents could hardly be accused of moving secretly.
29. While the opposition was primarily domestic, it was not exclusively so, and appears to have included expatriate advisors to President Nazarbayev (see Hoffman, et al., 1999; and Spiecker and Zwiener, 1997). Hoffman's group argued that the reform would not address the problem of arrears, and would be likely to fail; Spiecker and Zwiener made similar points, and also emphasized the transition funding costs and the adverse distributional effects.
30. GoK, Decree #1733, *On the Accounting and Remittances of Mandatory Pension Contributions . . . by the SPPC,* December 10, 1997; amended by GoK decrees on January 21, 1998; March 11, 1998; and December 22, 1998. The decree has since been revoked.
31. GoK, Decree #1396, *Regarding Licensing of Accumulative Pension Funds and Conduct of Pension Payments*, September 30, 1997; amended by GoK, Decree #1258 of November 26, 2002, and revoked by GoK, Decree #124 of February 9, 2005.

32. Subsequently, the APF became a powerful lobbying tool for the pension funds in their attempts to replace the regulatory burden of MLSP by an independent financial regulator, as evidenced by a public letter from APF Chairman A. Alibayev to President Nazarbayev on June 7, 2000.
33. NPA, Order #3-p, *Requirements for Following the Rules of Accumulative Pension Funds,* August 27, 1997.
34. GoK, Decree #1355, *On the Rules of Payments from the Accumulative Pension Funds,* September 21, 1997.
35. NSA, Decree #133, *On Investment Activity of Asset Management Companies,* August 21, 1997.
36. NSA, Decree #133, *Order and Forms for Reporting on Investment Management of Pension Assets,* August 21, 1997.
37. These returns are referred to in the regulations as the "income coefficient," rather than the "return on pension assets." See NSA Decree #133, *Prudential Norms for Asset Management Companies,* August 21, 1997.
38. No pensions would be paid from Accumulative funds in a periodic form prior to January 1, 2001.

Chapter 4

1. The KAZAK1 modification of PROST was conducted by Charles Becker, Ai-Gul Seitenova, and Dina Urzhumova. Initial support was provided by USAID, but most of the analysis was performed for the Kazakhstan ministries of finance, and labor and social protection, in order to satisfy World Bank conditionalities.
2. This was especially the case for the KAZAK2 simulations, which covers several different reports and underlying simulations over a three-year period. While all of these simulations used the same core version of PROST (itself updated from the version used by KAZAK1), subroutines were added and parameter values were updated over this period.
3. For a brief overview, see http://siteresources.worldbank.org/INTPENSIONS/Resources/395443-1121194657824/PRPNoteModeling.pdf.
4. An accurate measure of potential expenditures must include contingent liabilities that will accrue if individuals fail to save an adequate amount in their accumulation accounts. This liability depends on the distribution of earnings at any instant, as well as labor force participation incidence for different groups over time. PENMODEL did not include these estimates.
5. Wiener (1998:1) writes, "The pension program in effect on April 1, 1997 was not sustainable for many reasons," including high overall payroll tax rates, poor Solidarity collection rates, excessive premature retirement, absence of a "direct link between contributions and benefits," "projected revenue shortfalls [that] are expected to increase significantly in the years ahead," and "the structure of the pension system [that] reflects the Socialist model, and is inappropriate for a market economy driven by profit motives." Thus, "The goal of this task order was to redesign the pension system to put it on a sound financial basis, and so it helps the overall productivity, economic growth, and savings rate of Kazakstan. It must be designed to work well within the framework of a market economy. To accomplish this, requires the design of the public program, and the introduction of a private, tax favored pension program as well."

   Many of these claims are either untrue and misleading or undocumented. But, together, they comprise a good summary of the benefits of Accumulative "second-pillar" system pension reform as espoused by the international community. They also suggest why GoK policymakers would have ignored Wiener's actuarial forecasts, since he apparently did so himself. Rather, they would have had the word of the sole actuary present at the time that an Accumulative reform was necessary, and likely assumed that he had insights into the forecasts that were not transparent.

Chapter 6

1. GoK *Regulation No. 564* (issued June 11, 2003) increased Solidarity pensions based on personal participation coefficients and 2002 wages by economic branch.
2. Women with five or more children are allowed to retire between ages 50 and 53 (Pension Law, Article 9, point 3). Regulations permit early retirement (45–48 for women and 50–53 for men) for those who lived in nuclear zones for at least ten years during the period August 29, 1949–July 5, 1963, and with complete LOS in concordance with RK Law No. 1787-XII dated December 18, 1992, *On the Social Protection of Citizens, Suffering from the Consequences of Nuclear Exposure in the Semipalatinsk Experimental Nuclear Polygon* (Pension Law, Article 9).
3. As Pragma Corporation (2005: 9) notes, "Ministry of Labor *Decree 1241* requires new retirees to purchase guaranteed lifetime annuities with their pension accumulations beginning in 2006. The same decree, however, establishes a grace period only before the end of which the annuities must be purchased. The grace period for females is 9 years until age 67; for males, 7 years until age 70."
4. Population life tables recently have been calculated for Kazakhstan, but these are for entire rather than contributing (insured) populations and do not project future changes—a huge issue in a country with rapidly changing mortality risk. The most detailed tables, by both gender and oblast, are in SARK (2005).
5. Expenses incurred by insurance companies would include bank commissions for fund transfers from the company to annuitants' accounts. The fee charged by local banks for a tenge funds transfer is equal to 0.15%–0.20% of the amount, with a minimum charge of $0.7–0.8. For small accumulations, the present value of these expenses amounts to a significant percentage of the annuity premium.
6. This 21% rate applies to regular nonagricultural employees. Foreign administrative and technical staff are taxed at 11%; agricultural enterprises make quarterly general tax payments based on output.
7. The method for determining the size of government social allowances appears in RK law *On the State Social Disability, Survivorship, and Old-Age Allowances in the Republic of Kazakhstan* (June 19, 1997). Several articles, including Article 12(only for disability allowances), were changed according to the RK law No. 101-III of December 15, 2005, *Concerning Amendments to Some Legislative Acts Regarding Social Provision Issues*. These amendments substituted the official subsistence level for RCI.
8. It should be emphasized that these figures are economy-wide averages. The cost of living varies considerably across cities and regions. The average pension offers a fairly impressive income in smaller towns and rural areas, but not in cities such as Almaty, Astana, or Atyrau. On the other hand, medical care and social services are weaker in poorer regions.
9. RK Law No. 177-III-ZRK, July 7, 2006, *On Amendments to Some Regulations on Tax Regulations.*

Chapter 8

1. "Legal entities, excluding those financed by founders, by government bodies, or which are otherwise specified, will answer for their obligations with all property belonging to them." (RK Civil Code, Article 44(1)).

"Property is declared ownerless in the event that it does not have an owner, or for which the owner is unknown, or is something for which the owner refuses the rights of ownership." (RK Civil Code, Article 242(1)).

"The right to ownership of unowned moveable property can be obtained under the authority of customary use (RK Civil Code, Article 241(2)).

"A citizen or legal entity, not themselves the owners of a property, but in good faith, openly and uninterruptedly having under their control real estate property for the duration of 15 years, or any other property for no less than five years, obtains the right of ownership of that property." (RK Civil Code, Article 240(1)).

2. "The government guarantees to recipients the security of obligated pension receipts held in Accumulative pension funds in the amount of actually deposited pension receipts, taking into account the level of inflation at the moment at which the rights to receive pension payments are secured by the recipient, as defined by the present Law and other legal acts of the Republic of Kazakhstan" (Law of the Republic of Kazakhstan on Pension Guarantees No. 136-1, enacted July 20, 1997, Article 6(1)).

Chapter 9

1. Vito Tanzi, "Things will Fall Apart but It Is the Aftermath that Matters," *Financial Times*, February 24, 2006, p.15, provides an analysis of the consequences of growing organizational complexity without structural refinement that is consistent with this approach.

Chapter 10

1. This vague statement in fact follows from the standard assumptions in microeconomic theory that agents seek to maximize expected utility rather than expected income, that the von Neumann-Morgenstern expected utility theorem applies, and that intertemporal preferences are convex, or are closely contained in a convex hull.

Chapter 11

1. One can easily compare system characteristics via publications (in particular, Whitehouse, 2007; the earlier Palacio and Pallarès-Miralles, 2000, remains useful as well) and websites (that of the international division of the US Social Security Administration, http://www.ssa.gov/policy/docs/progdesc/ssptw, is particularly useful). For lists of lessons, see Andrews (2006) and Kay and Sinha (2008).
2. For example, in his survey of fully funded, defined contribution pension system reformers, Catalán (2004) specifies the group as including Hungary (1997), Poland (1999), and Croatia (2000) among transition economies; Chile (1981), Peru (1991), Argentina (1994), Colombia (1994), Uruguay (1997), Mexico (1997), and El Salvador (1998) as the first wave of Latin American reformers, and Costa Rica, the Dominican Republic, and Nicaragua as the second Latin wave.
3. Charlton and McKinnon, 2001, especially pp. 78–82 and 116–122, serve as the source for most of the discussion in this section. Their measured scepticism can be offset by reading Pinera (2004), who, as the reform's architect, serves as an enthusiastic if uncritical cheerleader; he also maintains an informative website http://www.pensionreform.org. Mesa-Lago (2001) and Acuña and Iglesias (2001) provide detailed critical analyses that

serve as an excellent introduction, while Kay and Sinha (2008) provide a current discussion of Accumulative reform issues in Latin America.

4. See www.proteccionsocial.cl. The SPS, covering 2002, 2004, and 2006, is described in detail in Arenas de Mesa et al., 2008, which provides the data that follow.
5. To contrast this performance a decade after initiation with that of Chile in 1991, one finds 4.1 million APF members (in a national population of about 13 million), or 62.5% of the labor force, with pension fund values, in US$2000, of 10.004 billion, equal to 31% of GDP. Some 38% of APF holdings were in government instruments, and from 1992 to 1998 this proportion ranged from 39% to 42%, suggesting continued dependence on public debt (Acuña and Iglesias, 2001).

References

Abuhatba, Mario, and Marcela Ruiz-Tagle. 1996a. "Regulations of private voluntary pension fund." Almaty: USAID/DAI Kazakhstan Pension Reform Project.

———. 1996b. "Pension scheme regulations." Almaty: USAID/DAI Kazakhstan Pension Reform Project.

Acuña, Rodrigo R., and Augusto P. Iglesias. 2001. "Chile's pension reform after 20 years." Washington, D.C.: World Bank, Social Protection discussion paper no. 0129.

Anderson, Joseph M. 1996. "Pension reform for Kazakstan: Background, concepts, and strategy." Bethesda, MD: DAI, report to the U.S. Agency for International Development.

Anderson, Joseph M., Jon Eivind Kolberg, Wayne Vroman, and Trevor Evans-Young. 1997. "The pension system of the Republic of Kazakstan: policy, structure, operations, reform." Bethesda, MD: DAI, Report to the Ministry of Labor and Social Protection.

Andrews, Emily S. 2001. "Kazakhstan: An ambitious pension reform." Washington, D.C.: World Bank, paper prepared for the World Bank Pension Primer on Country Experiences in Europe and Central Asia.

———. 2006. "Pension reform and the development of pension systems: An evaluation of World Bank assistance." Washington, D.C.: World Bank.

Anusić, Zoran, Philip O'Keefe, and Sanja Madzarević-Šujster. 2003. "Pension reform in Croatia." Washington, D.C.: World Bank, Social Protection discussion paper no. 0304.

Asian Development Bank. 2002. *People's Republic of China—old age pensions for the rural areas: From land reform to globalization.* Manila: ADB.

Auty, Richard. 1998. "Mineral wealth and the economic transition: Kazakhstan." *Resources Policy* 24 (4): 241–49.

Bacon, Roger, and Silvana Tordo. 2006. "Experiences with oil funds: Institutional and financial aspects." Washington, D.C.: World Bank ESMAP Report 321/06.

Baimateyeva, Gulnar K. 2002. "Pension reform in Kazakhstan: Cost-benefit analysis." Almaty: KIMEP, paper presented at the fifth International Conference on Public Sector Transition, St. Petersburg.

Baskakov, Valerii. 2006. "On the social efficiency of Russia's pension system" (O sotsial'noj effektivnosti pensionnoi sistemy Rossii). *Pensionnye Fondy Investitsii* 1 (25): 50–57.

Becker, Charles M., and Sergey V. Paltsev. 2001. "Macro-experimental economics in the Kyrgyz Republic: Social security sustainability and pension reform." *Comparative Economic Studies* 43 (4): 1–34.

———. 2004. "Economic consequences of demographic change in the former USSR: Social transfers in the Kyrgyz Republic." *World Development* 32 (11): 1849–70

———. 2006. "The (in)credibility of social security modeling in transition countries: Uncertainty analysis for Kyrgyzstan." Durham, NC: Duke University, Department of Economics, unpublished manuscript.

Becker, Charles M. and Ai-Gul S. Seitenova. 2006. "Fertility and marriage in Kazakhstan's transition period." In *Economics of Intergenerational Equity in Transition Economies* Masaaki Kuboniwa and Yoshiaki Nishimura, eds. Tokyo: Maruzen Publishers, chap. 13, pp. 341–57.

Becker, Charles M., Ai-Gul S. Seitenova, and Dina S. Urzhumova. 1999. "Government of Kazakhstan pension expenditure forecasts." Almaty: IMCC for USAID CAR, report to the National Bank of Kazakhstan.

———. 2000. "Adequacy of pensions for different groups of employees and recommendations for actions necessary to adequately address identified retirement income deficiencies." Astana, Kazakhstan: Ministry of Labor and Social Protection, second annual report to the World Bank in fulfillment of a conditionality for the continued disbursement of a PRIL (pension reform implementation) loan.

———. 2001. "Long-run fiscal costs of state pensions and social allowances." Astana, Kazakhstan: Ministry of Finance, final report to the World Bank in fulfillment of a conditionality for the continued disbursement of a PRIL (pension reform implementation) loan.

———. 2006. "Pension reform in Central Asia: An overview." In *Economics of Intergenerational Equity in Transition Economies*, ed. Masaaki Kuboniwa and Yoshiaki Nishimura. Tokyo: Maruzen Publishers, chap. 9, pp. 233–54.

Becker, Charles M., and Dina S. Urzhumova. 1998. "Pension burdens and labor force participation in Kazakhstan." *World Development* 26 (11): 2087–2102.

Becker, Charles M., and Dina S. Urzhumova. 2000. "Annuity and other retirement payout options in the Republic of Kazakhstan." Almaty: National Bank and IMCC/USAID.

Becker, Charles M., and Dina S. Urzhumova. 2005. "Mortality recovery and stabilization in Kazakhstan." *Economics & Human Biology* 3 (1): 97–122.

Bello, Omar. 2000. "Returns to human capital investment in Venezuela." Boulder, CO: University of Colorado at Boulder, Department of Economics, unpublished PhD. dissertation.

Brown, Robert L. 1997. "In defense of pay-as-you-go (Paygo) financing of social security." *North American Actuarial Journal* 1 (4): 1–20.

Calvo, G. A., and F. Coricelli. 1993. "Output collapse in Eastern Europe: The role of credit." *IMF Staff Reports* 40: 32–52.

Catalán, Mario. 2004. "Pension funds and corporate governance in developing countries: What do we know and what do we need to know?" *Journal of Pension Economics & Finance* 3 (2): 197–232.

Charlton, Roger, and Roddy McKinnon. 2001. *Pensions in Development.* Aldershot, UK: Ashgate.

Chen, Vivian. 2005. "A macro analysis of China's pension pooling system: financial problem and incentive issues." In Takayama, Noriyuki, ed. *Pensions in Asia: Incentives, Compliance and Their Role in Retirement.* Tokyo: Maruzen, chap. 2, pp. 11–38.

Chlon, Agnieszka, Marek Góra, and Michal Rutkowski. 1999. "Shaping pension reform in Poland: Security through diversity." Washington, D.C.: World Bank, Social Protection discussion paper no. 9923.

Clément, Matthieu, 2007. "Tentative evaluation of the impact of public transfers on the dynamics of poverty: The case of Russia." *International Social Security Review* 60 (1): 59–80.

DAI. 1996a. "Recommendations on taxation of the private pension system." Almaty: USAID/DAI Kazakhstan Pension Reform Project, unpublished document.

———. 1996b. "Financing of social security in Kazakhstan: State and regional problems." Almaty: USAID/DAI, Kazakhstan Pension Reform Project working report no. 9.

———. 1996c. "Annuity Payout Options for the Voluntary Pension Program." Almaty: USAID/DAI Kazakhstan Pension Reform Project, unpublished document.

De Broeck, Mark, P. De Masi, and V. Cohen. 1995. "Inflation dynamics in Kazakhstan." Washington, D.C.: IMF working paper no. 95/140-EA.

De Broeck, Mark, and K. Kostial. 1998. "Output decline in transition: The case of Kazakhstan." Washington, D.C.: IMF working paper no. 98/45.

De Mesa, Arenas, Alberto, David Bravo, Jere R. Behrman, Olivia S. Mitchell, and Petra E. Todd. 2008. "The Chilean pension reform turns 25: Lessons from the Social Protection Survey." In *Lessons from pension reform in the Americas*, ed. Stephen J. Kay and Tapen Sinha. Oxford: Oxford University Press.

Devesa-Carpio, José E., and Carlos Vidal-Meliá. 2002. "The reformed pension systems in Latin America." Washington, D.C.: World Bank, Social Protection discussion paper no. 0209.

Diamond, Peter A. 2002. *Social Security Reform*. Oxford: Oxford University Press.

Egert, Balázs 2006. "Investigating the Balassa-Samuelson hypothesis in Kazakhstan." Almaty: NBRK, unpublished report.

Égert, Balázs, and Carol Leonard. 2007. "Dutch disease scare in Kazakhstan: Is it real?" Munich: CES-IFO working paper no. 1967.

Eicher, Sharon. 2004. "What causes bank asset substitution in Kazakhstan? Explaining dollarization in a transition economy." Ann Arbor: University of Michigan, William Davidson Institute, working paper no. 688.

Elveren, Adem Y. 2008. "Assessing gender inequality in the Turkish pension system." *International Social Security Review* 61 (2): 39–58.

European Bank for Reconstruction and Development. 2002. "Strategy for Kazakhstan." London: EBRD. http://www.ebrd.com/about/strategy/country/kaza/kazakh.pdf.

Evans-Young, Trevor. 1996. "A review of the technical process of pensions of social protection in Kazakhstan: Financing of social security in Kazakhstan; State and regional problems." Almaty: USAID/DAI, Kazakhstan Pension Reform Project, Working Report no. 4.

Fitch Rating Agency. 2002. "Sovereign report: Republic of Kazakhstan," internal document, New York.

Fox, Louise. 2003. "Safety nets in transition economies: A primer." Washington, D.C.: World Bank Social Protection discussion paper no. 0306.

Fultz, Elaine, ed. 2004. *Pension reform in the Baltic States*. Geneva: ILO.

Giffen, James. 1998. "Budget and pension reforms in the Republic of Kazakhstan" (Byudzhetnye i pensionnye reformy v Respubliki Kazakhstan), internal document. Astana: GoK.

Gill, Indermit S., Truman Packard, and Juan Yermo. 2005. *Keeping the promise of social security in Latin America*. Palo Alto, CA, and Washington, D.C.: Stanford University Press and the World Bank.

Ghai, Dharam. 2002. "Social security priorities and patterns: A global perspective." Geneva: ILO International Institute for Labour Studies discussion paper DP/141/2002.

Government of Latvia. 2005. "Latvian National Report on Adequate & Sustainable Pensions." Unpublished document. Brussels: European Commission. http://ec.europa.eu/employment_social/spsi/docs/social_protection/2005/lv_en.pdf.

Gray, J. 2000. "Kazakhstan: A review of farm restructuring." Washington, D.C.: World Bank Technical Paper no. 458.

Habibov, Nazim, and Lida Fan. 2007. "Social protection and poverty in Azerbaijan, a low-income country in transition: Implications of a household survey." *International Social Security Review* 60 (4): 47–68.

Hinz, Richard P., Asta Zviniene, and Anna-Marie Vilamovska. 2005. "The new pensions in Kazakhstan: Challenges in making the transition." Washington, D.C.: World Bank, Social Protection Discussion Paper No. 0537.

Hoelscher, David. 1998. "Banking system restructuring in Kazakhstan." Washington, D.C.: IMF Working Paper No. 98/96.

Hoffman, Lutz, Peter Bofinger, Geiner Flassbek, and Alfred Schtainher. 1999. "The state of pension reform in Kazakhstan." Astana: Report to the government of the Republic of Kazakhstan, unpublished document.

———. 2001. *Kazakhstan, 1993–2000.*" Heidelberg, Germany: Physica–Verlag.

Holmes, Martin R. 2003. "Methods for stochastic trust fund projection." Policy Simulation Group working paper, Washington, DC: Social Security Administration and US Department of Labor. http://www.polsim.com/stochsim.pdf.

Holzmann, Robert, Mitchell Orenstein, and Michal Rutkowski, eds. 2003. *Pension Reform in Europe: Process and Progress.* Washington, D.C: World Bank.

IMF. Staff Country Report No. 00/29: kazakhstan–selected issues and statistical appendix, March 2000.

IMF. 2005. "Republic of Kazakhstan: Selected Issues." Washington, D.C: International Monetary Fund, IMF country report no. 05/240.

Institute of Macroeconomics Research (Development and Reform Committee) [IMR]. 2008. "Research on rural old age insurance in Hebei." Shijiazhuang, China: Hebei Provincial Government, IMR (in Chinese).

IMCC. 1997a. "Financial and actuarial analysis of Kazakstan's pension reform legislation." Almaty: USAID CAR mission, unpublished document.

IMCC. 1997b. "Developing a pension regulatory and supervisory capacity in Kazakhstan." Almaty: USAID Central Asia—IMCC, unpublished document.

Infante, Maria Teresa. 1998. "How the system came into being." *AFP: A three-letter revolution*, ed. CILDLSS. Santiago, Chile: Fyrma Gruf for CILDLSS, chap. 1.

Ivliev, V. "The conception of the establishing of the analogy of trust relationship in the Republic of Kazakhstan." Pension reform project, 1997.

James, Estelle. 1997. "New systems for old age security—theory, practice and empirical evidence." Washington, D.C., World Bank Working Paper No. 1766.

James, Estelle, Alejandra Cox Edwards, and Rebeca Wong. 2003. "The gender impact of pension reform." *Journal of Pension Economics & Finance* 2 (2): 181–219.

James, Estelle, and Sarah Brooks. 2001. "The political economy of structural pension reform." In *New Ideas about Old Age Security*, ed. Robert Holzmann and Joseph Stiglitz. Washington, D.C.: World Bank.

Kazakhstan Today. 2006. March 30, Astana.

Kotlikoff, Lawrence. 1999. "The World Bank's approach and the right approach to pension reform." Boston: Boston University Department of Economics, unpublished manuscript.

Kuboniwa, Masaaki, and Yoshiaki Nishimura, eds. 2006. *Economics of Intergenerational Equity in Transition Economies.* Tokyo: Maruzen.

Lee, Ronald. 2004. "Quantifying our ignorance: Stochastic forecasts of population and public budgets." University of California, Berkeley: Center for the Economics and Demography of Aging, CDA paper 2004-0001.

Lee, Ronald, and Shipad Teljapurkar. 1998. "Uncertain demographic futures and social security forecasts." *American Economic Review* 88 (2): 237–41.

Leckie, Stuart, and Yasue Pai. 2005. *Pension funds in China—a new look.* Hong Kong: ISI Publications.

Lim, Jiunken. 2005. "Pension reform in Russia and Kazakhstan." Philadelphia: University of Pennsylvania, *Wharton Research Scholars Journal* (online). http://repository.upenn.edu/wharton_research_scholars/27/.

Madrid, Raul L. 2003. *Retiring the State: The Politics of Pension Privatization in Latin America and Beyond.* Stanford, CA: Stanford University Press.

Marchenko, Grigori A. 2002. "Pension reform: Results of the first five years." Almaty: National Bank of the Republic of Kazakhstan, press release, July 30.

Matysiak, Anna, and Beata Nowok. 2007. "Stochastic forecast of the population of Poland, 2005—2050." *Demographic Research* 17 (11): 301–38.

McKinnon, Roddy, Roger Charlton, and Lukasz Konopielko. 1999. "Non-state pension funds: Private sector developments in transition economies." Glasgow: Glasgow Caledonian University, Faculty of Business, Working Paper no. 17.

McLure, Charles, J. Martinez-Vazquez, and S. Wallace. 1999. *Fiscal transition in Kazakhstan.* Manila: Asian Development Bank.

Mesa-Lago, Carmelo, 2001. "Structural reform of social security pensions in Latin America: Models, characteristics, results and conclusions." *International Social Security Review* 54 (4): 67–92.

Mesa-Lago, Carmelo. 2007. "The extension of healthcare coverage and protection in relation to the labour market: Problems and policies in Latin America." *International Social Security Review* 60 (1): 3–32.

Mikheeva, L. Yu. 1999. "Property trust management." In *Yurist* (The Jurist), ed. V. M. Chernov. Moscow: Nauka, pp. 1–27.

Moody, Stephen S. 2005. "Kazakhstan's term structure of interest rates." Almaty: Pragma, unpublished manuscript.

———. 2007. Private communication.

Müller, Katharina. 2003. "The making of pension privatization in Latin America and Eastern Europe." In *Pension reform in Europe: Process and progress,* ed. Robert Holzmann, Mitchell Orenstein, and Michal Rutkowski. Washington, D.C: World Bank.

Natali, David. 2004. "Latvia: The reformed pension system." Brussels: Observatoire social europeén, unpublished document, http://www.ose.be/files/mocpension/ LatviaOMC.pdf.

National Bank of Kazakhstan. 2002. Statistical Bulletin 11 (96). Almaty, Kazakhstan.

———. 2006. "Financial Stability Report." Almaty: NBRK.

———. 2007. *Statistical Bulletin* 147 (2). Almaty: NBRK (in Kazakh and Russian).

———. 2008. *Statistical Bulletin* 2 (159). http://www.nationalbank.kz/cont/publish 567096_4415.pdf.

Olcott, Martha Brill. 2002. *Kazakhstan: Unfulfilled promise.* Washington, D.C.: Carnegie Endowment for International Peace.

Orenstein, Mitchell A. 2000. "How politics and institutions affect pension reform in three postcommunist countries." Washington, D.C.: World Bank, Development Research Group, Policy Research working paper no. 2310.

Palacios, Robert, and Roberto Rocha. 1998. "The Hungarian pension system in transition." Washington, D.C: World Bank, Social Protection Discussion Paper no. 9805.

Palacios, Robert, and Aleksandra Posarać. 2000. "Options for pension reform in Georgia." Washington, D.C: World Bank, Pension Reform primer paper.

Palacios, Robert, and Montserrat Pallares-Miralles. 2000. "International patterns of pension provision." Washington, D.C.: World Bank Social Protection Discussion Paper no. 0009.

Palmer, Edward. 2007. "Pension reform and the development of pension systems: An evaluation of World Bank assistance." Washington, D.C: World Bank, Independent Evaluation Group.

People's Republic of China, State Council. 2004. "China's social security and its policy." White paper. http://english.gov.cn/official/2005-07/28/content_18024.htm.

Piñera, José. 1997. *Testimony* before the Senate Committee on Banking, Housing and Urban Affairs Subcommittee on Securities, June 26.

———. 2004. "Empowering workers: The privatization of social security in Chile." In *Social security and its discontents,* ed. Michael B. Tanner. Washington, D.C.: Cato Institute.

Pomfret, Richard. 1995. *The economies of central Asia.* Princeton, NJ: Princeton University Press, p. 216.

Pragma Corporation (Stephen Moody, lead author; Dina Urzumova, actuary). 2005. "Recommendations for the State Annuity Company and the Kazakhstan Life Insurance and Annuity Market." Almaty: Pragma/USAID, unpublished report to the Financial Supervisory Agency.

Rajnes, David M. 1999. "Privately-managed pension funds: The Chilean model." Almaty, Kazakhstan, and Arlington, VA: IMCC for USAID/CAR, unpublished document.

Ramia, Gaby, Gloria Davies, and Chris Nyland. 2008. "The compliance challenge: Implications for social security in the People's Republic of China," *International Social Security Review* 61 (1): 1–20.

Rocha, Roberto, Richard Hinz, and Joaquin Gutierrez. 1999. "Improving the regulation and supervision of pension funds: Are there lessons from the banking sector?" Washington, DC: World Bank Social Protection Discussion Paper no. 9929.

Rodriguez, Lourdes. 2005. "Overview on China's social security system reform." Houston, TX: University of Houston, Department of Economics, unpublished manuscript.

Sah, Raaj, and Joseph E. Stiglitz. 1992. *Peasants versus city-dwellers: Taxation and the burden of economic development.* Oxford: Clarendon Press.

Salditt, Felix, Peter Whiteford, and Willem Adema. 2007. "Pension reform in China: Progress and prospects." Paris: OECD Social Employment & Migration working paper no. 53.

Schiff, Jerald, Niko Hobdari, Axel Schimmelpfennig, and Roman Zytek. 2000. "Pension reform in the Baltics." Washington, D.C.: IMF occasional paper no. 200.

Seitenova, Ai-Gul S., and Charles M. Becker. 2004. "Kazakhstan's pension system: Pressures for change and dramatic reforms." *Hitotsubashi Journal of Economics* 45 (2): 151–87.

Seitenova, Ai-Gul S., and Becker, Charles M. 2008. "Disability in Kazakhstan: An evaluation of official data." Washington, D.C.: World Bank, Social Protection Discussion Paper no. 0802.

Seitenova, Ai-Gul S., and Dina S. Urzhumova. 2003. Actuarial assessment of pension system options in Kazakhstan. Almaty: Kazakhstan Actuarial Center, unpublished report to World Bank.

Sipos, Sándor. 2003. Improving pensions and facilitating pay out from the new funded pension system in Kazakhstan: The challenges of transition. Washington, D.C.: World Bank ECSHD/ECA, unpublished report.

Srinivas, P.S., Edward Whitehouse, and Juan Yermo. 2001. "Regulating private pension funds, structure, performance, and investments: Cross-country evidence." Washington, D.C.: World Bank, Social Protection discussion paper no. 0113.

Spiecker, Friederike, and Rudolf Zwiener. 1997. "Are funded pensions better than a pay-as-you-go system—a critical view on Kazakhstan's pension reform." *Kazakhstan Economic Trends* IV.

State Social Protection Fund of the Republic of Azerbaijan (SSPF). No date; "Historical path of development" (in Russian). http://www.azerbaijan.az/_StatePower/_ CommitteeConcern/committeeConcern_10_r.html#6, accessed on April 25, 2008.

Statistical Agency of the Republic of Kazakhstan (SARK). 2005. *Demograficheskii Ezhegodnik Kazakhstana 2004.* Almaty: SARK.

Sycheva, Lyudmila, and Leonid Mikhailov. 2006. *Reform and challenges for private pensions in Russia.* Paris: OECD.

Tafradjiyski, Borislav. 2002. "The pension reform in Bulgaria—two years after the start." Tokyo: Hitotsubashi University Institute of Economic Research Discussion Paper no. 64.

Tang, H., E. Zoli, and I. Klytchnikova. 2006. "Banking crises in transition countries: Fiscal costs and related issues." Washington, D.C: World Bank Policy Research working paper.

Tsyganov, Oleg, and Shamil' Mejidov. 2007. "Azerbaijan State Social Protection Fund Chairman Salim Muslimov: 'We have succeeded in creating an efficient, realistic national model of the social system.'" *Izvestiya,* May 30 (in Russian). http://www. izvestia.ru/azerbaijan/article3104724/ .

Urzhumova, Dina S. 2000. "Some issues of pension provisions in the Republic of Kazakhstan." Unpublished report submitted to the Ministry of Labor.

Utro.ua (*Morning Ukraine* website). 2008. "The Ministry of Labor carries out pension reform" (Mintruda provodit pensionnuyu reformu). http://www.utro.ua/articles/2008/01/11/71855.shtml.

Van der Mensbrugghe, Emmanuel, et al. 2001. "Kazakhstan." Washington, D.C.: IMF Country Report no. 01/20.

Verme, P. 2001. *Transition, recession and labour supply.* Aldershot, UK: Ashgate.

Walker, Eduardo, and Fernando Lefort. 2002. "Pension reform and capital markets: Are there any (hard) links?" Washington, D.C.: World Bank Social Protection Discussion Paper no. 0201.

Weiner, Mitchell. 1997. "Developing a pension regulatory and supervisory capacity in Kazakstan." Almaty: IMCC, unpublished report to USAID.

Weiner, Mitchell. 1998. Pension reform project final tour of duty report. Arlington, VA: IMCC, unpublished document.

Whitehouse, Edward. 2007. *Pensions panorama: Retirement-income systems in 53 countries.* Washington, D.C: World Bank.

Williamson, John B., Stephanie A. Howling, and Michelle L. Maroto. 2006. "The political economy of pension reform in Russia: Why partial privatization?" *Journal of Aging Studies* 20 (2): 165–175.

World Bank. 1993. "Kazakhstan: The transition to a market economy." Washington, D.C.: World Bank (World Bank Country Study).

———. 1994. *Averting the old age crisis.* New York: Oxford University Press.

———. 1997a. "Aide-mémoire of the 1st World Bank pension reform mission." Washington, D.C.: World Bank, unpublished document, May 12–19, 1997.

———. 1997b. "Aide-mémoire of the 2nd World Bank pension reform mission." Washington, D.C.: World Bank, unpublished document, July 21–August 2, 1997.

———. 1997c. *China 2020: Old-age security.* Washington, D.C.: World Bank.

———. 1997d. *Kazakhstan: Transition of the state.* Washington, D.C.: World Bank (World Bank Country Study).

———. 1998a. "Kazakhstan: Pension reform adjustment loan, appraisal mission." Washington, D.C.: World Bank, unpublished document, February 5–19, 1998.

———. 1998b. "Aide-mémoire, Kazakhstan: Pension reform adjustment loan, appraisal mission." Washington, D.C.: World Bank, unpublished document, March 30–April 3, 1998.

———. 2004. "The new pensions in Kazakhstan: Challenges in making the transition." Washington, D.C: World Bank, Europe and Central Asia Region, Human Development Sector Unit, report no. 30873-KZ.

———. 2006. "Ukraine—creating fiscal space for growth: A public finance review." Washington, D.C.: World Bank, ECA Region, ECSPE report no. 36671-UA.

———. 2007. "Project information document (PID) appraisal stage: Pension administration project." Washington, D.C.: World Bank, ECA Region, report no. AB2407.

World Bank Pension Reform Mission [WBPRM] (Bernard Funk, Emily Andrews, Dimitri Vittas, Zhanar Abdildina, Robert Holzmann). "Aide-Memoire." Washington, D.C.: World Bank, unpublished manuscript, May 12–19, 1997.

Yan, Wang, Xu Dianqing, Wang Zhi, and Zhai Fan. 2001. "Implicit pension debt and transitional cost in China's pension reform—a CGE analysis." Washington, D.C.: World Bank.

Yi, Zeng. 2005. "Estimating the impacts of demographic and policy changes on pension deficit rates: A simple model and application to China." Durham, NC: Duke University, China Population and Socio-Economic Studies Center, unpublished manuscript.

Zaman, Gheorghe, and Valentina Vasile. 2001. "Intergenerational problems in Romania with a special view on pension system reform." Tokyo: Hitotsubashi University Institute of Economic Research discussion paper no. 20.

Zhao, Yaohui, and Xu, Jianguo. 2002. "China's urban pension system: Reforms and problems." *Cato Journal* 21 (3): 395–414.

Zhu, Yukun. 2002. "Recent developments in China's social security reforms." *International Social Security Review* 55 (4): 39–54.

Index